Lecture Notes of the Institute for Computer Sciences, Social Informatics and Telecommunications Engineering 413

More information about this series at https://link.springer.com/bookseries/8197

Wei Xiang · Fengling Han ·
Tran Khoa Phan (Eds.)

Broadband Communications, Networks, and Systems

12th EAI International Conference, BROADNETS 2021
Virtual Event, October 28–29, 2021
Proceedings

Editors
Wei Xiang
La Trobe University
Bundoora, VIC, Australia

Fengling Han
RMIT University
Melbourne, VIC, Australia

Tran Khoa Phan
La Trobe University
Melbourne, VIC, Australia

ISSN 1867-8211   ISSN 1867-822X (electronic)
Lecture Notes of the Institute for Computer Sciences, Social Informatics
and Telecommunications Engineering
ISBN 978-3-030-93478-1   ISBN 978-3-030-93479-8 (eBook)
https://doi.org/10.1007/978-3-030-93479-8

This Springer imprint is published by the registered company Springer Nature Switzerland AG
The registered company address is: Gewerbestrasse 11, 6330 Cham, Switzerland

Preface

We are delighted to introduce the proceedings of 12th EAI International Conference on Broadband Communications, Networks, and Systems (BROADNETS 2021). This conference brought together researchers, developers, and practitioners around the world who are leveraging and developing smart communications networks with a particular focus on 5G applications. The theme of BROADNETS 2021 was 'Beyond 5G (B5G) Enabled Advanced Manufacturing'.

5G mobile networks and beyond (B5G) provide high bandwidth capacity, low latency, and connectivity to enable a new generation of applications, services, and business opportunities that have not been seen before. Smart sensors, enabled by 5G/B5G, are coordinated and communicate in real time to complete the manufacturing process. These smart sensors will be able to assess the quality of components that are being manufactured in real time, reducing re-working requirements. This has the potential to revolutionize modern industrial processes and applications including agriculture, manufacturing, and business communications through a combination of AI-based planning, edge computing, high bandwidth with low latency, connected machines, AR-enabled workers, and integrated logistics. Beyond 5G, one can anticipate that there will be a more dynamic, self-regulating, and self-adjusting process that will translate into agility, speed, and higher productivity.

The technical program of BROADNETS 2021 consisted of 24 full papers. The conference also features two international workshops on 5G-enabled Smart Building: Technology and Challenge, and 5G: The Advances in Industry. Aside from the high-quality technical paper presentations, the technical program also featured two keynote speeches by distinguished researchers Qing-Long Han (Swinburne University of Technology, Australia) on 'Multi-agent Systems Based Distributed Control, Optimization, and Energy Management in Smart Grids' and Mehdi Bennis (University of Oulu, Finland) on 'Communication-efficient and Distributed ML Over Wireless Networks'.

Coordination with the steering chair, Imrich Chlamtac, was essential for the success of the conference. We sincerely appreciate the chair's constant support and guidance. It was also a great pleasure to work with such an excellent organizing committee team for their hard work in organizing and supporting the conference. In particular, we are grateful to the Technical Program Committee, who have completed the peer-review process for technical papers and helped to put together a high-quality technical program. We are also grateful to the conference managers for their support and all the authors who submitted their papers to the BROADNETS 2021 conference and workshops.

We strongly believe that BROADNETS provides a good forum for all researchers, developers, and practitioners to discuss all science and technology aspects that are relevant to broadband communications networks. We also expect that the future

BROADNETS conferences will be as successful and stimulating as this year's, as indicated by the contributions presented in this volume .

Wei Xiang
Fengling Han
Lei Pan
Khoa Phan

Organization

Steering Committee

Imrich Chlamtac (Chair)	University of Trento, Italy
Honghao Gao	Shanghai University, China

Organizing Committee

General Chair

Wei Xiang   La Trobe University, Australia

General Co-chair

Fengling Han   RMIT University, Australia

Technical Program Committee Chair

Lei Pan   Deakin University, Australia

Sponsorship and Exhibit Chair

Son Hoang Dau   RMIT University, Australia

Local Chair

Yun Yang   Swinburne University of Technology, Australia

Workshops Chair

Margaret Hamilton   RMIT University, Australia

Publicity and Social Media Chair

Peng Cheng   La Trobe University, Australia

Publications Chair

Khoa Phan   La Trobe University, Australia

Web Chair

Maria Spichkova   RMIT University, Australia

Posters and PhD Track Chair

Ke Deng   RMIT University, Australia

Demos Chair

Li Li   Monash University, Australia

Industrial Chairs

Xiaoqi Chen   Swinburne University of Technology, Australia
Bing Chen   Shenzhen Benchuang Information Technology Pty Ltd.,
                              China

Technical Program Committee

Aravinda Rao   University of Melbourne, Australia
Biplob Ray   Central Queensland University, Australia
Bruce Gu   Victoria University, Australia
Chao Chen   James Cook University, Australia
Gaowei Zhang   Nanyang Technology University, Singapore
Jaime Martins   University of Algarve, Portugal
Keshav Sood   Deakin University, Australia
Mahmoud Khasawneh   Jordan University of Science and Technology, Jordan
Michael Hobbs   Deakin University, Australia
Mohammad Abu Shattal   Franklin University, USA
Nan Sun   Deakin University, Australia
Pablo Fondo-Ferreiro   University of Vigo, Spain
Pedro Castillejo   Universidad Politécnica de Madrid, Spain
Punit Rathore   Massachusetts Institute of Technology, USA
Rory Coulter   Swinburne University of Technology, Australia
Shigang Liu   Swinburne University of Technology, Australia
Sutharshan Rajasegarar   Deakin University, Australia
Tony de Souza-Daw   Melbourne Polytechnic, Australia
Xi Zheng   Macquarie University, Australia
Xiao Chen   Monash University, Australia
Ziyuan Wang   Swinburne University of Technology, Australia

Contents

Broadband Communications, Networks, and Systems: Theory and Applications

A Machine Learning-Based Elastic Strategy for Operator Parallelism in a Big Data Stream Computing System

Wei Li[1], Dawei Sun[1(✉)], Shang Gao[2], and Rajkumar Buyya[3]

[1] School of Information Engineering, China University of Geosciences,
Beijing 100083, People's Republic of China
{leeway, sundaweicn}@cugb.edu.cn
[2] School of Information Technology, Deakin University,
Melbourne, VIC 3216, Australia
shang.gao@deakin.edu.au
[3] Cloud Computing and Distributed Systems (CLOUDS) Laboratory,
School of Computing and Information Systems,
The University of Melbourne, Melbourne, Australia
rbuyya@unimelb.edu.au

Abstract. Elastic scaling in/out of operator parallelism degree is needed for processing real time dynamic data streams under low latency and high stability requirements. Usually the operator parallelism degree is set when a streaming application is submitted to a stream computing system and kept intact during runtime. This may substantially affect the performance of the system due to the fluctuation of input streams and availability of system resources. To address the problems brought by the static parallelism setting, we propose and implement a machine learning based elastic strategy for operator parallelism (named Me-Stream) in big data stream computing systems. The architecture of Me-Stream and its key models are introduced, including parallel bottleneck identification, parameter plan generation, parameter migration and conversion, and instances scheduling. Metrics of execution latency and process latency of the proposed scheduling strategy are evaluated on the widely used big data stream computing system Apache Storm. The experimental results demonstrate the efficiency and effectiveness of the proposed strategy.

Keywords: Operator parallelism · Runtime awareness · Resource allocation · Machine learning · Stream computing · Distributed system

1 Introduction

In recent years, big data has driven the rapid advances in distributed systems. There are generally two processing methods for big data: batch processing and stream processing [1]. Compared with batch processing, stream processing is more suitable for real-time applications. Distributed stream processing platforms enable big data applications to process continuous stream data and obtain near real-time feedback [2]. At present, the mainstream distributed stream processing platforms include Apache Storm [3], Apache

W. Xiang et al. (Eds.): BROADNETS 2021, LNICST 413, pp. 3–19, 2022.
https://doi.org/10.1007/978-3-030-93479-8_1

Flink [4], Apache Spark (Spark Streaming) [5], Apache Samza [6], Apache Apex [7], and Google Cloud Dataflow [8]. Through an elastic execution engine, Flink can support batch processing tasks and stream processing tasks at the same time, as well as state management. It suits projects that require high throughput, low latency and demand state management or window statistics. Storm requires to design a topology first and then assign the topology to Execution nodes in a cluster, making it more suitable for small independent projects with low latency. Spark Streaming divides the input data stream into multiple batches through micro-batch processing, which is more suitable for projects in the Spark ecosystem. The work in this paper is optimized based on the widely used Storm platform, but the entire design, its strategy and model are not only limited to the Apache Storm platform. It can be applied to a variety of related streaming computing environments.

With the Storm default scheduling, if there are idle resources, uneven load and overload problems may occur [9, 10]. If no idle resources, there might be poor resource distribution caused by computing and communication bottlenecks in heterogeneous clusters [11]. The fundamental problem is that once the relevant parameter configuration is determined, the system cannot optimize parameter configuration during runtime. To support elastic adjustment, we face the following challenges: first, our solution must be compatible with the mainstream streaming computing platforms, such as Apache Flink, Apache Storm, and Apache Spark Streaming; the second is that the entire process must be monitored in real time to achieve true self-regulation; finally, the problem that needs to be solved is when using high-overhead pluggable scheduling, it is likely to introduce a new bottleneck affecting the whole performance [12].

1.1 Contributions

Motivated by the above discussion, we propose an elastic scaling strategy for operator parallelism (Me-Stream). It supports self-adjustment during runtime, can effectively optimize resource allocation and ensure the smooth operation of the system. In this paper, all the three aspects of Me-Stream are discussed, summarized as follows:

(1) We provide a formal definition of the elastic scaling strategy for operator parallelism, and realize the complete process of self-adjustment in operation.
(2) We design the architecture of the parallelism strategy for elastic scaling operations to solve new bottlenecks caused by pluggable scheduling.
(3) We evaluate the optimization performance of the strategy by metrics of execution latency and process latency on Storm to demonstrate the effectiveness of the proposal.

1.2 Paper Organization

The rest of the paper is organized as follows. In Sect. 2, Me-Stream, together with a model for intelligent tuning solution are introduced. Section 3 focuses on the detailed discussion of Me-Stream and the algorithm design, where a machine learning model is adopted to find the better parallel migration path and resource allocation without manual intervention. Section 4 introduces the experimental environment, parameter settings and performance evaluation of Me-Stream. Section 5 reviews related work on runtime elastic optimization of parallelism in distributed systems. Finally, conclusions and future work are presented in Sect. 6.

2 Me-Stream Architecture

This section mainly focuses on the parallelism optimization of streaming application topology for dynamic data streams. An intelligent optimization solution to the parallelism of running instances without manual intervention is provided. The proposal is to solve the inability of self-adjustment during operation after the relevant parameter configuration is determined.

As shown in Fig. 1, first of all, at the runtime, a monitoring process needs to obtain bolts related data in real time [13]. The data set can be obtained through IO or crawlers. Then, based on the flow perception, the data set is cleaned in real time and output to the parallel degree bottleneck identification to obtain the bottleneck level. When the preset conditions are met, the monitoring process executes rebalance to redistribute slots. The whole process does not require manual intervention. Storm's default scheduling does not consider inter-process optimization or inter-node optimization, which will result in poor configuration of instance parameters with the same computing resource consumption [14, 15]. Through the parallelism bottleneck identification, the topology bottleneck level can be identified, then it is passed into the parameter plan generation together with all-slots. A topology parameter plan is created, and the resources are reallocated according to the default schedule.

At this time, if a scheduling with a large overhead is produced, it is likely to become a new bottleneck. Therefore, it is necessary to design a matching instance scheduling that has better performance than the default scheduling of Storm on the basis of generalization. Through the parameter migration conversion, the topology parameter plan is converted into a migration plan and stored in the routing table. By now, the resource reallocation is completed according to the migration plan.

An intelligent tuning solution model is designed to solve the problem of the parallelism of running instances without manual intervention. The whole process is as follows:

(1) Obtain relevant data of bolts;
(2) Identify parallel degree bottleneck;
(3) Generate parameter plan;
(4) Conduct parameter migration and transformation;
(5) Schedule instances;
(6) Execute the rebalance command;
(7) Complete resource redistribution.

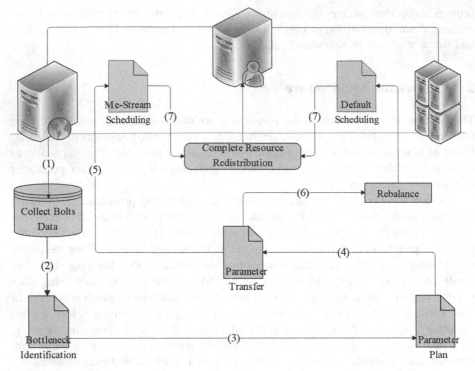

Fig. 1. Elastic scaling process of operator parallelism strategy (Me-Stream).

3   Me-Stream Framework

This section introduces in detail the processes of parallelism bottleneck identification, parameter plan generation, parameter migration, instances scheduling and how to complete the parallelism optimization for running instances using the elastic scaling strategy (Me-Stream).

3.1   Parallel Bottleneck Identification

First, the strategy traverses the nodes and the executed tasks in each topology in turn, quantifies the bottlenecks existing in the current topology through the execution latency, and calculates the maximum execution latency as the bottleneck. After all the topology traversal is completed, the bottleneck levels are sorted according to the execution latency, from the highest to the lowest. Among them, T_{calc} represents the calculation time for task c_j on node n_i, m function represents the required processing power under the complexity of current task, x function represents the complexity of the calculation task, and p function represents the ability of the assigned executor to process n_i. The preliminary deduction formula is defined by (1).

$$T_{calc}(n_i, c_j) = \frac{m(x(c_j))}{p(n_i)}. \tag{1}$$

Secondly, considering the communication bottleneck factors between nodes in different network environments, the strategy sequentially traverses the nodes and the executed tasks in each topology in different network environments, quantifies the bottlenecks in the current topology through the process latency, and calculates the maximum process latency as the bottleneck. After all the topology traversal is completed, the bottleneck levels are sorted according to the process latency. Among them, T_{comm} represents the communication time from n_{i-1} to n_i and n_i to n_{i+1}, m function represents the required processing capacity under the complexity of the calculation task, and l represents transmission link bandwidth. The preliminary deduction formula can be described by (2).

$$T_{comm}(n_i, c_j) = \frac{m(c_j)}{l_{i-1,i}} + \frac{m(c_j)}{l_{i,i+1}} = \frac{m(c_j)(l_{i-1,i} + l_{i,i+1})}{l_{i-1,i} l_{i,i+1}}. \tag{2}$$

In summary, the formula for calculating the sum of the parallel bottleneck time of tasks on all nodes is described by (3) (the maximum of calculation time and the communication time is the bottleneck time).

$$T = \max \begin{cases} Sum(T_{calc}(n_i, c_j)), \\ \frac{Sum(T_{comm}(n_i, c_j))}{2}. \end{cases} = \max \begin{cases} Sum(\frac{m(x(c_j))}{p(n_i)}), \\ \frac{Sum(m(c_j)(l_{i-1,i} + l_{i,i+1}))}{2l_{i-1,i} l_{i,i+1}}. \end{cases} \tag{3}$$

The above explains how to identify the main bottlenecks from communication bottlenecks and calculation bottlenecks in a cluster environment.

Next, we need to know when to perform the reallocation. In order to know this threshold accurately, we design a threshold identification function based on the linear regression. The specific steps are as follows:

(1) First, according to the above parallel bottleneck identification method, a first-order binomial linear regression equation is created. The data set (t, γ) is obtained by collecting, classifying, and labeling the original data (original data is obtained through crawlers and hooks), where t represents the original data timestamp, and γ represents the average delay at timestamp t.

$$\frac{1}{m} \sum_{i=1}^{m} (f(t) - \gamma_i)^2 = e(f, \gamma). \tag{4}$$

Where $f(t)$ is the threshold identification function, γ_i is the actual value, $e(f, \gamma)$ is the mean value distribution, defined as the mean error. The smaller the mean error, the more accurate $f(t)$ is. It is the linear regression function produced on the training set.

(2) Then, according to the principle of linear regression:

$$\frac{1}{m}\sum_{i=1}^{m}(wt_i + b - \gamma_i)^2 = e(f,\gamma). \tag{5}$$

(3) Next, the partial derivatives of w and b can be obtained by the linear regression function of the first-order binomial linear equation:

$$w = \frac{\sum_{i=1}^{m}\gamma_i(t_i - \bar{t})}{\sum_{i=0}^{m}t_i^2 - \frac{1}{m}(\sum_{i=1}^{m}t_i)^2}, b = \frac{1}{m}\sum_{i=1}^{m}(\gamma_i - wt_i). \tag{6}$$

(4) Finally, using the least squares method to calculate the w and b. when the sum of the Euclidean distance between the training set and the fitted linear labeling function is the smallest, the labeling function is the threshold identification function. When the fitting function becomes stable, the non-monitoring period can be entered, which can effectively reduce training overhead and release resources. The threshold identification function is associated with topologies and can be cached. Therefore, each threshold identification function does not depend on the selection of the training set, and can be used in parallel with the operator of another system in the current cluster. However, each threshold identification result is generated in the current topology instance and destroyed at the end of the topology's life cycle.

(5) After obtaining threshold identification function, Me-Stream records the reference bottleneck by comparing the value of the threshold identification function f and the actual value γ in real time. If the mean error $e(f,\gamma)$ between the value of the function and the actual value is positive under the accuracy requirement, record the value as an effective bottleneck value. We take the maximum effective bottleneck value in the bottleneck interval as the reference bottleneck (the bottleneck time interval depends on the data set interval and automatic redistribution time setting. The default is 1 min).

(6) When the reference bottleneck occurs multiple times in an interval and the bottleneck time obtained by the threshold identification function is in the same order of magnitude, reallocation is performed.

Algorithm 1 Bottleneck Identification Algorithm

Input:

n_i, c_j: Node i,task j.

w, b: partial derivative w,b.

T: the maximum bottleneck time between n_{i-1}.and n_i.

l: Transmission link bandwidth.

$T_C(n_i, c_j)$: the average computing time for task j on node i.

$T_t(n_i, c_j)$: the sum of the average transmission time from the preceding node to the succeeding node.

$x(c_j)$: the complexity of computing task j.

$m(x(c_j))$: the function that calculates the amount of processing power required under the complexity of the task.

Tr,e(f, y): Reference bottleneck linear regression function.

$T_{bottleneck}$: Bottleneck time list.

Output: $l_{bottleneck}$:Bottleneck level list.

1: **procedure** Bottleneck Identification Algorithm

   //Training function

2: **Calculate** $\frac{1}{m}\sum_{i=1}^{m}(f(x) - y_i)^2 = e(f, y)$

3: **from** $\frac{1}{m}\sum_{i=1}^{m}(wx_i + b - yi)^2 = e(f, y)$

4: **Calculate** $w = \frac{\sum_{i=1}^{m} y_i(x_i - \bar{x})}{\sum_{i=0}^{m} x_i^2 - \frac{1}{m}(\sum_{i=1}^{m} x_i)^2}$, $b = \frac{1}{m}\sum_{i=1}^{m}(y_i - wx_i)$

   //Cycle comparison

5: **while**(START FLAG)

6: **Calculate** $T_C(n_i, c_j) = \frac{m(x(c_j))}{p(n_i)}$

7: **Calculate** $T_t(n_i, c_j) = \frac{m(cj)}{l_{i-1,i}} + \frac{m(cj)}{l_{i,i+1}} = \frac{m(cj)(l_{i-1,i} + l_{i,i+1})}{l_{i-1,i}l_{i,i+1}}$

8: T = max(T_C, T_t)

9: Tr = e(f, y)

   //Compare T AND Tr

10: **if** T/Tr < 10 **then**

    //Judge the magnitude of the same number

11: $T_{bottleneck}[i] = T$

12: i++

13: **end if**

14: **end while**

    //After sorting,

    //the sequence number is regarded as the bottleneck level in turn

15: SORT($T_{bottleneck}$) GET $l_{bottleneck}$

16: **return** $l_{bottleneck}$

3.2 Parameter Plan Generation

Bottleneck level priority: The task with the highest bottleneck level gets slots allocated first, then the remaining slots are allocated in turn to tasks with lower bottleneck levels.

This allocation strategy considers the weight of bottleneck level more, and is suitable for situations where the difference of bottleneck time between topologies is large. The bottleneck time is calculated for different topologies. Each topology calculates the bottleneck time and then sorts them globally.

$$\overline{N}_{Task} = \varphi \frac{N_{Executer} + N_{Bottleneck}}{N_{Executer}} N_{Task}. \tag{7}$$

Parameter planning priority: According to the bottleneck levels from high to low, the previous executor number is added to the bottleneck level multiplied by the coefficient (default 1). At the same time, the number of tasks is increased by the corresponding multiple times. This allocation strategy controls the weight of the bottleneck level by a coefficient φ, and is suitable for situations where the bottleneck time between topologies has little difference. The bottleneck level and parameter schedule on the example WordCount instance are as follows (Table 1):

Table 1. Bottleneck level and parameter schedule on the WordCount instance

Topology	Worker number	Executor number	Task number	Bottleneck level
T1	3	8	16	4
T2	5	10	10	2
T3	3	5	10	1
T4	6	10	20	3

Algorithm 2 Parameter Plan Algorithm

Input:
N_{Task}: Number of resources allocated to previous tasks.
$\overline{N}_{Task}$: Number of resources allocated to current tasks.
$l_{bottleneck}$: Bottleneck level list.
φ: Allocation coefficient
Output: $\overline{N}_{Task}$: Transmission link bandwidth.

1: **procedure** Parameter Plan Algorithm
    //Add the previous number of executors to the number of bottleneck levels multiplied by a factor (default 1)
2: **Calculate** $\overline{N}_{Task} = \varphi \frac{N_{Executer} + l_{Bottleneck}}{N_{Executer}} N_{Task}$
3: **return** $\overline{N}_{Task}$

3.3 Parameter Migration and Conversion

Parameter migration conversion is conducted based on parameter planning. Its process is as follows:

(1) When Me-Stream program is started, the table columns N(k,v) and P(k,v) will be created automatically;
(2) At runtime, the current node and port are saved into the corresponding keys;
(3) Before redistribution, a new operator allocation is generated based on the parameter schedule;
(4) After completing the allocation, the node and port from the new allocation result are assigned to replace the corresponding value in the routing table;
(5) After N (k, v) and P (k, v) are updated, they are provided as a migration path on the example WordCount instance to the new scheduling (Table 2).

Table 2. Parameter plan and migration path on the WordCount instance

Topology	Executor number	Task number	Operator number	Slots		Migration path	
				Node	Port	N (k,v)	P (k,v)
T1	1	1	{ [1, 2]...}	S1	6700	(1, 3)	(1, 3)
	1	2		S1	6700	(1, 3)	(1, 3)
...							
T2	2	3	{...[3]...}	S2	6701	(2, 2)	(2, 1)
...							
T3	3	9	{...[9, 10]...}	S3	6702	(3, 1)	(3, 2)
	3	10		S3	6702	(3, 1)	(3, 2)

Algorithm 3 Migration Algorithm

Input:
k, v: Key,value.
n_i, p_j: Node i,port j.
$\bar{n}_i$, $\bar{p}_j$: Node i,port j.
Output: N(k,v): Node migration path.
P(k,v): Port migration path.

1: **procedure** Migration Algorithm
   //During operation, the current node and port are stored in the corresponding keys.
2: **while**(!EMPTY)
3:   N(k, v).put(n_i, $\bar{n}_i$)
4:   P(k, v).put(p_j, $\bar{p}_j$)
5:   i++
6:   j++
7: **end while**
8: **return** N(k,v),P(k,v)

3.4   Instances Scheduling

Bottlenecks may be created during the optimization process because of the computing and communication bottlenecks on heterogeneous cluster nodes, the stateful and stateless instances at the instance layer [16, 17], and some complex pluggable scheduling. As such, an instance scheduling that can directly identify the migration table is designed, and the corresponding configuration is provided as the default setting. The specific instance scheduling steps are executed as follows:

(1) Call the cluster's *needsSchedualerTopologies* method to obtain the topology that needs to be assigned with tasks, and store all the topologies in the keys of N (k, v) and P (k, v) according to the bottleneck level.
(2) Call the cluster's *getAvailableSlots* method to obtain the resources available in the current cluster, return them in the form of a collection of <node, port>, and allocate them to available slots.
(3) Call the cluster's *compute-executors* method to convert the topological executor information into a collection of <start-t ask-id, end-task-id> and store it in all executors.
(4) Call the *getAliveAssignedNodeAndPort* method of *eventScheduler* to obtain the resources acquired by the current topology, and return the <node + port, executor> collection and store it in *alive-assigned*.
(5) Call the overriding *slot-can-ressign* method in Me-Stream to determine whether the Slots information is active, then select the slot that can be reassigned and store it in the *can-ressigned* variable.
(6) Call the overriding *bad-slot* method in Me-Stream to calculate the number of slots that can be released in the current topology. If it is greater than the number of slots currently allocated, call the cluster's *freeSlots* method to release them.
(7) Call the *migration-path* method in Me-Stream and allocate all execution programs based on the N (k, v) and P (k, v) records calculated by all topologies before scheduling.

4   Performance Evaluation

In this section, the experimental environment and parameter settings are first discussed, followed by the analysis of performance evaluation results.

4.1   Experimental Environment and Parameter Settings

The proposed Me-Stream system is implemented on Storm 2.1.0, and installed on top of Ubuntu 20.04.1. Real-life data experiments are conducted on the computing cluster at Alibaba Cloud Computing. The cluster consists of 28 machines, with 1 designated machine serving as the master node, running Storm Nimbus, 2 designated as Zookeeper nodes, and the rest 25 machines working as Supervisor nodes. The software configuration of Me-Stream platform is shown in Table 3.

Table 3. Software configuration of Me-Stream.

Software	Version
OS	Ubuntu 20.04.1 64bit
Storm	Apache-Storm-2.1.0
JDK	Jdk1.8 64bit
Zookeeper	Zookeeper-3.4.14
Kafka	Kafka-2.3.0
Redis	Redis-6.0.5

Moreover, one DAG with WordCount function is submitted to the computing cluster. The logic graph of WordCount is shown in Fig. 2.

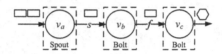

Fig. 2. Logical graph of WordCount in Me-Stream

In Storm, the WordCount instance is used to simulate random words input into Spout through Kafka, and messages from different partitions are evenly distributed to different executors for consumption. When Spout parallelism is set to 1, there is no need to adjust the parameters. Therefore, our focus is to test the system performance when the spout has multiple executors. Under normal circumstances, the Capacity value range is between 0.0x and 0.2. When the value is close to 1, it indicates that the load is severe and the degree of parallelism needs to be increased. At the same time, when the failure value is not 0, it means that the load is serious and there are tuples that experience failure or time out. At this time, the parallelism of Spout should be increased accordingly. We simulate a normal situation where the Capacity value is small and Failure value is 0. The following describes the experimental verification in detail, and the parameter table applied in the entire experimental process is shown in Table 4.

Table 4. Table of parameter settings in the experiments.

Parameter	Explain
Emitted	Number of tuples launched to date
Transferred	Number of tuples successfully transferred to the next bolt to date
Complete latency (ms)	The average time taken for each tuple to be fully processed in tuple tree to date
Acked	Number of tuples successfully processed to date
Failed	Number of tuples failed or timed out to date

4.2   Performance Results

We consider the average delay data set of topologies within 38min ∼ 50min under the default Storm scheduling strategy and Me-Stream optimization strategy for comparison. The experimental settings contain two evaluation parameters: execute latency EL and process latency PL.

(1) Execute latency.

Execute latency reflects the overall execution time for all running DAGs, and it is evaluated by the timestamp from the execution of the function to the end of per DAG. The smaller the execution latency, the stronger the data processing ability of the elastic stream computing system.

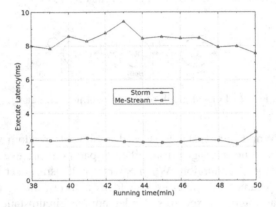

Fig. 3. Comparison of execute latency between the default scheduler and Me-Stream on the WordCount instance.

When the data input rate is stable, Me-Stream has a lower execution latency comparing to the *DefaultScheduler* on Storm platform. As shown in Fig. 3, with the capacity remains unchanged during the whole process, the average execute latency by Me-Stream and by the default scheduler at the stable stage are 2.3886 ms and 8.3267 ms, respectively. It demonstrates that the execution latency by Me-Stream is lower than that of the default scheduler on the given instance when the input rate is stable.

(2) Process latency.

Process latency reflects the overall processing time for all running DAGs, and it is evaluated by the timestamp of each DAG passed from the tuple arrival to the ack. The smaller the processing latency, the stronger the data processing ability of the elastic stream computing system.

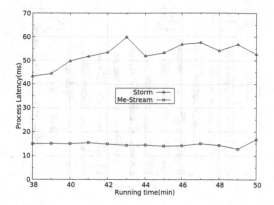

Fig. 4. Comparison of process latency between the default scheduler and Me-Stream on the WordCount instance.

When the data input rate is stable, Me-Stream has a lower process latency comparing to the *DefaultScheduler* on Storm platform. As shown in Fig. 4, with the capacity remains unchanged during the whole process, the average process latency by Me-Stream and by default Storm strategy at the stable stage are 14.6867 ms and 52.7333 ms, respectively. It demonstrates that the process latency by Me-Stream is lower than that of the default Storm strategy on the given instance when the input rate is stable.

We also respectively collect statistics on execute delay, process delay and total delay data sets of the *DefaultScheduler* and the Me-Stream optimization strategy, as shown in Fig. 5 and 6.

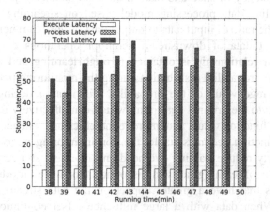

Fig. 5. Statistics of execute delay, process delay and total delay data sets of the default scheduler on the WordCount instance.

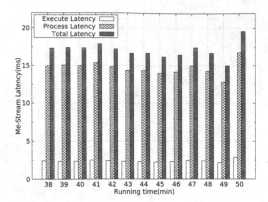

Fig. 6. Statistics of execute delay, process delay and total delay data sets of the Me-Stream optimization strategy on the WordCount instance.

5   Related Work

The application of machine learning models can produce better parallel migration paths and better resource allocation without manual intervention. However, the time-consuming training process greatly limits the efficiency of machine learning methods, and the inconsistency of state and data can also cause considerable overhead. Researchers have been trying to address these issues.

In [18], a double exponential smoothing method was proposed to predict abnormal events, which solves the shortcoming of the Markov model that requires a training process. By designing a seven-phase protocol for traffic-aware active migration, it handles the inconsistency of state and data in the load balancing partition.

In [19], a pipeline data processing model based on streaming applications was mentioned. When the ratio of input data to output data of upstream neighbor operations is known, the input data of downstream neighbor operations can be obtained in advance. The linear relationship is obtained through learning and analysis, and the average value of the probability distribution during the monitoring period is taken. The concept of the average value of the probability distribution during the monitoring period is also added to the original algorithm, which can effectively reduce the error of the data set and the function value, and improve the efficiency and accuracy of training. When the fitting function becomes stable, the non-monitoring period can be entered, which can effectively reduce training overhead and release resources.

In [20], the ideas of learning rate and discount factor were introduced on the basis of fitting. Data sets that have a greater impact on the data stream are stored in the evaluation table. When data with a large influence offset continuously appears, its weight can be added to influence according to the evaluation result, so as to achieve the purpose of better training the result function.

In [21], a cost-effective resource allocation model was proposed. Its purpose is to allow users to automatically and efficiently deploy applications in local or cloud clusters, and developed a profiler for Spark, which can analyze applications in actual clusters according to different resource allocation schemes and input workloads. Based on the application profile received from the profiler, dSpark uses the proposed resource allocation model to select a cost-effective resource allocation plan based on the deadline in order to deploy the application to the cluster.

The above prior works provide valuable insights into the potential solutions to the static parallelization setting problems using elastic strategies of machine learning. However, for big data stream applications, innovative methods need to be developed, and the characteristics specific to the big data flow computing environments need to be considered when exploring elastic non-manual intervention. A summary of the comparison between our work and other closely related works is given in Table 5.

Table 5. Comparison of Me-Stream and related work

Parameter	Related work				Me-Stream
	[18]	[19]	[20]	[21]	
Versatility	✗	✓	✓	✗	✓
Parallelism	✓	✓	✓	✓	✓
Machine learning	✗	✓	✓	✗	✓
Cost saving	✗	✓	✗	✓	✓
Resource saving	✗	✗	✓	✓	✓

6   Conclusions and Future Work

In this paper, an elastic scaling strategy for operator parallelism Me-Stream is proposed. It can intelligently perform instance parallelism without manual intervention at runtime. Starting from the Storm Instance parameter level, we first initiate a monitoring process to obtain the bolts-related data in real time through traffic sensing, then analyze and use them, followed by self-optimizing the resource allocation from time to time. This paper mainly solves the following problems:

(1) It is not transparent for Storm users to use API to set parallelism for operators in a topology at runtime, that is, users need to run the API frequently to change the configuration of their applications.
(2) Storm users may not know how to optimally adjust the parallelism. We use a machine learning model to achieve a better parallel migration path. The model can achieve a better effect in terms of resource allocation without manual intervention, and has a certain learning ability.
(3) Storm distributes instances to work programs and work program nodes in a round-robin manner by default. The number of configured work programs is still evenly distributed. The instance scheduling we designed can achieve better compatibility with the intelligent tuning scheme under the premise of ensuring good generalization.

Future work will focus on the following aspects:

(1) Adapt Me-Stream to other big data stream computing environments.
(2) Deploy Me-Stream in a real big data stream computing environment.

Acknowledgements. This work is supported by the National Natural Science Foundation of China under Grant No. 61972364, the Fundamental Research Funds for the Central Universities under Grant No. 2652021001, and Melbourne-Chindia Cloud Computing (MC3) Research Network.

References

1. Cao, H., Wu, C.E.Q., Bao, L., Hou, A., Shen, W.: Throughput optimization for Storm-based processing of stream data on clouds. Future Gener. Comput. Syst. **112**, 567–579 (2020)
2. Paris, C., Stephan, E., Gyula, F., Seif, H., Stefan, R., Kostas, T.: State management in Apache Flink: consistent stateful distributed stream processing. Proc. VLDB Endow. **10**(12), 1718–1729 (2017)
3. Apache, Storm. http://storm.apache.org
4. Flink. https://flink.apache.org/
5. Spark Streaming. https://spark.apache.org/streaming/
6. Samza. http://samza.apache.org/
7. Apex. https://apex.apache.org/
8. Google Cloud Dataflow. https://cloud.google.com/dataflow/
9. Deng, S., Wang, B., Huang, S., Yue, C., Zhou, J., Wang, G.: Self-adaptive framework for efficient stream data classification on storm. IEEE Trans. Syst. Man Cybern. Syst. **50**(1), 123–136 (2020)
10. Li, C., Zhang, J., Luo, Y.: Real-time scheduling based on optimized topology and communication traffic in distributed real-time computation platform of storm. J. Netw. Comput. Appl. **87**, 100–115 (2017)
11. Muhammad, A., Aleem, M., Islam, M.A.: TOP-Storm: a topology-based resource-aware scheduler for Stream Processing Engine. Cluster Comput. **24**(1), 417–431 (2020). https://doi.org/10.1007/s10586-020-03117-y
12. Pathan, R., Voudouris, P., Stenstrom, P.: Scheduling parallel real-time recurrent tasks on multicore platforms. IEEE Trans. Parallel Distrib. Syst. **29**(4), 915–928 (2018)
13. Li, H., Wu, J., Jiang, Z., Li, X., Wei, X.: Task allocation for stream processing with recovery latency guarantee. In: Proceedings of the 2017 IEEE International Conference on Cluster Computing, CLUSTER 2017, pp. 379–383. IEEE Press,September 2017
14. Zhang, J., Li, C., Zhu, L., Liu, Y.: The real-time scheduling strategy based on traffic and load balancing in storm. In: Proceedings of the 18th IEEE International Conference on High Performance Computing and Communications, HPCC 2016, pp. 372–379. IEEE Press, January 2017
15. Muhammad, A., Aleem, M.: A3-Storm: topology-, traffic-, and resource-aware storm scheduler for heterogeneous clusters. J. Supercomput. **77**(2), 1059–1093 (2020). https://doi.org/10.1007/s11227-020-03289-9
16. You, Y., Demmel, J.: Runtime data layout scheduling for machine learning dataset. In: Proceedings of the 46th International Conference on Parallel Processing, ICPP 2017, pp. 452–461. IEEE Press,September 2017

17. Al-Sinayyid, A., Zhu, M.: Job scheduler for streaming applications in heterogeneous distributed processing systems. J. Supercomput. **76**(12), 9609–9628 (2020). https://doi.org/10.1007/s11227-020-03223-z
18. Cheng, D., Wang, Y.: Adaptive scheduling parallel jobs with dynamic batching in spark streaming. IEEE Trans. Parallel Distrib. Syst. **29**(12), 2672–2685 (2018)
19. Wei, X.: Pec: proactive elastic collaborative resource scheduling in data stream processing. IEEE Trans. Parallel Distrib. Syst. **30**(7), 1628–1642 (2019)
20. Wang, W., Zhang, C.:An on-the-fly scheduling strategy for distributed stream processing platform. In: IEEE International Conference on Parallel & Distributed Processing with Applications, Ubiquitous Computing & Communications, Big Data & Cloud Computing, Social Computing & Networking, Sustainable Computing & Communications (2018)
21. TawfiqulIslam, M., Karunasekera, S., Buyya, R.: dSpark: deadline-based resource allocation for big data applicationsin apache spark. In: IEEE 13th International Conference on e-Science, 24–27 October 2017

End-to-End Dynamic Pipelining Tuning Strategy for Small Files Transfer

Shimin Wu[1], Dawei Sun[1(✉)], Shang Gao[2], and Guangyan Zhang[3]

[1] School of Information Engineering, China University of Geosciences,
Beijing 100083, People's Republic of China
{wushimin,sundaweicn}@cugb.edu.cn
[2] School of Information Technology, Deakin University, Victoria 3216, Australia
shang.gao@deakin.edu.au
[3] Department of Computer Science and Technology, Tsinghua University,
Beijing 100084, China
gyzh@tsinghua.edu.cn

Abstract. Improving the transmission efficiency for small files over a wide area network is always challenging. Time may be wasted when waiting for transmission commands due to the design of transfer protocols, which in turn increases the Round-trip time (RTT). GridFTP is widely deployed as a transfer protocol in the grid era, where a concept of pipelining is proposed to improve the transmission efficiency for small files. Based on the GridFTP protocol, we design a smart data structure to classify files and propose a corresponding scheduling algorithm to tune the pipelining parameters, making them more reasonable and adaptive to different transmission scenarios. Bandwidth usage is optimized when a large number of small files are transferred with our strategy by combining the optimal pipelining and concurrency parameters. A method to optimizing the throughput for high-priority file transfer is also proposed. By adjusting the pipelining parameter dynamically, the throughput is increased by almost 10% compared with other methods. Moreover, our method achieves better performance even with a smaller concurrency setting. The favorable throughput is maintained when transferring high-priority files.

Keywords: GridFTP · Throughput optimization · Pipelining and concurrency · Lots of small files · Network protocols

1 Introduction

In this fast-developing era, a variety of new concepts and technologies are emerging. Massive volume of data ranging from GB to PB is generated every day, such as scientific experimental and e-commerce data. Most of the data are small files consisting of pictures and text information. For example, in BLAST [1], the bioinformatic data generated and required by experiments is usually string

W. Xiang et al. (Eds.): BROADNETS 2021, LNICST 413, pp. 20–36, 2022.
https://doi.org/10.1007/978-3-030-93479-8_2

data. The data needs to be transferred between sites before the experiments are conducted. Moreover, a research report from the Pacific Northwest National Laboratory in the United States showed that there were 12 million files in their system, 94% of which were smaller than 64 MB, and 58% were smaller than 64 KB [2]. Similar situations also exist in other systems and become more and more common. E.g. the meteorological data in a meteorological communication system [3] has the characteristics of large amount of output, diverse value types and small file sizes. With such data characteristics, the system needs to transfer them to the National Weather Information Center for further processing. There are priority or dependency relationships among these small files in some scenarios. For example, the model parameters of certain scientific experiments should be transmitted as soon as possible to start the next experiments.

When transferring different types of files, insufficient utilization of bandwidth on WAN has always been a problem under discussion. This phenomenon is more obvious when transferring data sets composed of small files like the aforementioned meteorological data. The low utilization of bandwidth might be caused by many reasons, such as the overhead of channel connection/disconnection, the transfer protocols which cannot make full use of the network bandwidth due to the time spent on waiting for the confirmation of transmission commands between two parties. Furthermore, the total idle time of a data channel will increase with the RTT (Round-Trip Time) and the number of files. For such scenarios, GridFTP supports a pipelining [4] parameter to ease the bandwidth under-utilization problem when transferring a large number of small files. However, how to find the best pipelining parameter is still a challenging problem to solve. Pipelining can neither make full use of bandwidth when the parameter value is too small, nor improve the utilization further when it is too large. Sometimes it may even consume more system resources (e.g. more storage and CPU to analyze the additional transmission commands). Moreover, the optimization of pipelining parameter often vary with the characteristics of file sets and network conditions.

The paper designs a smart data structure and an algorithm to find an optimal pipelining parameter value for different types of file sets by rearranging a transfer queue, while keeping the consumption of system resources as low as possible. The proposed algorithm not only suits for the transmission of static file sets, but also works well for the dynamic ones. The rest of the paper is organized as follows: Sect. 2 briefly introduces the background of GridFTP and related work. Section 3 describes the design and implementation of our structure and algorithm. Section 4 presents the experimental results. Section 5 concludes the paper and discusses future work.

2   Background and Related Work

In this section, we introduce the background knowledge of GridFTP. Furthermore, we review the typical existing methods for improving the GridFTP protocol and analyze their advantages and disadvantages.

2.1   GridFTP

GridFTP [5–7], as a part of the Globus Toolkit [8] project, is a high-performance, secure and reliable data transfer protocol optimized for high-bandwidth wide area networks. It is an extension to FTP [9] protocol and defined for high-performance operation and security purposes. GridFTP contains many new features such as automatic negotiation of TCP socket buffer size, third-party control of file transfer and partial file transfer, etc. GridFTP's parallelism, concurrency and pipelining [10] are three powerful parameters to improve bandwidth utilization for different scenarios.

Parallel streams have a positive impact on the transmission of a single large file. The provision of parallel streams is mainly through the establishment of multiple data channels for single file transmission, where a file is divided into multiple parts, and each data channel transmits one part. This approach can quickly transit through the slow start-up phase and make full use of network bandwidth. Parallel streams are controlled by the parallelism parameter in GridFTP. Many scholars use socket buffer size adjustment technology together with parallelism to resolve the deficiencies of TCP [11–13]. There is an optimal value for the parallelism parameter in a given scenario. An excessively large parallelism value cannot increase the transmission throughput, and sometimes has negative effects.

Concurrency supports transmission of multiple files simultaneously through the establishment of multiple control channels. Therefore, the overall utilization of bandwidth is improved. In most cases, the effect of concurrency parameter is better than that of parallelism [14]. Increasing the value of concurrency parameter can significantly improve the throughput, but the use of concurrency parameters may be constrained by resources such as CPU and file system processes.

Pipelining is mainly used to solve the problem of transferring a large number of small files. By allowing the client to have multiple unconfirmed transfer commands at once, the idle time between transmission is reduced as much as possible. Before reaching the formulated number of unconfirmed commands, the client can send transmission commands at any time, and the server processes the requests in the arrival order of the commands. Similar to the other two parameters, how to find the best pipelining parameter for different file sets and network conditions is challenging.

2.2   Related Work

There are many research aiming at finding an optimal value for the GridFTP parallelism parameter to improve the throughput of large file transmission over WAN. A formula was proposed in [15] to get the throughput of multiple parallel streams, followed by a series of transmission experiments conducted on WAN to evaluate how parallel streams could improve the throughput. [16] further studied the relationship between packet loss rate, RTT and parallel flow. It proposed a prediction formula for parallel flow. Based on the research of [15,16], a new model was proposed in [17] to approximate the optimal number of parallelism with the least historical information and the lowest prediction overhead.

Although there have been some optimization studies on GridFTP parameters, most of them aimed at large file transmission scenarios. With the development of technologies, the problem of lots of small files (LOSF) transmission should also be taken into consideration. The pipelining of GridFTP is a powerful tool to improve the efficiency of small file transmission, but it has the same problem as the parallelism parameter, i.e. how to determine an optimal pipelining parameter value.

In Globus Online [18], a static method was proposed for setting pipelining parameter according to file size and quantity. If there are more than 100 files for transmission in a file set, and the average file size is less than 50 MB, the pipelining parameter is set to 20. If all files are larger than 250 MB, the pipelining parameter is 5. Otherwise, the default value is 10. This algorithm does not consider the factor that the pipelining parameter is not only related to file characteristics, but also related to network characteristics. Too large a pipelining parameter value may have a negative impact on throughput, and even waste system resources.

Many scholars have conducted further research to explore the combined use of the three parameters. [19] proposed a model that adjusted the values of the three parameters based on historical information. [20] found that when transferring LOSF, pipelining did not work well with parallelism, because the implementation of parallelism transmission is based on the establishment of multiple TCP transmission channels, which will further reduce the size of the transmitted file and exacerbate the problem of bandwidth under-utilization. Therefore, for LOSF transmission scenarios, better to use the pipelining parameter and concurrency parameter together. Based on this finding, a Recursive Chunk Division (RCD) algorithm was proposed in [20] to calculate the best pipelining parameter value. The advantage of this algorithm is that the pipelining parameter value can be obtained according to different network conditions and file set characteristics. However, this algorithm could easily reach the maximum pipelining parameter value (e.g. 20) when processing KB-level files, and it will take up a lot of resources when the number of server requests increases. In some cases, even setting with the maximum pipelining parameter value, the file clusters could not take up most of the link bandwidth, resulting in a waste of bandwidth.

3   Optimal Pipelining Adjustment

When transmitting LOSF, the file composition of different file sets might be different. For example, some may have files of similar sizes, while others might have high variance in file size. So how to deal with file sets with different characteristics and determine the best pipelining parameter value for them is difficult. In this section, we design a smart data structure to address this problem, and propose an algorithm to determine an optimal pipelining parameter value based on this structure.

3.1 Pipelining Calculation

File size is the main factor to consider when setting an optimal pipelining value, especially for long RTT networks. Regardless of the file size, transmission at different pipeline levels will experience a similar slow start phase. The key point is whether each transmission after the slow start phase can reach the maximum number of bytes under current network condition. If the file size is larger than the BDP [21] (Bandwidth-Delay Product), the bandwidth of each transmission can be fully utilized. If the file size is smaller than the BDP, the link might not be fully used, or there will be under-utilization of bandwidth. With an optimal pipelining parameter value, each transmission will more likely reach the maximum link bandwidth to reduce any waste and increase the throughput. However, under special circumstances, if there are a large number of extremely small files, even if the maximum pipelining value is adopted, the link still cannot be fully utilized. For this kind of scenarios, this paper designs a new data structure, called bucket structure, to store files with different characteristics. On top of it, a Bucket Divide (BD) algorithm is proposed to tune the optimal pipelining parameter value and rearrange the file transmission queue according to that value.

The original intention of bucket design is to reduce the time complexity of sorting files. Similar to the RCD algorithm, accurate sorting based on file size is required for getting an optimal pipelining parameter. The buckets are used to hold different sized files. If the file sorting is not desirable, the files combined from the buckets for transmission may not match the target BDP well, resulting low bandwidth utilization. To reduce the influence of imprecise sorting, we increase the denominator of the pipelining parameter calculation. The pp (pipelining parameter) value calculated in formula (1) is an initial value. It will be fine tuned when the files in the bucket structure meet certain conditions.

The pp calculation formula is listed as formula (1):

$$pp = 3 * BDP/MF - 1 \tag{1}$$

where the BDP is Bandwidth-Delay Product and MF is the mean file size of the files smaller than BDP. One reason why the denominator is set to triple BDP is to reduce the effect of phenomenon when the size of file combination cannot match the BDP well. Secondly, we hope that the transmission can be stabilized over the slow start phase, and the TCP stream needs to transmit about three times [22] BDP to fill the channel. The difference between our formulation and RCD algorithm is the RCD algorithm divides the files of similar sizes into a file cluster and calculates the best pp value based on this cluster, while our formulation uses all the files smaller than BDP in the bucket structure (to be introduced later in detail) to calculate the pp. If a file set contains some files whose sizes are close to the BDP, the MF can be increased significantly. The calculated pp is smaller than that of the RCD algorithm, giving us an opportunity to increase the denominator and improve transmission performance.

3.2   File Classification

The design of the new data structure mainly adopts the idea of bucketing used to store files by size. When the number of buckets increases, the file sizes in each bucket become more closer. Allocating files to these buckets is like sorting the file set. To improve the bandwidth utilization, we can deliberately select files from these buckets and make the combined file size as close as possible to the BDP. But the drawback is using a large number of buckets for sorting all files of the file set will increase time complexity. We need to use less buckets to decrease time complexity. The algorithms discussed in Subsect. 3.3 are proposed to address this problem: first allocating files into different sized buckets, then selecting files from proper buckets and creating file combination with the right size.

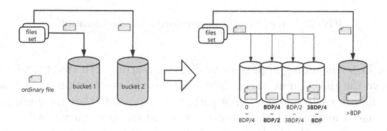

Fig. 1. The process of ordinary file classification

As shown in Fig. 1, bucket 2 is used to load files larger than BDP, while bucket 1 keeps the files smaller than BDP. All the files stored in bucket 1 are small files, which are the main factor to derive the best pp value. We further divide bucket 1 into multiple smaller buckets. One thing to note is that the number of smaller buckets is to be carefully selected as it impacts on the size accuracy of the file combination. The larger number of buckets is adopted, the more accurate size of file combination we have. In extreme cases, all the same sized files are allocated to one bucket. The fewer the number of buckets, the more files placed in each bucket. This results in greater size difference in a bucket and larger size deviation to BDP for the file combination being created by selecting files from different buckets. Since the files in each bucket are randomly placed and not ordered purposely, this randomness lowers the probability of selecting multiple smallest files for one pp transmission. Moreover, the performance improvement brought by a large number of buckets is not very outstanding. We tested the performance with different bucket numbers and found that when the number of buckets exceed 10, there was almost no improvement. We recommend that 4–10 buckets is normally a good choice. The following analysis and description will use 4 buckets as an example.

As shown in Fig. 1, bucket 1 is equally divided into 4 small buckets, represented by No.1–No.4. The size ranges of files stored in each bucket are 0–BDP/4, BDP/4–BDP/2, BDP/2–3BDP/4 and 3BDP/4–BDP, respectively. Bucket 2 (No. 5) is used to store files larger than BDP. The files in the 4 small buckets (No. 1–4) are mainly used to calculate the pp value. The files in the bucket 2 (No. 5) is to supplement the file combination, offsetting the gap between the pipelining files and the BDP, and increasing the pipelining transmission bandwidth.

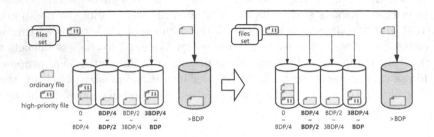

Fig. 2. The process of high-priority file classification

For a file set including high-priority files, we rearrange the file transfer queue to improve the throughput and deliver them to the destination as fast as possible. As files in each bucket are not sorted, it is possible that the high-priority files are placed at the end of the bucket file transmission queue. Although the transmission of a small file does not take too much time, given a large number of small files are to be transmitted, the files placed at the end of transmission queue may still take a considerately long time to be delivered. As such, the transmission order is important for the high-priority files. If we simply insert the high-priority files to the front of the queue without specific ordering, their transmission might not consume the ideal bandwidth, which in turn reduces the total throughput.

To reduce the potential bandwidth waste when transferring large number of high-priority files, we cannot simply put them at the front of the queue. The best arrangement should be transferring them as soon as possible without significant decrease of bandwidth utilization. To do that, we arrange the high-priority files to the No. 1, No. 4 and No. 5 buckets because the files transmission priority of these buckets are set higher. Furthermore, we put the files to the front of these bucket queues. As shown in Fig. 2, the file replacement operation is performed after the files are sorted into buckets. If there is a non-prioritized ordinary file in front of the high-priority file sorted into No.1 bucket, that ordinary file will be swapped with the high-priority file. The right side of Fig. 2 shows the status after the replacement.

To ensure the pipelining transmission size as close to the BDP as possible, each transmission chunk may mix several ordinary files. The mixing of several non-prioritized ordinary files will not consume too much time. The transmission speed of high-priority files is still improved without notable total throughput drop.

3.3 File Queue Rearrangement

Our Bucket Divide (BD) has 2 steps: File Bucket Divide (Algorithm 1 FBD) and Transmission Queue (Algorithm 2 TQ). The proposed bucket structure is used to support file classification from line 1 to 13, as shown in Algorithm 1. After the file classification, the files are put into corresponding buckets by size.

The OPTIMALPP function is used to calculate the pp value based on the status of $bucketNum[0]$ to $bucketNum[4]$ (e.g. No. 1–5 bucket), as shown from lines 16 to 23 of OPTIMALPP function. The variable $times$ in OPTIMALPP represents the number of rounds that the files in $bucketNum[4]$ (e.g. No. 5 bucket) can be transferred for a pp value. N is the total file number in $bucketNum[4]$. The pp value will be fine tuned if N and $time$ meet certain conditions, which will be discussed in Algorithm 2.

Algorithm 1. File Bucket Divide(FBD)

Input: $file$ list, $bucketNum[0] \rightarrow bucketNum[4]$, BDP
Output: $bucketNum[0] \rightarrow bucketNum[4]$, N, pp, $times$
 1: **while** $file$ list **do**
 2:      **if** $0 < file[i].size <= BDP/4$ **then**
 3:          $bucketNum[0] \leftarrow file[i]$
 4:      **else if** $BDP/4 < file[i].size <= BDP/2$ **then**
 5:          $bucketNum[1] \leftarrow file[i]$
 6:      **else if** $BDP/2 < file[i].size <= 3BDP/4$ **then**
 7:          $bucketNum[2] \leftarrow file[i]$
 8:      **else if** $3BDP/4 < file[i].size <= BDP$ **then**
 9:          $bucketNum[3] \leftarrow file[i]$
10:      **else** $file[i].size > BDP$
11:          $bucketNum[4] \leftarrow file[i]$
12:      **end if**
13: **end while**
14: OPTIMALPP $(bucketNum[0] \rightarrow bucketNum[4])$
15:
16: **function** OPTIMALPP$(bucketNum[0] \rightarrow bucketNum[4])$
17:      Calculate $Nums \leftarrow$ the number of files except for $bucketNum[4]$
18:      Calculate $meanFileSize \leftarrow$ mean file size except for $bucketNum[4]$
19:      Calculate $N \leftarrow$ the number of files in $bucketNum[4]$
20:      Calculate $pp \leftarrow [3BDP/meanFileSize] - 1$
21:      Calculate $times \leftarrow Nums/(pp + 1)$
22:      **return** N, pp, $times$
23: **end function**

The Algorithm 2 Transmission Queue (TQ) aims to establish a file transmission queue by taking out files from buckets selectively, so that the pp transmission can match the BDP as close as possible. The rule to take out files is determined by $times$, pp and N from Algorithm 1.

As shown in Algorithm 2, the value of maxPP is set to 20 (an empirical setting). Given N is the number of files contained in $bucketNum[4]$, when the value of "times" is greater than N, it means that the files in the $bucketNum[4]$ are not enough to make the pipelining transmission match BDP optimally. In this case, we perform the function EQUALTRANSFER in Algorithm 2, which uses the large files in $bucketNum[4]$ to consume small files as much as possible for decreasing the effect of small files in subsequent transmission and increase the probability of the remaining file combination matching the BDP.

Algorithm 2. Transmission Queue(TQ)

Input: $bucketNum[0] \rightarrow bucketNum[4]$, $maxPP$, N, pp, $times$
Output: $queue$
 1: **if** $times > N$ **then**
 2:      EQUALTRANSFER($bucketNum[0] \rightarrow bucketNum[4], pp$)
 3: **else**
 4:      $newPP \leftarrow pp + [N/times]$
 5:      **if** $newPP < maxPP$ **then**
 6:          INEQUALTRANSFER($bucketNum[0] \rightarrow bucketNum[4], newPP, pp$)
 7:      **else**
 8:          $newPP \leftarrow maxPP$
 9:          INEQUALTRANSFER($bucketNum[0] \rightarrow bucketNum[4], newPP, pp$)
10:      **end if**
11: **end if**
12: **function** EQUALTRANSFER($bucketNum[0] \rightarrow bucketNum[4], pp$)
13:      initialize an empty $queue$
14:      $left = 0$, $right = 3$ and $big = 4$
15:      **while** $bucketNum[0] \rightarrow bucketNum[4]$ is not empty **do**
16:          **if** the file number is zero in bucketNum[left] or bucketNum[right] **then**
17:              $left ++$ or $right --$
18:          **end if**
19:          **if** $bucketNum[big]$ is not empty **then**
20:              $queue \leftarrow pp$ number of files from bucketNum[left]
21:              $queue \leftarrow$ one file from bucketNum[big]
22:          **else if** $(pp + 1)$ is even **then**
23:              $queue \leftarrow (pp + 1)/2$ number of files from bucketNum[left]
24:              $queue \leftarrow (pp + 1)/2$ number of files from bucketNum[right]
25:          **else if** $(pp + 2) <= maxPP$ **then**
26:              $queue \leftarrow (pp + 2)/2$ number of files from bucketNum[left]
27:              $queue \leftarrow (pp + 2)/2$ number of files from bucketNum[right]
28:          **else**
29:              $queue \leftarrow (pp + 1)/2$ number of files from bucketNum[left]
30:              $queue \leftarrow [(pp + 1)/2] + 1$ number of files from bucketNum[right]
31:          **end if**

32:          remove the files in queue from bucketNum[left-big]
33:      **end while**
34:      **return** *queue*
35: **end function**
36: **function** INEQUALTRANSFER(*bucketNum*[0] → *bucketNum*[4], *newPP, pp*)
37:      initialize an empty *queue*
38:      *left* = 0, *right* = 3, *big* = 4
39:      **while** *bucketNum*[0] → *bucketNum*[4] is not empty **do**
40:          **if** the file number is zero in bucketNum[left] or bucketNum[right] **then**
41:              *left* + + or *right* − −
42:          **end if**
43:          **if** (*pp* + 1) is even **then**
44:              *queue* ← (*pp* + 1)/2 number of files from bucketNum[left]
45:              *queue* ← (*pp* + 1)/2 number of files from bucketNum[right]
46:              *queue* ← *newPP* − *pp* number of files from bucketNum[big]
47:          **else**
48:              *queue* ← [(*pp* + 1)/2] + 1 number of files from bucketNum[left]
49:              *queue* ← (*pp* + 1)/2 number of files from bucketNum[right]
50:              *queue* ← *newPP* − *pp* number of files from bucketNum[big]
51:          **end if**
52:          remove the files in queue from bucketNum[left-big]
53:      **end while**
54:      **return** *queue*
55: **end function**

If the value of *times* is less than or equal to N, the function INEQUAL-TRANSFER in Algorithm 2 is called. It indicates that the number of files in *bucketNum*[4] is sufficient to support all the pipelining transmissions and the files in *bucketNum*[4] can be used as supplementary to help the transmission size match BDP. In order to ensure the transmission reaches the maximum link bandwidth, the *pp* should be changed to *newPP* in this situation.

The detailed arrangement of transmission queue is shown in line 12–35 of EQUALTRANSFER function and line 36–55 of INEQUALTRANSFER function. The line 16 and 40 check if there are no more files in current bucket, the adjacent non-empty bucket's files are transferred. In EQUALTRANSFER function, if the file number in *bucketNum*[4] is not large enough to participate pp transfer from beginning to end, the pp is not changed, and the queue arrangement is as shown from line 19–31. In INEQUALTRANSFER function, if *bucketNum*[4] contains many files larger than BDP, the transmission queue can make full use of the files in *bucketNum*[4] from beginning to end. The queue arrangement is shown from line 43 to 51. With the TQ algorithm, we get a transmission queue that makes each pp transfer match BDP as much as possible, which in turn improves the throughput.

For high-priority file transmission, the first thing is to ensure they are transmitted as soon as possible. The second thing is the throughput should not decrease drastically. The first answer can be found based on high-priority file's size. If the file size is less than or equals to BDP/2, it should be put into the $bucketNum[0]$ (e.g. No. 1 bucket). If the file size is in range BDP/2 and BDP, it should be put into the $bucketNum[3]$ (e.g. No. 4 bucket), the other files are put into $bucketNum[4]$ (e.g. No. 5 bucket). The purpose of this classification is to place the high-priority files to the front of the transmission queue in the buckets. Another purpose is to ensure the size of the pipelining file combination is as close as possible to BDP. When the number of high-priority files in buckets No. 1, No. 4 and No. 5 are similar, it can be guaranteed that the high-priority files will be transmitted before all the other files. In some extreme cases, the files in No.1 bucket are all high-priority files, and there are no high-priority files in No. 4 or No. 5 bucket. In this case, the transmission time of the last high-priority file may be delayed. But when the high-priority files are evenly distributed, our algorithm achieves good performance.

4   Experiment

4.1   Experiment Environment

The experimental environment consists of three servers running CentOS7 operating system and xfs file system. One server works as the GridFTP server and the other two work as client1 and client2. The bandwidth bottleneck is 100 Mbps from the server to the clients. The RTT is 50 ms from client1 to the server and 100 ms from client2 to the server. The buffer size is set to BDP in all experiments.

The throughput with different file sets are tested on this two-clients/server network. We also test the performance when transferring small file sets with simple pipelining settings. The pp is set to static value 2 as the baseline experiment, called DEFAULT when referred to. Furthermore, the RCD algorithm mentioned above is implemented and its throughput is tested in the same environment as our BD algorithm and DEFAULT. Simultaneously, we test the performance of transferring high-priority files and the impact brought by the combination of pipelining parameter and concurrency parameter, followed by the comparison of the mentioned algorithms and analysis of the outcomes produced by different algorithms.

4.2   Performance Analysis

As shown in Fig. 3, the experiments are carried out under different RTT conditions (50 ms and 100 ms). Given the max bandwidth is 100 Mbps, the test file set consists of 500 0 KB–100 KB files and 500 1 MB–2 MB files that are generated randomly. It can be found that the throughput of different methods (Default, BD and RCD) when the RTT is 50 ms are all higher than those when the RTT is 100 ms in Fig. 3. The reason behind is simple: the BDP increases accordingly with the increase of RTT. The probability of bandwidth loss will increase when the KB files are transmitted with the DEFAULT method and the RCD method.

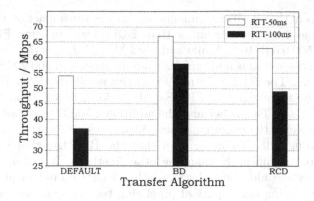

Fig. 3. The impact of different RTT

This leads to a decrease of the overall throughput. The BD algorithm, through the rearrangement of file orders, makes the transferred file size under a pp value match the BDP as close as possible. However, the throughput of BD decreases because the difficulty of making the pp transmission better match the BDP size also rises when the BDP increases. But compared to other methods, it only reduces the total throughput at about 8%, while the DEFAULT and RCD reduce about 17% and 14%, respectively. When the RTT is 50 ms, the throughput gap between BD and RCD is not too large. The reason is that RCD can fill up the link easily by using the maximum pp value at the early stage under 50 ms RTT. However, the ability of RCD to process extremely small files is weakened with the increase of BDP, so the throughput of RCD drops significantly when RTT increases to 100 ms.

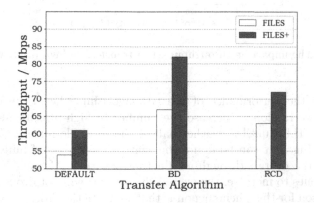

Fig. 4. The impact on throughput by different file sizes

On the basis of the above experiments, we explore the impact on transmission throughput when file sizes are larger than BDP. The condition FILES set in Fig. 4 includes 500 0 KB–100 KB files and 500 1 MB–2 MB files that are generated randomly. FILES+ set adds additional randomly generated 500 2 MB–4 MB files on top of FILES. The RTT is 50 ms. From the result shown in Fig. 4, it can be seen that the throughput of FILES+ all perform better than those under condition FILES set. This is because the additional 500 files are all larger than BDP, which increases the maximum bandwidth transmission time and improves the overall throughput. It can be seen that the BD algorithm improves the throughput more significantly than the other methods. It is because the BD algorithm uses all the additional files larger than BDP to supplement the transfer of small files, reducing the impact of pipelining transmission not matching the BDP, thereby increasing the overall throughput. RCD and DEFAULT algorithm only extend the maximum bandwidth transfer time under FILES+ compared to those under FILES transfer.

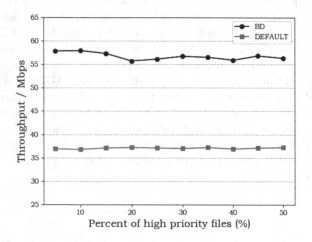

Fig. 5. The impact on throughput when transferring high-priority files

To explore the performance of the BD algorithm when transferring high-priority files, we randomly increase the number of high-priority files based on the condition FILES until it reaches half of the total file number. The RTT is 100 ms. From Fig. 5, it can be found that with the increase of number of high-priority files, the overall throughput fluctuates within 3% range. Even if the number continues to increase, the overall throughput will not drop significantly. The main reason for this phenomenon is that we force the order arrangement for high-priority files and put them into the side buckets (e.g. bucket No.1, No. 4 and No. 5) to make them first transferred before other bucket files. Moving these high-priority files from the middle buckets (e.g. bucket No. 2 and No. 3) to the side buckets makes the size of the high-priority file combination match BDP easily, but this file movement will also increase the size variance in the side buckets, making it harder to match BDP for the immediate following combinations, which in turn causes a slight throughput loss.

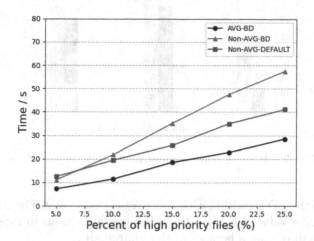

Fig. 6. The transmission time of high-priority files

As shown in Fig. 6, we increase the percentage of high-priority files based on the condition FILES when RTT is 100 ms. AVG-BD represents the case where the sizes of high-priority files are evenly distributed among the overall 1000 files, and we use BD algorithm to transfer the file set. Non-AVG-BD represents that the sizes of high-priority files are only within the range of 500 0 KB–100 KB. When the size distribution of high-priority files is even, AVG-BD performs best. For Non-AVG-BD, its high-priority file transmission time is longer than that of the Non-AVG-DEFAULT. The reason is with an uneven file size distribution, the BD algorithm will have to select a large number of ordinary files to meet the BDP requirement, leaving the high-priority files waiting in the queue for preferred file combination, and affecting their transmission order. Under an even file size distribution, the BD algorithm is able to improve the throughput and transmit the high-priority files promptly.

No comparison to RCD is provided here is because RCD does not consider the high-priority files in a file set. After the file set is split by RCD, the high-priority files are distributed to each file cluster and their delivery priority demands are no longer supported.

As the implementation of parallelism has a negative impact on the throughput when processing small file transmission, we test the performance of combining the concurrency parameter (cc) and pipelining parameter together. As shown in Fig. 7, when RTT is 50 ms, it can be seen that the cc has a very obvious impact on the throughput, but compared to the DEFAULT and RCD algorithm, the BD algorithm has a stable throughput when the concurrency parameter is set to 2. When the cc increases to 4 and 6, the improvement on throughput is minimal. The DEFAULT method with concurrency value 6 can only reach almost identical

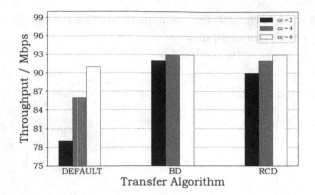

Fig. 7. The state of throughput under different cc values

throughput to the BD algorithm with concurrency value of 2. The BD algorithm requires a smaller value of cc than the other two algorithms in most situations and saves system resources because of this characteristic.

From the above experiments, it can be found that the throughput of the BD algorithm is better than those of the DEFAULT and RCD when transmitting small files, regardless of whether the pipelining parameter is used alone or in combination with the concurrent parameter. With the increase of transfer delay time and number of large files, the performance of BD algorithm is further improved without notable increase of resource assumption.

5   Conclusion and Future Work

As a high-performance transmission protocol, GridFTP provides three parameters for transmission optimization. In different file transmission scenarios, the optimal parameter values are not the same. If the parameters are not set properly, the improvement on the throughput will be compromised, and sometimes may even have negative effects. In this paper, a smart bucket structure is designed for GridFTP. It is mainly used to perform file classification operation based on their size. On top of the bucket structure, a BD algorithm is proposed to conduct corresponding bucket division and queue arrangement operations on files. With the bucket structure and the BD algorithm, we can not only find optimal pipelining parameter values, but also optimize the transmission throughput for LOSF with low resource consumption. Furthermore, more than 90% of the total throughput can be easily achieved when our BD algorithm is used with the concurrency parameter.

In terms of future work, the following points are worth further exploring: the first is to refine the model to make the rearrangement of various special files more accurate; the second is to update the parameters for continuous influx of files in real time.

Acknowledgement. This work is supported by the National key R&D Program of China under Grant 2018YFB0203902, the National Natural Science Foundation of China under Grant No. 61972364; and the Fundamental Research Funds for the Central Universities under Grant No. 2652021001.

References

1. Altschul, S.F., Gish, W., Miller, W., et al.: Basic local alignment search tool. Journal of molecular biology **215**(3), 403–410 (1990)
2. Mackey, G., Sehrish, S., Wang, J.: Improving metadata management for small files in HDFS. In: IEEE International Conference on Cluster Computing and Workshops, IEEE, pp. 1–4 (2009)
3. Wang, F.: WMO information system: Beijing global information system center. Bull. Am. Meteorol. Soc. **94**(7), 991–994 (2013)
4. Bresnahan, J., Link, M., Kettimuthu, R., et al.: Gridftp pipelining. In: Proceedings of the 2007 TeraGrid Conference (2007)
5. Allcock, W.: GridFTP: protocol extensions to FTP for the Grid. http://www.ggf.org/documents/GFD.20.pdf (2003)
6. Bresnahan, J., Link, M., Khanna, G., et al.: Globus GridFTP: what's new. In: Proceedings of the First International Conference on Networks for Grid Applications, pp. 1–5 (2007)
7. Allcock, W., Bresnahan, J., Kettimuthu, R., et al.: The globus striped GridFTP framework and server. In: Proceedings of the 2005 ACM/IEEE Conference on Supercomputing, SC 2005. IEEE, pp. 54–54 (2005)
8. Foster, I.: Globus toolkit version 4: software for service-oriented systems. J. Comput. Sci. Technol. **21**(4), 513–520 (2006)
9. Postel, J., Reynolds, J.: File transfer protocol (1985)
10. Liu, Y., Liu, Z., Kettimuthu, R., et al.: Data transfer between scientific facilities–bottleneck analysis, insights and optimizations. In: 2019 19th IEEE/ACM International Symposium on Cluster, Cloud and Grid Computing (CCGRID), pp. 122–131. IEEE (2019)
11. Ito, T., Ohsaki, H., Imase, M.: On parameter tuning of data transfer protocol GridFTP for wide-area networks. Connections **3**, 9 (2008)
12. Choi, K.M., Huh, E.-N., Choo, H.: Efficient resource management scheme of TCP buffer tuned parallel stream to optimize system performance. In: Enokido, T., Yan, L., Xiao, B., Kim, D., Dai, Y., Yang, L.T. (eds.) EUC 2005. LNCS, vol. 3823, pp. 683–692. Springer, Heidelberg (2005). https://doi.org/10.1007/11596042_71
13. Data Intensive Distributed Computing: Challenges and Solutions for Large-scale Information Management: Challenges and Solutions for Large-scale Information Management. IGI Global, Hershey (2012)
14. Kosar, T., Balman, M., Yildirim, E., et al.: Stork data scheduler: mitigating the data bottleneck in e-science. Phil. Trans. R. Soc. Math. Phys. Eng. Sci. **2011**(369), 3254–3267 (1949)
15. Hacker, T.J., Athey, B.D., Noble, B.: The end-to-end performance effects of parallel TCP sockets on a lossy wide-area network. In: Proceedings 16th International Parallel and Distributed Processing Symposium, 10p. IEEE (2002)
16. Lu, D., Qiao, Y., Dinda, P.A., et al.: Modeling and taming parallel TCP on the wide area network. In: 19th IEEE International Parallel and Distributed Processing Symposium, 10 p. IEEE (2005)

17. Yildirim, E., Balman, M., Kosar, T.: Dynamically tuning level of parallelism in wide area data transfers. In: Proceedings of the 2008 International Workshop on Data-Aware Distributed Computing, pp. 39–48 (2008)
18. Allen, B., Bresnahan, J., Childers, L., et al.: Software as a service for data scientists. Commun. ACM **55**(2), 81–88 (2012)
19. Kim, J.: Tuning GridFTP pipelining, concurrency and parallelism based on historical data. IEICE Trans. Inf. Syst. **97**(11), 2963–2966 (2014)
20. Yildirim, E., Arslan, E., Kim, J., et al.: Application-level optimization of big data transfers through pipelining, parallelism and concurrency. IEEE Tran. Cloud Comput. **4**(1), 63–75 (2015)
21. Yildirim, E., Kim, J., Kosar, T.: Optimizing the sample size for a cloud-hosted data scheduling service. In: Proceedings of the 2nd International Workshop on Cloud Computing Science Application (2012)
22. Cardwell, N., Savage, S., Anderson, T.: Modeling the performance of short TCP connections. Techical Report (1998)

Containers' Privacy and Data Protection via Runtime Scanning Methods

Francisco Rojo(✉) and Lei Pan

Deakin University, Geelong, VIC 3220, Australia
{frojorosales,l.pan}@deakin.edu.au

Abstract. Docker containers' privacy and data protection is a critical issue. Unfortunately, existing works overlook runtime scanning methods. This paper proposes a novel lightweight and rapid scanning model under a framework covering assertion techniques during the container's runtime, defined as *vulnerability scanning framework* VSF. Our framework includes identifying vulnerability, scanning security exposures, conduct analysis, and call-back notifications to the requestor asynchronously. In addition, the proposed scanning model is compared against other tools of similar and complementary objectives. The framework is modeled using *nmap* scripting engine NSE for its active scanning building block. It applies network port scanning and security assertion techniques to rapidly discover security vulnerabilities in a running Docker container environment for a proactive testing approach as a security engine. Also, providing an active trust model developed for Docker containers whether containers are *black-listed* or *grey-listed*. It was developed over a framework for DevSecOps environments and DevOps teams as the persona on its adoption. The empirical case studies demonstrate the capability of our scanning model, including standalone, CI/CD pipelines, and security containerized environment. The case studies revealed no tangible difference in the performance but the flexibility driven by the modeled architecture. The experiments presented a velocity of $1.15 \frac{scans}{sec}$. However, the execution time is directly proportional to the complexity of the vulnerability on the Docker ecosystem and its related attack vector complexity. Its core capability resides on the artifacts developed as part of the Art per relevant CVE via *nmap* NSE scripts.

Keywords: DevSecOps · DevOps · Containers · Docker · Containers security · Docker security · Containers vulnerability scanner · Containers vulnerability assertion · Vulnerability scan

1 Introduction

Information Technology (IT) ecosystems that are generally considered secure with a full spectrum of security measures can be exposed to vulnerabilities natively available in container environments, on either: the container host, guest

W. Xiang et al. (Eds.): BROADNETS 2021, LNICST 413, pp. 37–56, 2022.
https://doi.org/10.1007/978-3-030-93479-8_3

daemon, and the image. Large Enterprise, Banking, Government, Telco, Public Cloud, Entertainment amongst key players in today's economy, are widely adopting containers platforms as an emerging technology due to its native benefits; driving microservices architectures adoption in a vast range of organisations such as Amazon, Twitter amongst a few [13]. Some key drivers in the emergence of containerised environments include simplicity, flexibility derived from a microservices architecture, shared compute underlying options, and easy adoption requirements.

DevOps teams are surging as digital technology enablers across organisations and using containers as a crucial component. The organisational size and business requirements drive the container's orchestration needs, where advanced environments will consume containers via a clustered orchestration layer, such as Kubernetes. Some other players will deploy isolated container hosts to meet their needs on a smaller scale. Despite the approach taken, the key issue remains the same, caused by the existing vulnerabilities in the runtime containers' abstraction layer.

DevOps environments tend to adopt conventional security measures and passive image scanning, where related work presents novel active and passive security methods that aim to provide a secure and trusted environment. The Docker environments rely on Docker Hub as the sole repository of public Docker images, including non-official nor verified images available. Once a Docker image is loaded into a Docker Host, Docker does not provide a method to prove the image authenticity in runtime. However, Guo et al. [5] proposes a PKI under a container attestation service. The ability to deploy unverified Docker images presents a security risk in any Docker environment, given published images are public, uncontrolled, nor digitally signed.

The DevSecOps paradigm arises on protecting a DevOps tool-chain if the tool-chain runs on containers or uses containers as an underpinning technology. How can the containers be trusted? This paper proposes to black-list containers that are directly pulled from the Docker Hub until verified under the proposed *vulnerability scanning framework* VSF. It grey-lists the relevant containers launched in runtime with active software scanning techniques. It allows validating vulnerabilities present in the running container like CVE (Common Vulnerabilities and Exposures) and consequently trusts the container in the containers' network environment.

The experiments were conducted on Amazon AWS EC2 compute running CentOS 7 instances. The case studies are considered typical scenarios for DevOps teams; DevOps teams are considered the key stakeholder group for adopting the proposed work. VSF's key features aligns with the flexibility sought in DevOps environments for container runtime vulnerability scanning.

Our research work found that: **(a) runtime assertion testing for vulnerability scanning in Docker environments** is an active technique to mitigate native security risks associated with the ability of Docker to deploy images that are not verified nor signed directly from Docker Hub. **(b) A trust model** can be leveraged via the assertion testing with using an accuracy factor to determine whether the *grey-listed/black-listed* classification for a Docker container is certain against some conditions. **(c)** Any active Docker vulnerability scanning techniques can be adopted by DevOps teams via a **vulnerability scanning framework** as needed in DevSecOps environments.

In the following section, we present the *related work*, where we cover the classification of the tools and approaches used to date in security-relevant to containers environments. Next, we present our *proposed framework* (VSF), some experiments, and analysis. The experiments cover the *scanning engine* selection and the case studies used to demonstrate VSF. Later on, the *results* are presented to include a summary of the finding of the case studies plus our *recommendations*; finally, our *conclusions* are presented with future work.

2   Related Work

Container environments have been rapidly adopted in the industry, especially in DevOps teams, for accelerating development and its lightweight release cycle [10]. However, this approach increases surface attacks and further security exposures. Evidence of this adoption relates to Docker Hub's recording over four million images in the Docker Hub by March 2021, with an increase of 77% in three years, when compared to 2018 as per Martin et al. [10]. The key attributes of container adoption in DevOps environments include: an abstraction level in computing architecture, optimization of computing resources, and segmentation provided at the service level in a micro-services architecture [13].

Applications and services are transformed with the adoption of containers as seen in DevOps environments [10]; from edge computing to adaptive applications, when conventional security does not address the attack surface in an agile manner, a lightweight runtime scanner is required, as detailed by Merino et al. [1], as evidence on security concerns around the utilisation of containers technologies.

Containers, when compared to its predecessor technology *virtualisation* (virtual machines - VMs), drive abstraction into a micro-services domain but running on a Linux baseline kernel host. It opens up flexibility but implies fewer controls in a non-specific purpose kernel [15]. Containers have not been designed with a robust security framework, instead conventional Linux hardening and configuration options are available. Consequently, the are problems with security risks associated with the utilisation of the containers technology as applications can have direct access to the host kernel; thus, an attacker can reach the host environment from the container layer [15]. Merino et al. [1] exemplifies the need for a runtime scanning method.

We classify the related work in *hardware-software based*, or *active-passive*; being *hardware-based* dependant on compute hardware; *software-based* dependant on a software defined approach; or as *active* if it interacts with container in runtime; or *passive* when interacts with components prior attestation of containers.

Hardware-based security techniques for containers include the following: Schwarz and Lipp [12] demonstration on how side-channel attack vectors can target Intel SGX (Software Guard Extensions) chipset and how to protect it via the deployment of an enclave which proxies communications to an encrypted section of DRAM on any computing; containers can still be targeted. Guo et al. [5] developed a trust model based on remote attestation techniques for containers via vTMP (Virtual Trust Platform Modules) requiring modification of the host and container image. These use cases covered hardware-based protection on general SGX computes or attestation via vTMP, respectively, affecting container environments. In addition, Guo et al. [5] uses a PKI (Public Key Infrastructure) model during the attestation of containers. The PKI is positioned between the Host and Containers as a trust model, where the root certificate is self-signed, and certificate exchange occurs. Their method represents an active hardware technique to provide data protection with enforcement of a PKI within the container's ecosystem.

Software-based security deployments are used to protect either host, container, application, and permutations of these, including industry container hardening techniques, container isolation, vulnerabilities patching via container's lightweight images upgrades, modifications in the kernel or container images with a secure Linux load, with image vulnerability scanning occurring before the container's attestation [2,5]. Sultan et al. [13] excluded from their work the orchestration layer security and mentioned the decentralized attestation via blockchain as needing further development. Furthermore, Xu et al. [14] uses blockchain to decentralize the container image trust or other data types but developing an image trust model. Kong et al. [7] presents a secure containers' deployment method using genetic algorithms via Secure Container Deployment Strategy (SecCDS). Li et al. [9] applied a DDoS (Denial of Service) mitigation mechanisms for low rate DDoS attacks over a simulation, demonstrating that the isolation of affected containers in an environment improves the quality of service of the model via *white-listing* requests into the containers environment.

On the other hand, broader security exposure analysis reveals multi-dimensional exposures in Docker as covered by Martin et al. [10]; it highlights the importance of runtime scanning techniques. Berkovich [2] argued that scanning Docker container images as binaries are a critical security activity in DevOps environments, such as CI/CD pipelines. Yasrab [15] described the issues on the Docker container level due to the large number of sensitive services running, including the container service, application, and Host OS. A *vulnerability assessment framework* is presented by Mostajeran et al. [11] which includes three key components related to containers on their work: (1) configuration, (2) images, (3) deployed services.

A Docker Thread Detection Framework acting as a software-based system is presented by Huang et al. [6]; the framework analyses the Docker image and the container's running IP/DNS requests. Similar to IP addressing scanning, other industry players target development environments with tools such as *Kali-Linux* to target containers environments. However, this active testing is related to legacy scanning methods.

Passive scanning techniques relate to those that do not actively interact with the security exposure or presence of the condition that defines the attack vector in runtime. Guo et al. [5] that enables a trusted environment incurring in modification of the kernel and container's attestation service via a state challenge protocol. As per Kwon et al. [8] by enabling a Docker Image Vulnerability Diagnostic System (DIVDS) for containers. As well as, Berkovich et al. [2] running a container's image vulnerability scanning tool known as *Ultimate Benchmark for Container Image Scanning* (UBCIS).

On the other hand, **Active scanning techniques** relate to those which actively interact with the Docker Host and/or Docker containers in runtime to detect a condition that defines the attack vector, including work such as Mostajeran et al. [11] with their *vulnerability assessment framework* that presents a runtime fixed container security benchmark tool as a risk assessment tool. Merino et al. [1] described in its managed container layers: application, namespace, control groups, amongst others to detect containers anomalies in runtime. Alternatively, it is the potential to detect co-resident containers security exposures, according to Gao et al. [3]. Kong et al. [7] used a genetic algorithm defence system, or Huang et al. [6] which uses their *Docker thread detection framework* to complete hardware checks against computing resources and network port scanning.

Table 1 lists key comparison features in related work highlighting the *defence* as a key attribute being developed, followed by the *scanning, attack* and *runtime* capabilities.

Table 1. Related work comparison

Related work/Capability	Scanning	Defence	Attack	Runtime
Two-stage defense approach [3]	No	Yes	No	Yes
DIVDS [8]	Yes	No	No	No
Docker thread detection framework [6]	Yes	Yes	No	No
SecCDS [7]	No	Yes	No	No
Security assessment framework [11]	Yes	No	No	Yes
UBCIS [2]	Yes	No	No	No
Managed container framework [1]	No	Yes	No	No
Container state attestation [5]	No	Yes	No	Yes

Amongst the overall security approach discussed earlier and summarised in Table 1, the **scanning engine** is a pivotal component. Key industry players in cloud containerization as Google have developed tools such as *tsunami* [4] which can be used to develop vulnerability scanning. In our experiments section, we will compare and select a scanning engine for our proposed framework.

This work focuses on developing a lightweight security framework encompassing runtime security vulnerability scanning of the container service abstraction layer within a Docker environment as an active software-defined approach.

In particular, using the CVE disclosed vulnerabilities against Docker to enable DevSecOps practices. The framework is to be used in line with the operations of the DevSecOps environment for detecting possible attack surfaces exposed by the Docker Host or Docker Images in runtime as an active scanner. Also, it assumes that DevOps teams know the CVEs to test using VSF on the Docker environment. This method is not described in related literature, as it conducts software assertion tests of the relevant CVEs into the Docker Host or specific Docker containers in runtime.

3   Security Framework for Containers Environments

The runtime *vulnerability scanning framework* VSF for Docker containers pinnacles its capability in the active assertion testing against a Docker runtime environment in a lightweight manner. This security framework has been defined modularly to aggregate active software scanning. The active approach aims to detect existing vulnerabilities in a running Docker container environment as part of an Incident Response Procedure, Proactive testing practices, and the state of the Art container practice due to the atomic nature of the container's environment of short lifespan; and with an increased level of difficulty in its tracing and tracking capabilities once the containers are destroyed.

Initially, the positioning of the security framework is defined in the container's abstraction layer and identified as the Docker Engine; the application runs as a container via the *containerd* daemon. Thus, to complete the vulnerability assertion testing, VSF provides a binary response: *true-positive* if the container is vulnerable, or *true-negative* when the container is not vulnerable against the CVE. Hence, the container can be *grey-listed*.

Figure 1 shows a representation of VSF and its modules, including `core`, `fetch`, `runner`, `callback`, and `connection`. These modules represent specific functions underpinned by *nmap* to complete the scanning function. The framework include the following five components:

- `Core`: The core engine for the scanner like *nmap*.
- `Fetch`: A plugin for fetching the CVEs related to the Docker image.
- `Runner`: Individual scripts running as assertion techniques against the vulnerability in runtime.
- `Callback`: A notification means to the requestor.
- `Connection`: Underlying Host packages that enables the presentation OSI layer of the framework with a type of connection handled by the core engine, e.g., SSH.

`Core` is considered the core engine of the framework. It could be regarded as an orchestrator on demand to interface with all other components in the framework. Some of its features include orchestration, scanning engine, telemetry, analytics, scheduler, trust, and queuing. The emphasis in the component is given to the *scanning engine* where a substantial section of the core development takes place.

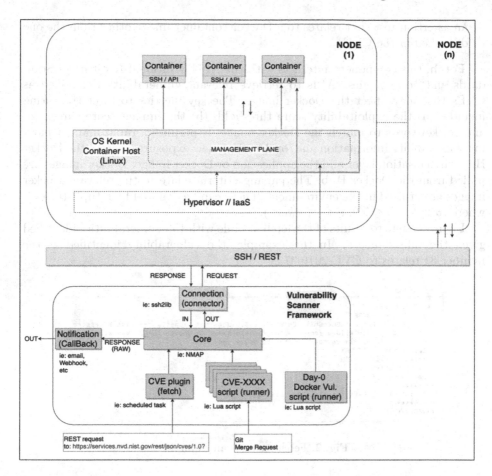

Fig. 1. Docker containers *vulnerability scanning framework*—Framework

VSF proposes to *black-list* containers that returned *true-positive* as a result of the assertion testing and also to those containers which has not been tested via VSF. On the other hand, if the assertion test results as a *true-negative* containers can be *grey-listed* and digitally signed; however, if the Accuracy Factor of the assertion testing is lower than 75%, then the image is *black-listed* due to its low certainty on the trust of the running container.

The container's digital certificate signing request will adopt the DevSecOps environment PKIs as required, and the certificate can be made available via the container's secret exchange method of choice.

The Accuracy Factor (AF) is a metric measured in percentage that indicates the certainty of the runtime assertion test completed given some conditions, including:

- An AF value lower than 75% results into a *black-listed* docker container;
- An AF value between 75% and 100% is considered as a true result;

- An assertion test that relates to a Docker container image other than the one described in the CVE.

Fetch, this component interacts with the NIST (National Institute of Standards and Technologies) APIs to retrieve relevant vulnerabilities classified as CVEs that may affect the Docker image. The key metrics to filter the rating includes (a) the exploitability score threshold, (b) the impact score threshold, and (c) keywords to match the Docker image. It permits a rapid manner parsing vulnerability information and/or detecting new exposures, across the Docker Host virtualisation layer and the application or Docker image. Docker images are pulled from the Docker Hub. The parsing criteria relate to the relevant Docker images are utilised in the environment. These can be denoted by a tuple (a, b, c), where $(a \geq 1.8,\ b \leq 5.9,\ c =$ "*docker*").

Figure 2 refers to results of the fetch module with 153 vulnerabilities identified given the values (a, b, c). In this example, the vulnerability identified as the number 81 relates to CVE-2016-3728.

```
*** ( 81 ) ***
CVE:  CVE-2016-3738
Description:  Red Hat OpenShift Enterprise 3.2 does not properly restrict access to
 STI builds, which allows remote authenticated users to access the Docker socket an
d gain privileges via vectors related to build-pod.
attackVector:  NETWORK
attackComplexity:  LOW
exploitabilityScore:  2.8
impactScore:  5.9
*********
Pages: 1, Total CVEs scanned: 153, Listed: 81 **
*********
***EOF***
```

Fig. 2. Fetch results—an example

The fetch module could be exchanged if the CVEs were unknown, with the DIVDS system proposed by Kwon et al. [8] amongst one of the passive models to detect impacting vulnerabilities in containers via *white-listing*. Hence, the *fetch* component is presented as a lightweight alternative that assumes pre-existing knowledge on the CVEs and exposures to Docker containers environment, typically the case in DevOps teams. However, VSF aims to *grey-list* despite the DIVDS approach.

Runner uses the *nmap scripting engine* (NSE) to execute the assertion testing on a specific vulnerability relevant to the Docker Host environment or Docker image. The Art defines the artifacts that include each vulnerability assertion test in an independent NSE script. The NSE scripts are executed in runtime within the Docker environment. The *Runner* component contains a collection of NSE scripts that will be classified based on the CVE id. Should the *Core* component consider necessary to validate this vulnerability, it would then execute the *nmap* script and obtain the response of the assertion test. Results are to be retrieved and identified as binaries, *true-positive* or *true-negative*.

An example of a *Runner* NSE script for CVE-2020-35195 is detailed below. It conducts assertion testing against the existence of a blank root password in the container in runtime for a *haproxy* image.

```
if conn:password_auth(user, passw) then
   local A1 ... = conn:run_remote(cmd)
   local A2 ... = conn:run_remote(cmd2)
   local _A2, _y = string.find(A2, _blankpw)
if _A2 == 1 then
   stdnse.verbose("Passed␣assertion␣test")
return "CVE␣assertion␣test␣Passed"
```

Callback relates to a notification mechanism to inform on the outcome of the assertion testing completed by the *runner*. The *core* component would have captured the assessment completed, and this is to be reported asynchronously back to the requestor. Notifications are to be sent as webhooks.

Connection contains underlying Host OS packages required to interact at a network layer with the Docker host, in order to enable connectivity of the *core*, *runner* components. Two options can be chosen, including *libssh2* and *openssl*.

The components of the *vulnerability scanning framework* (VSF), as previously defined, present a lightweight novel security framework for Docker container environments. Its purpose is to provide runtime Docker host and container's vulnerability software scanning capability to offer Privacy and Data Protection via completing active assertion testing techniques that would *grey-list* running containers. It assumes pre-existing knowledge of the CVEs, as in the case of DevOps teams. The modularity of VSF resides on its capability to exchange some of the methods, i.e., the *fetch* and *core* components, could be interfaced with the DIVDS system defined by Kwon et al. [8], or with the certificate exchange proposed by Guo et al. [5] respectively.

4   Experiments

We present the experiments in two sections, the underlying scanning engine with the *initial experiment*, followed by the *case studies* and subsequent *analysis*.

4.1   The Scanning Engine Selection—Experiment

The *initial experiment* for the vulnerability scanner consisted of testing the underlying agent that would be running the assertion testing. In this case, we selected *tsunami* and *nmap* (NSE) as two well-known tools in the open-source community.

Our experiment with *tsunami* and *nmap* comprised of installing the each tool on disparate AWS EC2 CentOS 7.0 instances. The execution time for *tsunami* is comparable to those seeing in *nmap*, with 12.355 s to run. Table 2 compares the two scanning engines, with the capabilities as detailed below:

- *Open source*, *nmap* is a well-known network security scanning tool; and *tsunami*, is a Google initiative that allows development of network security scanning.
- *Programmatic development*, is the capability to developing vulnerability assertion tests over a programmatic approach. *nmap* is implemented in Lua and *tsunami* in Java.
- *Response time*, is the execution time of a one scanning job. Both tools are of comparable execution time as per our experiment; with 12.355 s on *tsunami* and 1.86 s on *nmap*. This is a metric that can vary, and it is dependant on the complexity of the scan as observed later in the case studies.
- *Lightweight*, is the ability to consume the tool across a wide range of environment in a simple manner. The experiment revealed that *tsunami* has a large set of dependencies when compared to *nmap*; which makes *nmap* considerably easier to deploy and portable across environments. We consider as a result of the experiment that *nmap* is a *lightweight* tool.
- *Network port scanning*, is the ability to run active network port scanning on a target system. Both *tsunami* and *nmap* cover this capability.
- *Relevance in the Industry*, is the presence and relevance of the tool in the industry. We define this capability as a measure of the risk to adopt the tool given its wide spread in the industry. We consider both tools *tsunami* and *nmap* offer low risk.

The previous capability analysis offers comparable characteristics for the selection of the scanning engine, between *tsunami* and *nmap*. However, the lightweight capability of *nmap*, its execution simplicity, and portability distinctively enable the proposed framework for rapid development on its scanning component. Thus *nmap* NSE is VSF's *scanning engine*.

Table 2. Scanning engine comparison

Tools	Open source	Programmatic	Response time	Lightweight	Port scanning	Relevance
nmap	Yes	Yes	Yes	Yes	Yes	Yes
tsunami	Yes	Yes	Yes	No	Yes	Yes

4.2   Case Studies

The presented *case studies* assume that VSF is used by a DevOps team across various scenarios, including Standalone and CI/CD pipelines. Hence, CVEs are known or checked via the *fetch* component of VSF. The container signing request and secrets management methods detailed in the *core* component are not represented and outside of the scope of the experiments in the *case studies*.

The experiments follow the same execution principle against different running Docker containers, Docker host, and emulation scenarios. Firstly, we develop individual *nmap* NSE scripts per CVE. These scripts are written in Lua-NSE and reference each relevant CVE attack vector against a target running container. Our approach consists of the following steps per NSE script as detailed below and as shown in Fig. 3:

Step 1, to complete a Docker host or Docker container network port scanning against common network ports relevant to the communications;
Step 2, to authenticate into the Docker host; the NSE script to authenticate into the Docker host using the root credentials;
Step 3, to gain privilege access into Docker host;
Step 4, to identify the relevant Docker container id (as optional step);
Step 5, to run Docker remote commands from the host into the target Docker container, or to run Docker local commands in the Docker host;
Step 6, to navigate through the conditions as defined in the impacting CVE that makes the running target container vulnerable;
Step 7, to match the assertion criteria for the impacting CVE;
Step 8, to present the scan result as *true-positive* or *true-negative* with an accuracy factor; then repeat from *Step 1* to complete next scan.

Direct access via the container's network interface (CNI) is not used, as in specific container images, this capability is disabled. As detailed before, the *Anatomy* of VSF includes the artefacts that leverage *nmap*'s ability to scan ports and define network connectivity (i.e., *libssh2*) to reach the container; then define the rule sets and followed by actions and logic to determine whether the running environment is vulnerable or not with an accuracy factor.

The accuracy factor (AF) is a metric we use to measure the certainty of the scan; i.e., if the scan targets the specific Docker container image relevant to a CVE and the matching criteria are validated, the AF value is 100%. However, if the vulnerability scan is run against a different image than the one referenced in the CVE, we estimate that the AF is 50%, as the certainty is lower given the CVE conditions are not fully met.

The *Art* defines the artefacts in the *runner* component, which include the development for the following shortlisted CVEs for Lua-NSE development:

- CVE-2020-35467, relates to a "Docker docs" container image vulnerability,
- CVE-2020-35195, relates to a "haproxy" container image vulnerability,
- CVE-2020-15157, relates to a "containerd" vulnerability,
- CVE-2016-3697, relates to a Docker "runC" vulnerability,
- CVE-2021-21284, relates to a "libcontainerd" vulnerability.

The performance of each case study is checked against one metric. It is defined as the *velocity* during scanning, which is the number of scans in the environment against the execution time in seconds. Depending on volume, this will incur in greater overall execution time that will impact the case study. $\overline{A}$ would be relevant within the DevOps team context as it impacts the pipeline execution.

$$\frac{\Delta \overline{A}}{\Delta \overline{t}} = \lambda$$

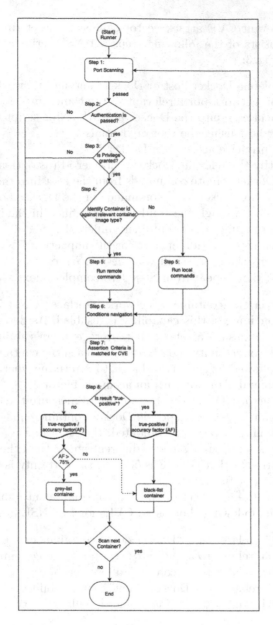

Fig. 3. Vulnerability scanning

- $\overline{A}$, the number of assertion tests in a period of time,
- $\overline{t}$, the execution time of a NSE script,
- λ, the number of test over period of time, velocity.

A *velocity* of 1.5 assertion tests is achieved via VSF given the detailed *runner* artefacts (Table 3). The velocity would vary depending on the vulnerability complexity and compute required in the execution of the NSE. The execution time does not fall into a distribution or statistical relationship as shown in Fig. 4; instead these are derived from the complexity of the vulnerability on the Docker ecosystem and its related attack vector complexity as execution time associated with the scan type.

Table 3. Experiment results: execution time

Scan type	Performance (s)
CVE-2020-35467	0.68
CVE-2020-35195	0.68
CVE-2020-15157	0.57
CVE-2016-3697	1.86
CVE-2021-21284	0.56

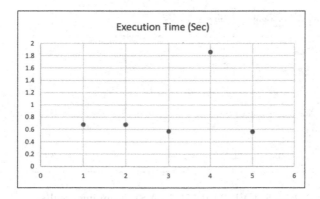

Fig. 4. Experiment results: execution time plot

The case studies are detailed as follows, where we act as a DevOps team across multiple scenarios.

Standalone, this case study encompasses the use of VSF in a standalone Docker environment, such as a software developer's IDE (integrated development environment). The case study assumes that an IDE runs in a Linux-based Operating System to leverage VSF components' capabilities. Our Docker container environment included the following running containers as active:

- *docker.io/centos*
- *docker.io/docs/docker.github.io*
- *docker.io/haproxy*

CVE-2020-15157, as demonstrated in Fig. 5 the NSE script shows a matching CVE condition which asserts a *true-positive* result in runtime with an AF value of 100%. Implying that the active Docker container is running a configuration in runtime that points to an external source, as per test case **A3** in Table 4. In this case instead of reading the offline image manifest, VSF validates the runtime foreign layer by reading the active *config.json* file per container on each *libcontainerd* process and returning a *true-positive* result, as per path: /run/docker/libcontainerd/[id]/config.json

Fig. 5. CVE-2020-15157—VSF scanning results

Similarly, we completed the CVE-2020-35195 and CVE-2020-35467 assertion testing procedures related to the *haproxy* and *Docker Docs* active containers as per test cases **A1** and **A2** respectively. Our assertion testing results (See Table 4) revealed that our running container are set with no-password for the root user, resulting in an AF value of 100% for each scan. Our VSF assertion demonstrates *true-positive* results, as per the path /etc/shadow and condition root:!::0::::: .

Our test case **A5** CVE-2021-21284, requires the utilisation of *namespaces* within the Docker containers environment via root user privilege access. In this test case, our standalone environment did not have enabled *namespaces* so resulted in nonvulnerable assertion testing as a *true-negative*. The recorded AF value is 80%, and this container would still be *grey-listed*. We refer to Table 4 as an impact on the Docker host.

```
--userns-remap
# cat /etc/docker/daemon.json
{
 "userns-remap":"admin"
}
```

Finally, in test case **A4** related CVE-2016-3697 attempts to capture numeric UID as usernames. This test case resulted in non-vulnerable assertion testing as a *true-negative*, given that none of the containers captured these running conditions as per the below path. The recorded AF value is 100%.

```
libcontainer/user/user.go
```

Table 3 shows the maximum value to the run time execution time on the local CI/CD pipeline, which is 1.86 s. In addition, to identifying *true-positive* assertion test results against the CVEs rule sets as defined in VSF. Test Cases **A4** and **A5** relate to conditions within the Docker Host. Whereas **A1**, **A2** and **A3** relates to Docker containers as described in the experiments. The key benefits of the proposed methods arise in the ability to rapidly validate vulnerability exposures in the Docker Host and running Docker containers which as per results presented in Table 4.

Table 4. Experiment results: CVE assertion testing—*runner* component

Test case (runner)	A1: CVE-2020-35467
Test result	*true-positive*
Impact	container: docker.io/docs/docker.github.io
Performance	0.68 s
Accuracy	100%
Trust	*black-listed*
Test case (*runner*)	**A2**: CVE-2020-35195
Test result	*true-positive*
Impact	container: docker.io/haproxy
Performance	0.68 s
Accuracy	100%
Trust	*black-listed*
Test case (*runner*)	**A3**: CVE-2020-15157
Test result	*true-positive*
Impact	host: Docker host
Performance	0.57 s
Accuracy	100%
Trust	*black-listed*
Test case (*runner*)	**A4**: CVE-2016-3697
Test result	*true-negative*
Impact	host: Docker host
Performance	1.86 s
Accuracy	100%
Trust	*grey-listed*
Test case (*runner*)	**A5**: CVE-2021-21284
Test result	*true-negative*
Impact	host: Docker host
Performance	0.56 s
Accuracy	80%
Trust	*grey-listed*

As a summary of the experiment results, our standalone Docker environment is *black-listed* given the results of test cases **A1**, **A2** and **A3**. Also as per Fig. 6 the assertion testing accuracy is high with existing *true-positive* Docker containers. Hence, our IDE require container images updates or configuration updates to mitigate these risks as identified in the Docker environment.

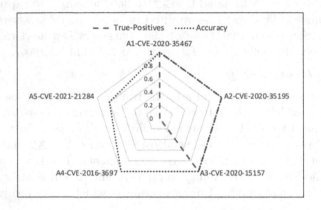

Fig. 6. Standalone assertion results VS accuracy

CI/CD Pipelines, this case study involves a dynamic insertion of VSF within a CI/CD pipeline tool-chain, with containers being used for infrastructure platform orchestration. The case study assumes we are a DevOps team that is using *Jenkins* as a typical CI/CD pipeline in a DevSecOps environment to manage infrastructure platform orchestration. Our Docker environment is used for code promotion during pipeline testing. The following container image was loaded in Docker as available in Docker Hub[1] (A 2 years old image).

In test case **B1**, we deploy the *Jenkins* Docker container and launch VSF in the Docker Host environment. VSF does not contain a specific CVEs NSE script for the *Jenkins* container image. Nevertheless, we complete runtime scanning against known vulnerabilities as we consider it relevant to this image. In our test case, we target the *Jenkins* workload as the target container and validate that the running container may have exposure as related to known vulnerability CVE-2020-25195 related to blank password condition for the root user, as per the path and matching condition shown below:

```
/etc/shadow
root:!::0:::::
```

Table 5 presents the result of the test case **B1**, and demonstrates the runtime execution of VSF. The assertion testing on the *jenkins* image against CVE-2020-35195 resulted in a *true-negative* and an AF of 80% due to the condition that the scan CVE is related to a different image *haproxy*. Our testing classifies the *jenkins* container as *grey-listed*.

---

[1] *docker.io/jenkins:2.60.3.*

Table 5. Experiment results: CVE assertion testing against *jenkins* image—*runner* component

Test case (*Runner*)	**B1**: CVE-2020-35195
Test result	*true-negative*
Impact	container: docker.io/jenkins:2.60.3
Performance	0.71 s
Accuracy	80%
Trust	*grey-listed*

5   Analysis

The case studies demonstrated how Docker active containers are *grey-listed* or *black-listed* against relevant CVEs. The accuracy factor (AF) is found as a required metric to validate the assertion test upon a criterion within VSF. It was proven to be an effective metric in test case C1 when a *grey-listed* container was rated with an AF of 80% equal to a lower certainty.

The experiments presented a velocity of $1.15 \frac{scans}{sec}$ and the samples captured as per the plot shown in Fig. 4 does not fall into a statistical relationship. However, the execution time is directly proportional to the complexity of the vulnerability on the Docker ecosystem and its related attack vector complexity as the CVE detailed in the *fetch* component as per Fig. 2.

The first case study was the **standalone**, where a typical IDE environment for a DevOps team member pulls containers from Docker Hub. VSF offered a capability to rapidly complete CVE assertion testing in runtime to validate if the running container is vulnerable. Table 4 present the result where *true-positive* events were detected on test cases **A1**, **A2** and **A3**. Test Case **A3** CVE-2020-15157 matches the CVE condition which asserts in runtime that the Docker image is running a configuration from an image that points to an external source in a known CVE. Consequently this container is *black-listed* until resolved and VSF scan presents a *true-positive* result with an AF value of 100%, as a defence mechanism to vulnerable container images.

The **CI/CD pipeline** applied test cases **B1**. In this case, the DevOps teams considered that the condition was relevant for *Jenkins* container images, with an AF factor of 80%. The trust result shows that the *Jenkins* container is *grey-listed*. It is indicative of the potential, portability, and flexibility of VSF for DevOps teams.

Table 6 presents a **comparative analysis** across four key capabilities, including *scanning, defense, attack* and *runtime*; when compared to related work as per previous sections. VSF demonstrates a robust reach across the security portfolio of a DevSecOps environment as the only tool with three categories, including scan, defense, and runtime. Even though the runtime capability overlaps with other frameworks, VSF is unique in its ability to complete Docker Host and container's **software** vulnerabilities scanning in runtime, not evidenced in related work.

Table 6. Comparative analysis

Related work/Capability	Scanning	Defence	Attack	Runtime-Hardware	Runtime-Software
VSF	Yes	Yes	No	No	Yes
Two-stage defense approach [3]	No	Yes	No	Yes	No
DIVDS [8]	Yes	No	No	No	No
Docker thread detection framework [6]	Yes	Yes	No	No	No
SecCDS [7]	No	Yes	No	No	No
Security assessment framework [11]	Yes	No	No	No	Yes
UBCIS [2]	Yes	No	No	No	No
Managed container framework [1]	No	Yes	No	No	No
Container state attestation [5]	No	Yes	No	Yes	No

6   Results

VSF's execution performance in runtime has no impact on the execution time of the container. In fact, the execution time and scanning velocity of the *vulnerability scanning framework* VSF are directly proportional to the complexity of the vulnerability and its attack surface.

The experiments consisted of two stages. In the first stage, the focus was to baseline the *scanning engine* tools that can effectively perform security vulnerabilities scans against container environments running Docker. The second stage consisted of utilizing the tool in a software-driven approach over a proposed framework (VSF) to *grey-list* or *black-list* active Docker containers as a trust model.

Nmap NSE was *scanning engine* shortlisted due to its lightweight capability on the initiation of the engine. Our testing revealed that *tsunami* could perform scanning functions; however, its interdependencies in the installation may encounter issues for adoption as a lightweight tool. Whereas *nmap* is widely available as a native tool in many security infrastructures, libraries are available and have proven their usability as per the case studies. VSF leverages *nmap* NSE for containers *privacy* and further covers the capability of detecting vulnerabilities that would affect the containers and its *data* from know exposures as detailed in CVEs.

Our case studies obtained a trust posture of each Docker environment presented via the assertion testing of the VSF engine that resulted in *grey-listing* or *black-listing* the target Docker container. The trust was cross-referenced against an accuracy factor that indicates the certainty of the result given explicit conditions. The combination of the two metrics allowed us to obtain a runtime vulnerability assessment of each Docker container. In addition, the flexibility of VSF has proven that it can be used on multiple scenarios, with a central view on the DevSecOps environment.

6.1   Recommendations

VSF has proven to fulfill a function not found in related work due to its software vulnerability scanning capability in runtime for Docker containers. Whether used as a framework or as a discrete tool per component, it can complement other security initiatives within a DevSecOps strategy agenda as a lightweight tool for a Docker containers environment. Some highlighted recommendations include:

1. On the *Framework*, by improving the credentials management during assertion testing; and adding a containers' signing request capability as a functional addition to the framework.
2. On the *Usability*, by facilitating an easy deployment approach for DevOps teams to deploy the tool in DevSecOps environments; and by adding automation to VSF in order to facilitate the operational requirements of the adopting team.
3. On the *Accuracy Factor model*, by gathering a larger data set that allows for a higher volume of assertion testing results.

7 Conclusions

This paper proposed the *vulnerability scanning framework* (VSF) as a novel lightweight toolset for DevSecOps environments. VSF targets DevOps teams as the key audience. VSF delivers software vulnerability scanning capability to Docker container environments in runtime, leveraging *nmap* NSE scripts to deploy discrete assertion testing to relevant CVEs.

Further work is required on Docker containers security to enrich the trust model in runtime and orchestration. We will adapt VSF components to fit specific requirements generic to DevOps teams in software development CI/CD pipelines or infrastructure as code scenarios. Improving the trust model via the *greylisting* objective will also improve its accuracy factor module. Last but not least, we will add the feature of containers signing requests to the Docker containers environment.

References

1. Aguilera, X.M., Otero, C., Ridley, M., Elliott, D.: Managed containers: a framework for resilient containerized mission critical systems. In: Proceedings of the 2018 IEEE 11th International Conference on Cloud Computing (CLOUD 2018), pp. 946–949 (2018)
2. Berkovich, S., Kam, J., Wurster, G.: Ubcis: ultimate benchmark for container image scanning. In: Proceedings of the 13th USENIX Workshop on Cyber Security Experimentation and Test (CSET 2020), co-located with USENIX Security 2020 (2020)
3. Gao, X., Gu, Z., Kayaalp, M., Pendarakis, D., Wang, H.: Containerleaks: emerging security threats of information leakages in container clouds. In: Proceedings of the 47th Annual IEEE/IFIP International Conference on Dependable Systems and Networks (DSN 2017), pp. 237–248 (2017)
4. Google: Tsunami. https://github.com/google/tsunami-security-scanner. Accessed 3 Mar 2021

5. Guo, Y., Yu, A., Gong, X., Zhao, L., Cai, L., Meng, D.: Building trust in container environment. In: Proceedings of the 2019 18th IEEE International Conference on Trust, Security and Privacy in Computing and Communications/13th IEEE International Conference on Big Data Science and Engineering (TrustCom/BigDataSE 2019), pp. 1–9 (2019)
6. Huang, D., Cui, H., Wen, S., Huang, C.: Security analysis and threats detection techniques on docker container. In: 2019 IEEE 5th International Conference on Computer Communication, ICCC 2019, pp. 1214–1220 (2019). https://doi.org/10.1109/ICCC47050.2019.9064441
7. Kong, T., Wang, L., Ma, D., Xu, Z., Yang, Q., Chen, K.: A secure container deployment strategy by genetic algorithm to defend against co-resident attacks in cloud computing. In: 2019 IEEE 21st International Conference on High Performance Computing and Communications; IEEE 17th International Conference on Smart City; IEEE 5th International Conference on Data Science and Systems (HPCC/SmartCity/DSS), pp. 1825–1832 (2019). https://doi.org/10.1109/HPCC/SmartCity/DSS.2019.00251
8. Kwon, S., Lee, J.H.: DIVDS: Docker image vulnerability diagnostic system. IEEE Access **8**, 42666–42673 (2020)
9. Li, Z., Jin, H., Zou, D., Yuan, B.: Exploring new opportunities to defeat low-rate DDoS attack in container-based cloud environment. IEEE Trans. Parallel Distrib. Syst. **31**, 695–706 (2020). https://doi.org/10.1109/TPDS.2019.2942591
10. Martin, A., Raponi, S., Combe, T., Di Pietro, R.: Docker ecosystem-vulnerability analysis. Comput. Commun. **122**, 30–43 (2018)
11. Mostajeran, E., Mydin, M.N.M., Khalid, M.F., Ismail, B.I., Kandan, R., Hoe, O.H.: Quantitative risk assessment of container based cloud platform. In: Proceedings of the 2017 IEEE Conference on Application, Information and Network Security (AINS), pp. 19–24. IEEE (2017)
12. Schwarz, M., Lipp, M.: When good turns evil using intel SGX to stealthily steal bitcoins. In: Black Hat Asia 2018 (2018). https://i.blackhat.com/briefings/asia/2018/asia-18-Schwarz-When-Good-Turns-Evil-Using-Intel-SGX-To-Stealthily-Steal-Bitcoins-wp.pdf
13. Sultan, S., Ahmad, I., Dimitriou, T.: Container security: issues, challenges, and the road ahead. IEEE Access **7**, 52976–52996 (2019)
14. Xu, Q., Jin, C., Rasid, M.F.B.M., Veeravalli, B., Aung, K.M.M.: Blockchain-based decentralized content trust for docker images. Multimedia Tools Appl. **77**(14), 18223–18248 (2017). https://doi.org/10.1007/s11042-017-5224-6
15. Yasrab, R.: Mitigating docker security issues. arXiv preprint arXiv:1804.05039 (2018)

Digital Twin for Cybersecurity: Towards Enhancing Cyber Resilience

Rajiv Faleiro, Lei Pan$^{(\boxtimes)}$ ⓘ, Shiva Raj Pokhrel ⓘ, and Robin Doss ⓘ

School of IT, Deakin University, Geelong, VIC 3220, Australia
{rfaleiro,l.pan,shiva.pokhrel,robin.doss}@deakin.edu.au

Abstract. Digital Twin (DT) impacts significantly to both industries and research. It has emerged as a promising technology enabling us to add value to our lives and society. DT enables us to virtualize any physical systems and observe real-time dynamics of their status, processes, and functions by using the data obtained from the physical counterpart. This paper attempts to explore a new direction to enhance cyber resilience in the perspective of cybersecurity and Digital Twins. We enumerate definitions of the Digital Twin concept to introduce readers to this disruptive concept. We then explore the existing literature to develop a holistic analysis of the DT's integration into cybersecurity. Our research questions develop a novel roadmap for a promising direction of research, which is worth exploring in the future and is validated by an extensive and systematic survey of recent works. Our research has aimed to properly illustrate the current research state in this area and can benefit both community and industry to further the integration of Digital Twins into Cybersecurity.

Keywords: Digital Twin · Cybersecurity · Cyber resilience

1 Introduction

Every company is now concerned about cybersecurity and the resilience of their infrastructure, and we anticipate that new technology like digital twin may contribute significantly to a robust online defense. Therefore, we envision creating a virtual framework of our information technology (IT) network to identify security flaws, create attack scenarios, avoid expensive attacks, and improve resilience before our security infrastructure is deployed into the real network system.

We start with the basic idea and concept of Digital Twin. First, what is a Digital Twin (DT)? In general, *"Digital Twin"* [25] refers to developing a highly complex computer image that is the replica (or twin) of a physical object. For example, a physical object can be an automobile, a house, a bridge, or a jet engine. DT's underlying idea employs the virtual computer image model to project the sensor data gathered from the connected physical objects.

Different industry verticals define DT in a slightly different fashion. IBM defines DT as[1] *"a virtual representation of an object or system that spans its life*

---

[1] https://ibm.co/3vCiwl5.

Published by Springer Nature Switzerland AG 2022. All Rights Reserved
W. Xiang et al. (Eds.): BROADNETS 2021, LNICST 413, pp. 57–76, 2022.
https://doi.org/10.1007/978-3-030-93479-8_4

cycle, is updated from real-time data, and uses simulation, machine learning, and reasoning to help decision-making." Gartner[2] defines DT as *"a software design pattern that represents a physical object with the objective of understanding the asset's state, responding to changes, improving business operations and adding value."* Furthermore, Gartner says that 13% of industry verticals undertaking Internet of Things (IoT) projects are using DTs in 2021, and 62% are in the process of doing so or intend to do so soon. Our study indicates that DTs can best complement Cyber Security as an Intrusion Detection System due to the bi-directional flow of real-time data. We have elaborated more on this in Sect. 2, according to the chart provided below:

Fig. 1. Digital Twin for cybersecurity use cases

With the increasing application of DT in manufacturing and industry 4.0 [25], organizations have realized that developing a digital replica of their resources, processes, and, most importantly, cybersecurity systems is always advantageous. The cases of cyber attacks increased at an unprecedented pace during the epidemic, prompting some to call it a *cyber pandemic*. As soon as more businesses migrate their digital assets to the web and their IT network becomes increasingly prevalent, cyber criminals are becoming more interested in exploiting unprotected nodes, systems, and repositories. Being a relatively new topic, DTs' importance to enhance cybersecurity has been poorly understood. By using simulated attacks over the DT, companies can identify security gaps that are currently neglected [25].

Considering one of the critical infrastructure sectors such as power homes, schools, critical infrastructures, healthcare, energy sectors, and their data from physical assets' sensors and/or cyber assets' controllers used to efficiently operate them in a low-risk domain [51,60]. Distributed control systems are highly vulnerable to cyber threats. The need to protect them has risen due to ongoing malicious damages. In such systems, data encryption, certificate authentication, and control system resiliency can be used to improve the resilience. However, extensive research has been lacking to monitor, manage, and mitigate the multiple coordinated attacks on such distributed systems [55]. A conceptual framework proposed in [55] hints at the potential of DTs for improving the level of cyber resilience.

This paper's primary objective is to explore and exploit the current state of DT research for cybersecurity to investigate whether resilience has been completely covered. To start with, we use the Scopus database and search for the

---

[2] https://gtnr.it/337j7Py.

term "Digital Twin", which hits over 1,500 papers in 2020. Next, we search for the two terms "cybersecurity" and "Digital Twin," which found only 13 papers of 2020. These statistics demonstrate that DTs are explored for several applications in different industry verticals, but not enough has been investigated regarding cybersecurity. This observation provides us the confidence to analyze the following two research questions: i) *How DT contributes to cybersecurity and Resilience?*, ii) *What is the state of cybersecurity in DT?*

2   Digital Twin for Cybersecurity

Our first main research question is: **"How does DT currently contribute to cybersecurity?"**

We witnessed several notorious cyber attacks over the past decade targeting ICS. In 2010, the Stuxnet computer worm successfully compromised an Iranian nuclear plant. The Ukrainian power grid was compromised by the black energy malware attack. Recent cyber-attacks on U.S. natural gas pipelines took place in 2020 [37]. The introduction of DTs as digital counterparts of physical assets could prevent a repeat of the above attacks by continuously monitoring the DTs to improve the detection of malicious threats and actors. In 2017, the use of DTs was proposed in [66] to enhance cybersecurity. More papers have been published on DTs since 2017. As of early 2021, 21 publications related to the topic were found.

Intrusion Detection Systems. The intrusion detection system (IDS) is commonly used to protect a network from malicious external attacks [36]. The use of an IDS improves the reliability and resilience of a system by detecting and reacting to behaviors that might endanger the system [73]. An IDS system has two varieties: 1) Anomaly or profile-based detection uses heuristics and behavior-based patterns to identify the activities that deviate from the normal usage. 2) In contrast, signature-based detection identifies threats in a system by matching known attack scenarios and subsequently raises an alert [4,36]. Intrusion detection systems are leveraging artificial intelligence to pinpoint system deviations and detect anomalies within a system's normal functioning from the collected data.

DTs enable us to mirror the internal environment and behavior of physical systems through creating exact virtual replicas [23]. DT's property allows us to implant an intrusion detection algorithm within the DT and test this virtual counterpart instead of the physical system without interrupting the live environment [3]. The latter can be considered a separate enhancement to cybersecurity. The DT can collect data from the physical twin and compare any deviations from the expected values, which can help determine failures within the system [35].

Rubio *et al.* [54] advocated to use DTs to provide IDS services in the context of Industry 4.0. Eckhart *et al.* [21] demonstrated how to implement a knowledge-based IDS using a DT together with knowledge-based rules, as shown in Fig. 2.

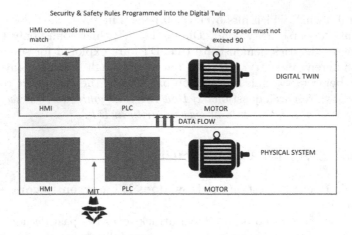

Fig. 2. Rule-based IDS for a DT

These rules were specified using AML and encompassed safety and security rules that the DT must follow. The safety rule ensured that the maximum velocity of the motor controlled by a PLC stayed within a specified threshold; and the security rule checked for consistency between the human-machine interface that sets the motor's velocity and the PLC that controls the motor velocity. These two rules were checked continuously for any violations. This experiment was more concentrated on simulating the system rather than incorporating real-time data into the DT. The operator will be alerted for any MITM attack that injects malicious commands, if it deviates from the defined rules.

A passive state replication approach was proposed in [20], where the DT virtually mirrored the behavior of the physical asset during its operation. It helped realize the intrusion detection use case. Here, the IDS was a behavior specification-based IDS that relied on the system's normal functioning to be predefined, which always yields a low false-negative rate and detects unknown attacks when the predefined system behavior was set. It was assumed that the system's correct behavior has already been created during the engineering phase. This method allows for identifying an intrusion by comparing the inputs and outputs of the physical asset to their counterparts of the DT. However, this approach can only copy a limited amount of data of the physical twin, resulting in a gap between the state of the physical twin and the DT. An improved architecture was proposed to allow a DT to constantly mirror the physical twin's behavior. This architecture is further equipped with a novel intrusion detection algorithm that can detect attacks on the ICS promptly in [3] and proposes a method to diagnose the detected attack type via classification using a Kalman filter.

Saad *et al.* [55] have introduced an IoT-based DT for cyber-physical networked microgrids to increase their cyber resiliency on physical sensors and control agents. A cloud-based platform was proposed in [49] to provide a central view for a networked microgrid system. This DT generates a digital replica for the interactions between the physical and cyber layers. The proposed DT framework by the authors detects false data injection (FDIA) and denial of service (DoS) attacks on the control system in case of a single or a coordinated attack and allows for corrective action to be taken by the user.

Dietz *et al.* [19] propose and demonstrate how a DT can be integrated into a Security Operation Centre (SOC) and Security Incident and Event Management (SIEM) to enhance cybersecurity. The SOC is responsible for providing a visualization of the procedures, technologies, and people within an enterprise [56] by integrating all security-relevant systems and events in a single point. Its main task is to identify and handle alerts while taking corrective actions to protect the organization's assets and data. A SIEM collects data like logs and network flows from different heterogeneous sources and collates them into a single view [68] and apply transfer learning with multipath communication [47] for accelerating the performance of DT along with the SIEM system.

SOCs face an increase in responsibility with the integration of industrial systems with corporate security. The current security strategies cannot keep pace with the growing attack surface of convergence of IT infrastructure and industrial systems that use sensors connected to enterprise networks [19]. Dietz *et al.* [19] have developed a process-based security framework to support SOCs using DT security and create a proof of concept. Using a Man-in-the-Middle attack simulation, they demonstrate how this integration can generate system logs provided to SIEM systems to build rules and take corrective action against attacks. Enterprises use a SOC supported by a SIEM to leverage capabilities ranging from security analysis to enforce rules and detect patterns to manage security-relevant data.

Authors in [17] apply simulations of security incidents in the DT and pass on the collected information to the SOC and a test SIEM system. The test SIEM is used to avoid negatively affecting the production environment during the simulation. SIEM security monitoring rules are created in advance by the experts who are assumed to be present in the SOC. The experts decide on the simulation parameters (e.g., a man-in-the-middle attack) within the DT, and the simulations settings. The output is the incident information artifact used within the test SIEM to verify whether it detects the security incident. Once this is verified, the logic/patterns identified can be passed onto the real SIEM and added into its monitoring rules to prevent similar real-world attacks in the future. Hence, DT focuses more on a particular asset than the attack itself [17]; see the identification of patterns—signature-based, behavior-based, specification-based, or hybrid [32], and a realistic attack demonstrated in [19] using ARP spoofing.

Simulation, Testing and Training. The authors in [17,20,21] propose various DT applications to enhance security in terms of historical data analysis and emulated environments to simulate attack testing. Testbeds help provide the security assessment of planned infrastructure, and cyber ranges help develop IT systems or infrastructures in a virtual environment for vulnerability assessment. Both testbeds and cyber rangers can serve as a training environment to improve the security, stability, and performance of the targeted infrastructure [44]. While testbeds are used to avoid damage or interruptions to the physical systems, this exercise can be costly and time-consuming to accurately represent the CPS in operation [9,21].

More importantly, another interest in using the DT with the above technologies is that it covers the entire life cycle of its physical twin. It begins with the planning and design phase to gather data as early as possible, even before the physical component exists. The inclusion of a DT enables the secure-by-design paradigm where the DT simulates the functioning of its physical counterpart and identifies security-related vulnerabilities before the physical asset is manufactured and begins to operate [59]. DT can incorporate security testing from the design phase onwards to fix any early identified vulnerabilities and continue into the following stages of the product life cycle to enable the secure by design paradigm to be a part of the CPS [22].

All CPS and IoT devices need to be tested to capture their effects on the underlying DT architecture. A complete rigorous testing should involve hundreds and maybe thousands of devices being a part of the test simulation. It is expensive in terms of the IoT test and evaluation costing and management but is a crucial aspect to study their large-scale effects [41]. In [40], the authors discussed how DTs can be used to replicate the behavior of IoT devices by multiplying them in a simulation environment to study large-scale effects of the IoT devices. A cyber-attack is modeled on a cluster of smart devices (smart thermostats) and examines their effects on a simulated environment.

Mittal *et al.* [40] conducted experiments on a NEST thermostat embedded in a local environment. This environment consists of multiple input sources such as the house environment, its occupancy, weather, and remote operations via a mobile application. The remote operations in this scenario open the possibilities of the thermostat being hacked. By observing how an attack influences the connected smart system, the DT owner incorporates simulations to enhance the infrastructure security during its deployment in the physical environment.

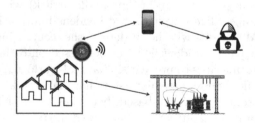

Fig. 3. An example of exploiting of SMART thermostat

As shown in Fig. 3, a SMART nest thermostat is connected to multiple households and can also be accessed via a mobile app, which opens the possibility of a hacker gaining access credentials and causing malicious damage. While a single app being hacked could cause a minor energy spike in the connected power grid, a hack involving multiple households' thermostats to be simultaneously switched on can be disastrous.

The DT generated from specification can simulate plant operation and generate the network traffic flows. This activity can allow an analyst to discover unused and unnecessary services within the system, thereby minimizing the attack surface of the plant [21]. This simulation can be complemented with logic and network features that allow security testing in a layer-wise fashion, which could indicate how an attacker can pivot through different system components and help realize a defense in depth strategy [21].

DT can be geared towards hardware and software misconfiguration. Since the DT is a replica of its physical twin, the DT should mimic the functionality of the physical asset (e.g., in terms of its communications interface, I/O modules in the hardware layer, and execution of control logic in the case of a PLC). We can expect to observe common features between both twins. Any deviation from the configurations in the hardware or software layer implies malicious activity. This use case is similar to implementing a behavior-specification-based IDS from DTs, which checks for differences in the functioning of the physical twin from the DT. Software manipulations can be detected by comparing configuration data between the twins [21]. In this case, the twin would need to be set up in an isolated environment to ensure that a malicious actor cannot make changes to the twin and mask their exploit if they could access the DT in the worst case.

To minimize the managing cost of a DT that mirrors its physical counterpart at all times, an economical method is proposed in [9]. A cost-effective DT within a budget only accounts for specific security tests that fit within the specified budget. Alternatively, DTs are integrated into a cyber range to test defense tactics and train users on cyber incident responses before the product's release into the production environments [7]. In this case, attacks could be launched against the DT from the cyber range itself. The cyber range can serve a range of use cases aside from training cybersecurity professionals. New cyberattack detection algorithms are developed before being released to production by using virtual hosts to showcase new security products [67]. DT serves as a source of data generation that is realistic enough to train AI algorithms [26], provides a testing environment for security equipment [69] and performs as environments to test out incident response plans before they are finalized.

The primary purpose of a CR is for cyber defense, focusing on network and information security [63]. CRs are adapting their offerings to support an OT and ICS use case [8]. Upon integrating a DT into a cyber range, we can obtain the performance of a DTs application to safety and the CRs application to security together. The DT will provide information to the CRs about the chain of impacts of an incident, and the CR can provide the source of the incident along with its nature (malicious/accidental) for a detected anomaly. In simpler terms, DTs can provide information about the physical processes and function of the system while the CR can report on the network traffic and bridge the gap between the digital and physical layers [8].

System testing is a part of their proposed DT framework in [21]. For testing purposes, real devices can be interfaced with the DT. Eckhart *et al.* [21] introduce the concept of CPS Twinning, which can allow testing of the network and logic layer of the CPS. The network layer of the CPS is emulated on Mininet, which allows the emulation of logic specific to a variety of devices like PLCs, HMIs, and motors. According to [22], DTs can be used as training exercises for Red and Blue teams for security testing purposes. The red team can uncover flaws and vulnerabilities from the current system configuration and state. The blue team would improve upon their incident response capabilities in response to the Red team. The data collected over these kinds of simulations and events can contribute to risk assessments to motivate cybersecurity uplift activities.

Cyber resilience is described in [71] as the ability of a system to maintain a stable level of control of physical processes while under attack. A four-step method is proposed to improve cyber resilience—risk assessment, resilience engineering, resilience operation, and resilience enhancement. This method lowers the probability of an attack, its impacts, and the recovery time needed to recover from an attack. The DT can actively support this process by providing an isolated environment to test for process control [22]. This iterative simulation on the DT can also identify potential losses during an attack and facilitate the creation of a containment and response plan tailored to different attacks.

Privacy and Legal Compliance. Recently, monitoring the CPS's security and safety posture during operation is regarded as a critical task in [62]. The monitoring activity could provide evidence of meeting security standards like IEC 62443, which would assist organizations in complying with legal requirements. According to [62], the DTs may provide an accurate reflection of CPSs throughout their entire lifecycle for continuous monitoring and documentation of security and safety aspects. The NIS directive (European Parliament and the Council of the European Union 2016) has brought about an increase of regulatory requirements for operators of CPS, which requires integrating security and legal compliance support into DTs.

DTs were used in [16] to enable automated privacy assessments and protect the privacy of smart car drivers, as shown in Fig. 4. A DT of the car continually receives data from the different sensors within the smart vehicle.

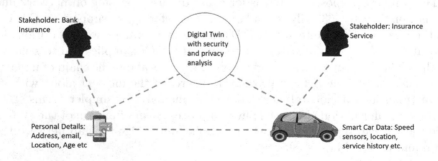

Fig. 4. Privacy protection and compliance via DTs

An example of anonymizing customer data was provided in [16], where DT can assist controllers and processors in fulfilling the general data protection regulation (GDPR) requirements. The customers' data is anonymized to preserve the customers' privacy rights before being sent to insurers.

This approach can be extended to other types of CPSs such as [48]. Privacy-enhancing techniques based on DTs for smart grids, medical CPSs, and smart transport are areas that need to be further explored due to the large volume of the produced data [22].

Security for the Factory of the Future (FoF) and a System of Systems (SoS). A factory of the future (FoF) DT technology was proposed in [8] to enhance cybersecurity resilience. DTs can be integrated into cyber ranges. Cyber range products are used for cybersecurity simulation and training [7], but using DTs will help better understand how cyber events are represented between the physical asset and the digital counterpart. Hence, combining DTs and cyber ranges benefits safety monitoring, predictive decision making, and SoS architecture decision support. Moreover, human behavior can be integrated into the DT for security testing. Nearly 60% of all cyber-attacks involve a human (intentionally or unintentionally), the inclusion of human behavior modeling will enhance the cyber resilience capability of the FoF [74].

3   Cybersecurity of Digital Twin

The second important research question in this work is: **"What is the current state of cybersecurity for the DT?**

With the growing convergence of information technology (IT) and operation technology (OT) [46], the evolution of intelligent manufacturing and industry 4.0 automation have increased the cyber attack surface dramatically. As manufacturing assets become increasingly interconnected, decision-making will be more reliant on DTs, and the increasing use of cloud manufacturing services increases the attack surface [8], a new attack fractal.

DTs have been considered by organizations to add to the current fractal and they must be subject to security measures to prevent an entry point for cyber attackers [7]. When machines are unprogrammable and relied mostly on electric power, the security issue is not important because they were isolated from the organizational infrastructure. However, with the introduction of the internet to the manufacturing industry has opened many security challenges [46,47]. Therefore, it is worth considering that the introduction of the DT will enlarge the attack surface. Therefore its weakened security requires additional measures and enhancements. Our main finding is that the decision to adopt and deploy DT in organization and industries poses additional challenges in security and privacy [43], which is the main focus of this section.

Along with all of the benefits and opportunities that DT brings, new attack vectors are also exposed. Adopting DT is a promising performance enhancement, and there has been an impeding demand from academic and industrial research.

But, quantification of security challenges and potential solutions should be investigated thoroughly before the adoption of DT [39]. When an attacker gets access to a DT of the system, great care should be taken to prevent the attackers getting into the physical twin and compromising them [39]. As mentioned earlier, we consider DTs of cars and/or remote surgery, which requires bidirectional communication links, therefore security needs are to be given equal attention to that of performance improvements for improved seamless migration to DTs.

Data Security Involving Personally Identifiable Information. DTs present privacy issues. Due to a large amount of data collected from users, especially in AVs or digital healthcare, the information may allow insights into people's behavior and usage patterns without their consent. The data could help target specific advertising at the users or even inflate insurance and healthcare. Similar to security and privacy regulations present in most of the standards followed in IT and OT, regulatory mechanisms need to enable usage of DT while preventing its misuse [10].

While the DT aims to represent its physical counterpart as accurately as possible, it raises the possibility of the collected data related to individuals' life, behavioral patterns, intellectual property, or combined. Currently, no regulations explicitly govern the ownership of data within a DT. As this paradigm further evolves and permeates into sectors like smart cars and smart health, data ownership will become increasingly important since the participant is part of the DT with significant data contribution in both cases—health and AVs. However, third parties are involved in the administration and management. Further questions include—who owns the data, who are allowed to access it, and when the access is granted [28]?

The DT environment must be developed with a strong resilience towards viruses and malicious activities. Compromising the private, sensitive, and confidential information within the DT can damage all sources of the physical twin that are communicating with the DT. A focus needs to be given to the DTs in the medicine and healthcare sectors regarding data security and privacy [6]. A security layer was introduced to a DT model in [18] for secure data sharing in the DT environment. And the security layer is used to protect the sensitive data transmitted between the DT and its physical counterpart.

Intellectual Property Protections. DTs raise the need for intellectual property protections. Intellectual property protection mechanisms like watermarking [29] and digital rights management (DRM) [53] can protect the DT and its organizational specific knowledge. However, watermarking and DRMs can be bypassed.

Trusted Platform Module Use. Further security protections for a DT may limit its use to a specific set of hardware or specific machines using a trusted platform module (TPM). The secure execution of DT is ensured via a successful cryptographic exchange between the hardware and software.

Software Security within the DT. An end-to-end scheme for cyber resilience was proposed in [75] to enable the security of DT software. The scheme identifies vulnerable functions in DT software projects for healthcare. A deep code attention technique was employed to explore the context code relationships between vulnerability-related keywords. The results of empirical studies showed superior performance to some state-of-the-art deep learning methods.

4   Challenges and Future Directions

The proliferation of IoT-enabled CPS induces multiple complexities. Since CPS are key components of a DT, the associated risks and vulnerabilities need to be better understood. The security-by-design is achieved through considering security and incorporating it from the design phase of a technology. While technology is moving at an accelerated rate and the transmission and supervision of vast quantities of data is supported by a sturdy infrastructure, the standards which govern data transactions are outpaced by the rise of smart technologies and their inclusion into different smart sectors [15]. The inter-connectivity of different smart sectors increases the threat surface and may lead to a severe security breach [1].

IDS Challenges. SIEMs are too complex for us to create intrusion detection and correlation rules [19]. Future research is needed to define complex rules in simple code to reduce the requirements of SIEM experts' familiarity with the SIEM syntax. Thus, more and more security personnel may contribute to the improved lightweight framework.

Physical Twin Vulnerabilities Affecting the DT. Cybersecurity risks present themselves to the DT paradigm [27]. Since the DT becomes a repository for enormous amounts of data via collection from sensors, a successful compromise of the system can result in the loss of sensitive data and financial damage. As DTs are used to predict and provide suggestions based on the acquired information, the compromise can also lead to the loss of business secrets and processes. When a hacker has attained access to the DT, the attackers may find a rich data asset, including a blueprint of the entire system and the possessed data on the DT, and a viable method of influencing the real twin in the case of a bidirectional twin [27].

Security gaps between DT and real twin were identified with examples of failing to replicate a microcontroller's security protection in the real twin within the DT. While there has been an increasing amount of research on the DT paradigm, there is little research on the actual security of the DT itself.

Security issues of a DT are similar to the security concerns observed in IoT, since they are connected as key components to a DT. The security issues include data encryption, access privileges, principle of least privilege, labelling known device, and vulnerabilities.

Threat modeling of the different components that make up a DT needs to be carried out to enable a secure by design DT that can mitigate the cyber risks currently present within it [1]. Within the smart healthcare sector, security threats were identified in [72] on smart devices, including hardware exploitation, backdoors, software exploitation, and many more.

CPS can attract compromised-key attacks due to authenticity requirements among different sensors using the handshake protocols. It can be problematic since CPS are key components of the DTs, especially since the supporting infrastructure can be manipulated to enable a backdoor [31] to the system for future access or potential intellectual property (IP) theft.

Data and Information Privacy Challenges. In [76], a DT was used to protect human safety in an airport cargo scenario. This work can be extended to include individual health status like blood pressure and heart rate, which can develop normal patterns of human behavior to check for anomalies and challenges.

Healthcare DTs applications will require massive development in terms of cyber resilience [14] due to the volume of patient data that is collected, moving in transit, and processed between the digital and physical twin. The information like personal data about a patient and their current state of health, needs to be handled with the utmost care, so hospitals and organizations must ensure the data security and integrity [75]. Vulnerability detection is a crucial requirement for cyber resilience in healthcare DTs [34] since an exploited vulnerability in the medicine DT can pose threats to its many users.

In [10], the privacy concerns were explored for DT in healthcare. Since a DT in medicine can be used to create the 'virtual patient', governance and due diligence will need to be used to safeguard the rights of a DT user. The governance can use processes from how biobanks or medical banks are inspected, designed, and regulated. Data protection will be a vital concern of the DT paradigm being used in medicine due to the sensitive nature of the data.

Human Errors. The human factor in any technology is currently overlooked as an inherent weakness and underestimated in the cyber-physical networks. The increasing number of phishing attacks to exploit this vulnerability are a severe threat, given that smart devices and the emerging use of IoT are targeted extensively. Another vector to be considered is the threat of the malicious insider [2], resulting in non-compliance, fraud, industrial espionage, or even plain human error. A baseline needs to be established to distinguish normal and malicious behaviors and integrated into the DT IDS [13]. Since a DT forms part of an organization's proprietary technology, it requires stringent IP protection.

Integration of Legacy Systems with a DT. With CPSs having a long life cycle, implementing the DT on brownfield sites will be a large area of interest [22]. Older systems are often insufficiently documented, which may affect the DT model's accuracy. It can lead to a dysfunctional DT representation of the system. The challenge will be to determine the use case of the DT. According to [12,22], a specification mining approach was proposed to implement an IDS of automation systems. Further research needs to be conducted on how legacy systems and DTs can be integrated to enhance the cyber resilience.

Enabling a Factory of the Future DT. Currently, the scope of DT is tied to a single asset. According to [8], the narrow scope is a limitation with current DTs. More research is needed to release the DT beyond the limits of an individual physical asset and eventually span the complete System of Systems [61]. The System of Systems is not a sum of isolated assets but a complete network of factories [38].

4.1 Potentials of DTs with Cybersecurity

Cybersecurity professionals shall establish an online digital clone for each physical device in the world through cyber DTs. As mentioned, such automated emulation simulates cyber attacks, circumvent vulnerabilities and spots possible threats before the actual production environment is effected. To this end, we have identified the following avenues for future research.

Attacks to/from DTs. When machines were not programmable and only relied on electricity powering them, there was little concern about their security since they were isolated from the organizational infrastructure. The introduction of the internet to the manufacturing industry has opened many challenges in terms of security and the many opportunities it presents. More research is required on the attacks against DTs or even attacks that can be carried out using the DT itself [22]. Since the DT is a replica of the system and is used to provide a digital replica of the physical counterpart, a capable attacker can manipulate the data in the DT to hide their traces within the physical counterpart go undetected. Alternatively, if the DT can issue automated commands based on the actions of the physical system, a compromised DT can be used by an attacker to issue malicious commands back to the physical asset and cause it to go to an unsafe state. The security and privacy concerns will be a key discussion factor in the future development of DTs. Its current level of maturity indicates a strong presence in industry 4.0 and the automation of manufacturing [33].

To thoroughly examine the security for a manufacturing system, five levels were proposed in [30] for the CIM model [64]. The five levels of the CIM model can be applied to the DT since it replicates the physical twin. By ensuring that security rules are defined, established, and implemented at each level, security within an organization could be addressed from a high-level view to more granular aspects of the system. The five levels are: i) **Enterprise or Corporate level:** Decision related to workflows and operational management are defined that span the complete process from production to the finalised product; ii) **Plant Management level:** The decisions that affect management of a single plant; iii) **Supervisory level:** The decisions that affect the manufacturing cells that come under a single supervisory process; iv) **Cell Control level:** This decision at this level effect a single process and its performed actions; v) **Sensor Actuator level:** This level consists of the most granular aspects of the system which could consist of the sensors, actuators and controllers that integrate to perform the physical process

Protocols used to support the manufacturing infrastructure like modbus, distributed network protocol (DNP3), industrial Ethernet, PROFIBUS, building automation, and control networking (BACnet) are mainly used for supervisory controls and not security. They cannot provide authentication, confidentiality, integrity, non-repudiation, and the ability to detect anomalies [30]. Manufactures are exposed to cyber liabilities like non-availability of systems, data breaches, intellectual property theft, and third-party damage.

Securing DTs with Authentication Measures. With the authors in [31] using DTs as a use case in remote control for surgery, they emphasize a strong need for authentication on each site where the DT is operating. Using state-of-the-art techniques like multi-factor authentication (MFA) and biometric authentication [65,70] should be made mandatory in addition to the application of physical access controls to the DT system. Any physical access to the facilities should be restricted and supported by strong multi-factor or biometric authentication [1]. A malicious actor could wreak havoc if they were to gain access to the system and affect all the connected systems and those that are linked to the DT. While there is very little research in authentication measures for a DT, research into this would provide an added layer of security that would make the DT harder to compromise and add to the defense-in-depth approach taken to secure it.

Knowledge-Based IDS for DTs. Multiple articles attempted to identify and mitigate cyber-attacks by using DTs as an IDS system. In [52,57], many IDSs have revolved around behavior-based systems because knowledge-based systems need historical data of realistic previous exploits to establish rules. DTs can be used as testbeds to obtain the required system behavior and data and can also be used as testbeds to simulate realistic incidents.

Scope and Optimality of DT. While the DT is meant to be a digital mirror image of its physical counterpart, it should only provide support to its physical twin and not be a redundancy backup that replicates the CPS in its entirety [22]. While a cost-effective method for operating a DT is proposed in [9], there is no current standard for how accurately a DT is supposed to mirror its physical twin. It is challenging to build a DT with sufficient capabilities [20]. Due to this pursuing the balance between budget and twin similarity is a direction worth pursuing.

DT-Based Honeypots. Honeypots are employed as baiting mechanisms to attract hackers by emulating a real-world environment. The primary use of honeypots is to serve as deception devices and discover attackers' tactics, techniques, and procedures. The use of hardware automation can enhance their similarity to real-time systems to enhance the credibility [45]. While we found no publication in this area, the results and learnings from integrating a DT with a cyber range can help create an accurate representation of the physical environment as a honeypot.

Secure Decommissioning with DT. Simulation has not been used for decommissioning an asset, even at the peak of its research [42] except for when it is an asset of high risk like a nuclear power plant [50]. Any high-risk asset requires to be securely decommissioned. It also holds for the DT that is accompanying a high-risk asset through its production life cycle. The DT needs to be decommissioned securely and avoid any instances of unauthorized access [22]. Since the DT has been leveraged in different phases of the systems' life cycle, Eckhart *et al.* [22] advocate to include the DT in the last stage of the life cycle (the decommissioning stage). Moreover, the inclusion of DT in the prior stages will allow a holistic view of how a DT can be used to its full capacity.

Human Behavior with DT for IDS. Human behavior modeling is in a very early stage of development within the DT concept [11,24]. Human behavior may have a massive impact on any manufacturing process since interfaces that require human input can be error-prone. A tired worker can lose focus and cause a problem with a machine [58], and it is challenging to distinguish as a malicious act or an accident. Nevertheless, it requires an understanding of human intention compared to normal behavior addressed by techniques like User and Entity behavior Analysis (UBEA) [5]. It has not been explored across cyber ad physical spheres yet. The authors in [8] propose that interactions with equipment (systems, applications, mouse, and keyboard) can be used to build a worker's profile which will establish a normal baseline of their activities and patterns of work and isolate any anomalies that might arise from the safety and security point of view; see a DT-enabled tracking framework [76] and the reference therein.

DT, SOC, and SIEM Integration. In [19], a DT was integrated with a SOC and SIEM to detect a MITM attack. It created new rules for the SIEM to assist with attack detection. This paradigm could be extended further by the data provided to the SOC from the DT or even the addition of cyber threat intelligence (CTI) and the common vulnerabilities and exposures (CVE)s. The integration of these could be used to simulate various scenarios in the DT and make it as realistic as possible. It could also be supplemented using data that has been obtained from honeypots about the attacker's TTPs. A point of convergence between the DT and CRs was forecasted in [7]. However, no research publication has been found for connecting security tests and simulations in a DT setup in early 2021 [8].

5 Conclusion

Over the past decade, fast advances in machine learning, artificial intelligence, IoT, and others have played a part in the emergence of the DT and will continue to do so for the upcoming decade. The advancement of technologies has led to the DT applied in broad fields, including manufacturing, aviation, automobiles, medicine, the design of cities, and many more. This paper has explored how the DT can be utilized further by enhancing cybersecurity measures.

This paper answered the two research questions: *How does a DT currently contribute to cybersecurity? What is the current state of cybersecurity for the DT?* We have examined some promising frameworks in the literature and have provided insights into the different use cases where DTs can enhance cybersecurity. Regarding the DT's security, some methods are used to prevent access of the DT from falling into malicious hands, but further research is required. In conclusion, this study has provided challenges faced by the use of DT and open research areas worth exploring to further this concept.

References

1. Ahmadi-Assalemi, G., et al.: Digital twins for precision healthcare. In: Jahankhani, H., Kendzierskyj, S., Chelvachandran, N., Ibarra, J. (eds.) Cyber Defence in the Age of AI, Smart Societies and Augmented Humanity. ASTSA, pp. 133–158. Springer, Cham (2020). https://doi.org/10.1007/978-3-030-35746-7_8
2. Ahmadi-Assalemi, G., Al-Khateeb, H.M., Epiphaniou, G., Cosson, J., Jahankhani, H., Pillai, P.: Federated blockchain-based tracking and liability attribution framework for employees and cyber-physical objects in a smart workplace. In: Proceedings of the 2019 IEEE 12th International Conference on Global Security, Safety and Sustainability (ICGS3), pp. 1–9. IEEE (2019)
3. Akbarian, F., Fitzgerald, E., Kihl, M.: Intrusion detection in digital twins for industrial control systems. In: Proceedings of the 2020 International Conference on Software, Telecommunications and Computer Networks (SoftCOM), pp. 1–6. IEEE (2020)
4. Aldwairi, T., Perera, D., Novotny, M.A.: An evaluation of the performance of restricted Boltzmann machines as a model for anomaly network intrusion detection. Comput. Networks **144**, 111–119 (2018)
5. Babu, S.: Detecting anomalies in Users-An UEBA approach. In: Proceedings of the International Conference on Industrial Engineering and Operations Management, pp. 863–876 (2020)
6. Barricelli, B.R., Casiraghi, E., Fogli, D.: A survey on digital twin: definitions, characteristics, applications, and design implications. IEEE Access **7**, 167653–167671 (2019)
7. Becue, A., et al.: Cyberfactory# 1-securing the industry 4.0 with cyber-ranges and digital twins. In: Proceedings of the 2018 14th IEEE International Workshop on Factory Communication Systems (WFCS), pp. 1–4. IEEE (2018)
8. Becue, A., Maia, E., Feeken, L., Borchers, P., Praca, I.: A new concept of digital twin supporting optimization and resilience of factories of the future. Appl. Sci. **10**(13), 4482 (2020)
9. Bitton, R., et al.: Deriving a cost-effective digital twin of an ICS to facilitate security evaluation. In: Lopez, J., Zhou, J., Soriano, M. (eds.) ESORICS 2018. LNCS, vol. 11098, pp. 533–554. Springer, Cham (2018). https://doi.org/10.1007/978-3-319-99073-6_26
10. Bruynseels, K., Santoni de Sio, F., van den Hoven, J.: Digital twins in health care: ethical implications of an emerging engineering paradigm. Front. Genet. **9**, 31 (2018)
11. Buldakova, T., Suyatinov, S.: Hierarchy of human operator models for digital twin. In: Proceedings of the 2019 International Russian Automation Conference (RusAutoCon), pp. 1–5. IEEE (2019)
12. Caselli, M., Zambon, E., Amann, J., Sommer, R., Kargl, F.: Specification mining for intrusion detection in networked control systems. In: Proceedings of the 25th USENIX Security Symposium (USENIX Security 16), pp. 791–806 (2016)
13. Cheh, C., Keefe, K., Feddersen, B., Chen, B., Temple, W.G., Sanders, W.H.: Developing models for physical attacks in cyber-physical systems. In: Proceedings of the 2017 Workshop on Cyber-Physical Systems Security and Privacy, pp. 49–55 (2017)
14. Chen, X., et al.: Android HIV: a study of repackaging malware for evading machine-learning detection. IEEE Trans. Inf. Forensics Secur. **15**, 987–1001 (2019)
15. Coppinger, R.: Design through the looking glass [digital twins of real products]. Eng. Technol. **11**(11), 58–60 (2016)

16. Damjanovic-Behrendt, V.: A digital twin-based privacy enhancement mechanism for the automotive industry. In: 2018 International Conference on Intelligent Systems (IS), pp. 272–279. IEEE (2018)
17. Dietz, M., Pernul, G.: Unleashing the digital twin's potential for ICS security. IEEE Secur. Priv. **18**(4), 20–27 (2020)
18. Dietz, M., Putz, B., Pernul, G.: A distributed ledger approach to digital twin secure data sharing. In: Foley, S.N. (ed.) DBSec 2019. LNCS, vol. 11559, pp. 281–300. Springer, Cham (2019). https://doi.org/10.1007/978-3-030-22479-0_15
19. Dietz, M., Vielberth, M., Pernul, G.: Integrating digital twin security simulations in the security operations center. In: Proceedings of the 15th International Conference on Availability, Reliability and Security, pp. 1–9 (2020)
20. Eckhart, M., Ekelhart, A.: A specification-based state replication approach for digital twins. In: Proceedings of the 2018 Workshop on Cyber-Physical Systems Security and Privacy, pp. 36–47 (2018)
21. Eckhart, M., Ekelhart, A.: Towards security-aware virtual environments for digital twins. In: Proceedings of the 4th ACM Workshop on Cyber-physical System Security, pp. 61–72 (2018)
22. Eckhart, M., Ekelhart, A.: Digital twins for cyber-physical systems security: state of the art and outlook. In: Security and Quality in Cyber-Physical Systems Engineering, pp. 383–412. Springer, Cham (2019). https://doi.org/10.1007/978-3-030-25312-7_14
23. Farsi, M., Daneshkhah, A., Hosseinian-Far, A., Jahankhani, H.: Digital Twin Technologies and Smart Cities. Springer, Cham (2020). https://doi.org/10.1007/978-3-030-18732-3
24. Graessler, I., Pöhler, A.: Integration of a digital twin as human representation in a scheduling procedure of a cyber-physical production system. In: Proceedings of the 2017 IEEE International Conference on Industrial Engineering and Engineering Management (IEEM), pp. 289–293. IEEE (2017)
25. Grieves, M., Vickers, J.: Digital twin: mitigating unpredictable, undesirable emergent behavior in complex systems. In: Kahlen, F.-J., Flumerfelt, S., Alves, A. (eds.) Transdisciplinary Perspectives on Complex Systems, pp. 85–113. Springer, Cham (2017). https://doi.org/10.1007/978-3-319-38756-7_4
26. Hallaq, B., Nicholson, A., Smith, R., Maglaras, L., Janicke, H., Jones, K.: CYRAN: a hybrid cyber range for testing security on ICS/SCADA systems. In: Cyber Security and Threats: Concepts, Methodologies, Tools, and Applications, pp. 622–637. IGI Global (2018)
27. Hearn, M., Rix, S.: Cybersecurity considerations for digital twin implementations. IIC J. Innov. 107–113 (2019)
28. Jones, D., Snider, C., Nassehi, A., Yon, J., Hicks, B.: Characterising the digital twin: a systematic literature review. CIRP J. Manuf. Sci. Technol. **29**, 36–52 (2020)
29. Katzenbeisser, S., Petitcolas, F.: Digital Watermarking. Artech House, London 2 (2000)
30. Kaur, M.J., Mishra, V.P., Maheshwari, P.: The convergence of digital twin, IoT, and machine learning: transforming data into action. In: Farsi, M., Daneshkhah, A., Hosseinian-Far, A., Jahankhani, H. (eds.) Digital Twin Technologies and Smart Cities. IT, pp. 3–17. Springer, Cham (2020). https://doi.org/10.1007/978-3-030-18732-3_1
31. Laaki, H., Miche, Y., Tammi, K.: Prototyping a digital twin for real time remote control over mobile networks: application of remote surgery. IEEE Access **7**, 20325–20336 (2019)

32. Liao, H.J., Lin, C.H.R., Lin, Y.C., Tung, K.Y.: Intrusion detection system: a comprehensive review. J. Network Comput. Appl. **36**(1), 16–24 (2013)
33. Lim, K.Y.H., Zheng, P., Chen, C.H.: A state-of-the-art survey of digital twin: techniques, engineering product lifecycle management and business innovation perspectives. J. Intell. Manuf. **31**(6), 1–25 (2019)
34. Liu, L., De Vel, O., Han, Q.L., Zhang, J., Xiang, Y.: Detecting and preventing cyber insider threats: a survey. IEEE Commun. Surv. Tutorials **20**(2), 1397–1417 (2018)
35. Liu, M., Fang, S., Dong, H., Xu, C.: Review of digital twin about concepts, technologies, and industrial applications. J. Manuf. Syst. **58**, 346–361 (2020)
36. Lv, L., Wang, W., Zhang, Z., Liu, X.: A novel intrusion detection system based on an optimal hybrid kernel extreme learning machine. Knowl. Based Syst. **195**, 105648 (2020)
37. Malik, N.S., Collins, R., Vamburkar, M.: Cyberattack pings data systems of at least four gas networks (2018)
38. Mennenga, M., Cerdas, F., Thiede, S., Herrmann, C.: Exploring the opportunities of system of systems engineering to complement sustainable manufacturing and life cycle engineering. Procedia CIRP **80**, 637–642 (2019)
39. Minerva, R., Lee, G.M., Crespi, N.: Digital twin in the IoT context: a survey on technical features, scenarios, and architectural models. Proc. IEEE **108**(10), 1785–1824 (2020)
40. Mittal, S., Tolk, A., Pyles, A., Van Balen, N., Bergollo, K.: Digital twin modeling, co-simulation and cyber use-case inclusion methodology for IoT systems. In: Proceedings of the 2019 Winter Simulation Conference (WSC), pp. 2653–2664. IEEE (2019)
41. Mittal, S., Zeigler, B.P., Tolk, A., Ören, T.: Theory and practice of M&S in cyber environments. In: The Profession of Modeling and Simulation: Discipline, Ethics, Education, Vocation, Societies and Economics. Wiley Online Library (2017)
42. Mourtzis, D., Doukas, M., Bernidaki, D.: Simulation in manufacturing: review and challenges. Procedia CIRP **25**, 213–229 (2014)
43. Parmar, R., Leiponen, A., Thomas, L.D.: Building an organizational digital twin. Bus. Horiz. **63**(6), 725–736 (2020)
44. Pham, C., Tang, D., Chinen, K.i., Beuran, R.: CYRIS: a cyber range instantiation system for facilitating security training. In: Proceedings of the Seventh Symposium on Information and Communication Technology, pp. 251–258 (2016)
45. Piggin, R., Buffey, I.: Active defence using an operational technology honeypot (2016). https://bit.ly/3njohBz
46. Pokhrel, S.R., Garg, S.: Multipath communication with deep Q-Network for industry 4.0 automation and orchestration. IEEE Trans. Ind. Inform. **17**(4), 2852–2859 (2020)
47. Pokhrel, S.R., Pan, L., Kumar, N., Doss, R., Le Vu, H.: Multipath TCP meets transfer learning: a novel edge-based learning for industrial IoT. IEEE Internet Things J. **8**(13), 10299–10307 (2021)
48. Pokhrel, S.R., Qu, Y., Gao, L.: QoS-aware personalized privacy with multipath TCP for industrial IoT: analysis and design. IEEE Internet Things J. **7**(6), 4849–4861 (2020)
49. Pokhrel, S.R., Vu, H.L., Cricenti, A.L.: Adaptive admission control for IoT applications in home wifi networks. IEEE Trans. Mob. Comput. **19**(12), 2731–2742 (2019)
50. Polenghi, A., Fumagalli, L., Roda, I.: Role of simulation in industrial engineering: focus on manufacturing systems. IFAC Pap. OnLine **51**(11), 496–501 (2018)

51. Poon, J., Jain, P., Konstantakopoulos, I.C., Spanos, C., Panda, S.K., Sanders, S.R.: Model-based fault detection and identification for switching power converters. IEEE Trans. Power Electron. **32**(2), 1419–1430 (2016)
52. Roosta, T., Nilsson, D.K., Lindqvist, U., Valdes, A.: An intrusion detection system for wireless process control systems. In: Proceedings of the 2008 5th IEEE International Conference on Mobile ad hoc and Sensor Systems, pp. 866–872. IEEE (2008)
53. Rosenblatt, B., Trippe, B., Mooney, S., et al.: Digital Rights Management. New York (2002)
54. Rubio, J.E., Alcaraz, C., Roman, R., Lopez, J.: Analysis of intrusion detection systems in industrial ecosystems. In: SECRYPT, pp. 116–128 (2017)
55. Saad, A., Faddel, S., Youssef, T., Mohammed, O.A.: On the implementation of IoT-based digital twin for networked microgrids resiliency against cyber attacks. IEEE Trans. Smart Grid **11**(6), 5138–5150 (2020)
56. Schinagl, S., Schoon, K., Paans, R.: A framework for designing a security operations centre (SOC). In: Proceedings of the 2015 48th Hawaii International Conference on System Sciences, pp. 2253–2262. IEEE (2015)
57. Shin, S., Kwon, T., Jo, G.Y., Park, Y., Rhy, H.: An experimental study of hierarchical intrusion detection for wireless industrial sensor networks. IEEE Trans. Ind. Inform. **6**(4), 744–757 (2010)
58. Shultz, K.S., Wang, M., Olson, D.A.: Role overload and underload in relation to occupational stress and health. J. Int. Soc. Investig. Stress **26**(2), 99–111 (2010)
59. Tao, F., Cheng, J., Qi, Q., Zhang, M., Zhang, H., Sui, F.: Digital twin-driven product design, manufacturing and service with big data. Int. J. Adv. Manuf. Technol. **94**(9), 3563–3576 (2018)
60. Tao, F., Zhang, H., Liu, A., Nee, A.Y.: Digital twin in industry: state-of-the-art. IEEE Trans. Ind. Inform. **15**(4), 2405–2415 (2018)
61. Tao, F., Zhang, M.: Digital twin shop-floor: a new shop-floor paradigm towards smart manufacturing. IEEE Access **5**, 20418–20427 (2017)
62. Tauber, M., Schmittner, C.: Enabling security and safety evaluation in industry 4.0 use cases with digital twins. ERCIM News (2018)
63. Tian, Z., et al.: A real-time correlation of host-level events in cyber range service for smart campus. IEEE Access **6**, 35355–35364 (2018)
64. Tuptuk, N., Hailes, S.: Security of smart manufacturing systems. J. Manuf. Syst. **47**, 93–106 (2018)
65. Tuyls, P., Akkermans, A.H.M., Kevenaar, T.A.M., Schrijen, G.-J., Bazen, A.M., Veldhuis, R.N.J.: Practical biometric authentication with template protection. In: Kanade, T., Jain, A., Ratha, N.K. (eds.) AVBPA 2005. LNCS, vol. 3546, pp. 436–446. Springer, Heidelberg (2005). https://doi.org/10.1007/11527923_45
66. Uhlemann, T.H.J., Lehmann, C., Steinhilper, R.: The digital twin: realizing the cyber-physical production system for industry 4.0. Procedia CIRP **61**, 335–340 (2017)
67. Urias, V.E., Stout, W.M., Van Leeuwen, B., Lin, H.: Cyber range infrastructure limitations and needs of tomorrow: a position paper. In: Proceedings of the 2018 International Carnahan Conference on Security Technology (ICCST), pp. 1–5. IEEE (2018)
68. Vielberth, M., Menges, F., Pernul, G.: Human-as-a-security-sensor for harvesting threat intelligence. Cybersecurity **2**(1), 1–15 (2019)
69. Vykopal, J., Ošlejšek, R., Čeleda, P., Vizvary, M., Tovarňák, D.: Kypo cyber range: design and use cases. In: Proceedings of the 12th International Conference on Software Technologies, pp. 310–321. SciTePress (2017)

70. Wayman, J., Jain, A., Maltoni, D., Maio, D.: An introduction to biometric authentication systems. In: Wayman, J., Jain, A., Maltoni, D., Maio, D. (eds.) Biometric Systems, pp. 1–20. Springer, London (2005). https://doi.org/10.1007/1-84628-064-8_1

71. Wei, D., Ji, K.: Resilient industrial control system (RICS): concepts, formulation, metrics, and insights. In: Proceedings of the 2010 3rd International Symposium on Resilient Control Systems, pp. 15–22. IEEE (2010)

72. Wurm, J., et al.: Introduction to cyber-physical system security: a cross-layer perspective. IEEE Trans. Multi Scale Comput. Syst. 3(3), 215–227 (2016)

73. Yahalom, R., Steren, A., Nameri, Y., Roytman, M., Porgador, A., Elovici, Y.: Improving the effectiveness of intrusion detection systems for hierarchical data. Knowl. Based Syst. **168**, 59–69 (2019)

74. van Zadelhoff, M.: The biggest cybersecurity threats are inside your company. Harvard Bus. Rev. **19** (2016)

75. Zhang, J., Li, L., Lin, G., Fang, D., Tai, Y., Huang, J.: Cyber resilience in healthcare digital twin on lung cancer. IEEE Access **8**, 201900–201913 (2020)

76. Zhao, Z., Shen, L., Yang, C., Wu, W., Zhang, M., Huang, G.Q.: IoT and digital twin enabled smart tracking for safety management. Comput. Oper. Res. **128**, 105183 (2021)

Differential Privacy-Based Permissioned Blockchain for Private Data Sharing in Industrial IoT

Muhammad Islam[1](✉), Mubashir Husain Rehmani[2], and Jinjun Chen[1]

[1] Swinburne University of Technology, Hawthorn, VIC 3122, Australia
[2] Munster Technological University, Rossa Avenue, Bishopstown, Cork, Ireland

Abstract. Permissioned blockchain such as Hyperledger fabric enables a secure supply chain model in Industrial Internet of Things (IIoT) through multichannel and private data collection mechanisms. However, the existing data sharing and querying mechanism in Hyperledger fabric is not suitable for supply chain environment in IIoT because the queries are evaluated on actual data stored on ledger which consists of sensitive information such as business secrets, and special discounts offered to retailers and individuals. To solve this problem, we propose a differential privacy-based permissioned blockchain using Hyperledger fabric to enable private data sharing in supply chain in IIoT (DH-IIoT). We integrate differential privacy into the chaindcode (smart contract) of Hyperledger fabric to achieve privacy preservation. As a result, the query response consists of perturbed data which protects the sensitive information in the ledger. We evaluate and compare our differential privacy integrated chaincode of Hyperledger fabric with the default chaincode setting of Hyperledger fabric for supply chain scenario. The results confirm that the proposed work maintains 96.15% of accuracy in the shared data while guarantees the protection of sensitive ledger's data.

Keywords: IIoT · Hyperledger fabric blockchain · Privacy preservation · Differential privacy · Supply chain · Industrial data sharing

1 Introduction

Blockchain is an emerging technology which has the desirable features of decentralization, tracking, immutability, verification, security, and fault-tolerance [1]. Therefore, since its development in financial sector, its adoption in other domains such as IoT, IIoT, e-health, smart grid, and smart city has grown exponentially in the last few years. Due to its attractive and salient features, blockchain is integrated with Industrial Internet of things (IIoT) which results in blockchain-based IIoT. Blockchain-based IIoT enables connectivity of industry partners such as manufacturer, retailer, distributor, and end consumers, to realize a robust supply chain management [2]. However, among the two types of blockchain, i.e., permissioned and permissionless the permissionless blockchain has been criticized

W. Xiang et al. (Eds.): BROADNETS 2021, LNICST 413, pp. 77–91, 2022.
https://doi.org/10.1007/978-3-030-93479-8_5

for public accessibility. Furthermore, it has several issues such as susceptibility to 51% attack, low transaction processing rate, and reveal of privacy [1,3].

In supply chain model, different industry partners come together with a shared business interest but have different requirements and policies for privacy preservation of sensitive and secret business data. As a result, certain partners are not willing to share their private and confidential data i.e., business secrets, special offers to certain retailers in a public ledger which is visible to other partners and competitors. For example, in food industry, three separate groups can be considered which are farmer-distributor, distributor-wholesaler, and distributor-retailer. Companies included in these groups would not be willing to share their business secrets with other participants in the network. In another case, supply chain partners can be competitors and they would not let competitors to see their business plans.

To address these issues, permissioned blockchain such as Hyperledger fabric provides two private data sharing mechanisms which are querying mechanism and multichannel mechanism [4]. Through querying mechanism, application clients (including third parties) can send queries which are evaluated on the ledger's data. Similarly, in multichannel mechanism for private data sharing between blockchain peers, two levels of privacy and confidential exchange of data exists in Hyperledger fabric which are application-level and data-level. Application-level privacy means a group of participants from network having same business interest come together and establish a private subset of communication which is called channel. Several subsets of private communications are known as multichannel concept in Hyperledger fabric which results in private communication and data sharing. As a result, communications are limited to valid group members in a channel. A separate and independent ledger is maintained for each such channel. Similarly, for privacy at data-level, Hyperledger fabric uses the concept of private data collection, hash, and transient field in transactions. In this way, only certain participants can see private contents while others can just see hash of the data.

However, both data sharing mechanisms have serious issues in relation to privacy, utility and transparency of data which need to be addressed. Querying mechanism evaluates query on actual data stored on the ledger through chaincode (smart contract) installed on each peer which makes it inadequate for supply chain environment in IIoT because query response can be utilized by adversaries and suspicious applications to infer sensitive information such as business secrets and special discount offers. Clearly, it needs improvement to make it suitable for supply chain in IIoT. Similarly, multichannel mechanism and private data collection limit utilization of data because the data is confined between restricted parties. As a result, it increases risk of black market and invalid transactions because peers other than restricted group members cannot see the contents of transactions which makes it difficult to verify transactions. In addition, the auditability and accountability are also impacted which are necessary for supply chain such as food industry [1,5].

It is evident from the above discussion that both mechanisms i.e., querying mechanism and multichannel mechanism need further improvement. This is the main motivation of our work in which we target the first mechanism i.e., querying mechanism for improvement in the context of supply chain in IIoT. The reason is that an improved (privacy preserving) querying mechanism enables the supply chain partners to share and access private data of others, which increases the transparency of activities across the network of supply chain partners. As a result, the risk of fraud and black market issues by keeping the data 100% private from other partners is reduced. The contribution of this work is as following: we propose a differential privacy-based permissioned blockchain for private data sharing in the context of supply chain in IIoT by integrating differential privacy into the chaincode of Hyperledger fabric which protects sensitive Industrial data stored on the ledger from linking attacks by adversaries and suspicious applications. We also present an algorithm for accessing the ledger's data in a privacy preserving manner. Similarly, we evaluate the proposed work by implementing a permissioned blockchain using Hyperledger fabric and integrate differential privacy in its chaincode. A privacy threat model based on linking attack is also implemented to evaluate privacy preservation of sensitive data in the context of supply chain in IIoT. Finally, the results are compared with default setting of Hyperledger fabric chaincode (non-privacy preserving) to validate the privacy preservation and utility of data. We prove that the proposed work gets 96.15% of accuracy in the shared data for $\epsilon = 0.5$ while guarantees the privacy preservation at the same time.

The rest of the paper is organized according to the following sequence: in Sect. 2, a literature review of the previous works in the related domain is presented. In Sect. 3, we present the proposed work (DH-IIoT) in detail including the working and time complexity analysis of the proposed algorithm whereas Sect. 4 presents evaluation and simulation results. Finally, Sect. 5 concludes this work.

2   Literature Review

In [6], a blockchain-based smart factory architecture is proposed with a privacy model to enhance security and privacy. The proposed architecture is lightweight, partially decentralized, easily expandable and have better privacy and security. However, their privacy model is limited to availability, integrity, and confidentiality through encryption, which is an old concept known as confidentiality, integrity, availability (CIA). In [2], a blockchain-based data sharing scheme in supply chain in IIoT environment is proposed. Attribute-based encryption is adopted to manage the access control of data in IIoT. To automate the flow of goods, smart contract is used in the proposed scheme. However, encryption is used for security of the system and privacy attack model is missing. Apart from this, in recent times, IoT is managed through cloud computing [7–9], and grid computing [10,11] to enable business-oriented environment. Furthermore, real-time streaming data along with IoT enables efficient Industrial control and management [12].

Similarly, the work in [13] has proposed an efficient credit-based proof of work (PoW) consensus for resource constrained environment in IIoT. In addition, a data authority management system is used to protect privacy of sensitive information. The adoptive control of difficulty of puzzle solving in PoW is used which decreases difficulty for honest nodes and increase it for malicious nodes. As a result, the overall efficiency in the system for honest behaviour is enhanced. The throughput of the system is enhanced using directed acyclic graphs instead of conventional blockchain. However, the PoW allows every participant to append a block and validate transactions in which contents of transactions are visible to every node in consensus phase. In addition, encryption is used to protect privacy which is cumbersome to implement.

A similar idea has been proposed in [14] which works on the principle of rewarding normal behaviour of nodes and punishing abnormal behaviour. The unique feature of their work is that it can be integrated with state-of-the-art PoX protocols. However, privacy concerns associated with PoX protocols are not addressed. A modified bitcoin system known as "Monero" has been proposed in [15]. Monero ensures privacy and unlikability of transactions to its sender and receiver and protecting balances of participants. However, it uses cryptographic algorithms to hide sending and receiving addresses and balances which are cumbersome to implement. In [16], a smart manufacturing supply chain based on blockchain with traceability and verifiability features has been proposed. The complex and private data sharing is performed by blockchain in a secure manner which enable participants to control data sharing in supply chain. However, the privacy and confidentiality are based on inherent encryption techniques of blockchain and addressing the privacy concern in consensus mechanism is missing. Similarly, the work in [5] also uses encryption techniques along with Hyperledger fabric to overcome privacy issue during the consensus phase. Finally, Hyperledger fabric adopts hashing and multichannel mechanism to enable private data exchange [4]. However, encryption techniques not only significantly impact the utility of data in blockchain but are costly in terms of computation.

3   Proposed Scheme: DH-IIoT

3.1   System Model

The proposed system model is shown in Fig. 1. The system model is composed of client applications, endorsing peers, privacy preserving module, orderer peers and finally the applications which reside on top of these components. The existing Hyperledger fabric architecture is customized, and a privacy preserving module based on differential privacy is added into the chaincode (smart contract) of Hyperledger fabric. The supply chain participants and third parties act as client applications and a collaboration scenario is also considered in which participants share their data and access data from others through query transactions. Client applications send transaction proposals to peers such as query

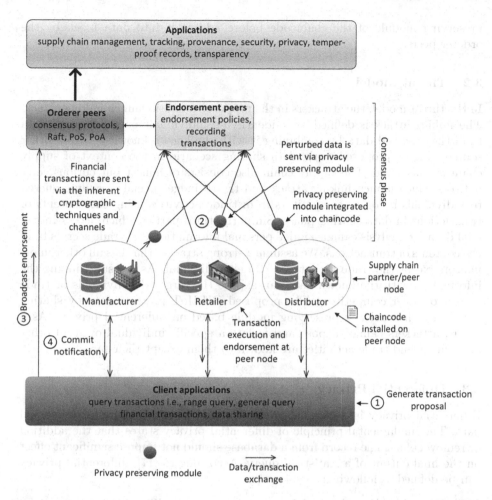

Fig. 1. System model of transactions flow in privacy preserving chaincode in DH-IIoT.

transactions, range transactions, financial transactions, and data sharing. The transaction proposals are endorsed by the available pool of endorsing peers.

It is assumed that the peers can differentiate between the mentioned transaction types. As a result, for financial transactions, inherent features of cryptographic techniques and channels are used whereas other transactions are sent via privacy preserving module. In addition, for query transactions only statistical queries are considered in this work, which can be extended for other transaction types as well. An example of a statistical query is how many customers have purchased more than 100 items of a product? The query transaction is represented as $T_q = \{f_1, f_2, f_3...f_n\}$ where $f_1, f_2, f_3...f_n$ represent queries to be evaluated on the ledger data. Similarly, the chaincode instance of the peer evaluates the query on the ledger which is denoted as $R_q = \{f_1^*, f_2^*, f_3^* ... f_n^*\}$ where $f_1^*, f_2^*, f_3^*, f_n^*$ are the answers to queries. This transaction is executed and sent via privacy preserving module of the chaincode before adding it into data block by the orderer peers.

3.2 Threat Model

In the threat model, the attackers in the proposed scenario launch linking attack. The linking attack is defined as re-identifying individuals or anonymized data from the observed data by combining it with the known knowledge from other sources. In the proposed work, data sharing scenario in the context of supply chain is considered. The supply chain also consists of honest but curious competitors which launch linking attack and try to judge special discounts offered to individuals by other competitors from trade activities using the contents of transactions in data sharing phase. Similarly, third parties which access Industrial data for analysis can also judge personal information and trade secrets from the contents of transactions. We assume a strong attacker that has all other information except the trade activities of target individual. As a result, linking the information with the known data can expose the targeted individuals or trade secrets of other competitors. The proposed DH-IIoT protects data by sharing data through a privacy preserving module based on differential privacy. As a result, attackers cannot expose and isolate a specific individual even all other individuals and trade activities are known to them except their target.

3.3 Differential Privacy

Differential privacy is a popular privacy preservation technique for numerical data. The fundamental principle of differential privacy states that the addition or removal of a single record from a database should not impose significant effect on the final output of a statistical query. According to [17], differential privacy can be defined as following:

Definition 1. *"A randomized function Q satisfies ϵ-differential privacy if for all datasets D_i, D_j which differs in one record, and for all $S \subseteq Range(Q)$, the following holds [17]:"*

$$P[Q(D_i) \in S] \leq e^\epsilon \times P[(Q(D_j) \in S] \qquad \text{(according to [17])} \qquad (1)$$

Where Range (Q) is range of all possible outputs of function Q. ϵ is known as privacy budget. Moreover, smaller value of the privacy budget is desired to get good privacy. Furthermore, in the literature, two mechanisms have been widely adopted to guarantee differential privacy which are Laplace mechanism and exponential mechanism [18]. In this work, we consider the scenario of numerical data sharing, i.e., products rating, number of transactions, count of products, and number of customers. Therefore, we adopt Laplace mechanism because it is suitable for numerical data perturbation [19]. The Laplace distribution function is given as following:

$$f(x, \mu, \lambda) = \frac{1}{2\lambda} e^{\frac{-|x-\mu|}{\lambda}} \qquad (2)$$

Where λ is Laplace scale and μ is mean for Laplace distribution. Furthermore, $\lambda = \frac{\Delta f}{\epsilon}$. In addition, Δf is the maximum difference of two queried results from adjacent datasets D_i and D_j. It is called sensitivity and for D_i and D_j differing in one record it is denoted as following [17,19]:

$$\Delta f = |f(D_i) - f(D_j)|_1 \tag{3}$$

Consequently, the random noise generated from Laplace distribution on scale λ is represented as $Lap(\lambda)$ which then added to the actual result.

3.4   Working of DH-IIoT

In Hyperledger fabric, the inclusion of transactions in blocks and validation are performed by separate peers known as orderers and validating or endorsing peers, respectively. This concept enables Hyperledger fabric to get high transaction validation rate and throughput. The working of the proposed DH-IIoT consists of four steps namely: (1) transaction proposal, (2) transaction endorsement and privacy preservation, (3) execution of ordering service, and, (4) transaction validation and commit. In the following, we discuss all these phases along with processing steps and Algorithm 1 for the proposed DH-IIoT in detail.

3.4.1   Transaction Proposal
In the first step, application clients send transaction proposal to endorsing peers. In this phase, ordering service is not involved and it only consists of interaction between application clients and endorsing peers regarding the chaincode function invocation. The set of endorsing peers independently invoke the chaincode with proposal. The set of endorsing peers is chosen according to the endorsement policy defined for the chaincode i.e., one peer from each organization must endorse transaction proposal. Similarly, single endorsing peer can also be targeted which requires only that specific node to endorse the transaction proposal. In proposed scenario, query transaction proposal is considered which is sent to targeted peer or organisation. The ledger state is not altered in this phase because the ordering service is not involved.

3.4.2   Transaction Endorsement and Privacy Preservation
In our proposed DH-IIoT, the invocation of chaincode with proposal is followed by execution of privacy preserving module as shown in Fig. 1. In this step, the chaincode evaluates query response against the private data stored on the local ledger of the peer. Algorithm 1 which is implemented as a chaincode function is used to add noise to the true answer of query. The query evaluation and noise addition are shown in Fig. 2. Finally, the perturbed response is returned to the requesting client application with endorsement. It is assumed that peer can differentiate between pure financial transaction and a data sharing or query transaction. In this way, financial transactions follow the same existing steps in

---

Algorithm 1: Differential privacy-based privacy preserving algorithm for DH-IIoT

    Input: Ledger data L_d, query transaction with n
    queries $T_q = \{f_1, f_2, f_3 \ldots f_n\}$
    Output: Differential private query response $R_q = \{f_1^*, f_2^*, f_3^* \ldots f_n^*\}$
    Initialization: Iteration $i = 1$, random variable x, $noise = 0$, mean $\mu = 0$,
    Laplace scale $\lambda = \frac{\Delta f}{\epsilon}$, privacy budget ϵ as given in equation 2

1 **while** $i \leq n$ **do**
2   Execute query f_i on the original ledger data L_d
3   **Call** LaplacianFunction()
4   Add noise to perturb query response $f_i + noise$
5     $i = i + 1$
6 **end**
    FUNCTION $\rightarrow LaplacianFunction()$
7   Calculate Laplacian noise using $f(x;\mu,\lambda)$ from equation 2
8   **return** $noise$
9 **return** $R_q = \{f_1^*, f_2^*, f_3^* \ldots f_n^*\}$

Hyperledger fabric whereas other query transactions are evaluated using differential privacy module. As a result, every client application can send request to peers for private data access even outside the members list of the channel.

3.4.3 Execution of Ordering Services

In step 3, on receiving the transaction response and enough endorsement from the peers, it is sent to ordering service. The ordering service receives transactions from all channels and combine them in blocks. The ordering service perform sequencing of transactions received from all channels and package them in blocks. Hyperledger fabric gives different options for ordering nodes to carry out consensus on sequencing of transactions i.e., Raft, Kafka, Solo etc. Raft and Kafka both offers fault-tolerance which is beneficial for robust applications across the industry environment. For simplicity reason in proposed work, we adopted single ordering node. In the proposed scenario, the risk of reading the contents of transactions by ordering nodes is avoided by including the perturbed data.

3.4.4 Transaction Validation and Commit

In this step, blocks are broadcasted to peers for validation. Each peer validates transactions included in the block and ensures that it meet the endorsement policy. After successful validation, the blocks are committed to peers. The committed blocks are added to the chain which update the status of the ledger. In addition, the blocks which fail the validation phase are not added to the chain. Finally, the application clients are notified of their successful transactions.

4   Performance Evaluation

4.1   Experimental Setup

The proposed blockchain network consists of two organizations having one peer and a Couch database. A single channel is maintained between the nodes with one chaincode installed on each peer. The endorsement policy is set to require endorsement of at least one of the two peers. Fabric is used as software under test (SUT) with SDK version 1.4.11. In addition, the Caliper version 0.4.0 is used for evaluation of SUT [20]. We used Ubuntu-18 64-bit operating system for our experimental setup. The hardware configuration includes Intel(R)Core (TM) i5-8250U CPU @ 1.6 GHz processor with 8 GB of installed physical memory.

4.2   Benchmark and Transaction Configuration

The benchmark configuration includes two rounds which are initialization of ledger and querying the ledger. In the first round, a test with five workers is configured to send input transactions with fixed rate in the range of 10–50 tran/sec to the SUT and a total of 500 transactions are sent to initialize the ledger. In the second round, query transaction is configured in which the ledger state is queried by the client application by sending input transactions with fixed rate in the range of 10–50 tran/sec for a total of 15 s.

It is assumed that the minimum and maximum quantity of product which can be purchased in a single write transaction are 1 and 100, receptively. Similarly, the customer name (owner) in the transactions will be selected from {Bob, Claire, David, Ali, Alice} whereas the colours of the product will be selected from {red, blue, green, black, white, pink, rainbow}. In query transaction, the sum of total products purchased by a customer is requested. The differential privacy budget ϵ is varied in the range 0.5–2.5 to perturb the query response before sending it to the client applications. Moreover, the sensitivity of differential privacy in Eq. 3 is assigned a value of 100 i.e., $\triangle f = 100$. The reason is that a single transaction removal in the proposed scenario causes a maximum difference of 100 on the sum of total products purchased by a customer.

4.3   Complexity Analysis

In this section, time complexity of Algorithm 1 is discussed. The proposed algorithm consists of a single *While* loop which executes according to the number of queries which is denoted as n i.e., for each query the loop executes once. Furthermore, each line in the body of the loop takes $O(1)$ time to execute. As a result, the time complexity of Algorithm 1 is $O(n)$. Therefore, Algorithm 1 maintains the high transaction processing rate of Hyperledger fabric.

4.4   Simulation Results and Discussion

In this section, simulation results obtained from the implementation of the proposed DH-IIoT are presented. The evaluation is performed over four parameters

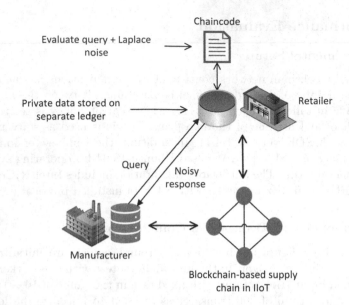

Fig. 2. Demonstration of query evaluation through chaincode on private data in DH-IIoT.

i.e., (1) privacy preservation (2) relative error (3) throughput, and (4) latency of transaction. In the following section, details of the mentioned parameters with comparison results are provided.

4.4.1 Privacy Preservation

In proposed DH-IIoT, supply chain partners keep separate ledgers for private and public data based on Hyperledger fabric channels and private data collection mechanism. The data stored on public ledger is visible to all other partners however, data stored on private ledger is only visible to restricted members of the channels. For instance, in the group of three supply chain partners namely manufacturer, distributor and retailer, the distributor and retailer maintain a separate private data collection. This data collection is only visible to distributor and retailer. On the other hand, manufacturer can only see the hash of the data [4]. In the proposed scenario, manufacturer needs statistical results evaluated on this data to improve its performance. However, both members of the private collection are not welling to share actual data.

To access private data of supply chain partners (distributor and retailer in this case), application clients from requesting party (manufacturer in this case) send queries to the peers of associated supply chain partners for customers trade activities and number of items purchased. The ledger is populated through write transactions as discussed in Sect. 4.2. In this way, the data of trade activities of all customers is maintained in private ledger which results in a dataset with rows and columns. A row represents a write transaction by a customer whereas column is defined according to the transaction fields i.e., product name,

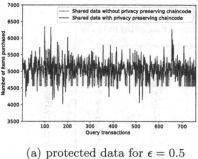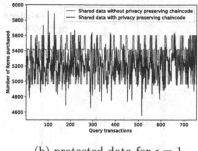

(a) protected data for $\epsilon = 0.5$ (b) protected data for $\epsilon = 1$

Fig. 3. Comparison of privacy preserving chaincode (DH-IIoT) with non-privacy preserving chaincode.

customer name, product quantity, and colour. The query transaction requests the sum of quantity i.e., number of items purchased in all transactions by a specific customer. The chaincode executes the query on local ledger of the peer and add random noise generated from Laplace distribution to the true answer using Algorithm 1. The demonstration of query evaluation and noise addition is shown in Fig. 2. The sample noisy responses to query transactions are plotted with varying differential privacy budget ϵ for default setting of non-privacy preserving chaincode in Hyperledger fabric and privacy preserving chaincode in the proposed DH-IIoT as shown in Fig. 3.

It is evident from the comparison results of both chaincodes that increasing the privacy parameter ϵ decreases the difference between the actual query response and the noisy query response i.e., for $\epsilon = 0.5$, the variation in query responses is frequent as compared to query responses for $\epsilon = 1$, as shown in Fig. 3a and Fig. 3b, respectively. However, the privacy preservation guarantee for $\epsilon = 1$ is less than $\epsilon = 0.5$. The reason is that less noise is added for higher values of ϵ. In this way, the adversary is deceived by sending the perturbed query responses in DH-IIoT whereas maintaining almost the same pattern in the shared data. As a result, the adversary will not be able to link it with known data to expose individual's private data i.e., special discount from retailer. Similarly, exposing the individual spending trends or shopping activities are also avoided. However, the addition of noise also impacts the accuracy (utility) of query responses which impacts the utility of data for service and management improvements, future forecast, and quality enhancements through data sharing and data analysis by honest supply chain partners. The more noise added to the data, the lower will be the accuracy and vice versa. The trade-off between privacy and accuracy is presented in the next section.

4.4.2 Relative Error

The accuracy of results is measured from the magnitude of relative error in the query response. A high magnitude of relative error means lower accuracy and vice versa. The relative error is defined as following [21]:

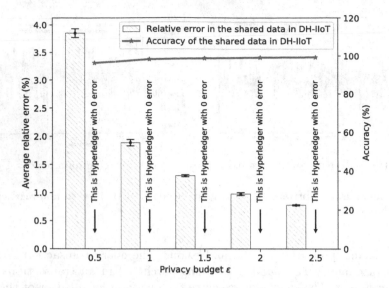

Fig. 4. Relative error in query response with varying differential privacy parameter ϵ. The results are within 95% of confidence interval.

$$\text{Relative error} = \frac{|a - a'|}{a} \times 100\% \tag{4}$$

Where a is the actual value of query response and a' is the perturbed value of query response. Here, 100 is multiplied to get percentage relative error. The average relative error is evaluated with varying ϵ and the results are shown in Fig. 4. It is evident from the results that increasing the differential privacy parameter ϵ decreases the relative error in the shared data through query responses i.e., from 3.85% to almost 0.75%. Similarly, the accuracy is increased from 96% to 99%. However, the guarantee of privacy preservation is reduced because less noise is added for higher values of ϵ. Therefore, a trade-off between privacy preservation and accuracy in the shared data exists which should be agreed upon by the data sharing parties. Figure 4 also shows that more privacy preservation is achieved for sacrificing the accuracy in the query results. As a result, a suitable value of ϵ should be considered and agreed upon by the data sharing parties.

4.4.3 Throughput

In this section, throughput of the proposed DH-IIoT is evaluated. In the experimental setup, five workers were configured to send query transactions to the blockchain network (SUT). The chaincode (smart contract) query function is invoked to read the required data from local ledger in a privacy preserving manner using differential privacy module as shown in Fig. 2. The transaction input rate is varied, and the throughput of the blockchain network is evaluated using the Hyperledger Caliper for both Init (write) and query transactions. The results are shown in the Fig. 5. It can be seen from the results that throughput for both

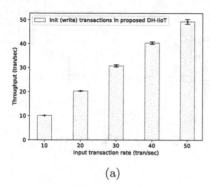 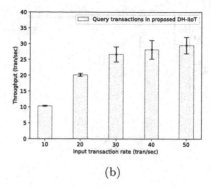

(a)   (b)

Fig. 5. Evaluation of throughput in DH-IIoT. The results are within 95% of confidence interval.

Init (write) and query transactions increases with the increase in input transaction rate. The gradual increase in throughput is aligned with the fact that more input transactions in a unit time increase the throughput under the maximum capacity of the network. A maximum throughput of almost 50 tran/sec is achieved in case of write transactions for input transaction rate of 50 tran/sec. Similarly, for query transactions, the maximum throughput is almost 30 tran/ for the same input transaction rate.

4.4.4   Latency of Transaction

In this section, latency of transactions in proposed scenario is evaluated. The experimental setting is configured as described in Sect. 4.1. The latency for both Init (write) and query transactions is evaluated, and the results are shown in Fig. 6. It can be seen from the results that latency for Init (write) transactions decreases until 40 tran/sec however, it shows an increase beyond this point. The reason is that below the input transaction rate of 40 tran/sec, blockchain network is under the maximum processing capacity and hence transactions take less time for processing. Similarly, the latency of query transactions shows steep increase beyond input transaction rate of 20 tran/sec. The reason is that on this point, the blockchain network reaches its maximum capacity of processing query transactions and hence beyond this point the transactions latency increases.

It is evident from the results of evaluation and comparison that our proposed DH-IIoT enables privacy preservation in a collaborative setting in the context of supply chain in IIoT with inherent features of blockchain such as tracking, validation, querying and recording of transactions. In addition, we improved the performance of existing Hyperledger fabric to enable privacy preservation for marginally compromising the accuracy of shared data. We get 96.15% of accuracy with $\epsilon = 0.5$ which gives sufficient guarantee of privacy preservation in the shared data. Furthermore, the proposed DH-IIoT enables supply chain partners to record the query response in the ledger which can be used for similar queries sent by other application clients. As a result, it increases the usability

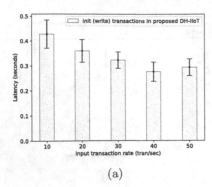 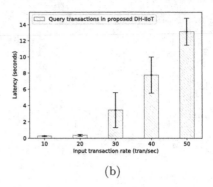

(a)   (b)

Fig. 6. Evaluation of latency of transactions in DH-IIoT. The results are within 95% of confidence interval.

of data by re-using the query responses. Finally, DH-IIoT enables supply chain partners and applications to access real-time data recorded on the ledger.

5   Conclusion

In this work, a differential privacy-based permissioned blockchain using Hyperledger fabric for private data sharing (DH-IIoT) is proposed to solve the issue of exposure of sensitive information in statistical query transactions in the context of supply chain in IIoT. Hyperledger fabric uses two mechanisms for private data sharing which are query mechanism and multichannel mechanism with private data collection for controlling access of confidential data in the network. However, both mechanisms need further enhancement for practical scenarios. In this work, we targeted the querying mechanism of Hyperledger fabric for improvement in the context of supply chain in IIoT. We integrated differential privacy into chaincode of Hyperledger fabric to provide perturbed query responses and protect the original data stored on the ledger. We proved that DH-IIoT maintains 96.15% accuracy in the shared data for $\epsilon = 0.5$ which provides sufficient privacy preservation guarantee. The results validated that the proposed DH-IIoT preserves the privacy of sensitive information while maintaining high throughput of the system and improves the performance of Hyperledger fabric.

References

1. Ali, M.S., Vecchio, M., Pincheira, M., Dolui, K., Antonelli, F., Rehmani, M.H.: Applications of blockchains in the Internet of Things: a comprehensive survey. IEEE Commun. Surv. Tutor. **21**(2), 1676–1717 (2019)
2. Wen, Q., Gao, Y., Chen, Z., Wu, D.: A blockchain-based data sharing scheme in the supply chain by IIoT. In: IEEE International Conference on Industrial Cyber Physical Systems (ICPS), pp. 695–700. IEEE (2019)

3. Xiao, Y., Zhang, N., Lou, W., Hou, Y.T.: A survey of distributed consensus protocols for blockchain networks. IEEE Commun. Surv. Tutor. **22**(2), 1432–1465 (2020)
4. Hyperledger fabric documentation. https://hyperledger-fabric.readthedocs.io/en/release-2.2/. Accessed 26 Mar 2021
5. Yasusaka, Y., Watanabe, C., Kitagawa, H.: Privacy-preserving pre-consensus protocol for blockchains. In: IEEE International Conference on Big Data and Smart Computing (BigComp), pp. 1–8 (2019)
6. Wan, J., Li, J., Imran, M., Li, D.: A blockchain-based solution for enhancing security and privacy in smart factory. IEEE Trans. Ind. Inf. **15**(6), 3652–3660 (2019)
7. Liu, X., Yuan, D., Zhang, G., Chen, J., Yang, Y.: SwinDeW-C: a peer-to-peer based cloud workflow system. In: Furht, B., Escalante, A. (eds.) Handbook of Cloud Computing, pp. 309–332. Springer, Boston (2010). https://doi.org/10.1007/978-1-4419-6524-0_13
8. Qi, L., Dou, W., Zhang, X., Chen, J.: A QoS-aware composition method supporting cross-platform service invocation in cloud environment. J. Comput. Syst. Sci. **78**(5), 1316–1329 (2012)
9. Song, X., Dou, W., Chen, J.: A workflow framework for intelligent service composition. Future Gener. Comput. Syst. **27**(5), 627–636 (2011)
10. Wang, L., Jie, W., Chen, J.: Grid Computing: Infrastructure, Service, and Applications. CRC Press, p. 528 (2009). ISBN-13: 978-1420067668
11. Chen, J., Yang, Y.: Temporal dependency based checkpoint selection for dynamic verification of fixed-time constraints in grid workflow systems. In: ACM/IEEE 30th International Conference on Software Engineering, pp. 141–150. IEEE (2008)
12. Puthal, D., Nepal, S., Ranjan, R., Chen, J.: DLSeF: a dynamic key-length-based efficient real-time security verification model for big data stream. ACM Trans. Embed. Comput. Syst. **16**(2), 1–24 (2016)
13. Huang, J., Kong, L., Chen, G., Wu, M., Liu, X., Zeng, P.: Towards secure industrial IoT: blockchain system with credit-based consensus mechanism. IEEE Trans. Ind. Inf. **15**(6), 3680–3689 (2019)
14. Wang, E.K., Liang, Z., Chen, C.M., Kumari, S., Khan, M.K.: PoRX: a reputation incentive scheme for blockchain consensus of IIoT. Future Gener. Comput. Syst. **102**, 140–151 (2020)
15. Monero. https://www.getmonero.org/get-started/what-is-monero/. Accessed 18 Nov 2020
16. Assaqty, M.I.S., et al.: Private-blockchain-based industrial IoT for material and product tracking in smart manufacturing. IEEE Netw. **34**(5), 91–97 (2020)
17. Dwork, C.: Differential privacy. In: Bugliesi, M., Preneel, B., Sassone, V., Wegener, I. (eds.) Automata, Languages and Programming, pp. 1–12. Springer, Heidelberg (2006)
18. Zhu, T., Li, G., Zhou, W., Philip, S.Y.: Differentially private data publishing and analysis: a survey. IEEE Trans. Knowl. Data Eng. **29**(8), 1619–1638 (2017)
19. Dwork, C., Roth, A., et al.: The algorithmic foundations of differential privacy. Found. Trends Theor. Comput. Sci. **9**(3–4), 211–407 (2014)
20. Hyperledger caliper. https://www.hyperledger.org/use/caliper. Accessed 26 Mar 2021
21. Xiao, X., Bender, G., Hay, M., Gehrke, J.: iReduct: differential privacy with reduced relative errors. In: Proceedings of the 2011 ACM SIGMOD International Conference on Management of Data, SIGMOD 2011, pp. 229–240. Association for Computing Machinery, New York (2011). https://doi.org/10.1145/1989323.1989348

Efficient Privacy-Preserving User Matching with Intel SGX

Junwei Luo(✉), Xuechao Yang, Xun Yi, Fengling Han, and Andrei Kelarev

School of Computing Technologies, RMIT University,
Melbourne, VIC 3000, Australia
{junwei.luo,xuechao.yang,xun.yi,fengling.han,
andrei.kelarev}@rmit.edu.au

Abstract. User matching is one of the most essential features that allows users to identify other people by comparing the attributes of their profiles and finding similarities. While this facility enables the exploration of friends in the same network, it poses serious security concerns over the privacy of the users as the prevalence of modern cloud computing services, companies outsource computational power to untrusted cloud service providers and confidential data of the users can be exposed as the data storage is transparent in the remote host server. Encryption can hide the user data, but it is difficult to compare the encrypted profiles. While solutions utilising the homomorphic encryption can overcome such limitations, they incur significant performance overhead, which is impractical for large networks. To overcome these problems, we propose an efficient privacy-preserving user matching protocol with Intel SGX. Other techniques such as oblivious data structure and searchable encryption are deployed to resolve security issues that Intel SGX has suffered. Our construction relies on secure hardware which guarantees the integrity and confidentiality of the code execution, which enables the computation of similarities between the profiles of the users. Moreover, our protocol is designed to provide protection against several types of side-channel attacks. The security analysis and experimental results presented in this paper indicate that our protocol is efficient, secure, practical and prevents side-channel attacks.

Keywords: Privacy-preserving user matching · Intel SGX · Oblivions data structure · Searchable encryption · Social network security

1 Introduction

Modern social networks such as Facebook and Instagram allow people to connect with each other in a virtual space, enabling them to make new friends in different parts of the world. While this facility enables the exploration of friends in the same network, it poses serious security concerns over the privacy of the users. With the increasing demands on modern cloud computing services, companies outsource computational power to untrusted cloud service providers and

© ICST Institute for Computer Sciences, Social Informatics and Telecommunications Engineering 2022
Published by Springer Nature Switzerland AG 2022. All Rights Reserved
W. Xiang et al. (Eds.): BROADNETS 2021, LNICST 413, pp. 92–111, 2022.
https://doi.org/10.1007/978-3-030-93479-8_6

confidential data of the users can be exposed as the data storage is transparent in the remote host server. Social network service providers have become targets of adversaries who try to exploit the service and attempt to steal sensitive information, data breaches for social networks have greatly impacted the society in a negative way. A group named "The Impact Team" breached a dating social network Ashley Madison and released over 30 million of users' data to the public in July 2015. Several unconfirmed suicides that occurred in the following days were believed to be linked to the cyber incident as some victims were not able to undertake the social impacts and public shaming that implied to them.

Such data breaches raise concerns about the privacy of social networks as the network holds sensitive information that users might want to keep it secret. While encryptions seem to be an answer to such cyber incidents, encrypted data are difficult to process and features such as user matching that allows the discovery of people with similar interests are hard to implement. So far, many efforts have been made to overcome such limitations. Agrawal et al. [1] proposed a model that allows certain information to be exchanged without disclosing others. Freedman et al. [7] proposed a solution using polynomial evaluation to allow user profile matching to be done securely. The paper [7] was extended later by [10] that adds supports for set intersection matching. These solutions support binary matching, in which matching result shows whether or not users have a matching. Yi et al. [28] introduced a user matching scheme that uses multiple parties to compute the shared secret via homomorphic encryption, and later, extended in [29] to improve efficiency. The solution was implemented in [12] using Intel SGX to improve security.

However, solutions mentioned above are far from practical as they impose expensive computational overhead, due to the constraints of the involved cryptosystems. In [12], the authors proposed a user matching protocol that takes advantage of Intel SGX. This has made a reduction to the computation overhead compared to the use of traditional asymmetric cryptosystems. The results of [12] show that the system remains impractical and further improvements to security and performance remain desirable.

The present paper proposes a novel approach to the design of a privacy-preserving user matching protocol by simultaneously employing Intel SGX, oblivious data structure, searchable encryption and other techniques for enhancing security and performance. Our novel solution aims to provide user profile matching with better accuracy and ensure protection against several types of side-channel attacks while minimising the computational cost.

It is known that SGX is vulnerable to many side-channel attacks (see, [4, 8, 13, 26, 27]). Side-channel attacks such as cache-timing attack can be used to extract the secret key from a running program by observing the behaviour of a cryptographic algorithm to determine the secret [8]. Therefore, it is crucial to include protection against side-channel attacks. Our new protocol is designed to address these issues.

A brief overview of our solution is presented as follows: a user on a social network platform has a profile with one or more attributes representing the characteristics or interests of the user. All the attributes of the user are encrypted with the own symmetric key of the user that was generated during the registration process, and is known to the user and the secure enclave thereby guaranteeing integrity. All users communicate with Intel SGX via secure communication channel. Intel SGX securely places data into the untrusted domain after encryption to minimise leakages. All sensitive computation is done in the secure enclave where the integrity and privacy of code execution are guaranteed. We strengthen the confidentiality of our system by introducing oblivious mechanisms to prevent unnecessary leakage via side-channel attacks.

To summarise, our contributions include the following:

1. We design a novel privacy-preserving user matching protocol, which has several stages incorporating Intel SGX, oblivious data structure, searchable encryption and other security-strengthening techniques to expedite the computation of privacy-preserving profile matching on social networks.
2. Our protocol is designed to provide protection against several types of side-channel attacks. While one component in searchable encryption leaks information about users, we incorporate a data oblivious scheme to mitigate the leakage.
3. We implement a prototype of proposed protocol and evaluate the performance of our protocol in terms of memory usage, matching time, and compare its effectiveness with previous alternative options.

The organisation of this paper is as follows: Sect. 2 presents the related work, followed by the overview of system architecture in Sect. 3. The proposed protocol is presented in Sect. 4. Section 5 details the security analysis. Section 6 discusses the performance of the proposed protocol and Sect. 7 concludes the paper.

2   Related Work

Since the introduction of Intel SGX in 2014, many researchers have been exploring the possibility of utilising such feature to enhance security of their products [2,3,6,15,17,25]. Pbsx [9] is a secure boolean query retrieval model implemented using Intel SGX to protect the privacy of users data in an outsourced cloud environment. Pbsx corporates with components such as Bloom Filter, ORAM and Bitmap to provide query matching efficiently with various techniques to protect against cache-timing attacks [8]. Lightbox [6] is a software middleware that acts as a firewall to provide a pattern matching for detecting malicious packets within the secure hardware, allowing it to be outsourced to the cloud infrastructure where it can provide computational power as requested instead of building a server in-house.

Apart from the works that focus on data matching aforementioned, Intel SGX has also been applied to various industries where a trusted computation is needed. SCONE [3] is a OS-level virtualisation container project that utilises Intel SGX to preserve the privacy of the program running within in a cloud environment. Container such as Docker is a container-as-a-service that facilitates the development process by packing any dependencies required for a product to be deployed into a container and share between developers. VC3 [17] is a data analysis framework based on MapReduce that utilises Intel SGX for outsourced big data analysis with strong security guarantees. All data is encrypted and sent to the secure enclave where the integrity and confidentiality are held, using Remote Attestation to establish secure communication channel for key exchange as well as returning final results to the client, all is done without leaking information about what is being computed.

While researchers take advantage of secure enclave to enhance overall security of their proposed solutions, SGX has been known to be vulnerable for many side-channel attacks [4,8,13,26,27] that can leak information inside the enclave. Side-channel attacks such as cache-timing attack can be used to extract the secret key from a running program by observing the behaviour of a cryptographic algorithm to determine the secret [8]. Therefore, many works that focus on mitigating the side-channel attacks have been proposed [14,16] that provide mechanisms against various side-channel attacks such as cache-timing attack by hiding the access pattern with the help of Oblivious Random Access Memory (ORAM), or randomising the memory location whenever an enclave is created [18] using Address Space Layout Randomization technique (ASLR). Other side-channel attacks such as power analysis [26] has also been proven possible but is less practical compared to other attacks aforementioned.

3   System Architecture

3.1   System Design

Our new privacy-preserving matching protocol consists of three components: Users, a matching server and a secure enclave that co-exists within the matching server. Secure enclave is employed with Intel SGX to facilitate the cost of creating a Trusted Execution Environment. Figure 1 demonstrates the system architecture of proposed matching protocol. Users will be communicating directly with secure enclave via secure communication established using remote attestation. User data will be processed within the enclave to ensure its confidentiality and the matching server is solely responsible for persisting data for the enclave.

Matching Server. There exists a matching table MT in matching server that is constructed on basis of a SSE scheme [22]. The purpose of MT is to facilitate the process of encrypted queries about user matching in untrusted cloud environment, whereas sensitive information such as encryption keys for users are preserved within secure enclave as it guarantees integrity and confidentiality of the data within. As the profile of a user is processed within the enclave and sent back to matching server, it is persisted into the database for long-term storage.

Secure Enclave. The secure enclave will be responsible for computing sensitive information such as profile matching and constructing search tokens to enable

SSE scheme. There exists a key table KT within the secure enclave where it denotes all symmetric keys of users registered to the network. As the memory limitation implied to Intel SGX, performance will inevitably be hindered to the system, once the memory usage has reached to the point where the enclave triggers paging to encrypt and swap out unused memory to untrusted domain. We adopt an ORAM scheme to our key table KT later in our *Extended* scheme, where it adds communication overhead in flavour of mitigating memory paging issues. A simplified system workflow below demonstrates our matching protocol.

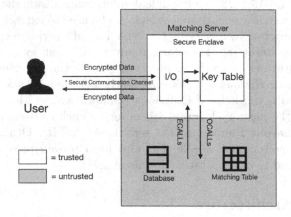

Fig. 1. System architecture.

Initialisation: Users begin by registration with secure enclave via secure communication channel after running remote attestation with the enclave to ensure the authenticity and validity of the system. A symmetric key for the registered user is randomly generated within the enclave and sent to the user. The symmetric key is managed within the secure enclave using a key table KT that contains tuples (U, K_U) where U is a unique identifier for the registered user, and K_U is the symmetric key for user U. A master key for secure enclave K_{SGX} is generated and managed within the enclave for encrypted querying. After registration, a profile P_U for the registered user is created, where P_U might contain one or more attributes A_U that represent the registered user U. Upon completing profile creation, P_U is then encrypted with K_U and sent to the enclave.

Processing: Once the profile is received by the secure enclave, it processes the profile by decrypting each attribute within the profile, and computes a search token that corresponds to the attribute. We adopt the SSE scheme [22] as a data structure that allows sensitive information to be stored securely in the matching server due to several constrains that imply to the secure enclave. Each search token corresponds to an attribute and acts an index to the SSE scheme, followed by encrypted user identifiers that can be used to query database which stores all encrypted profiles. However, the scheme that we adopt does not offer mechanisms against timing analysis, a technique that has been widely studied to exploit secure enclaves. We solve this issue by introducing a data-oblivious access scheme into a component within the SSE scheme where it is affected by timing analysis.

Matching: As the user matching begins, user specifies one or multiple attributes that describe her preferences in friend matching, attributes are encrypted and transmitted to the secure enclave. Upon receiving the preference, secure enclave decrypts and computes the corresponding search token for each attribute. Search tokens are then passed to matching server where the matching table exists and queries databases based on result sets from the matching table. Secure enclave is able to evaluate the result set from matching server to determine if one shares similar interests to the user who requests a profile matching. While our proposed protocol supports different matching algorithms based on the type of attributes, such as Euclidean Distance for numerical values, exact matching and Hamming Distance for others. Other schemes that allow semantic matching between two words can also be adopted to evaluate similarity of attributes.

3.2 SSE Construction

Searchable Symmetric Encryption (SSE) allows clients to outsource encrypted data to the cloud service providers while maintaining the ability to search for the encrypted data (cf. [5, 22]). Such constructions have been adopted to enable secure pattern matching such as deep packet inspection (DPI) [19], mobile cloud networks [11] and so on.

A SSE scheme defines the following operations:

Init: A security parameter λ, $K : \{0,1\}^{\lambda}$, a pseudorandom function that generates search token, $\langle k1, k2 \rangle = \mathsf{H}(K, w)$ where the search token $ST = \langle k1 \| k2 \rangle$ and $\|$ denotes concatenation.

Create: Client computes an inverted index for every word w within a document set DB, where $Inv(DB) = (w_i, (id_{i_0}, id_{i_1}, ...), ...)$ that denotes the occurrence of word w in id_i document. Client then builds an encrypted list L as follows: for every word w within the $Inv(DB)$, a counter c for word w is initialised and set to 1 and computes the following: $\langle k1, k2 \rangle = \mathsf{H}(K, w)$, $\ell = \mathsf{H}(k1, c)$ and $V = \mathsf{Enc}_{k2}(id_i)$. The process continues for every id that links to the word w, and the counter c is incremented by 1 for every computation until all id has been processed. Tuple $\langle \ell, V \rangle$ is stored in the list L and uploaded to the cloud. An index map manages all c for every word w to facilitate insertion when a new document is added.

Search: The client inputs K, w to generate $\langle k1, k2 \rangle = \mathsf{H}(K, w)$, the pair is sent to the server. Having received it the server computes $V = L.get(\mathsf{H}(k1, c))$, $id = \mathsf{Dec}_{k2}(V)$ and returns the appropriate documents with id attached to. The update step is usually performed by the clients downloading the list L stored in the cloud and reconstructing a new L'.

3.3 Design Choices

We adopt the SSE construction from [22] as to reduce overall computational overhead implied using traditional homomorphic encryptions [12, 29] while being able to search for information needed for matching. Original work of adopted SSE assumes that the client is honest and does not leak information that enables timing and pattern analysis, whereas in our protocol, secure enclave acts as the client which is situated in an untrusted environment. An adversary may observe the access pattern to the index map to deduce information based on access distribution. Works have been made to extract information simply by observing access patterns [4, 8, 21, 27]. We mitigate the issue by introducing a pattern-hiding technique that obfuscates access patterns of the index map, which will be discussed in the next section. Our construction allows such table to be outsourced in matching server due to the memory constrains implied to the secure enclave, while ensuring that adversaries cannot learn information by observing the access pattern to the index map.

3.4 Adversary Model

We define a powerful adversary controlling the host environment, where the secure enclave is deployed, including OS resource scheduling for the underlying applications. The adversary can intercept, record, and monitor the use of hardware resources and attempt to disclose the secret information running in the secure enclave via side-channel attacks. Only the code running in the secure enclave is trusted, whereas the rest remain untrusted. We assume that the execution environment that Intel SGX introduces guarantees the integrity, confidentiality and consistency of code execution. The adversary can behave maliciously by sending false requests to both the matching server and the secure enclave trying to reveal some information about the user and corresponding keys. However, we assume that the adversary cannot extract the data from a running processor via physical attacks. Other side-channel attacks such as power analysis are outside the scope of this paper.

4 Privacy-Preserving User Matching Protocol

4.1 Construction of Improved Index Map

As discussed aforementioned that information can be deduced by observing access patterns of the data structure, we adopt the idea of data obliviousness to components of the SSE that could potentially suffer from such attacks. More specifically, we modify the index map to enable oblivious operations in order to prevent timing attacks. In our matching protocol, the index map is to group users based on their interests, where the interests will serve as an index, followed by the group that contains user ids. Originally the index map is constructed similarly to a hash table, which offers better performance in the expense of memory usage and pattern leakage, we present our data oblivious scheme on basis of binary search tree, similar to [20, 23].

Construction: The original work of index map is constructed using a data structure similar to a hash table, we modify this by adopting a binary search tree T with additional mechanisms to tighten security. Unlike an ordinary binary search tree, each node within the tree is a bucket whose size is the multiple of a search token and its corresponding counter. This ensures that the size of each bucket in the tree is the same. Given a full binary tree T of depth D, we have 2^D leaf nodes and $P(l)$ is used to denote the path from root of the tree T to the leaf node l.

Within the secure enclave, there is a deterministic function $DF()$ that takes as input a search token ST and decides a leaf node l which the search token ST is assigned to. When a record is inserted, secure enclave first computes $l = DF(ST)$ which returns a leaf node indicating where the record is randomly inserted into one of the bucket along the way from root to the leaf node. Matching server then performs a scan from the root of the tree to the leaf node l, and stores every bucket along the way to the leaf node as $P(l)$.

To achieve obliviousness, every bucket will be examined in order to prevent attacks that utilise cache timing analysis. Searching and deletion also perform similarly to insertion, where $l = DF(ST)$ is computed in secure enclave and sent to matching server, $P(l)$ is then obliviously retrieved and sent to the secure enclave, which then the secure enclave iterates all buckets and retrieves or removes c that corresponds to the search token ST. It is worth noting that in order to prevent timing attacks, there is no early termination when performing either insertion or searching, meaning that regardless of whether or not the desirable result is found, the system continues to go through the rest of the bucket. If the operation is deletion, secure enclave simply returns the $P(l)$ after deletion, and lets matching server to overwrite its stale path.

Algorithm 1: Pattern-hiding Index Map Insertion

1 **Secure enclave:**
2   Computes $l = DF(ST)$ and sends l to the matching server.
3 **Matching server:**
4   Retrieves all buckets in path $P(l)$ from T
5   Sends $P(l)$ back to secure enclave.
6 **Secure enclave:**
7      $r = UniformRandom(\{0,1\}^D)$
8   **foreach** bucket **in** $P(l)$ **do**
9   **If** $bucket.depth$ equals to r **then**
10             $bucket = bucket.add(ST, c)$
11   **end**
12   sends $l, P(l)$ to matching server.
13 **Matching server:**
14   Overwrites $P(l)$ back to the l leaf of tree T.

Algorithm 2: Pattern-hiding Index Map Search

---

1 **Secure enclave:**
2   Computes $l = DF(ST)$ and sends l to the matching server.
3 **Matching server:**
4   Retrieves all buckets in path $P(l)$ from T
5   Sends $P(l)$ back to secure enclave.
6 **Secure enclave:**
7   **foreach** bucket **in** $P(l)$ **do**
8   If $bucket.contain(ST)$ **then**
9              $c = bucket.getAndRemove(ST)$
10   **end**
11   Runs code 7 - 14 in Algorithm 1 to overwrite the previous path.

4.2   Construction of Privacy-Preserving Matching Protocol

Initialisation. At initialisation, matching server initialises components such as database, matching table and index map for matching server, as well as setting up a secure enclave with Intel SGX that co-exists within matching server. Inside the secure enclave there exists a master key K_{SGX} and a key table KT that stores tuples consisted of $\langle U_i, K_{U_i} \rangle$, where U_i is the identity of a user and its encryption key K_{U_i} respectively.

Preprocessing. When a user U_i signs up on the network, a remote attestation is executed with the secure enclave to ensure the validity and authenticity of a running enclave. This process establishes a secure communication channel between the enclave and U_i. A symmetric key K_{U_i} is created and stored in the key table that exists in the enclave. The key K_{U_i} is sent back to the user U_i, and U_i can send her basic information along with her profile P_{U_i} to the enclave via secure communication channel.

A profile P_{U_i} of U_i in modern social networks is a digital representative of the user U_i that usually contains one or more attributes A_j^i, such as age and interests. The U_i can upload one or more A_j^i to the enclave every time, when finishing creating a profile, P_{U_i} is encrypted using the key K_{U_i} received previously to encrypt her profile,

$$\mathsf{Enc}_{K_{U_i}}(P_{U_i}) = (\mathsf{Enc}_{K_{U_i}}(A_1^i), \mathsf{Enc}_{K_{U_i}}(A_2^i), \cdots, \mathsf{Enc}_{K_{U_i}}(A_m^i)) \tag{1}$$

where m denotes the number of attributes. The encrypted profile $\mathsf{Enc}_{K_{U_i}}(P_{U_i})$ is then sent to secure enclave via the secure communication channel established after successful remote attestation. Preprocessing begins when the enclave receives encrypted profile $\mathsf{Enc}_{K_{U_i}}(P_{U_i})$ from U_i. A key for decrypting this profile is retrieved from key table using user's identity.

As the content of an attribute within the profile is vetted and padded, secure enclave generates a search token as follows: $ST_j = \mathsf{H}(K_{GSX} \| A_j^i)$, where K_{SGX}

is the master key for the enclave, and A_j^i is the j-th attribute of a profile P_{U_i}. This continues for every attribute within the profile P_{U_i}. For instance, the attribute that describes user's age is $A = 'AGE : 21'$, such attribute is appended to the master key of the enclave and digested using a Pseudorandom function $ST = H(K_{SGX} \parallel A)$, the result of the digest function gives us a search token ST for an attribute that describes age of 21. The secure enclave then follows Algorithm 2 to computes a leaf node l for index map for searching and/or insertion.

Once a search token is computed, secure enclave queries the index map stored in matching server to check if a counter c can be found for this specific search token. Index map stores tuples of $\langle ST, c \rangle$, where ST is the search token and c is the number of users with the same attribute settings. For example, the token computed above $ST = H(K_{SGX} \parallel A)$ describes an attribute of age with the value of 21, and c in this context is the number of users that shares the same attribute settings, namely age of 21.

When the leaf node l is given to the index map, it performs oblivious search over the map to check if c is present in the map. If c is not found, secure enclave runs codes 7 to 14 from Algorithm 1 to create a new tuple $\langle ST, c \rangle$, where the value of c is set to 1. This indicates that there exists one user who shares an attribute setting of age of 21 on the network. Such mechanisms allow secret to be stored and indexed in an untrusted environment without letting the server know about the content of the search token.

Following the previous example, if a tuple is found in the index map, secure enclave replaces the tuple with dummy data, updates the counter by $c = c + 1$ if the enclave receives a new profile that contains the same attribute settings, shifts the tuple into different position of the path and overwrites the entire path back to the index map.

Upon completion, secure enclave then encrypts the user id as follows: ST is broken down into two, where $ST = (ST_a \parallel ST_b)$, a new record A new record $\langle CA, CB \rangle$ is computed and inserted into the matching table MT, where $CA = H(ST^a \parallel c)$ and $CB = \text{Enc}_{ST^b}(U_i)$, where c is the counter retrieved from the index map using the corresponding ST.

This process continues for every attribute that exists in P_{U_i} until no remaining attribute requires processing, and the encrypted profile itself $\text{Enc}_{K_{U_i}}(P_{U_i})$ is sent back to the matching server.

To summarise, any new attributes submitted by users are classified to a group if the attribute settings are the same (e.g., same age) as each attribute results in the same search token ST. The index map is updated based on the search token ST generated, and returns a counter c that relates to ST, which is used to generate secret record $\langle CA, CB \rangle$ for the matching table. ST_x is split into ST_a and ST_b, $ST = (ST_a \parallel ST_b)$ and the secret record $\langle CA, CB \rangle$ can be computed based on the counter c returned from the index map, where $CA = H(ST_a \parallel c)$ and $CB = \text{Enc}_{ST_b}(U_i)$ respectively. Each $\langle CA, CB \rangle$ is sent to the matching server where the record persists in the matching table. Algorithm 3 demonstrates this procedure.

Algorithm 3: User registration.

---

1 **User U_i:**
2   Remote attestation with the SGX enclave. Retrieves K_{U_i}.
3   Computes $\text{Enc}_{K_{U_i}}(P_{U_i}) = (\text{Enc}_{K_{U_i}}(A_1^i), \cdots, \text{Enc}_{K_{U_i}}(A_m^i))$.
4   Sends $\text{Enc}_{K_{U_i}}(P_{U_i})$ to the enclave.
5 **SGX enclave:**
6   Receives $\text{Enc}_{K_{U_i}}(P_{U_i})$ from U_i.
7   Reveals $P_{U_i} = A_1^i, A_2^i, \cdots, A_m^i$ using K_{U_i} ▷ see Sect. 4.2.
8   **for** $j = 1$ **to** m **do**
9   Computes $ST = \text{H}(K_{SGX} || A_j^i))$
10        $l = DF(ST)$
11   **If** l exists in the index map **then**
12   Inserts $(ST, c + 1)$ for this ST
13   **Else**
14   Inserts $(ST, 1)$ in the index map.
15   **end**
16   Obtains the latest counter c for the ST.
17   Splits ST as $ST_a || ST_b = ST$.
18   Computes $\text{H}(ST_a || c)$, $\text{Enc}_{ST_b}(U_i)$, sends to the matching server.
19   **end**
20 **The matching server:**
21   Stores $\text{H}(ST_a || c)$, $\text{Enc}_{ST_b}(U_i)$ received from the enclave.
22   Stores $\text{Enc}_{K_{U_i}}(P_{U_i})$ in the user profile table

---

Matching. When user U_i wants to find other users who have similar attributes (e.g., age), U_i submits his/her own attribute value (e.g., age = 21) to the SGX, and a list of corresponding users is returned by the matching server. To do that, U_i specifies one or more attributes indicating the group of users U_i is looking for, encrypts it with K_{U_i} and sends the encrypted attributes along with U_i's profile to the enclave.

Once the enclave receives a matching request from U_i, each attribute can be revealed in the secure enclave by using the corresponding key of U_i from the key table (refer to Sect. 4.2). After that, it is similar to the registration process where a search token is computed based on the attribute A_j^i from the request and stored in a list $ST[]$. When the computation completes, $ST[]$ is sent to the matching server. In order to find the related users that contain the same attribute, the matching server splits the search token ST into two, ST^a and ST^b respectively, such that $ST = (ST^a || ST^b)$, for every ST in $ST[]$. A counter c is initialised and set to 0, and CA can be computed as $\text{H}(ST^a || c)$ where c increments until $\text{H}(ST^a || c)$ is not found in the matching table. Each $\text{H}(ST^a || c)$ that were found in the matching table returns an encrypted user identity $\text{Enc}_{ST^b}(\text{user ID})$, which can be decrypted using the key ST^b. This process continues for every ST that exists in the list $ST[]$, when the computation completes, the matching server queries its database to retrieve data using the decrypted user identity, a list of encrypted profiles $RST[]$ is then returned from the database and is sent to enclave for similarity computation.

Algorithm 4: User matching.

---

1 **User U_i:**
2   Computes $\mathsf{Enc}_{K_{U_i}}(A_1^i), \cdots$ as PT, send PT and $\mathsf{Enc}_{K_{U_i}}(P_{U_i})$ to SGX.
3 **SGX enclave:**
4   Receives PT and $\mathsf{Enc}_{K_{U_i}}(P_{U_i})$ from U_i.
5   Reveals $PT = \{A_1^i, \cdots\}$ using K_{U_i} as PT'.   ▷ see Sect. 4.2
6   Decrypts P_{U_i} as P'_{U_i} using K_{U_i}.
7   Creates an empty list of search tokens $ST[] = \emptyset$.
8   **foreach** A_j^i in PT' **do**
9   Computes ST (e.g., $ST = \mathsf{H}(K_{SGX}||'Age : 21')$).
10   Adds the computed ST to the list $ST[]$.
11   **end**
12   Sends the list $ST[]$ to the matching server.
13 **The matching server:**
14   Receives $ST[]$ from the SGX.
15   Creates an empty list of user IDs $U[] = \emptyset$.
16   **foreach** ST in $ST[]$ **do**
17   Sets counter $c = 0$.
18   Splits $ST = ST^a||ST^b$.
19   **while** $\mathsf{H}(ST^a||c)$ exists in the matching table **do**
20   Reveals user ID U from $\mathsf{Enc}_{ST^b}(U)$ using ST^b.
21   Adds revealed U to the user list $U[]$.
22   Updates counter $c = c + 1$.
23   **end**
24   **end**
25   Query the database with user IDs in $U[]$ and stored in $RST[]$.
26 **SGX enclave:**
27   Receives $RST[]$ from the matching server.
28   Defines an empty set $R[] = \emptyset$ of results.
29   **foreach** P in $RST[]$ **do**
30   Obtains K_p for profile P.
31          $P' = \mathsf{Dec}_{K_p}(P)$.
32   Computes the similarity score between P' and P'_{U_i}, stores it in $R[]$.
33   **end**
34   Sorts $R[]$ and sends it to the requesting user U_i.

As the list $RST[]$ consists of users with the similar attribute settings as U_i requests (e.g., same age), it is imperative to realise what users that potentially match better with U_i. To find out, similarity computation is required. Once the enclave receives the list $RST[]$, each profile is decrypted using the corresponding key from the key table and the decrypted profile is compared with user who requests the profile matching using several distance measurements algorithm.

For attributes that are not in numerical form, Levenshtein Distance is used to measure the similarity, and Euclidean Distance is used to measure the distance of two numerical attributes. Results of similarity score of two profiles are stored in $R[]$, which is sorted when the process completes. The enclave can optionally include some public information about the user in the list $R[]$ (e.g., the name) before sending the list back to user U_i.

5 Adversary Model and Security Analysis

Our protocol relies on the trusted execution environment provided by Intel SGX. Assuming that Intel SGX guarantees the integrity of code execution and content isolation, an attacker cannot directly expose the content of the protected memory section. Potentially, an adversary could try to exploit the system using various side-channel attacks. Our proposed user matching protocol remains secure against several types of side-channel attacks.

Theorem 1. *Improved Index Map is pattern-hiding and secure against timing analysis.*

The security of improved index map is defined as a game between an adversary $\mathcal{A}$ and a challenger $\mathcal{C}$. Let $\mathcal{P}$ be the access pattern which $\mathcal{A}$ can measure. The goal of the adversary is to evaluate access pattern of the data structure in order to learn what elements are visited and used. Adversary $\mathcal{A}$ starts the game by sending two search tokens ST_0 and ST_1 to the challenger. The challenger $\mathcal{C}$ then runs Algorithm 2 and generates two access patterns $\mathcal{P}_0$ and $\mathcal{P}_1$ that $\mathcal{A}$ is able to measure. In the end, the adversary wins the game if for all measured patterns, the probability of correctly identifying whether $\mathcal{P}_0$ belongs to the search token ST_0 or ST_1 by observing the pattern generated during the runtime is non-negligible.

Proof. According to Algorithm 1, for each insertion, there exists a deterministic function DF which decides which path $P(l)$ that the data should be inserted at the position chosen uniformly at random $r = UniformRandom(\{0,1\}^D)$. More specifically, when an element is accessed, either by searching or insertion, it is moved to another position r somewhere on the way from the root of the tree to the leaf l, where r is chosen uniformly at random. Moreover, all buckets on the path l are accessed as the search begins, this forces the processor to load all data into caches and prevents cache misses when processing.

Security of the SSE Scheme: As our proposed user matching protocol employs SSE scheme [22], it inherits all security guarantees from the original work, except for the index map where our improved index map mitigates issues with timing analysis. Most SSE schemes introduce a concept of leakage function, which defines the amount of information leaked at certain stages. Our adopted SSE scheme defines leakages as follows:

$leak_s(ST, S, t)$, where ST denotes the search token that is being searched for, S denotes a set of results related to the search token ST and the time t when the search is requested.

Such SSE holds forward privacy in $leak_s()$, this means that the result set S relates to the elements added prior to occurrence of the leakage only, meaning the items added after the leakage cannot be related until a new leakage is captured.

6   Experiments and Performance Analysis

Our system was developed in C and deployed on a device equipped with Intel Core i7-7700HQ with 32 GB of DDR4 2400 MHz memory and the host OS is Ubuntu 18.04 LTS with Intel SGX SDK 2.10 and OpenSSL 1.1.3c. For symmetric encryption scheme, we choose standard AES-NI implementation as it comes with the SGX SDK that prevents against various side-channel attacks, and the message digest algorithm for computing search token uses SHA256 from OpenSSL. Table 1 presents the overall complexity of our proposed system and compares with other alternative protocols.

Table 1. Comparisons with the protocols of [29] using asymmetric encryption with multiple servers, and [12]. The number of servers involved in profile matching is S. The number of profiles is n.

	Our protocols	[12]	[29]
Profile matching cost	$\mathcal{O}(2n)$	$\mathcal{O}(2n * S)$ (Exp.)	$\mathcal{O}(2n * S)$ (Exp.)
Profile storing cost	$\mathcal{O}(n)$	$\mathcal{O}(n * S)$ (Exp.)	$\mathcal{O}(n * S)$ (Exp.)
Communication cost	2 rounds	n * S rounds	n * S rounds
Cryptosystem used	Symmetric	Asymmetric	Asymmetric
Num of party participated	Two parties	Multi-party	Multi-party
SGX-enabled	Yes	Yes	No

While Intel SGX provides a secure environment for sensitive computation at minimum cost, systems that utilise secure enclave technology usually require to minimise the attack surface, that is, to reduce the memory usage to the point where only data that is absolutely necessary for computation is placed in Enclave Page Cache (EPC). EPC is a set of memory that is reserved and protected by CPU, any programs that attempt to read the protected memory is blocked in hardware level. Currently the maximum amount of memory allocated to secure enclave is 128 MB, approximately 90 MB of which is available for programs that run in the enclave mode, and the rest is reserved by hardware. If the program consumes more than the amount of EPC RAM allocated, an EPC paging occurs resulting in a huge performance penalty. Depending on the use case, the performance could be several times slower as the enclave encrypts and evicts the previously used data into untrusted memory section to make room for new data.

In our proposed protocol, the secure enclave is the component that runs in the matching server where the integrity and confidentiality are guaranteed. Inside the enclave there exists a key table with the main purpose of holding the keys of all users on the platform, as the enclave is the only trusted entity in our system. Although placing the key table inside the EPC memory grants security benefits, the limitation of EPC size eventually renders the system unusable once the registered users reach to a point where it exceeded the amount of EPC memory allocated, which triggers the EPC paging that mentioned above. To handle this, the key table needs to be stored in unprotected memory while ensuring that the privacy of users is not compromised.

A tree-based data structure that enables obliviousness without sacrificing too much performance was proposed in [23]. It was implemented using SGX in [16]. Using this data structure, the risk of exceeding the EPC memory is mitigated, with a small cost of reducing performance. In the experimental section, our protocols implements both data structures for the key table that exists in the enclave to evaluate the performance and space trade-off between two data structures.

We implement two different variants of our user matching protocols: the *Vanilla* version aims to provide maximum performance, whereas the *Extended* version takes advantage of various techniques to optimise the EPC memory usage in the enclave, as well as adding resistance to protect against some side-channel attacks, which Intel SGX is known to suffer for years. In the next sections, we discuss the overall EPC usage between *Vanilla* and *Extended* versions, as well as the overall performance of running user matching with given parameters. Finally, we discuss the improvements of our proposed protocol and compare it with the previous work [12] that also uses SGX as a trusted computation environment but applied expensive homomorphic encryption.

6.1 Space Complexity

Intel SGX ensures that the content stored in the EPC memory is protected. This allows sensitive information such as symmetric keys to be stored within. However, simply storing the keys in the EPC memory is suboptimal as the current limit of the EPC memory is 128 MB, and only around 90 MB of which is available for developers, a paging issue that heavily impacts the performance occurs if the system consumes more than the designed EPC memory. The *Vanilla* implementation stores the key table in the EPC memory, which gives great performance as the computational complexity of each operation such as search and add is always constant, with performance penalty once it exceeds the EPC memory. To facilitate this, the *Extended* version utilises Oblivious Binary Tree [16,23] that allows data to be stored securely in unprotected memory region in exchange for a small performance overhead.

In Fig. 2, the *Vanilla* implementation of our user matching protocols exceeds the maximum amount of EPC memory when the registered users reach 1 million, whereas the *Extended* implementation performs roughly 10 times better than *Vanilla* implementation, with around 9 MB of EPC memory usage even if the number of registered users reaches 2 million. The significance of the cost of EPC memory is obvious, that is, the *Extended* version certainly enables more users

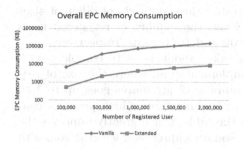

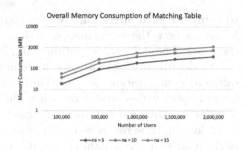

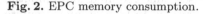

Fig. 2. EPC memory consumption.

Fig. 3. MT memory consumption for various numbers na of attributes in the profiles.

to sign up on the platform before reaching the limit of one enclave. However, the *Extended* implementation also comes with performance penalty whenever a user requests for user matching, because of the overhead of utilising untrusted memory and switching between trusted and untrusted environment, which can also be addressed by integrating switchless calls [24].

Memory consumption of the matching table MT in our proposed protocols is highly dependent on the number of attributes in a profile. In our experiments we choose the configuration that each profile contains 5,10 and 15 attributes, which result in 5, 10 and 15 secret pairs CA, CB that is stored in the matching table MT. Given the fixed numbers of users, we measure the memory consumption as described in Fig. 3. A profile requires more space to store if the number of attributes increase accordingly, with more than 2 million registered users and more than 30 million secret pairs, it consumes roughly around 1000 MB of RAM allowing a fast lookup when a profile matching is requested.

Note that the space complexity of the matching table is approximate without counting the overhead of the data structure and its objects as they are not easily measurable. The space consumption of the actual encrypted profile is dependent on database implementation, thus it cannot provide a reference to how much disk space the encrypted profiles take.

6.2 Performance of User Matching Protocols

When a user U wishes to look for new friends, U begins by sending a request to the enclave that indicates the type of people U is looking for, and the server receives and process the request. The secure enclave first decrypts the request and compute corresponding search token for the matching server to locate the targeted users in the matching table. The experimental variables are as follows: Given a request which contains 5 attributes indicating the type of people U is looking for, the enclave computes the corresponding search tokens for those 5 attributes, and let the matching server search the matching table and return the top rst of results, where $rst = [25, 50, 100]$. In Fig. 4, the x-axis indicates the number of profiles returned, whereas the y-axis indicates the time spent to complete each operation. We also generated three datasets of different sizes to assess how the performance changes when the number of registered users increases. These datasets contain 100k, 500k and 1m records, respectively.

As described in Fig. 4, user matching takes about 1 ms to complete on 3 different configurations for the *Vanilla* implementation, where the size of registered users varies, and 5 ms when the number of attributes goes up to 100. *Vanilla* implementations take advantage of hashing table which provides constant lookup time regardless of the size of the table, which greatly improves the performance of the matching, albeit with some compromises when it comes to leakage, which is discussed below. The increased time required for computing the secret corresponds to the amount of data needed to look up and compute, which believes to be reasonable and expected with the data structures involved.

The *Extended* implementation takes extra countermeasures to prevent potential data leaks via side-channel attacks, using oblivious data structure is the first counter-measurement that is used to resist cache-timing attacks, implementation of such data structure is presented in [16] with features that reduce the EPC usage by securely placing the data into untrusted regions after encryption. We measure the performance drop by up to 5 times compared to the *Vanilla* implementation that provides no protection against such attacks, from 5 ms to complete user matching with 25 returned users in the size of 100k users, all the way to 25 ms when the number of returned users is 100. This is due to the fact that oblivious data structure usually throttle the performance by a significant amount for security reason, and the most efficient oblivious data structure results in logarithmic complexity as supposed to constant found in *Vanilla* implementation. Context switching in the enclave also contributes to the longer execution time as the element in the key table needs to be encrypted before placing it outside the EPC memory section. In exchange for this degraded performance, we measure a significant drop in consumption of EPC memory in Fig. 2, allowing more users to sign up to the website while ensuring the enclave is resistant to some side-channel attacks.

Finally, we compare the performance of our new protocols with [12], another user matching scheme that utilises homomorphic encryption with multi-party settings that corporate with other servers to store and compute data for profile matching. The idea behind [12] is to split data into multiple servers to ensure the indistinguishability of data in the situation where some servers are compromised, while ensuring the data that stores across multiple servers can be securely computed using homomorphic encryption scheme, which imposes a huge computational overhead. Both [12,29] support matching profiles with numerical attributes only.

We measure the performance difference between our *Extended* implementation and [12] in Fig. 4 as an average in 30 tests, as [12] splits the secret into pieces, encrypts and distributes them to different servers using asymmetric encryption scheme, and combining them together when required by using the homomorphic property of the ElGamal encryption. When a user profile is requested by users, the user also submits their preferences to one of the servers, each server computes

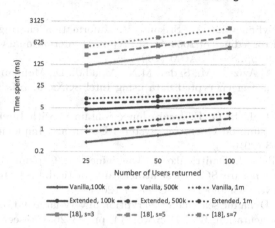

Fig. 4. Comparison of our protocol and alternatives using multiple servers and asymmetric encryption. The number of servers is denoted by s.

the partial similarity of the data and sends the intermediate result to the next server until all servers have completed computation, all intermediate results are then combined and revealed in secure hardware.

Finally, the users with the highest similarity score are returned to the requesting user. According to the experimental results in [12], it takes around 125 ms to compare 25 profiles, each profile with 5 attributes, on a configuration where the number of servers S is 3, and the number goes up to around 600 ms when S is 7. This computational overhead is mostly due to the complexity of computing exponentiation over large integers, and the experiments were conducted in a local network where the latency is minimised during the data transmission between multiple servers. Our new implementations outperform the solution [12] and in addition prevent several types of side-channel attacks.

7 Conclusion

In this paper, we design a privacy-protecting user matching protocol for modern social networks. It allows users to look for new friends without leaking any private information, while achieving reasonable performance so that it can be deployed in day-to-day use. Security analysis shows that the protocol is secure against various side-channel attacks and remains secure even when deployed in a public cloud. The security analysis and the outcomes of experiments presented in this paper demonstrate that our protocol is efficient, secure, practical and provides protection against side-channel attacks.

References

1. Agrawal, R., Evfimievski, A., Srikant, R.: Information sharing across private databases. In: Proceedings of 2003 ACM SIGMOD International Conference Management of Data, pp. 86–97. ACM (2003)
2. Ahmed, K.W., Al Aziz, M.M., Sadat, M.N., Alhadidi, D., Mohammed, N.: Nearest neighbour search over encrypted data using Intel SGXs. J. Inf. Secur. Appl. **54**, 102579 (2020)
3. Arnautov, S., et al.: SCONE: secure linux containers with Intel SGX. In: 12th USENIX Symposium on Operating Systems Design and Implementation, (OSDI 16), pp. 689–703 (2016)
4. Brasser, F., Müller, U., Dmitrienko, A., Kostiainen, K., Capkun, S., Sadeghi, A.R.: Software grand exposure: SGX cache attacks are practical. In: 11th USENIX Workshop on Offensive Technologies, WOOT 17 (2017)
5. Cash, D., et al.: Dynamic searchable encryption in very-large databases: data structures and implementation. In: NDSS, vol. 14, pp. 23–26. Citeseer (2014)
6. Duan, H., Wang, C., Yuan, X., Zhou, Y., Wang, Q., Ren, K.: Lightbox: full-stack protected stateful middlebox at lightning speed. In: Proceedings of the 2019 ACM SIGSAC Conference on Computer and Communications Security, pp. 2351–2367 (2019)
7. Freedman, M.J., Nissim, K., Pinkas, B.: Efficient private matching and set intersection. In: Cachin, C., Camenisch, J.L. (eds.) EUROCRYPT 2004. LNCS, vol. 3027, pp. 1–19. Springer, Heidelberg (2004). https://doi.org/10.1007/978-3-540-24676-3_1
8. Götzfried, J., Eckert, M., Schinzel, S., Müller, T.: Cache attacks on Intel SGX. In: Proceedings of the 10th European Workshop on Systems Security, pp. 1–6 (2017)
9. Jiang, Q., Qi, Y., Qi, S., Zhao, W., Lu, Y.: Pbsx: a practical private Boolean search using Intel SGX. Inf. Sci. **521**, 174–194 (2020)
10. Kissner, L., Song, D.: Privacy-preserving set operations. In: Shoup, V. (ed.) CRYPTO 2005. LNCS, vol. 3621, pp. 241–257. Springer, Heidelberg (2005). https://doi.org/10.1007/11535218_15
11. Li, H., Liu, D., Dai, Y., Luan, T.H.: Engineering searchable encryption of mobile cloud networks: when QoE meets QoP. IEEE Wirel. Commun. **22**(4), 74–80 (2015)
12. Luo, J., Yang, X., Yi, X.: SGX-based users matching with privacy protection. In: Proceedings of the Australasian Computer Science Week Multiconference, pp. 1–9 (2020)
13. Moghimi, A., Irazoqui, G., Eisenbarth, T.: CacheZoom: how SGX amplifies the power of cache attacks. In: Fischer, W., Homma, N. (eds.) CHES 2017. LNCS, vol. 10529, pp. 69–90. Springer, Cham (2017). https://doi.org/10.1007/978-3-319-66787-4_4
14. Oleksenko, O., Trach, B., Krahn, R., Silberstein, M., Fetzer, C.: Varys: protecting SGX enclaves from practical side-channel attacks. In: 2018 USENIX Annual Technical Conference, USENIX ATC 18, pp. 227–240 (2018)
15. Priebe, C., Vaswani, K., Costa, M.: Enclavedb: a secure database using SGX. In: 2018 IEEE Symposium on Security and Privacy (SP), pp. 264–278. IEEE (2018)
16. Sasy, S., Gorbunov, S., Fletcher, C.W.: ZeroTrace: oblivious memory primitives from Intel SGX. IACR Cryptol. ePrint Arch. 2017, 549 (2017)
17. Schuster, F., et al.: Vc3: trustworthy data analytics in the cloud using SGX. In: 2015 IEEE Symposium on Security and Privacy, pp. 38–54. IEEE (2015)

18. Seo, J., et al.: SGX-shield: enabling address space layout randomization for SGX programs. In: NDSS (2017)
19. Sherry, J., Lan, C., Popa, R.A., Ratnasamy, S.: BlindBox: deep packet inspection over encrypted traffic. In: Proceedings of the 2015 ACM Conference on Special Interest Group on Data Communication, pp. 213–226 (2015)
20. Shi, E., Chan, T.-H.H., Stefanov, E., Li, M.: Oblivious ram with $O((\log N)^3)$ worst-case cost. In: Lee, D.H., Wang, X. (eds.) ASIACRYPT 2011. LNCS, vol. 7073, pp. 197–214. Springer, Heidelberg (2011). https://doi.org/10.1007/978-3-642-25385-0_11
21. Spreitzer, R., Plos, T.: Cache-access pattern attack on disaligned AES T-tables. In: Prouff, E. (ed.) COSADE 2013. LNCS, vol. 7864, pp. 200–214. Springer, Heidelberg (2013). https://doi.org/10.1007/978-3-642-40026-1_13
22. Stefanov, E., Papamanthou, C., Shi, E.: Practical dynamic searchable encryption with small leakage. In: NDSS, vol. 71, pp. 72–75 (2014)
23. Stefanov, E., et al.: Path ORAM: an extremely simple oblivious RAM protocol. In: Proceedings of the 2013 ACM SIGSAC Conference on Computer & Communications Security, pp. 299–310 (2013)
24. Tian, H., et al.: Switchless calls made practical in Intel SGXs. In: Proceedings of the 3rd Workshop on System Software for Trusted Execution, pp. 22–27 (2018)
25. Tsai, C.C., Porter, D.E., Vij, M.: Graphene-SGX: a practical library OS for unmodified applications on SGX. In: 2017 USENIX Annual Technical Conference, USENIX ATC 17, pp. 645–658 (2017)
26. Van Bulck, J., et al.: Foreshadow: extracting the keys to the Intel SGX kingdom with transient out-of-order execution. In: 27th USENIX Security Symposium, USENIX Security 18, pp. 991–1008 (2018)
27. Wang, W., et al.: Leaky cauldron on the dark land: understanding memory side-channel hazards in SGX. In: Proceedings of the 2017 ACM SIGSAC Conference on Computer and Communications Security, pp. 2421–2434 (2017)
28. Yi, X., Bertino, E., Rao, F.Y., Bouguettaya, A.: Practical privacy-preserving user profile matching in social networks. In: 2016 IEEE 32nd International Conference on Data Engineering (ICDE), pp. 373–384. IEEE (2016)
29. Yi, X., Bertino, E., Rao, F.Y., Lam, K.Y., Nepal, S., Bouguettaya, A.: Privacy-preserving user profile matching in social networks. IEEE Trans. Knowl. Data Eng. **32**, 1572–1585 (2019)

Developing an Online Examination Timetabling System Using Artificial Bee Colony Algorithm in Higher Education

Kaixiang Zhu[(✉)], Lily D. Li, and Michael Li

Central Queensland University, Rockhampton, QLD 4702, Australia
{k.zhu,l.li,m.li}@cqu.edu.au

Abstract. Educational timetabling is a fundamental problem impacting schools and universities' effective operation in many aspects. Different priorities for constraints in different educational institutions result in the scarcity of universal approaches to the problems. Recently, COVID-19 crisis causes the transformation of traditional classroom teaching protocols, which challenge traditional educational timetabling. Especially for examination timetabling problems, as the major hard constraints change, such as unlimited room capacity, non-invigilator and diverse exam durations, the problem circumstance varies. Based on a scenario of a local university, this research proposes a conceptual model of the online examination timetabling problem and presents a conflict table for constraint handling. A modified Artificial Bee Colony algorithm is applied to the proposed model. The proposed approach is simulated with a real case containing 16,246 exam items covering 9,366 students and 209 courses. The experimental results indicate that the proposed approach can satisfy every hard constraint and minimise the soft constraint violation. Compared to the traditional constraint programming method, the proposed approach is more effective and can provide more balanced solutions for the online examination timetabling problems.

Keywords: Educational timetabling · Examination timetabling · Constraint satisfaction problem · Optimisation · Artificial bee colony algorithm

1 Introduction

Examination timetabling, course timetabling and school timetabling constitute educational timetabling [1] which is a fundamental task of schools and universities. According to Wren [2], "Timetabling is the allocation, subject to constraints, of given resources to objects being placed in space time, in such a way as to satisfy as nearly as possible a set of desirable objectives". A well-organised educational timetable ensures a sound operation of an educational institute. Educational Timetabling Problems (ETP) are considered the constraint satisfaction problems which involve multiple factors, such as educators, students, classrooms and teaching equipment, as a whole. ETPs have been widely studied with multiple artificial intelligence algorithms developed, mainly including heuristics algorithms, novel approaches and multi-agent systems [3]. Heuristics algorithms consist of meta-heuristics and hyper heuristics [4]. Novel approaches can be classified as hybrid approaches and fuzzy logic approaches

W. Xiang et al. (Eds.): BROADNETS 2021, LNICST 413, pp. 112–131, 2022.
https://doi.org/10.1007/978-3-030-93479-8_7

[3]. However, there is a lack of general solution solving a wide range of ETPs, resulted from the definition differences of hard and soft constraints in different universities [5]. Besides, each method has its applicability and strengths.

Currently, COVID-19 crisis challenges the traditional teaching format. Traditionally, ETP should consider teaching staff availabilities and infrastructure capability. However, as social distancing practices, schools and universities have to transfer face-to-face classes and assessments online, which causes the hard and soft constraints of ETP changed. Especially for examination timetabling problems, multiple new conditions emerge, such as non-invigilator, unlimited room capacity, technical issues and diverse exam durations. Those features, to the best knowledge of the authors, have not been studied in conventional ETP research, which inspires this research to investigate the Online Examination Timetabling (OET) problem and to develop a model for solving the problem.

The contributions of this research include a conceptual model for the OET problem, a conflict table for constraint handling and a modified Artificial Bee Colony (ABC) algorithm for solving the OET problem.

The organisation of this article is as follows: In Sect. 2, the existing approaches and algorithms for solving ETPs are reviewed. Section 3 proposes a conceptual model of the OET based on the discussion of the general features of the OET problems. A conflict table aiming to shrink the search space is introduced to handle the main hard constraint. In Sect. 4, a modified ABC algorithm is applied to solve the problem. The experiment based on the data from a local university for the proposed model is presented in Sect. 5. In order to further verify the effectiveness, the proposed approach is compared with the Constraint Programming (CP) method in Sect. 6. Section 7 concludes the article.

2 Literature Review

The approaches for solving ETPs have been studied over 50 years since Appleby, Blake and Newman [6] initiated a study in school timetabling. Around 3000 computational timetabling articles are published every year, within which university timetabling problems occupy over 85% proportion [5]. Educational Timetabling is to allocate a number of educational activities, such as exams, lectures, tutorials and meetings, into finite timeslots and/or room-slots [7]. Each activity has its unique conditions needed to be satisfied. The conditions are different from instance to instance depending on the priorities given by different educational institutes. Generally, those conditions could be categorised into hard constraints and soft constraints. Hard constraints decide the feasibility of a timetabling problem solution. Soft constraints impact the solution quality [8]. Schaerf [1] classified ETPs as course timetabling, school timetabling and examination timetabling problems. Course timetabling is to allocate lectures and tutorials to timeslots, classrooms or other teaching facilities avoiding an individual student taking more than one class at the same time. School timetabling, based on curriculum, assigns lecturers and tutors to a scheduled course timetable, taking their availabilities and specialisations as hard constraints [9]. Examination timetabling is to ensure no student taking two or more exams simultaneously and to optimise resource usage within an examination period [10]. Unlike course timetabling or school timetabling, in an examination, rooms or examiners could be assigned to different courses at the same time [8, 9]. For each type of the ETPs, the hard constraints are commonly defined as below.

Hard constraints for course timetabling problems [3, 11, 12]:

- No student can take more than one class at the same time.
- Only one course can be taught in one classroom at a time.
- Timeslots for assigning courses in are limited to one day.
- The number of students in a class cannot exceed the capacity of a classroom.
- All courses must be allocated in a regular basis as required.

Hard constraints for school timetabling problems [13–15]:

- No teacher can deliver more than one class at the same time.
- Teachers cannot be scheduled to timeslots when they are unavailable.
- Teachers must be allocated to the courses they are capable to deliver.
- For co-teaching classes, the teachers must be allocated in the same timeslots.

Hard constraints for examination timetabling problems [8, 16–19]:

- Every exam must be assigned in consecutive timeslots and cannot be split.
- Exams must be invigilated, meaning examiner(s) will be allocated.
- No student can sit more than one exam simultaneously.
- The number of examinees cannot exceed the capacity of the exam hall in a timeslot.
- Every exam must be scheduled.

Educational timetabling problems are NP-complete problems [20], meaning that it may be impossible to find a polynomial-time algorithm to solve the problem. In addition to the traditional constraint programming method, more and more researchers are interested in seeking stochastic methods in recent years [21]. Mainly, those methods are heuristic approaches and novel methods [3, 5, 21]. Heuristic approaches are problem-independent [22], including meta-heuristics and hyper-heuristics. Meta-heuristic approaches are known as approximate methods which aim at finding better solutions in a reasonable computational time rather than the best solution [23]. Meta-heuristics approaches are inspired by the nature mechanisms, such as biological systems, physical and chemical processes, for their success in solving multi-objective and combinational optimisation problems [24]. Hyper-heuristics is to heuristically choose a heuristic [25]. Instead of using a technique derived from specific scenarios, hyper-heuristics solve problems with more generalised solutions [26]. Novel methods include hybrid approaches, fuzzy logic approaches and Multi-Agent Systems (MAS). Hybrid approaches combine different approaches with the purpose to mitigate the weakness of a single approach. Fuzzy logic approaches focus on solving those problems which do not have a precisive classification [27, 28] resulting in the difficulty of quantitating and modelling. Multi-agent systems engage several artificial intelligence techniques, as agents, to collaboratively accomplish a common goal [29]. Every agent is independent, able to communicate with each other and to do tasks incompletely.

Based on the algorithms abovementioned, many applications have been evolved and developed. In heuristics scope, Soria-Alcaraz et al. [30] applied iterated local search, and Soria-Alcaraz, Özcan, Swan, Kendall and Carpio [31] adopted perturbative hyper-heuristics to solve course timetabling problems. Odeniyi, Omidiora, Olabiyisi and Aluko modified Simulated Annealing (SA) approach, while Kheiri and Keedwell [32] introduced a sequence-based selection hyper-heuristic framework to find solutions for school timetabling problems. Kasm, Mohandes, Diabat and El Khatib combined constructive heuristics with colour graphing [33], and Bykov and Petrovic developed Step Counting Hill Climbing to tackled examination timetabling problems. Hybrid approaches are approach combinations. Those combinations for solving ETPs include but are not limited to Artificial Bee Colony (ABC) with Hill Climbing (HC) [34], HC with SA [35], Cat Swarm Optimisation (CSO) with swap operator [13], tabu with genetic algorithm [36], ABC with Simple Local Search (SLS) and Harmony Search (HS) [37], and ABC with Great Deluge (GD) [38]. To deal with ill-defined problems [39], many fuzzy logic applications were developed to solve ETPs for universities, such as the University of Malaysia Sabah Labuan [40], Islamic Azad University [41], University of Eswatini and Uludag University [42]. Since, universities' resources, such as rooms, teaching facilities and teaching staff, are shared with different faculties, faculties need to negotiate with each other for different resources and bring discussion results to their administrations to come up with a solution. To mimic the negotiation processes, many universities have adopted MAS and let the agents play the roles of negotiators, administrators and planers [29]. For example, the University of Gdansk [43] utilised MAS to simulate administration, database, room and teacher agent and scheduler.

Due to the idiosyncrasy of ETPs, there is a lack of universal solutions for general ETPs. The key components of ETPs, such as rooms, teachers, courses, students and timeslots, are different from university to university. Universities prioritise and weigh those components differently. In addition, the university structures, educational policies and procedures diversify the differences dramatically. Therefore, a number of ETP approaches reviewed in this article were based on particular business scenarios.

This research will apply ABC algorithm to solve the online examination time-tabling problem driven by a local university's practice. The reasons for adopting ABC algorithm are: 1) ABC was proved to be an efficient algorithm for solving multivariable, multimodal optimisation problems [44]. 2) ABC algorithm is simple, efficient and effective in solving many optimisation problems compared to traditional algorithms, such as Differential Evolution, Genetic Algorithm, Particle Swarm Optimisation (PSO) [37]. 3) ABC algorithm is easy to be implemented with a few parameters [44].

3 A Conceptual Model of the Online Examination Timetabling

This section presents the features of the OET problem, conducts mathematically modelling and proposes a conceptual model for the OET problem including a novel approach for hard constraint handling.

To model and simulate the application, the word "unit" is used to represent a learning subject in the rest of the article, while other literature mentioned in Sect. 2 may use "course" for the subject.

3.1   OET Problems Features

Originated from the local university's conduct of online examination, the new features of OET problems are derived as below:

- Students participate in exams remotely. But students still cannot take two exams simultaneously. It is expected that students are not overloaded.
- Every exam only can be allocated once in the exam period.
- Exams are non-invigilated and open book. Similar to an assessment, but the timeframe is shorter. Through teaching and learning management systems, students can download the exam questions, and upload the answers within the designated exam durations. It is realised that the non-invigilated examination may cause academic integrity issues, however, this is not in the scope of this research.
- Although exams move online, an exam duration cannot be fragmented. That is, the exam duration should be continuous from the scheduling point of view.
- An exam duration could be extended up to 12 h. This is to consider the technical issues such as Internet connection failure and/or ICT system faults.
- Physical room capacity is not taken into account.
- Without the limitation of room capacity, the number of examinations to share the same timeslots is unlimited.
- Since the number of exams put in a day could be many, the administrative load would be increased. The examination downloading and uploading could intensify the traffic of the IT system. Therefore, to balance the ICT network traffic should be taken into consideration.

3.2   Symbols and Terms Definition

Parameters
P   Number of days of the whole exam period
N   Number of exam units to be allocated

Variables
t Duration (in hours) of each exam, $t \in \{1, \ldots, 12\}$
w Number of days a timetabling solution uses, $w \to P$
a set of exams allocated in one day, $a \in \{1, \ldots N\}$
v Average number of units distributed in w, $v = \frac{N}{w}$
x Number of exam units that cannot be allocated in P, $x = N - \sum_{i=1}^{w} a_i$.

3.3   Hard Constraints and Fitness Function

Eight hard constraints have been identified, as follows.

1. Each student cannot take more than one exam simultaneously.
2. Each unit only can be allocated once in the whole exam period.

3. All units must be allocated.
4. An exam whose duration is less than eight hours must be allocated in business hours.
5. An exam whose duration is less than or equal to twelve hours must be allocated in one day.
6. An exam cannot be allocated on a timeslot that is blocked by administration (e.g., a scheduled maintenance time).
7. The duration of an exam must be consecutive.
8. The whole period of the examination must not be greater than the designated days.

A feasible solution has to satisfy all the hard constraints. During the solution-seeking process, a formulation as in Eq. 1 is introduced to evaluate the fitness $f(w)$ of the current search node and then lead the algorithm to a feasible solution.

$$min \ f(w) = \begin{cases} \frac{\sum_{i=1}^{x} t_i}{\sum_{i=1}^{N} t_i} \times \frac{w-P}{P}, & if \ \ w > P \\ 0, & if \ \ w \le P \end{cases} \qquad (1)$$

The major goal of this project is to let the number of days (w) that a solution uses is no more than the number of days (P) that the examination administration designates. Therefore, w should be less than or equal to P, in other words, $f(w)$ is required to be zero. When w is greater than P, the proportions, that total hours of excessive exams to all exams and the number of excessive days to designated days, will jointly affect the fitness value. Seeking a feasible solution without hard constraint violation is the aim of this research. The purpose to establish Eq. (1) is to set up an intermediate value for bees to detect better food sources. The algorithm will chase the lesser $f(w)$ in the search space unit w equals to or smaller than P, then $f(w)$ will be set to zero directly. After that, all the solutions that have $f(w)$ equal to zero will be outputted as feasible solutions.

3.4 Soft Constraint

When multiple feasible solutions are found, the soft constraint will be applied to filter the most preferred one. In order to avoid exam data traffic congestion and reduce administrative workload, exams need to be levelly distributed to the whole designated exam period. To evaluate the evenness, Standard Deviation formulation (2) is adopted. The less the σ is, the more balanced solution will be. Thus, among feasible solutions, the solution with the least σ will be chosen as the best solution.

$$\sigma = \sqrt{\frac{\sum_{i=1}^{w} (a_i - v)^2}{w}} \quad where \ \ w \le P \qquad (2)$$

3.5 The Proposed Conceptual Model

The proposed conceptual model is illustrated in Fig. 1. Preliminarily, course data are retrieved from the student enrolment database, which includes student unique identifications and the courses they have enrolled in. Based on the retrieved course data, a conflict table can be constructed. The conflict table is introduced to shrink search space, which will be detailed in Sect. 3.6. After consulting the conflict circumstances, the exam profiles, such as exam duration, will be required. To seek solutions from the shrunk search space for OET problems, a modified ABC algorithm is applied. After that, all the solutions found will be filtered to output the best solution with a minimum soft constraint violation.

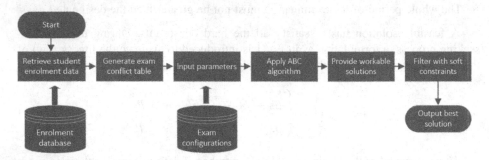

Fig. 1. The conceptual model of OET

The fundamental hard constraint of examination timetabling is that no one student can take more than one examination simultaneously. Consequently, every conflict between units should be known at the very beginning. For an individual student, all the units enrolled are conflicted with each other in the examination period. Therefore, the conflict unit table can be formed from all the students' unit enrolment data. A feasible examination timetable is to arrange, within a day, non-conflict exam units to share timeslots, and to avoid the timeslot overlap between conflict exam units. But the conflict exam units could be allocated consecutively. In other words, a solution is a combination of overlapping non-conflict and/or consecutive conflict units. As the number of possible combinations is vast, a Computational Intelligence algorithm is needed to get a better solution efficiently and effectively. Before the algorithm runs, parameters, such as the period of a whole examination and the duration of each unit exam, will be required.

3.6   Constraint Handling Approach

As mentioned earlier, the major hard constraint is to prevent any student from taking more than one examination at the same time. Based on this principle, a conflict table is established to restrain the search space. When seeking a solution, every two examination units conflicting in the conflict table will be kept from sharing timeslots. As the conflict table is an aggregation from the student enrolment database, the solution search space is largely shrunk.

The data structure of the conflict table is illustrated in Fig. 2 with Java language expression, which collects every exam unit as a unique data item and records all the conflict exam units to be its subset.

ConflictUnit <UnitItem> []{ UnitName; ConflictUnits<UnitName>{}}

Fig. 2. Data structure of conflict table

The conflict unit table is generated by consulting students' enrolment database. The flowchart of the conflict table construction is presented in Fig. 3.

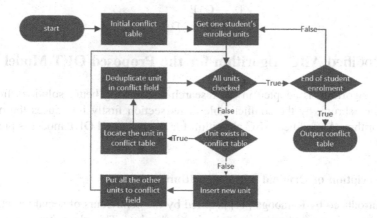

Fig. 3. Conflict table construction flowchart

The method will consult every student's data to get their unit enrolment situation. When a student's data is retrieved, each enrolled unit is compared with the existing conflict table. If the unit is not in the conflict table, this unit will be inserted into the table as a new item and the other units will be put into the conflict unit field. If the unit is found in the conflict table, then the other units will be added to this unit's conflict unit field but a deduplicating method will be implemented to ensure every unit in the conflict unit field is unique. When every student has been consulted, the complete conflict table is constructed.

A simplified example of constructing a conflict table is shown in Table 1 and Table 2. For instance, in Table 1, student S1 enrolled units A, B and C, and student S3 enrolled units A, C and E. Hence, it is known that unit A conflicts with units B, C and E. As result, units B, C and E have been placed into the conflict unit field of A in Table 2. After consulted students S1, S2 and S3, the conflict table for units A, B, C, D and E can be established.

Table 1. Example of unit enrolment

Student	Enrolled units		
S_1	A	B	C
S_2	C	D	E
S_3	A	C	E

Table 2. Example of conflict table

Unit	Conflict unit field			
A	B	C	E	
B	A	C		
C	A	B	D	E
D	C	E		
E	A	C	D	

4 A Modified ABC Algorithm for the Proposed OET Model

The ABC algorithm is adopted in the research for seeking better solutions from the search space shrunk by the conflict table. This section firstly introduces the original ABC algorithm. A modified ABC algorithm for the proposed OET model is presented afterward.

4.1 Description of Original ABC Algorithm

ABC is introduced by Karaboga [44] inspired by the behaviours of social insects. Self-organisation and labour division is its basic mechanism. This algorithm simulates the way that honeybees self-arrange to forage with four major traits, including positive feedback, negative feedback, fluctuations and multiple interactions. Positive feedback reinforces a foraging process, encouraging bees to create convenient paths. Negative feedback prevents positive feedback from saturation, such as food source exhaustion and over-population to a destination. Fluctuations help to discover new paths by randomly walking. Although fluctuations may cause errors, it is significant for creativity. Multiple interaction mechanisms ensure the information can be delivered to each node of the network. In the labour division, honeybees are categorised to be employed foragers and unemployed foragers. With the food sources, these two bee characters can form a minimal model of forage selection. Food sources stand for the possible solutions for the problems to be solved. Food sources are valued with many factors, such as the distances to the nest and the lavishness. Employed bees take the responsibility to investigate the food sources and then bring the information about the sources back to the nest. Unemployed bees consist of two groups: scouts and onlookers. Scouts search the surroundings of the nest to exploit new food sources while onlookers set in the nest to build up food sources from the information shared by employed bees. Onlookers determine the profitability of the food sources.

ABC algorithm includes four stages: 1) in the initialisation stage, several solutions (food resources) will be initialised; 2) in the employed bee stage, bees will be sent to the initialised solutions to implement search tasks; 3) in the onlooker bee stage, bees will select a better solution according to the solution fitness; 4) in scout bee stage, bees will explore new solutions. The equations of each stage are detailed below.

Solution Population

The number of solutions SN will be randomly generated with different dimension D. The solution generating rule as follows:

$$s_i^d = s_{min}^d + random(0,1)\left(s_{max}^d - s_{min}^d\right), \tag{3}$$

Where $i \in \{1, \ldots, SN\}, d \in \{1, \ldots D\}$. s_{max}^d and s_{min}^d is the upper bound and low bound for the dimension d.

After the population, solutions will be evaluated and randomly allocated with employed bees to be exploited. The exploitation process will be enforced repeatedly in R times. During the exploitation, scout bee(s) will explore new solution(s).

Employed Bee Stage

Based on the assigned solutions, employed bee *es* will generate a neighbour solution with the below equation.

$$es_i^d = s_i^d + \varphi_i^d\left(s_i^d - s_k^d\right) \tag{4}$$

Where $k \in \{1, \ldots, SN\}$ is randomly chosen and $k \neq i$. φ_i^d is randomly generated in the range of $[-1, 1]$. s_k^d is a neighbour of s_i^d.

The es_i^d will be evaluated and compared to s_i^d. If the fitness of es_i^d is better than or equals to s_i^d, then es_i^d will be chosen. Otherwise, s_i^d will be remained.

Onlooker Bee Stage

Onlookers will evaluate the possibility value (p) of each solution provided by employed bees. After the evaluation, onlooker bees will exploit the high possibility solution. The possibility equation is represented as below.

$$p_i = \frac{fit(es_i)}{\sum_{n=1}^{SN} fit(es_n)} \tag{5}$$

Where $fit(es_i)$ is the fitness of es_i generated in employed bee stage.

Scout Bee Stage

$$s_i = s_{min} + random(0,1)(s_{max} - s_{min}) \tag{6}$$

If any solution found by an employed bee has been abandoned in the onlooker stage because of its p, the owner of the abandoned solution will become a scout bee. This scout bee will look for a new solution in a way similar to the solution population, which is shown in Eq. 6.

Key parameters of the original ABC algorithm are:

- SN: number of populated solutions which equals to employed and onlooker bees.
- MAX-ITERATION: max number of exploitation cycle.

4.2   A Modified ABC Algorithm for OET

```
/**Initialise the search spaceand solution population**/
1. Generate Conflict Table
2. Set parameter: MAX_ITERATION, NUMBER_BEE, MAX_EXPOITATION
3. Populate food sources using Equation (3).
4. Send employed bees to explore the populated food sources.
5. Evaluate the solution fitness with Equation (1)
6. If a solution's f(w) is zero, then output it and populate a new one with Equation
   (3)
7. DO WHILE (ITERATION < MAX_ITERATION)
   /*Employed bee stage*/
8.    FOR (each employed bee)
9.       Find neighbours of the solutions explored from Step 4 using Equation (4).
10.      Evaluation the fitness of the solution by using Equation (1),
11.         IF fitness <> 0, apply greedy selection.
12.         ELSE output feasible solution and keep another one.
13.   Calculate the probability of each found solution with Equation (5)
   /*Onlooker bee stage*/
14.   Declare COUNTER //the exploitation counter
15.   FOR (each onlooker bee: I)
16.      For (each MAX_EXPOITATION)
17.        Generate a random number: RAN
18.        IF (RAN < probability of I)
19.          Send onlooker bees to exploit neighbours of solutions found in Step
             10.
20.          IF (fitness of new solution == 0) output as feasible solution
21.          ELSE IF (fitness of new solution < old one) select new one
22.          ELSE COUNTER +1;
23.   Memorise the best solution so far
   /*Scout bee stage*/
24.   Convert employed bees having MAX(COUNTER) to scout bees
25.   FOR (each scout bees)
26.      Scout bee randomly initialises a solution similarly to Step 3.
27.   ITERATION +1;
28. END WHILE
29. Evaluate soft constraint against every feasible solution with Equation (2).
30. Output the solution which has best soft constraint and least duration.
```

Fig. 4. Modified ABC algorithm for OET

ABC is adopted for OET problem in this research. The exam combination pool is the search space. As each exam can and only can be assigned once in the whole examination period, the allocated units have to be bypassed. Therefore, this research will modify Eq. 4 into Eq. 7, where $\vartheta \in \{1, \ldots, UN\}$, UN is the number of unvisited exams $UN \subset N$.

$$es_i^d = s_i^d + random(0, 1)\left(\vartheta_{Max}^d - \vartheta_{min}^d\right) \tag{7}$$

Unlike employed bees choosing a better solution with fitness Eq. 1, the key role of onlooker bees is to exploit the neighbourhood for a better solution by probability value with Eq. 5. In order to avoid overexploitation, a parameter called exploitation_counter is introduced. If a solution is exhaustedly exploited (exploitation_counter reaches maximum number which is defined as MAX_EXPOITATION in Fig. 4) without probability value improvement or the solution has the biggest local exploitation_counter, a scout bee would replace the onlooker bee to discover a new food source. Since the goal of this research is to obtain feasible solutions, when one of them is found, it will be outputted, and the related bee will be converted to a scout bee immediately. The modified algorithm pseudocode is represented in Fig. 4.

The major modifications are summarised as below:

- Preprocess original data to generate the conflict table to limit search space.
- Use modified Eq. 7 for neighbour search to avoid duplicated exploration.
- Use the exploitation-counter to abandon exhausted sources in order to avoid over-exploitation.

Output solutions anytime if a feasible solution is found, and the bee will be converted to be a scout bee immediately.

5 Experiment

5.1 Experimental Settings

This research obtained a large dataset from a local university, detailed as follows.

- Number of data items: 16,246
- Number of students: 9,399
- Number of examinations: 209
- Range of examinations that a student takes: 1 to 4
- The whole period of examination: 7 days (resulted from manual arrangement)

With the purpose to test the flexibility of the proposed algorithm, the experiment has been configured with extra conditions presented below.

- Range of examination duration: 3 to 12 h (detailed in Table 3)
- Timeslot limitation: examinations whose duration is less than or equals to 8 h must be allocated in the daytime. (Daytime: 8 am to 5 pm)

Table 3. Number of exam distribution in duration

Duration (hours)	3	4	5	6	7	8	9	10	11	12
Number of exams	19	23	22	18	22	28	24	19	15	19

Table 4. ABC algorithm parameter settings

Samples	Bees	Iterations	MAX_EXPOITATION
A	20	500	20
B	60	500	20
C	40	500	40
D	10	1000	20
E	20	1000	20
F	40	1000	40
G	60	1000	20
H	20	1000	100
I	80	1000	20
J	20	5000	20

The proposed approach was experimented with the below environment.

- Operation system: Windows 10 Education Edition
- Integrated development environment: IntelliJ IDEA Ultimate 2019.3
- Programming language: Java
- Computer hardware system: Intel® Core™ i5-9500 3.00 GHz; 16.0 GB memory; integrated graphics card

The algorithm has been experimented with ten samples as presented in Table 4. Each sample is set with different parameters in the number of bees, the number of iterations and the MAX_EXPOITATION. The number of bees represents the coverage of solution population in the search space; The number of iterations is expected to test whether the increase of searching rounds will improve the result; the MAX_-EXPOITATION is to decide the deep of exploitation. Each sample will be fed in the proposed algorithm ten times. To choose reasonable initial parameters, this research referenced the first ABC algorithm experiment conducted in [44] and configures the number of bees to be 20 and the number of iterations to be 500.

To evaluate the experiment result, three values have been recorded, including time-spent, days and soft constraint violations. The time-spent indicates how much time the algorithm used to seek a solution under a particular parameter setting; the days shows how many days the best solution needs to allocate all the examinations; The soft constraint violations refer to the fitness value of the best solution calculated with Eq. 2.

5.2 Experimental Results

The experiment results for each sample are shown in Table 5 with average value, the best value, standard deviation and Coefficient of Variation (CV), from which the following conclusions could be drawn.

Table 5. Experiment results (ten times runs)

Samples		Time-spent (second)	Days	Soft constraint violation
A	Average	75.9518	7	38.02756
	Best	74.2180	7	34.98571
	Std.Dev./CV	1.4557/1.92%	0/0%	2.2372/5.88%
B	Average	153.9567	6.6	36.74307
	Best	151.1280	6	34.61214
	Std.Dev./CV	2.3456/1.52%	0.5163/7.82%	1.4708/4.00%
C	Average	150.5761	6.3	37.62617
	Best	147.782	6	34.14674
	Std.Dev./CV	2.2246/1.48%	0.4830/7.67%	2.5541/6.79%
D	Average	117.0227	7	37.7743
	Best	110.119	7	34.89986
	Std.Dev./CV	4.1278/3.53%	0/0.00%	1.5995/4.23%
E	Average	149.5253	6.8	36.71512
	Best	141.21	7	33.70599
	Std.Dev./CV	3.5841/2.40%	0/0.00%	1.8711/5.10%
F	Average	299.5271	6.2	37.30763
	Best	293.362	6	34.16138
	Std.Dev./CV	3.9970/1.33%	0.4216/6.80%	1.8075/4.84%
G	Average	372.8681	6.4	36.1736
	Best	362.575	6	30.88689
	Std.Dev./CV	5.4304/1.46%	0.5163/8.07%	2.20376.09%
H	Average	446.7798	6.4	36.31801
	Best	437.548	6	34.05877
	Std.Dev./CV	5.8057/1.30%	0.5163/8.07%	1.8077/4.98%
I	Average	382.9436	6.375	34.88421
	Best	368.638	6	30.23243
	Std.Dev./CV	8.6314/2.25%	0.5175/8.12%	2.0953/6.01%
J	Average	762.8847	6.285714	34.99916
	Best	740.658	6	32.92416
	Std.Dev./CV	1.5754/0.21%	0.4879/7.76%	2.1523/6.15%

- The algorithm can obtain a feasible solution in a short time for a big dataset. In Sample A, the proposed algorithm reaches the best solution within 75 s.
- Increasing the number of iterations can minimise the soft constraint violation. Compared to Sample A who runs 500 iterations, Sample E executes two times of iteration (1000), which improves the soft constraint violation by 3.57% (from Sample A 38.02756 to Sample E 36.71591). However, significantly increasing number of iterations does not linearly improve the soft constraints. The number of iteration that Sample J operates is ten times greater than Sample A. But the improvement is merely 7.96% (from Sample A 38.02756 to Sample J 34.99916).

- Increasing the number of bees improves the result. Comparing to Sample E, Sample G and Sample I deploy three times and four times of bees respectively. The soft constraint violations improved 5.68% (from Sample E 38.35568 to Sample G 36.1736 on average) and 9.05% (from Sample E 38.35568 to Sample I 34.88421 on average).
- Deepening exploitation was not cost-effective. Compared to Sample E, Sample H inputs five times MAX_EXPOITATION, but the soft constraint violation only minimized by 5.3% (from 38.3556 to 36.3180)
- The proposed approach can stably output solutions with given parameters as the all the coefficient of variation (CV) is less than 10%.
- Overall, Sample A consumed the smallest population and achieved satisfactory results with the least iteration. Therefore, the settings are reasonable for the proposed OET model.

6 Comparison Study

The examination timetabling problem of this research is posed by the COVID-19 pandemic crisis, which makes it difficult to find a similar study to compare the experimental result. In order to verify the performance of the proposed approach in solving OET problem, a Constraint Programming (CP) [17] method is implemented for the comparison study as ETPs are considered constraint satisfaction problems. CP has been proved successful in solving various problems, such as vehicle routing and timetabling [45]. The flowchart of the CP for the proposed model is illustrated in Fig. 5.

Firstly, the exam and enrolment data are retrieved to construct the conflict table, which is the same as the processes described in Fig. 1 and Fig. 3. The program then creates a day and then selects an exam from the exam list in turn. If the selected exam does not conflict with other exams in that day slot, the exam will be allocated on the day. Otherwise, a consecutive exam in the exam list will be consulted. If all the unallocated exams have been visited and none of them can be assigned in the current day, a new day will be created for them. When a new day is created, if the number of days violates the hard constraint, the program will backtrack the exam list. When all the exams have been allocated without hard constraint violation, a feasible solution will be recorded. In order to find out all the feasible solutions that the proposed CP can come out with, this research will fully backtrack each exam in the exam list even a feasible solution is found. All the feasible solutions will be filtered by the soft constraint. Also, after an exam list is completely backtracked, the list will be arranged to form a new array by the way of moving the first element of the list to the end with the purpose to evenly expose each element in each variable selection phase. When every rearrangement is finished, in other words, the last element of the original list has reached the first position of the array, the program terminates.

To compare with CP, the proposed ABC approach uses Sample A in Table 4, which has the smallest population and iterations. The same university dataset in Sect. 5.1 is used in the experiment. The comparative items include the number of feasible solutions found, the elapsed time for seeking the first feasible solution, the number of days the solution uses to allocate all the exams, the time of the program execution, and the soft constraint violations. The comparison results are presented in Table 6. As CP selects exam units sequentially, its experimental results are almost the same in each execution, Table 6 lists only one set of CP results. On the contrary, ABC generates solutions randomly and outputs results differently in each execution. Therefore, this comparison study tests ABC ten times and lists the best and the average results respectively. Since in this comparison, the ABC is re-run, its results are slightly different from Table 5.

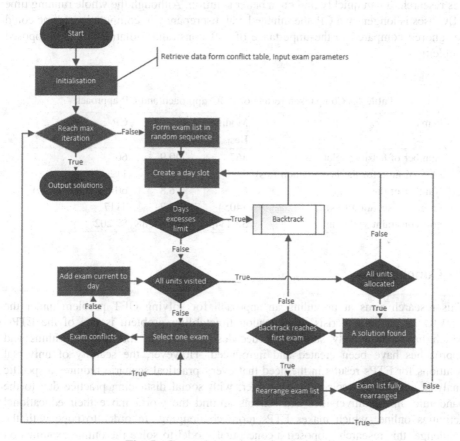

Fig. 5. Constraint programming flowchart

From Table 6 the following findings are observed.

- ABC can find out much more solutions than CP does. The number of solutions ABC found is 5.68 times more than the number of solutions CP did (340.9 compares to 60).
- ABC is 27.3 times faster than CP in finding the first feasible solutions (4.1 ms compares to 112 ms)

- ABC and CP are competitive in getting the best solution in the number of days used.
- ABC consumes a longer time than CP to complete the program execution. (74054 ms compares to 4117 ms).
- ABC approach has achieved a less soft constraint violation than the CP approach 2.35 times (37.84188 compares to 87.202). This indicates the applied ABC approach can even the examination density in the whole exam period.

Overall, the modified ABC algorithm can provide better results than CP method in this research. It can quickly find out a better solution. Although the whole running time ABC uses is longer than CP, the minute level discrepancy in computational time could be ignored compared to the importance of soft constraint violation for the proposed problem.

Table 6. Comparison results of ABC approach and CP approach

Items	Modified ABC		CP
	Best	Average	
Number of feasible solutions	467	340.9	60
Elapsed time for the first solution (ms)	3	4.1	112
Number of days	6	6.8	6(best)/6.8(average)
Program execution (ms)	74054	75613.2	4117
Soft constraint violation	32.4345	37.84188	87.202

7   Conclusions

This research aims at providing an approach for solving OET problem under the COVID-19 pandemic crisis. Examination timetabling problem is one of the ETPs, which has been widely studied for decades and therein multiple algorithms and approaches have been created and introduced. However, the scarcity of universal solutions for ETPs results in the need that every practical scenario requires a specific analysis and method selection. Moreover, with social distancing practice due to the pandemic, many universities and schools around the world move their educational activities online, which makes ETPs more challenging. In order to cope with the challenge, this research proposed a conceptual model to solve the online examination timetabling problems along with a conflict table constructed to handle the hard constraint. A modified Artificial Bee Colony algorithm was proposed to solve the OET problems. The proposed approach possesses multiple merits: 1) the conflict table proposed converts big volume raw data to be a shrunk search space; 2) the modified ABC algorithm changes neighbour search process to avoid over-exploration; 3) introducing MAX_EXPOITATION parameter lest overexploitation. The experimental result shows the proposed algorithm can effectively solve OET problems with several advantages: 1) quickness, the algorithm can reach a feasible solution in 4.1 ms on average, which is 27.3 times faster than CP does. 2) effectiveness, the algorithm provides feasible solutions 7.7 times larger than CP in solution volume. 3) reasonableness, the algorithm is able to gain more reasonable solutions in soft constraint violations, 2.3 times over CP.

The research can be applied to post-pandemic education as long as the examination is conducted online. The future works include more algorithm evaluation comparing with other evolutionary algorithms and extending the model to other educational timetabling problems such as school timetabling.

Acknowledgment. The authors would like to acknowledge CQUniversity to give permission to use the de-identified student enrolment data for the research.

References

1. Schaerf, A.: A survey of automated timetabling. Artif. Intell. Rev. **13**(2), 87–127 (1999). https://doi.org/10.1023/A:1006576209967
2. Wren, A.: Scheduling, timetabling and rostering—a special relationship? In: Burke, E., Ross, P. (eds.) Practice and Theory of Automated Timetabling. LNCS, vol. 1153, pp. 46–75. Springer, Heidelberg (1996). https://doi.org/10.1007/3-540-61794-9_51
3. Babaei, H., Karimpour, J., Hadidi, A.: A survey of approaches for university course timetabling problem. Comput. Ind. Eng. **86**, 43–59 (2015)
4. Burke, E., Kendall, G., Newall, J., Hart, E., Ross, P., Schulenburg, S.: Hyper-heuristics: an emerging direction in modern search technology. In: Glover, F., Kochenberger, G.A. (eds.) Handbook of Metaheuristics. ISOR, vol. 57, pp. 457–474. Springer, Boston (2003). https://doi.org/10.1007/0-306-48056-5_16
5. Zhu, K., Li, L., Li, M.: A survey of computational intelligence in educational timetabling. Int. J. Mach. Learn. Comput. **11**(1), 40–47 (2021)
6. Appleby, J., Blake, D., Newman, E.: Techniques for producing school timetables on a computer and their application to other scheduling problems. Comput. J. **3**(4), 237–245 (1961)
7. Song, T., Liu, S., Tang, X., Peng, X., Chen, M.: An iterated local search algorithm for the University Course Timetabling Problem. Appl. Soft Comput. **68**, 597–608 (2018)
8. Arbaoui, T., Boufflet, J., Moukrim, A.: Lower bounds and compact mathematical formulations for spacing soft constraints for university examination timetabling problems. Comput. Oper. Res. **106**, 133–142 (2019)
9. Kahar, M., Bakar, S., Shing, L., Mandal, A.: Solving kolej poly-tech mara examination timetabling problem. Adv. Sci. Lett. **24**(10), 7577–7581 (2018)
10. Valouxis, C., Gogos, C., Alefragis, P., Housos E.: Decomposing the high school timetable problem. In: Practice and Theory of Automated Timetabling (PATAT 2012), Son, Norway (2012)
11. Junn, K.Y., Obit, J.H., Alfred, R.: The study of genetic algorithm approach to solving university course timetabling problem. In: Alfred, R., Iida, H., Ag, A.A., Ibrahim, Y.L. (eds.) Computational Science and Technology. LNEE, vol. 488, pp. 454–463. Springer, Singapore (2018). https://doi.org/10.1007/978-981-10-8276-4_43
12. Jamili, A., Hamid, M., Gharoun, H., Khoshnoudi, R.: Developing a comprehensive and multi-objective mathematical model for university course timetabling problem: a real case study. In: Conference: Proceedings of the International Conference on Industrial Engineering and Operations Management, Paris, France (2018)

13. Skoullis, V., Tassopoulos, I., Beligiannis, G.: Solving the high school timetabling problem using a hybrid cat swarm optimization based algorithm. Appl. Soft Comput. **52**, 277–289 (2017)
14. Dorneles, Á., de Araújo, O.C., Buriol, L.: A column generation approach to high school timetabling modeled as a multicommodity flow problem. Eur. J. Oper. Res. **256**(3), 685–695 (2017)
15. Tassopoulos, I., Iliopoulou, C., Beligiannis, G.: Solving the Greek school timetabling problem by a mixed integer programming model. J. Oper. Res. Soc. **71**(1), 117–132 (2020)
16. Leite, N., Melício, F., Rosa, A.: A fast simulated annealing algorithm for the examination timetabling problem. Expert Syst. Appl. **122**, 137–151 (2019)
17. June, T.L., Obit, J.H., Leau, Y.B., Bolongkikit, J.: Implementation of constraint programming and simulated annealing for examination timetabling problem. In: Alfred, R., Lim, Y., Ibrahim, A., Anthony, P. (eds.) Computational Science and Technology. LNEE, vol. 481, pp. 175–184. Springer, Singapore (2019). https://doi.org/10.1007/978-981-13-2622-6_18
18. Güler, M., Geçici, E.: A spreadsheet-based decision support system for examination timetabling. Turk. J. Electr. Eng. Comput. Sci. **28**(3), 1584–1598 (2020)
19. Aldeeb, B., Al-Betar, A., Abdelmajeed, A., Younes, M., AlKenani, M., Alomoush, W.: A comprehensive review of uncapacitated university examination timetabling problem. Int. J. Appl. Eng. Res. **14**(24), 4524–4547 (2019)
20. Kaur, M., Saini, S.: A review of metaheuristic techniques for solving university course timetabling problem. In: Goar, V., Kuri, M., Kumar, R., Senjyu, T. (eds.) Advances in Information Communication Technology and Computing. LNNS, vol. 135, pp. 19–25. Springer, Singapore (2021). https://doi.org/10.1007/978-981-15-5421-6_3
21. Tan, J., Goh, S., Kendall, G., Sabar, N.: A survey of the state-of-the-art of optimisation methodologies in school timetabling problems. Expert Syst. Appl. **165**, 113943 (2021)
22. Memeti, S., Pllana, S., Binotto, A., Kołodziej, J., Brandic, I.: Using meta-heuristics and machine learning for software optimization of parallel computing systems: a systematic literature review. Computing **101**(8), 893–936 (2018). https://doi.org/10.1007/s00607-018-0614-9
23. Salhi, S.: Heuristic Search: The Emerging Science of Problem Solving. Springer, Cham (2017). https://doi.org/10.1007/978-3-319-49355-8
24. Gandomi, A., Yang, X., Talatahari, S., Alavi, A.: Metaheuristic algorithms in modeling and optimization. In: Metaheuristic Applications in Structures and Infrastructures, pp. 1–24 (2013)
25. Kim, J., Yang, H.: Effects of heuristic type on purchase intention in mobile social commerce: focusing on the mediating effect of shopping value. J. Distrib. Sci. **17**(10), 73–81 (2019)
26. Pillay, N., Rong, Q.: Hyper-Heuristics: Theory and Applications. Springer, Cham (2018)
27. Kouhbanani, S., Farid, D., Sadeghi, H.: Selection of optimal portfolio using expert system in mamdani fuzzy environment. Ind. Manag. Stud. **16**(48), 131–151 (2018)
28. Bělohlávek, R., Dauben, J., Klir, G.: Fuzzy Logic and Mathematics: A Historical Perspective. Oxford University Press, Oxford (2017)
29. Junn, K.Y., Obit, J.H., Alfred, R., Bolongkikit, J.: A formal model of multi-agent system for university course timetabling problems. In: Alfred, R., Lim, Y., Ibrahim, A., Anthony, P. (eds.) Computational Science and Technology. LNEE, vol. 481, pp. 215–225. Springer, Singapore (2019). https://doi.org/10.1007/978-981-13-2622-6_22
30. Soria-Alcaraz, J.A., et al.: Effective learning hyper-heuristics for the course timetabling problem. Eur. J. Oper. Res. **238**(1), 77–86 (2014)

31. Soria-Alcaraz, J., Ochoa, G., Swan, J., Carpio, M., Puga, H., Burke, E.: Iterated local search using an add and delete hyper-heuristic for university course timetabling. Appl. Soft Comput. **40**, 581–593 (2016)
32. Kheiri, A., Keedwell, M.: A hidden Markov model approach to the problem of heuristic selection in hyper-heuristics with a case study in high school timetabling problems. Evol. Comput. **25**(3), 473–501 (2017)
33. Kasm, O., Mohandes, B., Diabat, A., Khatib, S.: Exam timetabling with allowable conflicts within a time window. Comput. Ind. Eng. **127**, 263–273 (2019)
34. Bolaji, A., Khader, A., Al-Betar, M., Awadallah, M.: University course timetabling using hybridized artificial bee colony with hill climbing optimizer. J. Comput. Sci. **5**(5), 809–818 (2014)
35. Akkan, C., Gülcü, A.: A bi-criteria hybrid Genetic Algorithm with robustness objective for the course timetabling problem. Comput. Oper. Res. **90**, 22–32 (2018)
36. Sutar, S., Bichkar, R.: High school timetabling using tabu search and partial feasibility preserving genetic algorithm. Int. J. Adv. Eng. Technol. **10**(3), 421 (2017)
37. Bolaji, A., Khader, A., Al-Betar, M., Awadallah, M.: A hybrid nature-inspired artificial bee colony algorithm for uncapacitated examination timetabling problems. J. Intell. Syst. **24**(1), 37–54 (2015)
38. Fong, C., Asmuni, H., McCollum, B.: A hybrid swarm-based approach to university timetabling. IEEE Trans. Evol. Comput. **19**(6), 870–884 (2015)
39. Pappis, C.P., Siettos, C.I.: Fuzzy reasoning. In: Burke, E.K., Kendall, G. (eds.) Search Methodologies, pp. 437–474. Springer, Boston (2005). https://doi.org/10.1007/0-387-28356-0_15
40. June, T.L., Obit, J.H., Leau, Y.-B., Bolongkikit, J., Alfred, R.: Sequential constructive algorithm incorporate with fuzzy logic for solving real world course timetabling problem. In: Alfred, R., Lim, Y., Haviluddin, H., On, C.K. (eds.) Computational Science and Technology. LNEE, vol. 603, pp. 257–267. Springer, Singapore (2020). https://doi.org/10.1007/978-981-15-0058-9_25
41. Babaei, H., Karimpour, J., Hadidi, A.: Generating an optimal timetabling for multi-departments common lecturers using hybrid fuzzy and clustering algorithms. Soft. Comput. **23**(13), 4735–4747 (2018). https://doi.org/10.1007/s00500-018-3126-9
42. Cavdur, F., Kose, M.: A fuzzy logic and binary-goal programming-based approach for solving the exam timetabling problem to create a balanced-exam schedule. Int. J. Fuzzy Syst. **18**(1), 119–129 (2015). https://doi.org/10.1007/s40815-015-0046-z
43. Tkaczyk, R., Ganzha, M., Paprzycki, M.: AgentPlanner-agent-based timetabling system. Informatica **40**(1) (2016)
44. Karaboga, D.: An idea based on honey bee swarm for numerical optimization. Technical report-TR06, Erciyes university, Engineering Faculty, Computer (2005)
45. Bukchin, Y., Raviv, T.: Constraint programming for solving various assembly line balancing problems. Omega **78**, 57–68 (2018)

A Topology-Aware Scheduling Strategy for Distributed Stream Computing System

Bo Li[1], Dawei Sun[1(✉)], Vinh Loi Chau[2], and Rajkumar Buyya[3]

[1] School of Information Engineering, China University of Geosciences,
Beijing 100083, People's Republic of China
{libocn,sundaweicn}@cugb.edu.cn
[2] School of Information Technology, Deakin University,
Geelong, VIC 3216, Australia
vlchau@deakin.edu.au
[3] Cloud Computing and Distributed Systems (CLOUDS) Laboratory,
School of Computing and Information Systems, The University of Melbourne,
Parkville, Australia
rbuyya@unimelb.edu.au

Abstract. Reducing latency has become the focus of task scheduling research in distributed big data stream computing systems. Currently, most task schedulers in big data stream computing systems mainly focus on tasks assignment and implicitly ignore task topology which can have significant impact on the latency and energy efficiency. This paper proposes a topology-aware scheduling strategy to reduce the processing latency of stream processing systems. We construct the data stream graph as a directed acyclic graph and then, divide it using the graph Laplace algorithm. On the divided graph, tasks will be assigned with a low-latency scheduling strategy. We also provide a computing node selection strategy, which enables the system to run tasks on the topology with the least number of computing nodes. Based on this scheduling strategy, the tasks of the data stream graph can be redistributed and the scheduling mechanism can be optimized to minimize the system latency. The experimental results demonstrate the efficiency and effectiveness of the proposed strategy.

Keywords: Stream computing · Big data system · Topology-aware · Scheduling · Graph division

1 Introduction

With the increase in demand for real-time data processing especially in streaming applications, timeliness of data has become prominent with the rising number of applications deployed in streaming computing platforms across various fields such as finance and banking [1, 2], intelligent recommendation system [3], and Internet of Things [4]. Currently, many big data streaming solutions have been provided [1, 5], such as Storm, Flink, Spark Streaming, etc. Storm is one of the most popular open source big data stream computing systems [7]. It provides powerful distributed cluster management, millisecond latency, rich APIs and high fault tolerance mechanisms, and is widely used in the field of real-time data processing [8].

© ICST Institute for Computer Sciences, Social Informatics and Telecommunications Engineering 2022
Published by Springer Nature Switzerland AG 2022. All Rights Reserved
W. Xiang et al. (Eds.): BROADNETS 2021, LNICST 413, pp. 132–147, 2022.
https://doi.org/10.1007/978-3-030-93479-8_8

Storm's stream processing can be viewed as a directed acyclic graph (DAG) topology [5]. Stream is an abstraction of data transmission between different vertices. It is an unbounded sequence of tuples in time. Storm has two types of vertices: Spout and Bolt. Spout is the source representing the Stream and is responsible for emitting Streams from a specific data source of the topology. Bolt can receive any number of streams as input and then process the data. Bolt can also emit new streams to the downstream Bolt for processing.

System latency and system throughput are important metrics to measure the performance of a stream computing system [7–9]. Therefore, reducing system latency and improving system throughput are the major challenges for task schedulers. Task scheduling for stream computing systems is an effective way to achieve these goals. If tasks are assigned based on the transfer rate between them and the computing resources on the compute nodes, system latency and system throughput can be significantly improved.

The topology-aware scheduling policy is able to place tasks on the appropriate compute nodes based on the structure of the topology. To achieve this goal, we first need to construct DAGs and divide them rationally, and assign tasks to as few compute nodes as possible.

1.1 Contributions

In this paper, our primary focus is to reduce the time delay of distributed stream processing systems. Our contributions are as follows:

(1) We established the DAG model, and a graph partitioning method based on graph Laplacian which can be used to create high-quality partitioning results quickly and efficiently.
(2) Based on the partitioning results, tasks are allocated using a low-latency scheduling strategy. We then proposed a computing node selection strategy to run tasks on the topology with the least number of nodes. We named this approach Ts-Stream.
(3) We conducted experiments to evaluate system performance using time delay as a metric. The experiments demonstrated the effectiveness of our proposed strategy.

1.2 Paper Organization

The rest of the paper is organized as follows. Section 2 will explain DAG model and communication model. In Sect. 3, the graph partitioning method based on graph Laplacian and the Ts-Stream scheduling strategy are introduced. Section 4 dictates the experiment set up and report the evaluation results. Section 5, summarizes related studies on the scheduling problem. Finally, conclusions and future works are presented in Sect. 6.

2   Related Work

Computational models of Big Data can be divided into batch computing and streaming computing [10]. Batch computing are suitable for different big data application scenarios when data is first stored for computation and the real-time requirements are not a priority. Streaming computing is more suitable for the application scenarios that have strict real-time requirements and do not need to store data first [11].

At the time this work is conducted, researches related to large data batch processing and calculation is relatively mature, forming an efficient and stable batch computing system represented by Google's MapReduce programming model and the opensource Hadoop computing system [6, 12].

In streaming computing, it is impossible to determine the moment of arrival and the order of arrival of data, and it is also impossible to store all the data [13]. Many solutions have been proposed to solve this problem. Yahoo launched S4 Streaming Processing Computing System in 2010 [14], Twitter launched Storm Streaming Computing System in 2011 [5], and Flink originated from a research project called Stratosphere [4]. Storm, S4 and Flink have typical streaming data computing architecture, where data is computed in task topology and outputs valuable information, which has largely driven the development and application of big data streaming computing technology.

Scheduling problem of streaming applications is an active research area [16].

In [17], a Storm-based resource-aware scheduling policy, R-Storm, was proposed. R-Storm considers resource constraints in three main aspects: CPU, memory, and bandwidth. It focuses on memory constraints and considers CPU and network bandwidth constraints as soft constraints.

In [18], a dynamic resource scheduling DRS is proposed to meet the estimation of necessary resources required for real-time demand, effective and efficient re-resource provisioning and scheduling, and effective implementation of such scheduler in cloud-based DSMS.

In [19], a stream computing system T-Storm was proposed. T-Storm monitors data traffic and CPU load changes of each worker node in real time through an external plug-in to achieve fine-grained control and optimized resource usage of the worker nodes.

Thread-level task migration is also an important research direction for task scheduling. In [20], a thread-level task migration N-Storm is proposed, which can perform thread-level task migration without stopping the Storm, avoiding the time wastage due to unnecessary Executor and worker stops and restarts.

The detailed division of the topology is also an important direction to reduce the system delay. In [21], an adaptive hierarchical scheduling P-Scheduler was proposed, which reduces the system latency by dividing the topological graph using the open source graph partitioning software METIS and then dividing the tasks with tightly transmitted data among the same compute nodes after two levels of scheduling.

Ensuring that the system latency is in a reasonable range is also an important direction. In [22], the task assignment problem with delay guarantee (TAPLG) is introduced and two heuristic algorithms, AHA and PHA, are proposed, while considering the critical path of the topology to reduce the latency of the stream topology and reduce the energy consumption.

The above task scheduling works on Storm rarely considers the structure of the topology map. In this work, we proposed Ts-Stream strategy uses the graph Laplacian algorithm to quickly divide the task graph, and uses fewer computing nodes to run the topology, reducing the system latency of the system. The summary of the comparison between our work and other closely related works is given in Table 1.

Table 1. Comparison of Ts-Stream and related work

Parameter	Related work					Ts-Stream
	[17]	[18]	[19]	[20]	[21]	
Task scheduling	✓	✓	✓	✓	✓	✓
Communication saving	✓	✓	✓	✗	✗	✓
Latency saving	✓	✗	✓	✓	✓	✓
Topology aware	✗	✗	✗	✗	✗	✓
Graph partition	✗	✗	✗	✗	✓	✓

3   Problem Statement

This section introduces DAG model and communication model in big data stream computing environments.

3.1   DAG Model

The big data stream processing process can be represented by DAG, in which a vertex represents a Spout or a Bolt, and a directed edge between two vertices forms a Stream between them. Stream is an infinite sequence of tuples and can be considered as an abstraction of data communication between components (Spout or Bolt). A DAG can be represented as $G = (V, E)$, where $V = \{v_1, v_2, \ldots, v_n\}$ represents a finite set of n vertices and $E = \{e_{1,2}, e_{1,3}, \ldots, e_{n-i,n}\}$, $i \in \{1, 2, \ldots, n\}$ is a finite set of directed edges. The Spout component acts as a data source to send tuples to the topology, while Bolt implements the processing of data by the topology and passes the results to the downstream components. Each component can execute multiple tasks to increase the parallelism of the topology.

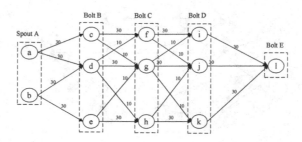

Fig. 1. A topology of storm

Figure 1 shows a topology with five components including one Spout and four Bolts. The number of vertices in each component is also the number of instances of the component.

We define r_{ij} as the transfer rate of tuples between two adjacent vertices, which is the number of tuples sent from v_i to v_j per unit time. Since the arrival rate of the data stream changes, when the data stream fluctuates greatly at a certain moment, if this value is taken at this point in time, the accuracy of the entire DAG will be affected. In order to avoid the effect of violent fluctuations in the data stream at a specific point in time, we take the mathematical expectation E_r of all r_{ij} in the statistical time as the data transfer rate between two vertices.

$$E_r = \frac{1}{n} \sum_{i=1}^{n} r_{ij}, \tag{1}$$

In term of resources required for a task, we only consider CPU to focus more on the scheduling issue. However, the proposed solution can be applied for other types of resources including memory and bandwidth. We denote R_{C_v} as the total amount of resources to be consumed by the whole topology and it can be represented by (2).

$$R_{C_v} = \sum_{i=1}^{n} R_{C_{v_i}}, \tag{2}$$

where $R_{C_{v_i}}$ is the CPU resources consumed by a task.

3.2   Communication Model

In a stream computing system, there are three types of communications causing the overhead problem: processes between compute nodes, processes within a compute node and threads within a process.

Processes between compute nodes usually have higher communication overhead than processes within a compute node. These first two type of communication overheads are more significant than the third type which happens between threads in a process [17]. Therefore, in this research, we will ignore the inter-threads communication and focus on solving the top two types.

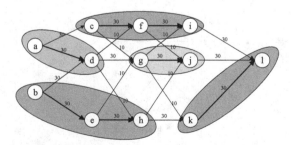

Fig. 2. Task assignment

As shown in Fig. 2, placing adjacent nodes with high communication rates in the same process or computing node can effectively reduce communication delays. $P = \{p_1, p_2, \ldots, p_u\}$ is used to denote the compute nodes in the cluster. The amount of data transfer between compute nodes in the cluster dtv_P is denoted by (3).

$$dtv_P = \sum_{i=1}^{u} \sum_{j=1}^{u} dtv(p_i, p_j), i < j, \tag{3}$$

subjected to

$$dtv(p_i, p_j) = \begin{cases} 0 & \text{no data transmission between } p_i \text{ and } p_j, \\ E_r \cdot q & \text{otherwise}, \end{cases} \tag{4}$$

where $dtv(p_i, p_j)$ denotes the data transfer rate between p_i and p_j, and q denotes the number of task pairs communicated between p_i and p_j.

Use $W = \{w_1, w_2, \ldots, w_h\}$ to denote the processes within the same compute node, and its total data transfer dtv_W is denoted by (5).

$$dtv_W = \sum_{i=1}^{h} \sum_{j=1}^{h} dtv(w_i, w_j), i < j, \tag{5}$$

subjected to

$$dtv(w_i, w_j) = \begin{cases} 0 & \text{no data transmission between } w_i \text{ and } w_j, \\ E_r \cdot a & \text{otherwise}, \end{cases} \tag{6}$$

where $dtv(w_i, w_j)$ denotes the data transfer rate between w_i and w_j, and a denotes the number of task pairs communicated between w_i and w_j.

dtv_S denotes the total data transmission and will be calculated as follows.

$$dtv_S = dtv_P + dtv_W, \tag{7}$$

If we can minimize the amount of data transferred between compute nodes and between processes, we can largely reduce the communication overhead of the system and reduce the system latency.

$$Min(S_{cd}) \Leftrightarrow Min(dtv_S), \tag{8}$$

where S_{cd} represents the system communication delay.

Therefore, we can reduce dtv_P by assigning tasks to as few compute nodes as possible. In the selection of compute nodes, compute nodes are selected in descending order for task assignment based on the amount of available CPU resources in the compute nodes. This approach allows a single compute node to accommodate more tasks, and in addition to further reducing the amount of data transfer between compute nodes, it also reduces system energy consumption by shutting down and hibernating idle compute nodes.

4 Ts-Stream Overview

Ts-Stream is a task scheduling strategy based on topology awareness. It is used to reduce the latency and energy consumption of distributed stream computing systems. This section focuses on a detailed discussion of Ts-Stream, including its system architecture, graph Laplacian-based graph partitioning approach, and task assignment strategy.

4.1 System Architecture

The Ts-Stream system adds a monitoring module, a database module, and a Ts-Stream scheduling generation module to the Storm system architecture, as shown in Fig. 3. The monitoring module regularly collects information from the system, such as the data transfer rate between executors, the load of executors and the load of worker nodes, and then stores them in the database. The Ts-Stream module reads this information from the database, first divides the different sub-topological graphs through the graph partitioning algorithm, and then generates a new schedule and delivers it to the Nimbus master node. To deploy our proposed task scheduling strategy, IScheduler will be implemented as an interface in Storm's custom scheduler.

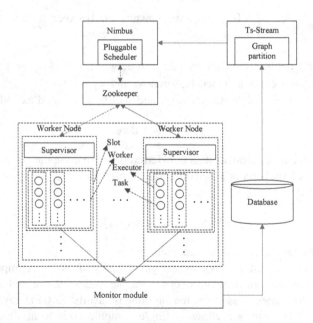

Fig. 3. Ts-Stream topology

In a distributed stream computing environment, the data stream rate and the load of the computing node are constantly changing. Moreover, due to the existence of a fault-tolerant mechanism, tasks may be restarted on other computing nodes. The existence of these problems will affect the performance of the system, so dynamic adaptive scheduling is essential. Ts-Stream will periodically check the operating status of the system. When the system is in a high-latency state for a long time or the remaining capacity of the computing node exceeds the threshold, it will generate a new schedule based on the topology information at this time.

4.2 Graph Division

Graph partitioning is used to divide the graph into two or k subgraphs to minimize the weights of the edges connecting different subgraphs and maximize the weights of the edges within the same subgraph. However, minimizing the value of cut edges can lead to some bad partitions, such as the partitioning of the topological graph into 1 vertex and $n - 1$ vertices in Fig. 4(a). In order to achieve a good partitioning as in Fig. 4(b), we can adjust the objective function, while making the sum of the edge weights in each part of the divided subgraphs as large as possible, the sum of the edge weights among the subgraphs is as small as possible. Using the Laplacian matrix, such segmentation results can be obtained simply and effectively.

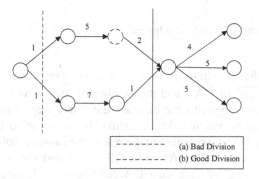

Fig. 4. Two different graph division results

In the graph partitioning phase, a graph partitioning method is described in Algorithm 1.

Algorithm 1: Graph partitioning algorithm based on graph Laplacian.

1.   **Input**: $E = \{e_{1,2}, e_{1,3}, \ldots, e_{n-i,n}\}, i \in \{1, 2, \ldots, n\}, k$.

2.   **Output**: k subgraphs after division, weights of cut edges.

3.   **for** M **do**

4. $m_{ij} = e_{ij}$

5.   **end for**

6.   **for** D **do**

7.   **if** $i = j$ **do**

8. $$d_{ij} = \sum_{j=0}^{n-1} m_{ij}$$

9.   **else**

10. $d_{ij} = 0$

11.   **end if**

12. **end for**

13. Calculate the eigenvalues and eigenvectors of L, Λ and Z_{nk}

14. $Z_{nk} = [y_1, y_2, \ldots, y_n]' \leftarrow Z_{nk} = [z_1, z_2, \ldots, z_k]$

15. **for** y_i **do**

16.   Perform k-means clustering on y_i'

17. $class(y_i) \leftarrow class(y_i')$

18. **end for**

19. **return** k subgraphs and cut edge value.

The input of the algorithm includes the edge weight set $E = \{e_{1,2}, e_{1,3}, \ldots, e_{n-i,n}\}$, $i \in \{1, 2, \ldots, n\}$ of DAG and the number of subgraphs k to be divided. The output is the divided k subgraphs and the cut edge value. Steps 2 to 14 are to generate the adjacency matrix M and the degree matrix D according to the weights of the directed edges of the DAG. According to the result, the Laplace matrix L is solved, and the first k minimum eigenvalues $\Lambda = \{\lambda_1, \lambda_2, \ldots, \lambda_n\}$ and the corresponding eigenvector $Z_{nk} = [z_1, z_2, \ldots, z_k]$ of L are solved. According to the Rayleigh-Ritz theory [23], k-means clustering is performed on the row vectors of the matrix composed of eigenvectors, and the results are mapped to the original graph to complete the division of DAG.

With this graph division method, adjacent tasks with high transmission rates can be allocated into the same node, and the amount of data transmission between computing nodes and between processes can be reduced, thereby realizing low-latency processing of the system.

4.3   Algorithm Description of Ts-Stream

In the task assignment phase, we propose a topology-aware task allocation strategy described in Algorithm 2.

Algorithm 2: Topology-aware task scheduling strategy.

1.   **Input:**   , and C_{cn}
2.   **Output**: data stream task scheduling based on topology awareness.
3. $V = \{v_1, v_2, \ldots, v_n\}$
4. $E = \{e_{1,2}, e_{1,3}, \ldots, e_{n-i,n}\ , i \in 1, 2, \ldots, n$
5. $G = \{G_1, G_2, \ldots, G_k \ \leftarrow G = \ V, E)$
6.   Arrange C_{cn} in descending order.
7.   **If** DAG $G = null \parallel C_n = null$ **then**
8.   **return** null;
9.   **end if**
10. **while** DAG $G! = null$ **do**
11.   Create a collection G_{ub};
12.   **for** $C_{cn_{max}}$ **do**
13.   Add the two subgraphs connected by the cut edge with the largest current weight to G_{ub};
14.   **while** $C_{G_{rub}}$ $C_{cn_{max}}$ **do**
15.   Add to G the subgraph with the largest weight of the edge connected to G_{ub};
16.   **end while**
17. $C_{cn_{max}} \leftarrow C_{G_{ub}}$;
18.   **end for**
19. $G = null$;
20. **end while**
21. **return** topology-aware task scheduling

First, the data transfer rate between tasks is collected by the monitoring module to construct a DAG. Although there can be multiple tasks on an executor, in our experiments, there is only one task on an executor by default. Then submit the DAG and the parameter k of the number of subgraphs that need to be divided to the graph partitioning module. Where k by (9).

$$k = \frac{n}{w_e}, \tag{9}$$

where w_e takes the value of the number of executors in the worker.

The graph segmentation module divides the DAG into k parts and arranges all the cut edges in descending order according to the cut edge weights. The working nodes are also arranged in the order of capacity from largest to smallest. First, the two subgraphs connected by the edge with the largest weight are selected and put into the first working node, and then the subgraphs connected by the edge with the largest weight of its adjacent edges are also assigned to this working node until this working node reaches the set threshold C_a. The value of C_a by (10).

$$C_a = C_{cn} \cdot \alpha, \tag{10}$$

where C_{cn} is the available computational resources of the node and alpha is factor for resource utilization (set to 0.7 by default).

Then the subgraphs are assigned to other compute nodes in turn until all subgraphs are assigned. This allows the allocation to be done using the least number of compute nodes, and the rest of the nodes are dormant or shut down, which has resulted in energy saving. This also reduces the cross-node communication and reduces the system latency.

5   Performance Evaluation

In this section, we evaluate our Ts-Stream system. We first discuss the experimental environment and parameter settings, and then analyze the performance results.

5.1   Experimental Environment and Parameter Setup

Our proposed Ts-Stream system is developed based on Storm 2.1.0 and installed on CentOS 6.8. This cluster has 9 nodes, where 1 node is designed as a Nimbus node, 2 nodes are designed as Zookeeper nodes and the remaining 6 nodes are designed as Supervisor nodes. The Nimbus node uses DELL's R410, equipped with 12 Intel(R) Xeon(R) CPU X5650 @ 2.67 GHz 6-core processors and 12 GB of memory. Zookeeper nodes and Supervisor nodes are virtual machines, equipped with 2 Intel(R) Xeon(R) CPU X5650 @ 2.67 GHz 2-core processors and 4 GB of RAM. Each machine uses Storm 2.1.0 as the base system and is coordinated by Zookeeper 3.4.14. The software configuration of the Ts-Stream platform is shown in Table 2.

Table 2. Software configuration of the Ts-Stream

Software	Version
OS	CentOS 6.8 64bit
Storm	apache-storm-2.1.0
JDK	jdk1.8 64bit
Zookeeper	zookeeper-3.4.14
Python	python 2.7.2
Maven	Maven 3.6.2
MySQL	MySQL-5.1.73

We evaluate the system latency and system throughput by running WordCount and Top-N task topology. The task topology of WordCount and Top-N is shown in Fig. 5.

5.2   Performance Results

The experimental setting contains two evaluation parameters: system latency and system throughput.

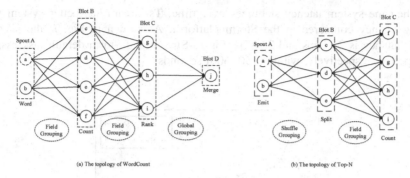

(a) The topology of WordCount   (b) The topology of Top-N

Fig. 5. The topology of WordCount and Top-N

(1) System latency

An important feature of stream computing systems is that they can process data in real time, so system latency is an important evaluation criterion. System latency is considered acceptable to users if it can be kept at the millisecond level. The lower the system latency, the better the real-time performance of the stream computing system. In Storm platform, the system latency can be obtained through Storm UI. We compare Ts-Stream with Storm's default scheduler. The processing latency metric is measured periodically over a period of 600 s.

In the WordCount experiment, the processing latency of the system fluctuated over time, but Ts-Stream's processing latency was lower than the default task policy of the Storm platform. As shown in Fig. 6, the processing latency of the TS-Stream policy and the default Storm policy are 1.91 ms and 2.72 ms, respectively. It is clear that the average system latency of Ts-Stream is smaller than the default Storm policy when the system is stable.

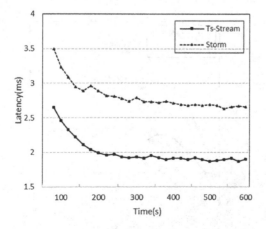

Fig. 6. System latency for running WordCount

When the system latency stabilizes over time, Ts-Stream has better system processing latency compared to the Storm platform. As shown in Fig. 7, the average system latency is 2.31 ms and 2.98 ms for Ts-Stream and Storm default task assignment policy, respectively, within [150, 600] seconds.

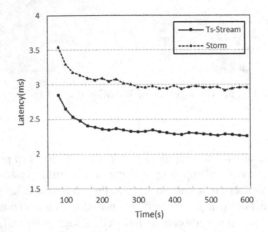

Fig. 7. System latency for running Top-N

(2) System throughput

System throughput reflects the system's ability to process data, which is estimated in terms of the number of tuples output by the DAG per second. The higher the system throughput, the better the stream computing system is able to process the data. In this set of experiments, we set the input rate of the data stream to 1000 tuples/s. The processing latency metric is measured periodically over 600 s.

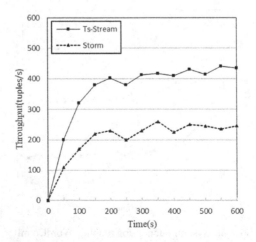

Fig. 8. System throughput for running WordCount

When the data transfer rate is kept stable, Ts-Stream has higher system throughput compared to the default Storm policy. As shown in Fig. 8, when the rate is set to 1000 tuples/s, the average system throughput of Ts-Stream and the default Storm policy during the stabilization phase is distributed as 412 tuples/s and 234 tuples/s. The average throughput of Ts-Stream proves to be higher than that of the default Strom policy.

As shown in Fig. 9, Ts-Stream has higher system throughput compared to the default policy of Storm when running the task topology of Top-N. During the stabilization phase of both policies, the average throughput of Ts-Stream and Storm's default policy are 405 tuples/s and 222 tuples/s, respectively.

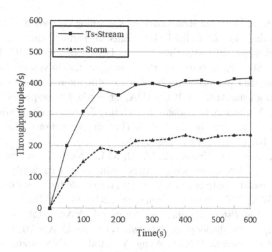

Fig. 9. System throughput for running Top-N

6   Conclusions and Future Work

We proposed a topology-aware task scheduling policy Ts-Stream. It uses a graph partitioning algorithm based on graph Laplacian to partition the task topology graph into k subgraphs with higher internal task communication. In the task scheduling phase, it minimizes the number of turned-on nodes by assigning tasks to the compute nodes with the highest capacity. Experimental results show that Ts-Stream performs significantly better than Storm's default scheduling, reducing system latency and improving throughput.

As part of future work, we will focus on the following areas:

(1) Consider other system resource constraints combined with the state of DAG vertices to further reduce the delay of the distributed stream computing system.

(2) Deploy Ts-Stream in the actual big data stream computing environment, such as intelligent recommendation system, real-time stock market analysis, embedded advertising and other scenarios.

Acknowledgements. This work is supported by the National Natural Science Foundation of China under Grant No. 61972364; the Fundamental Research Funds for the Central Universities under Grant No. 2652021001; and Melbourne-Chindia Cloud Computing (MC3) Research Network.

References

1. Chintapalli, S., Dagit, D., et al.: Benchmarking streaming computation engines: storm, flink and spark streaming. In: 2016 IEEE International Parallel and Distributed Processing Symposium Workshops, IPDPSW, Chicago, IL, USA, pp. 1789–1792. IEEE (2016)
2. Shih, D., Hsu, H., Shih, P.: A study of early warning system in volume burst risk assessment of stock with big data platform. In: 2019 IEEE 4th International Conference on Cloud Computing and Big Data Analysis, ICCCBDA, Chengdu, China, pp. 244–248. IEEE (2019)
3. Kridel, D., Dolk, D., Castillo, D.: Adaptive modeling for real time analytics: the case of "Big Data" in mobile advertising. In: 2015 48th Hawaii International Conference on System Sciences, Kauai, HI, USA, pp. 887–896 (2015)
4. Sharif, A., Li, J., Khalil, M., Kumar, R., Sharif, M.I., Sharif, A.: Internet of things — smart traffic management system for smart cities using big data analytics. In: 2017 14th International Computer Conference on Wavelet Active Media Technology and Information Processing, ICCWAMTIP, Chengdu, China, pp. 281–284 (2017)
5. Storm Homepage. http://storm.apache.org/. Accessed 25 Apr 2021
6. Hadoop Homepage. http://hadoop.apache.org/. Accessed 25 Apr 2021
7. Farahabady, M.R.H., Samani, H.R.D., Wang, Y., et al.: A QoS-aware controller for apache storm. In: 2016 IEEE 15th International Symposium on Network Computing and Applications, NCA, pp. 334–342 (2016)
8. Liu, Y., Shi, X., Jin, H.: Runtime-aware adaptive scheduling in stream processing. Concurrency Comput. Pract. Experience **28**(14), 3830–3843 (2016)
9. Dongen, G., Poel, D.: Evaluation of stream processing frameworks. IEEE Trans. Parallel Distrib. Syst. **31**(8), 1845–1858 (2020)
10. Benjelloun, S., et al.: Big data processing: batch-based processing and stream-based processing. In: 2020 Fourth International Conference on Intelligent Computing in Data Sciences, ICDS, Fez, Morocco, pp. 1–6 (2020)
11. Aniello, L., Baldoni, R., Querzoni, L.: Adaptive online scheduling in storm. In Proceedings of the 7th ACM International Conference on Distributed Event-Based Systems, pp. 207–218. ACM (2013)
12. Dean, J., Ghemawat, S.: MapReduce: simplified data processing on large clusters. Commun. ACM **51**(1), 107–113 (2008)
13. Mehmood, E., Anees, T.: Challenges and solutions for processing real-time big data stream: a systematic literature review. IEEE Access **8**, 119123–119143 (2020)
14. Xhafa, F., Naranjo, V., Caballé, S.: Processing and analytics of big data streams with Yahoo! S4. In: 2015 IEEE 29th International Conference on Advanced Information Networking and Applications, Gwangju, Korea (South), pp. 263–270. IEEE (2015)

15. Liu, Y., Buyya, R.: Resource management and scheduling in distributed stream processing systems: a taxonomy, review, and future directions. ACM Comput. Surv. **53**(3), 1–41. Article No. 50. ISSN 0360-0300 (2020)
16. Govindarajan, K., Kamburugamuve, S., Wickramasinghe, P., Abeykoon, V., Fox, G.: Task scheduling in big data - review, research challenges, and prospects. In: 2017 Ninth International Conference on Advanced Computing, ICoAC, Chennai, India, pp. 165–173 (2017)
17. Peng, Y., Hosseini, M., Hong, H., Farivar, R., Campbell, R.: R-Storm: resource-aware scheduling in storm. In: Proceedings of the 16th Annual Middleware Conference, pp. 149–161. Association for Computing Machinery, New York, NY, USA (2015)
18. Fu, T., Ding, J., Ma, R., Winslett, M., Yang, Y., Zhang, Z.: DRS: dynamic resource scheduling for real-time analytics over fast streams. In: Proceedings 2015 IEEE 35th International Conference on Distributed Computing Systems, ICDCS, pp. 411–420. IEEE (2015)
19. Xu, J., Chen, Z., Tang, J., Su, S.: T-Storm: traffic-aware online scheduling in storm. In: 2014 IEEE 34th International Conference on Distributed Computing Systems, Madrid, Spain, pp. 535–544. IEEE (2014)
20. Zhang, Z., Jin, P., Wang, X., Liu, R., Wan, S.: N-Storm: efficient thread-level task migration in apache storm. In: 2019 IEEE 21st International Conference on High Performance Computing and Communications, pp. 1595–1602. IEEE (2019)
21. Eskandari, L., Huang, Z., Eyers, D.: P-Scheduler: adaptive hierarchical scheduling in apache storm. In: Proceedings of the Australasian Computer Science Week Multiconference, p. 26. ACM (2016)
22. Wei, H., Wei, X., Li, L.: Topology-aware task allocation for online distributed stream processing applications with latency constraints. Phys. A Stat. Mech. Appl. **534**, 122024 (2019)
23. Luxburg, U.: A tutorial on spectral clustering. Stat. Comput. **17**, 395–416 (2007)

A Data Stream Prediction Strategy for Elastic Stream Computing Systems

Hanchu Zhang[1], Dawei Sun[1(✉)], Atul Sajjanhar[2],
and Rajkumar Buyya[3]

[1] School of Information Engineering, China University of Geosciences,
Beijing 100083, People's Republic of China
{zhanghanchu, sundaweicn}@cugb.edu.cn
[2] School of Information Technology, Deakin University,
Geelong, VIC 3216, Australia
atul.sajjanhar@deakin.edu.au
[3] Cloud Computing and Distributed Systems (CLOUDS) Laboratory,
School of Computing and Information Systems, The University of Melbourne,
Parkville, Australia
rbuyya@unimelb.edu.au

Abstract. In a distributed stream processing system, elastic resource provisioning/scheduling is the main factor that affects system performance and limits system applications. However, in the data stream computing platform, resource allocation is often suboptimal due to the large fluctuations of the data stream rate, which creates a performance bottleneck for the cluster. In this paper, we propose a data stream prediction strategy (Dp-Stream) for elastic computing system to mitigate the resource allocation issue. First, we establish a back propagation (BP) neural network prediction model based on genetic simulated annealing algorithm to predict the trend of the data stream rate in the next time window of the cluster; second, according to the time latency, the estimation model adjusts the resources allocated to the critical operations of the critical path in the Directed Acyclic Graph (DAG) and finally, the resource communication cost is optimized. We evaluate the prediction accuracy and system latency of the proposed scheduling strategy in Storm. The experimental results prove the feasibility and effectiveness of the proposed strategy.

Keywords: Data stream prediction · Resource scheduling · Stream computing · Back propagation neural network · Storm

1 Introduction

1.1 Background and Motivation

With the continuous development of science and technology, society has entered the era of big data, which is driven by a series of smart applications, smart devices, and smart services, including social networks, smart phones, and intelligent transportation [1]. In these scenarios, the amount of data is showing a trend of rapid growth, so it can be seen that the demand for real-time data stream processing services is also increasing.

W. Xiang et al. (Eds.): BROADNETS 2021, LNICST 413, pp. 148–162, 2022.
https://doi.org/10.1007/978-3-030-93479-8_9

There is no doubt that the analysis and processing of real-time data has a very broad application prospect, and it is also a huge challenge. Therefore, a large number of distributed stream processing real-time computing platforms represented by Storm [2] and Spark Streaming [3] are derived to address the problem of timeliness of data, so that these data can be processed quickly within the constraints of time.

In a distributed stream processing system, the transmission rate of data stream usually has high volatility, for example, data stream surges during e-commerce promotional activities. On the other hand, data streams are reduced during the emergency incidents of smart power system. In this case, if the stream processing system can adjust resources according to the data demand when the data stream fluctuates the resource utilization of the system will be improved, so the research on elastic resource scheduling is of great significance [4]. Although Storm can meet the basic needs of data stream processing, it has many shortcomings in supporting elastic resource scheduling. The ideal elastic resource scheduling should accommodate the data stream traffic increase, and adjust the system to increase the resource allocation in real time [5]; and when the data stream traffic drops, the system should reclaim part of resources, in a timely manner. At the same time, if the system's resources are adjusted when the changed data stream arrives in the system, it will greatly increase the system's response time. Therefore, if resources are adjusted in advance before the data stream rate changes, a lot of system response time utilized for resource adjustments upon data arrival can be salvaged, thereby reducing the latency of the system and improving the performance of the system. As a result, we can predict the rate of the data stream to deploy resources in advance.

1.2   Contributions

Based on the above background, we propose a data stream prediction strategy (Dp-Stream) for elastic stream computing system. We mitigate the problem by making the following contributions:

(1) We develop a BP neural network model based on genetic simulated annealing algorithm to predict the change in trend of the data stream rate in the next time window of the cluster;

(2) We propose a resource scheduling strategy from a systematic perspective, according to the latency estimation model, resources are adjusted for the critical operations of the critical path in the DAG to obtain a lower system latency and higher resource utilization.

1.3   Paper Organization

The organization of the rest of the paper is as follows: Sect. 2 introduces the related work. In Sect. 3, the application model, prediction model and latency estimation model are introduced. Section 4 focuses on Dp-Stream, including system architecture, data stream prediction algorithm and resource scheduling algorithm. Section 5 introduces the experimental environment, parameter settings and performance evaluation of Dp-Stream. Finally, Sect. 6 presents conclusions and future work.

2 Related Work

In stream processing systems, due to the volatility of data streams, insufficient system resources will cause system performance degradation. How to allocate resources effectively and reasonably is the main challenge faced by streaming computing platforms. At present, some researchers use predictive methods to optimize the allocation of system resources to improve system performance.

In [12], the authors used the model predictive control (MPC) method to design an elastic data stream processing strategy for multi-core systems, and proposed a tree structure to describe the search space, and used the branch and bound method to determine Optimal resource allocation, reducing MPC runtime overhead and optimizing throughput and latency performance.

[13] proposed the use of autoregressive integrated moving average (ARIMA) model to predict the input traffic changes in the working node, using the resource cost model to track and limit the node's CPU usage level within the acceptable range of strategies.

In [15], the authors used an integrated regression model to predict CPU and memory usage, and used incremental learning techniques to build the prediction model in real time. At the same time, according to the relative independence of different regression models, the weighted integral algorithm of the regression model is given, and the abnormal value detection mechanism is introduced to monitor the abnormal execution to improve the accuracy of prediction.

Table 1. Comparison of our work and other related work

Parameter	Related work				Dp-Stream
	[13]	[15]	[16]	[17]	
Prediction modelling	✓	✓	✗	✗	✓
Performance modelling	✓	✓	✓	✓	✓
Elastic strategy	✗	✗	✗	✓	✓
Resource saving	✓	✓	✗	✓	✓

At the same time, there are many researchers working on the scheduling strategy in distributed stream processing system. [16] proposed a dynamic resource scheduling strategy DRS based on cloud data stream management system. It analyzes each node in the task topology through the Erlang formula to obtain its data processing latency, and then uses the Jackson queuing network to aggregate the processing latency of the entire topology on a weighted average.

In [17], the authors proposed an adaptive online solution for scheduling and resource implementation on a stream processing framework. It can determine the number of resources required by each instance in a timely manner to handle unexpected load peaks without causing congestion, and wasteful allocation of resources. A resource cost-aware layout algorithm is proposed, which can minimize the number of affected worker threads.

In summary, the above solutions provide valuable insights for the elastic scheduling strategy of distributed stream processing systems, including prediction methods, resource scheduling, and resource allocation. However, the current methods still have some limitations, so it is necessary to develop novel methods to adapt to the era of big data. The comparison between our work and other closely related works is given in Table 1.

3   Problem Statement

In this section, we introduce the application DAG model, prediction model and latency estimation model in big data stream computing environments.

3.1   Application Model

Data stream processing systems model the logic of the real-time application as a DAG, represented by $DAG = (V(G), E(G))$, where $V(G) = \{v_1, v_2, \cdots, v_n\}$ is a set of n vertices, and each vertex represents a Spout or Bolt component. Spout is responsible for reading data from the data source and sending tuples (Tuple) to the Topology. Tuples are units of data processed by Storm. Bolt encapsulate processing logic, realize the specific processing of data, each processing a tuple. $E(G) = \{e_{1,2}, e_{1,3}, \cdots, e_{n-i,n}\}$ is a finite set of directed edges, the weight associated with a vertex or an edge respectively represents its computation cost or communication cost. A vertex in each component is an instance, and the number of vertices in a component is the number of instances of the component, which is also called the parallelism of the component. For each DAG, first use the graph-based depth fist traversal algorithm to find the largest path from v_1 to v_n. This maximum path is called the critical path of the topological graph, all nodes on the critical path are called Critical Operations (CO).

3.2   Prediction Model

We propose a BP neural network based on the genetic simulated annealing algorithm to predict the input rate of data stream r_{t+1} of the application in the future time window $t+1$ based on the historical input rate $R_{in} = (r_1, r_2, r_3, ..., r_t)$.In the BP neural network, the historical input rate of the application $R_{in} = (r_1, r_2, r_3, ..., r_t)$ is used as the input data of the neural network, $W = (\omega_1, \omega_2, \omega_3, ..., \omega_n)$ is the weight corresponding to the input data to the hidden layer, $H = (h_1, h_2, h_3, ..., h_n)$ is the output value of the hidden layer, $Y = (y_1, y_2, y_3, ..., y_k)$ is the output value of the output layer, and $T = (t_1, t_2, t_3, ..., t_k)$ is the target value of the output layer. The output result of the hidden layer can be calculated by (1).

$$h_n = f\left(\sum_{i=1}^{t} \omega_{ni} \cdot r_i\right),\tag{1}$$

where we use $f = \frac{1}{1+e^{-kx}}$ as the transfer function of the BP neural network. And the output of the output layer can be expressed by (2).

$$y_k = f\left(\sum_{n=1}^{N} \lambda_{nk} \cdot h_n\right),\tag{2}$$

where, λ_{nk} is the weight between the hidden layer and the output layer. Therefore, the error between the target output and the actual output can be obtained by (3),

$$b = \frac{1}{2}(T-Y)^2 = \frac{1}{2}\left[\sum_{k=1}^{K} t_k - f\left(\sum_{n=1}^{N} \lambda_n \cdot h_n\right)\right]^2.\tag{3}$$

Genetic algorithm is a kind of global search algorithm, which has strong global search ability, but it is prone to premature convergence, which leads to the problem of local optimal solution. In the process of searching for the optimal solution, the simulated annealing algorithm uses a certain probability to jump out of the local optimal solution to avoid the shortcomings of falling into the local optimal solution. In the forecasting process, the genetic simulated annealing algorithm is used to replace the back propagation process of the BP neural network. First, get the initial population from the initial solution $P(k)$ of the BP neural network according to the genetic algorithm, and then perform crossover and mutation operations on the initial population to obtain new individuals x'. At this time, the energy value of the system $E' = b'$ is obtained according to the simulated annealing algorithm. Then the energy difference can be expressed as $\Delta E = E' - E = b' - b$. Metropolis' probability acceptance criteria is used to determine whether to accept or reject the new state. The probability of the system accepting the state x' can be calculated by (4).

$$P = \begin{cases} 1, & if \ \Delta E < 0, \\ \frac{1}{z(t_k)} \exp\left(-\frac{\Delta E}{K t_k}\right), & otherwise, \end{cases} \tag{4}$$

where, K is Boltzmann's constant, t_k is the current temperature. If the probability P is an arbitrary random number in the interval $[0, 1]$, the new state x is accepted, otherwise the current state x is retained. In the iterative process of the algorithm, the solid molecules continue to move to a place with relatively low energy, and the state probability distribution of the energy E of the solid in a certain state tends to the Gibbs distribution can be calculated by (5),

$$z = \frac{1}{\sum_i \exp\left(-\frac{\Delta E_i}{t_k}\right)}. \tag{5}$$

The genetic simulated annealing algorithm makes the initial point of the iteration continue to iterate from an initial solution, and correct the weights and error thresholds of the BP network to gradually find the optimal solution. Finally, the output of the output layer is used as the input rate of the application in the time window $t + 1$ to be predicted.

3.3 Latency Estimation Model

In data stream processing system, for data tuples, the flag of processing completion is that it and all the intermediate tuples it produces are processed by its corresponding compute nodes. T is used to represent the time experienced from the data stream input tuple to the application to the completion of its processing by the last computing node. T_i is used to represent the time required for the v_i node to process the tuple. T_i including tuple processing time Tp_i, the time Ts_i required to transmit tuples from node v_i to v_j.

The tuple processing time is related to the processing rate of the task, therefore, the faster the processing rate, the shorter the processing time. Hence, it is inversely proportional to the average processing rate, that can be calculated by (6).

$$Tp_i = \frac{r_i \cdot \Delta t}{\sum_{k=1}^{k} p_{ik}}, \tag{6}$$

where p_{ik} is the tuple processing rate under the assumption that the instances of all nodes are homogeneous. It can be seen that when the processing rate of node v_i is larger, Tp_i is smaller. Therefore, when the current processing rate cannot achieve the lower processing time, we can increase the number of node instances (that is, increase the node parallelism) to reduce the processing time.

Then the time required to transmit tuples from node v_i to v_j is related to the network bandwidth, and if the instances of two nodes are on the same Worker node, the transmission time between them can be ignored. Therefore, Ts_i can be calculated by (7),

$$Ts_i = \begin{cases} \frac{r_i \cdot \Delta t}{B_{ij}}, & \text{if } i,j \text{ in different Worker node.} \\ 0, & \text{otherwise.} \end{cases} \tag{7}$$

The value T_i is the weight of the sum of the value of all calculated values, that can be expressed by (8).

$$T_i = w_i \cdot (Tp_i + Ts_i), \tag{8}$$

where, w_i is the weight of node v_i on the path.

In stream processing applications, the required time between data stream on the path is equal to the sum of the latency of the nodes with the longest required time on the path, that is, the sum of the latency of all nodes that belong to the critical operation on the critical path, so each input element in the application the response time T of the group can be expressed by (9),

$$T = \sum_i T_i, \quad v_i \in CO. \tag{9}$$

Therefore, the optimization goal of this paper can be defined as: in the case of meeting the predicted data input rate, find the appropriate number of instances (executor) for each critical operation node of the critical path on the DAG, so as to minimize the latency and meet the requirements of each Worker node resource capacity to improve resource utilization.

4 Dp-Stream Overview

Based on the relevant model discussed in the Sect. 3, we propose a scheduling strategy, namely, Dp-Stream. Dp-Stream is a resource scheduling strategy based on the prediction of data stream rate. For data stream rates that fluctuate drastically, it can adjust system resources according to the stream rate before the changing data stream arrives to ensure low latency. In order to provide an overview of Dp-Stream, this section focuses on Dp-Stream, including data stream rate prediction algorithms, resource scheduling methods based on predicted stream rates and its system architecture.

4.1   System Architecture

The basic structure of Storm includes Nimbus, Zookeeper and several Worker nodes. Nimbus is responsible for receiving the DAG submitted by the user and deploying it to each Worker node. Each Worker node runs a Supervisor to monitor the tasks assigned by Nimbus to the Worker node. Zookeeper is used to save the working status of Nimbus and Supervisor.

In order to implement Dp-Stream, the basic structure of Storm needs to be improved. The improved cluster mainly includes an input rate monitoring module, a prediction module, and a resource scheduling module. The input rate monitoring module is used to monitor the current stream rate of the system data stream and save the record in the database. The prediction module applies historical input rate from the database to perform forecasting according to the algorithm proposed in Sect. 4.2. The resource scheduling module uses the IScheduler interface to implement the scheduling strategy proposed in Sect. 4.3. The Dp-Stream deployment architecture is shown in Fig. 1.

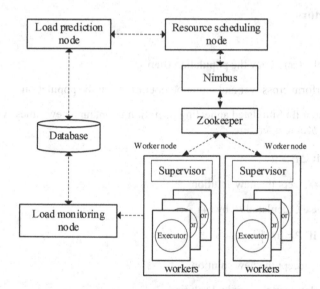

Fig. 1. Dp-Stream deployment architecture

4.2   Data Stream Prediction Algorithm

In order to realize a timely response of stream processing applications to rate changes, it is necessary to predict the data stream rate of the next time window through the prediction model, so as to allocate appropriate resources to the application in advance.

The genetic simulated annealing algorithm uses the annealing algorithm to find the optimal solution by adding the local optimal solution as a potential candidate, and then adjusting the entire search range with new candidates to improve the accuracy of the algorithm. BP neural network is prone to converge at the local optimal solution, so this paper proposes a BP neural network based on genetic simulated annealing algorithm as a prediction model, which is described in Algorithm 1.

156   H. Zhang et al.

Algorithm 1: Prediction algorithm of BP network based on genetic simulated annealing algorithm

---

1. **Input**: Population size S, iteration number N, crossover probability P_c, mutation probability P_m, simulated annealing initial temperature t_m, temperature decay function parameter α

2. **Output**: Data stream rate r_{t+1} in the t+1 time window

3. Initialize the BP network and encode the weight and threshold, and initialize the population $P(k)$ **then**

4. Use fitness function to evaluate current individuals $E = b$

5. **for** n<N **do**

6. **if** fitness value satisfies the termination condition **then**

7.   **return**

8. **else**

9.   Select and copy the population **then**

10.   Perform crossover and mutation operations on the population

11.   **then do** Simulated annealing operation to obtain a new fitness value $E' = b'$ at temperature t_k

12.   **if** $\Delta E > 0$

13.   Accept the new solution

14.   **else** Calculated P by (4)

15.   **if** $P \in [0,1]$

16.   accept the new solution

17.   **else** keep the original solution

18.   **then** gradually lower the temperature, $t_{k+1} = \alpha t_k$, $n = n+1$

19. **return**

In Algorithm 1, the initial solution of the algorithm is obtained by the BP neural network, and the initial population of the genetic algorithm is obtained (Step 3). Then a fitness function is used to evaluate the fitness value of the candidates in the population. If the fitness value meets the termination condition of the algorithm, the result will be output, otherwise the population will be cross-mutated (Step 4 to 10). At temperature t_k, calculate the fitness value of the individuals in the population after genetic manipulation and compare it with their respective parental fitness values, and decide whether to accept the individuals after genetic manipulation according to Metropolis acceptance criteria (Step 11 to 19). Then the population is cooled down.

4.3 Resource Scheduling

After predicting the rate of data stream, Dp-Stream will perform resource adjustment and scheduling operations based on the data stream rate in the next time window obtained by the prediction algorithm. Firstly, execute resource adjustment of the critical operation nodes on the critical path in the DAG, increase or decrease the number of instances of the component to match the changes in the coming data stream rate, so as to ensure a lower system latency. Then place the changed instance in the appropriate Worker node according to the remaining resource capacity on the Worker node to ensure the resource utilization of the system. The scheduling algorithm of the Dp-Stream is described in Algorithm 2.

Algorithm 2: Resource scheduling algorithm

---

1. **Input**: critical operation set CO, threshold ω and minimum value λ of critical operation T_i, set of Worker nodes W_j

2. **Output**: calculated time for critical operations T_i, the change number of instances of each critical operation node n_i, the placement of executor instances on each Worker node W_j'

3. **for** each $v_i \in CO$ **do**

4. calculate T_i by (8)

5. **if** $T_i > \omega$ **then**

6. **while** $T_i > \omega$ **do**

7. increase the number of instances $N_i = N_i + 1$, calculate T_i

8. **else if** $T_i < \lambda$ **then**

9. **while** $T_i < \lambda$ **do**

10. reduce the number of instances $N_i = N_i - 1$, calculate T_i

11. **for** each W_j **do**

12. calculate the remaining resource capacity R_j

13. **for** each n_i **do**

14. **if** $n_i > 0$ **then**

15. **if** the remaining capacity R_j is more than the resource requirement of the instance r_k and $R_j' = R_j - r_k$ is the smallest **then**

16. place an instance into, $R_j = R_j'$

17. **else if** $n_i < 0$ **then**

18. **if** W_j containing the instance and $R_j' = R_j + r_k$ is the biggest **hen**

19. release the instance form W_j', $R_j = R_j'$

20. **return** T_i, W_j'

In Algorithm 2, we adjust the resources of the critical operation nodes on the critical path in the DAG. First, calculate the latency of each critical operation node (Step 4). When the latency of the critical operation exceeds the threshold ω, add an Executor instance to the node until the latency is less than the threshold (Step 5 to 7). Similarly, when the latency of the critical operation is less than the minimum value λ, one Executor instance is reduced for the node until the latency is greater than the minimum value (Step 8 to 10). Then calculate the remaining resource capacity of each Worker node (steps 11–12). When an executor instance is placed, select a Worker node that meet the resource requirements of the instance and has the smallest remaining resource capacity after placing the instance to increase resource utilization (Step 13 to 16). Similarly, when releasing an executor instance, select the Worker node that contains the instance and the remaining resource capacity is the largest after the instance is released, so as to generate more resources to prepare for the subsequent placement of the instance (step 17–19).

5 Performance Evaluation

In this section, we first discuss the experimental environment and parameter settings, which is followed by analysis of performance evaluation results.

5.1 Experimental Environment and Parameter Setup

The proposed Dp-Stream system is developed based on Storm 2.1.0, and installed on top of CentOS 6.8. The cluster consists of 7 machines, with one designated machine serving as the master node, running Storm Nimbus, two designated as Zookeeper node, and the rest 4 machines working as Supervisor nodes. The Nimbus node is equipped with 12 Intel(R) Xeon(R) CPU X5650 @ 2.67 GHz 6-core processors and 12 GB of memory. Zookeeper nodes and Supervisor nodes are virtual machines, equipped with 2 Intel(R) Xeon(R) CPU X5650 @ 2.67 GHz 2-core processors and 4 GB of RAM. The software configuration of Dp-Stream platform is shown in Table 2.

Table 2. Software configuration of Dp-Stream

Software	Version
OS	CentOS 6.8 64bit
Storm	apache-storm-2.1.0
JDK	Jdk1.8 64bit
Zookeeper	zookeeper-3.4.14
Python	python 2.7.2
Maven	Maven 3.6.2
MySQL	Mysql 5.1.73

WordCount is an application used to count the frequency of words in English text. It consists of a Spout and two Bolt. Top-N is an application for counting trending topics, including one Spout and three Bolt. Here, we use WordCount and Top-N as the topology for our experiments.

5.2 Prediction Model Evaluation

In order to evaluate the accuracy of the prediction model for predicting the data stream rate, the experiment in this section simulates the phenomenon of violent rate fluctuations in the online business. The data stream rate is set as a random rate, and the arrival rate range of the random rate is set to [1000, 3000] tuple/s. First, collect the actual simulation value of 200 s as the training data of the neural network model. In order to describe the accuracy of the prediction algorithm more intuitively, we continuously collect 20 s predicted and true values of the data stream, we recorded the predicted values and actual values of 5 s, 10 s, 15 s, and 20 s, and calculated the mean absolute error (MAE), root mean squared error (RMSE) and mean relative error (MRE). The results are summarized in Table 3.

Table 3. Comparison of predicted value and actual value at different time and evaluation of prediction method

Time	Predicted value	Actual value
5	2101	2056
10	2511	2421
15	2114	2201
20	1864	1799
MAE 61.92	**RMSE** 66.76	**MRE** 0.031

In Table 3, both MAE and RMSE are around 60, and MRE < 0.05. Therefore, it can be concluded that our prediction method has a good accuracy and can meet the requirements of Dp-Stream for the accuracy of the prediction algorithm.

5.3 Resource Scheduling Strategy Evaluation

We apply the simulated data stream to the Dp-Stream and Storm's default scheduler, and observe the changes of system latency. The experiments evaluate the system latency under Dp-Stream and Storm default scheduler.

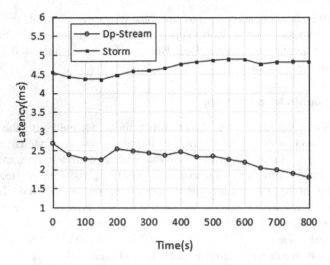

Fig. 2. System latency comparison when running WordCount

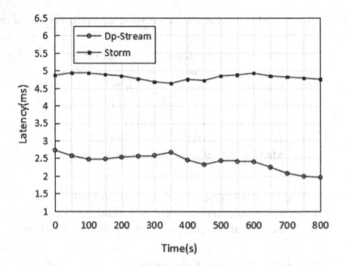

Fig. 3. System latency comparison when running Top-N

In Fig. 2 and 3, the horizontal axis represents the experiment time (s), and the vertical axis represents the waiting time (ms) of the Dp-Stream and Storm default scheduler. Figure 2 records the system latency comparison of Dp-Stream and Storm default scheduler when running WordCount application. Due to the constant fluctuation of the input rate of the data stream, during the 800s observation period, the average system latency of Dp-Stream is about 2.27 ms, and the average latency of Storm default scheduler is about 4.66 ms. Figure 3 records the system latency comparison of Dp-Stream and Storm's default scheduler when running Top-N application, and the average system latency of Dp-Stream is about 2.40 ms, and the average latency of Storm default scheduler is about 4.84 ms. It can be seen from these two figures that compared with the default scheduler of Storm the latency of Dp-Stream is much lower than the default scheduler. The Dp-Stream has been adjusted in advance to deal with rate changes, so the latency has only a small fluctuation and the overall trend is decreasing. However, the latency of the default scheduler is higher than Dp-Stream and the overall trend is increasing. This shows that our Dp-Stream is more effective.

6 Conclusions and Future Work

In a distributed stream processing system, in the face of continuous changes in the data stream rate of the data stream, if there is no proper resource scheduling strategy, the latency of the application will increase significantly. In this paper, we propose a data stream prediction strategy for elastic stream computing system (Dp-Stream), with the goal of allocating system resources in advance to ensure low system latency before changing stream arrive. Experimental results show that the prediction model proposed in this paper is more accurate, and the proposed scheduling algorithm reduces system latency compared with Storm's default scheduler.

In the future, we will focus on improving the prediction algorithm to improve the accuracy of prediction, and considering heterogeneous situation of Worker nodes in the resource scheduling strategy to make the scheduling strategy better.

Acknowledgements. This work is supported by the National Natural Science Foundation of China under Grant No. 61972364 and the Fundamental Research Funds for the Central Universities under Grant No. 2652021001. This work is also supported by Melbourne-Chindia Cloud Computing (MC3) Research Network.

References

1. Zhu, F., Lv, Y., Chen, Y., Wang, X., Xiong, G., Wang, F.Y.: Parallel transportation systems: toward IoT-Enabled smart urban traffic control and management. IEEE Trans. Intell. Transp. Syst. **21**(10), 4063–4071 (2020)
2. Toshniwal, A., et al.: Storm@twitter. In: 2014 ACM SIGMOD International Conference on Management of Data, SIGMOD 2014. ACM Press, pp. 147–156 (2014)
3. Chintapalli, S., et al.: Benchmarking streaming computation engines: storm, Flink and Spak streaming. In: 2016 IEEE International Parallel and Distributed Processing Symposium Workshops (IPDPSW), pp. 1789–1792 (2016)
4. Liu, X., Buyya, R.: Resource management and scheduling in distributed stream processing systems: a taxonomy, review, and future directions. ACM Comput. Surv. **53**(3), 1–41 (2020)
5. Zhang, J., Li, C., Zhu, L., Liu, Y.: The real-time scheduling strategy based on traffic and load balancing in storm. In: 2016 IEEE 18th International Conference on High Performance Computing and Communications, IEEE 14th International Conference on Smart City, IEEE 2nd International Conference on Data Science and Systems, Sydney, NSW, Australia, pp. 372–379 (2016)

6. Duan, W., Zhou, L.: Task scheduling optimization based on firefly algorithm in storm. In: 2020 IEEE 10th International Conference on Electronics Information and Emergency Communication (ICEIEC), pp. 150–154 (2020)
7. Heinze, T., Pappalardo, V., Jerzak, Z., Fetzer, C.: Auto-scaling techniques for elastic data stream processing. In: 2014 IEEE 30th International Conference on Data Engineering Workshops, Chicago, IL, USA, pp. 296–302 (2014)
8. Hidalgo, N., Wladdimiro, D., Rosasl, E.: Self-adaptive processing graph with operator fission for elastic stream processing. J. Syst. Softw. **127**, 205–216 (2017)
9. Cardellini, V., Nardelli, M., Luzi, D.: Elastic stateful stream processing in storm. In: International Conference on High Performance Computing and Simulation, pp. 583–590 (2016)
10. Chakraborty, R., Majumdar, S.: A priority-based resource scheduling technique for multitenant storm clusters. In: 2016 International Symposium on Performance Evaluation of Computer and Telecommunication Systems, pp. 1–6 (2016)
11. Zhou, Y., Liu, Y., Zhang, C., Peng, X., Oin, X.: TOSS: a topology-based scheduler for storm Clusters. In: 2020 IEEE International Parallel and Distributed Processing Symposium Workshops (IPDPSW), New Orleans, LA, USA, pp. 587–596 (2020)
12. Matteis, T.D., Mencagli, G.: Proactive elasticity and energy awareness in data stream processing. J. Syst. Softw. **127**, 302–319 (2017)
13. Farahabady, M.R.H., Samani, H.R.D., Wang, Y., Zomaya, A.Y., Tari, Z.: A QoS-aware controller for apache storm. In: 2016 IEEE 15th International Symposium on Network Computing and Applications (NCA), Cambridge, MA, USA, pp. 334–342 (2016)
14. Farahabady, M.R.H., Zomaya, A.Y., Tari, Z.: QoS-and contention-aware resource provisioning in a stream processing engine. In: 2017 IEEE International Conference on Cluster Computing (CLUSTER), pp. 137–146 (2017)
15. Wang, C., Meng, X., Guo, Q., Weng, Z., Yang, C.: OrientStream: a framework for dynamic resource allocation in distributed data stream management systems. In: 25th ACM International on Conference on Information and Knowledge Management. ACM Press, pp. 2281–2286 (2016)
16. Fu, T.Z.J., Ding, J., Ma, R.T.B., Winslett, M., Yang, Y., Zhang, Z.: DRS: dynamic resource scheduling for real-time analytics over fast streams. In: 2015 IEEE 35th International Conference on Distributed Computing Systems, Columbus, OH, USA, pp. 411–420 (2015)
17. Liu, S., Weng, J., Wang, J.H., An, C., Zhou, Y., Wang, J.: An adaptive online scheme for scheduling and resource enforcement in storm. IEEE/ACM Trans. Networking **27**(4), 1373–1386 (2019)
18. Wang, W., Zhang, C., Chen, X., Li, Z., Ding, H., Wen, X.: An on-the-fly scheduling strategy for distributed stream processing platform. In: 2018 IEEE International Conference on Parallel and Distributed Processing with Applications, Melbourne, VIC, Australia, pp. 773–780 (2018)
19. Liu, X., Buyya, R.: D-Storm: dynamic resource-efficient scheduling of stream processing applications. In: 2017 IEEE 23rd International Conference on Parallel and Distributed Systems, pp. 485–492 (2017)
20. De Matteis, T., Mencagli, G.: Elastic scaling for distributed latency-sensitive data stream operators. In: 2017 25th Euromicro International Conference on Parallel, Distributed and Network-based Processing (PDP), St. Petersburg, Russia, pp. 61–68 (2017)

Blockchain Enabled Integrity Protection for Bodycam Video

Michael Kerr$^{(\boxtimes)}$ ⓘ, Fengling Han ⓘ, and Ron Van Schyndel ⓘ

School of Science (Computer Science), RMIT University, Melbourne, Australia
{michael.kerr,fengling.han,ron.vanschyndel}@rmit.edu.au

Abstract. The prevalence of both documented incidents and anecdotal evidence perpetuate mistrust in video collected via Law Enforcement body worn recording devices. This paper examines the application of blockchain technology for the management of high volumes of video produced every day during the course of a police field officers' duties. We apply a comprehensive blockchain system developed specifically for law enforcement video collection to the body worn scenario and examine the protection level offered whilst considering the specific requirements and limitations of this mobile platform. Specific scenarios are examined and shown to offer a compelling level of assurance to mobile body worn video collection operations.

Keywords: Law enforcement · Bodycam · Video · Mobile · Digital watermarking · Blockchain

1 Introduction

Due to the rapid expansion of the use of body worn cameras (BWC, Bodycams) by Law Enforcement Agencies (LEA) worldwide [1,2] citizen groups and individuals alike have voiced concern over the proliferation of discrete, mobile and government controlled surveillance technology [2,3]. And rightly so, communities have the right to expect that their public infrastructure is there to service the people's best interests, in this context being public safety and security. It is not always immediately apparent that this is the case, which is unfortunate as this is undoubtedly the original intention of such technology. In order to assure community faith and comfort in the ubiquitous presence of mobile LEA captured video records there must be transparency in the collection, storage, retrieval and use of this data [4]. There is a strong and urgent requirement that collected video records are not only genuine, good faith representation of policing events, but that their collection is also a matter of public record; in addition to integrity checking mechanisms there must also be a record of creation, and in some legislative areas also a record of destruction. Goold [2] makes the profound argument that whilst body worn cameras share many similarities with existing deployed state sanctioned surveillance technology, they further encroach on individuals, as they are by definition mobile, and not only recording in public spaces, but

W. Xiang et al. (Eds.): BROADNETS 2021, LNICST 413, pp. 163–173, 2022.
https://doi.org/10.1007/978-3-030-93479-8_10

private locations like personal residences if the officer is called to such locations. One peak civil liberty group, the American Civil Liberty Union (ACLU) holds the sanguine position that body worn cameras have the potential to protect all involved parties, if only the integrity of the collected product can be assured [5]. The challenge of maintaining tight access control whilst also facilitating public accountability motivates the implementation discussed in this paper. The systems employed to meet these requirements must keep pace with the surveillance technologies themselves, and must be transparent and ubiquitous, so that in time communities can consider the audit functions as an equally integral component of the public safety and police accountability effort these body worn cameras are applied to.

1.1 Background

The clear requirement to protect the integrity of LEA collected footage is a good fit for Distributed Ledger Technology (DLT, or Blockchain) and there are currently several such research projects orientated towards CCTV in the public space, and of those some specifically intersect with to field of Bodycam video and blockchain technology. A common approach is to utilise public networks such as the ERC20 smart contract capability of the Ethereum network through 3rd party suppliers that leverage this network [6]. Our own earlier work outlined the utility of adapting existing audit frameworks within law enforcement procedure [7] and implemented these frameworks using complementary technologies of Blockchain ledgers and digital watermarking implemented on the camera itself [8]. This infrastructure applies itself well to not just general LEA surveillance operations, but specifically the challenges surrounding bulk collection of body worn video by officers in the field.

Whilst leveraging existing public blockchain networks is a valid strategy, advantages of our system include:

- Providing a self-contained Merkle-tree based blockchain system that has no reliance on the continued existence of any financially driven blockchain network.
- Being an entirely independent system that can be implemented at any required security classification or network.
- We further enhance the system by facilitating the on-camera creation of blocks.

Our system is applied here to protect the integrity of Bodycam video, as well as its associated metadata in a distributed fashion that is autonomous from public DLT networks, and can be distributed within LEA, governance authorities or independent third parties. Critically, it is also decoupled from the video data itself.

1.2 Bodycam Use Cases and Challenges

There are a multitude of developed Bodycam products in use worldwide. Mobile capture of video is a core feature, and devices can record locally in a range of resolutions, with some offering real time streaming over cellular and integration with local sensor networks, such as vehicle reed switches or Land Marine Radios (LMR). Scores of Bodycam devices collecting video every day generate vast amounts of data that is required to be centrally archived by the LEA. Different vendors approach this workflow with some variation of offloading data from the device at end of shift with the unit in a docking cradle or connected to a stations Wi-Fi network. Whilst some products can live stream when configured to do so, this is usually a tactical on demand function. Generally devices can be considered to be collecting video data in an independent manner and uploading centrally when a low cost, high bandwidth network becomes available.

Applicable Mechanisms from Camera to Client. Applying identification and integrity measures such as digital hashing, digital watermarking, or Distinctive DC Sequence operations on the camera itself can enable integrity protection at the earliest possible stage of the data's collection. Due to the partially offline, independent workflow of Bodycams in addition to the actual capture of video, there is increased requirement to *a.* Record the capture as an event, *b.* record video integrity information, *c.* Record any relevant metadata. We focus on how to process generated video and the immutable recording of this metadata, without impacting the device's image recording performance. Differing integrity protection mechanisms have their own practical implications to being deployed on the camera:

- Digital hashing mechanisms such as SHA or MD5 are well established and used heavily throughout the law enforcement and legal professions. They are well understood, and their output is widely accepted. Unfortunately hashing has significant limitations in our video scenario. Due to its binary output, in the event of a hash mismatch there is no information on where or how the data has altered from its original state, rendering the entire file suspect from an evidentiary perspective. Bodycams can be exposed to extreme environmental or tactical conditions, as well, this places particular risk on storage hardware and consequently hashing as a protective mechanism, even when deployed at the granular "key frame" level as is done in some video management systems.
- Digital Watermarking overcomes many of the issues surrounding the binary output of hashing. Many watermark schemes offer location based integrity information within the video down to inter frame location. Utilising watermarks trades the definitive nature of hashing for a metric capable of providing a level of confidence as well as information on what and where data could be modified, delivered within the above described volatile environment. This comes at a computational cost and it can be difficult to implement complex algorithms in real time on small, embedded hardware. Additionally, many vendors choose to deliver their own specific compression algorithms, complicating transform domain watermarking support across multiple vendors. This suggests that it is more practical to implement real time on-camera watermarking in the spatial domain as has been found by others specifically researching bench-marking [9]. After meeting implementation challenges it

needs to be also considered that, unsurprisingly, many CCTV vendors consider image quality a primary metric and differentiator to their products. This creates an imperative to minimise the introduction of noise into the video, further limiting the options of what watermark implementations are usable in a practical sense. For these reasons' visible watermarks, such as QR or bar codes can prove useful due to their known impact on the image, their ease of embedding and decoding and their open source.

In this system we utilise a visible watermark to link the video to a blockchain record, and within that record we store the sequence of DC values (position (0,0)) from each Discrete Cosine Transform (DCT) block within each triggered frame. At any subsequent point any user in possession of an enrolled video clip can query the blockchain and obtain metadata such as the distinctive DC Sequence (DCS) to examine the integrity of the video, without requiring access to the original device, video archive or any specifically protected metadata.

As a low complexity, multi-threaded operation that can be processed outside the multimedia pipeline of video capture our method of DCS enrolment is an integrity protection measure that can be implemented on small, embedded hardware, in real time and across many vendors, as it operates prior to, and independently of, the compression operation. Figure 1 shows the concurrent processing and creation of the blockchain data outside the multimedia pipeline of a Gstreamer implementation [10]. An attractive aspect for law enforcement is that, apart from the visible marking, this process in no way alters the main body of the frame and introduces no noise to the resulting video. It can therefore be presented in legal proceedings as unaltered with that caveat.

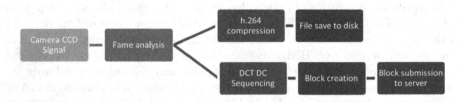

Fig. 1. Multi-threaded processing of frame for blockchain and video pipeline.

All of these options have some applicability and could be utilised to some effect. We have prioritised location based integrity checking with a minimum impact on image quality, and therefore combined a QR code with a DCS operation on keyframes as our method of identification and integrity checking. Our blockchain implementation utilises a Merkle tree structure that consists of blocks created on the camera in real time. Our previous work led to the adoption of a tree structured to create independent hash branches for each camera, merging into the root upon submission to the server, this flexibility is useful in some LEA operations where the camera must operate independently for some time before retrieval. Figure 2 shows the Merkle tree of two separate cameras generating their own blockchain records, with each block identifying hash, H_i, being hashed with the previous root hash, R_{i-1}, to form the Merkle root (R_i) of the system.

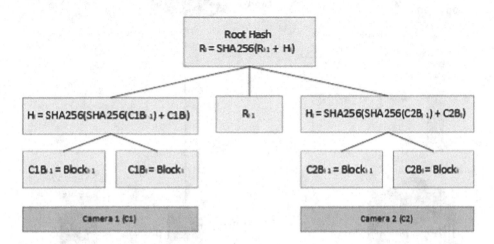

Fig. 2. Hash tree structure allowing for block records to be submitted in real time from multiple cameras, C1 and C2.

Figure 3 provides an overview of an operational system. Video is collected in the field and blockchain records are immediately transmitted to the DLT primary server using either the cameras own radio, or a tethered cellular or LMR communications device. The server infrastructure replicates DLT records, allowing for access from outside LEA networks. Third party clients can access and query the block's metadata using any DLT server without having access to the archived video.

1.3 Reference System

Our reference system contains the main components of Fig. 3. Our rugged wearable recording device utilises Wi-Fi to connect to a mobile bearer connecting to the Primary DLT server. Files are recorded locally and uploaded to central storage representing an end-of-shift LEA archive process. The Ledger is replicated to a Secondary DLT server, representing a 3rd party oversight authority. Our bespoke client application is used to search for blockchain records and verify both video and blockchain integrity. We examine the effectiveness in four distinct scenarios.

Scenario 1 (S1). Normal operation. Officer records video in the field. Each block creation event produces a block that is transmitted to the DLT primary server in real time.

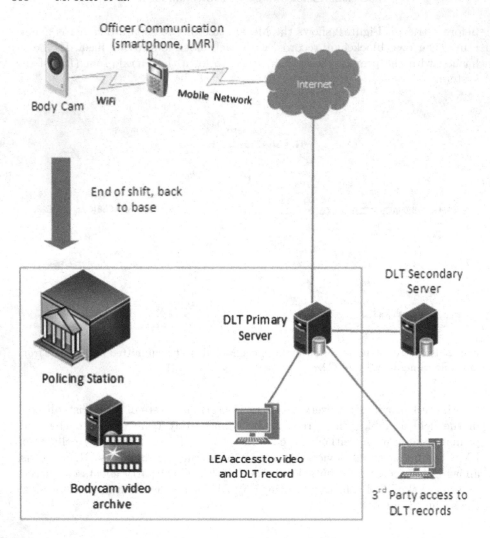

Fig. 3. System architecture overview.

As shown in Fig. 2, for Camera 1 (C1), the block hash C1H$_i$ is hashed with the Root, R$_{i-1}$, to produce R$_i$. We conducted three recordings of manually triggered events (E1, E2 & E3). A basic collection of metadata was added to each block: CameraID (C), BlockID (B), Creation Time (CT), DC Sequence (DCS), Event Code (E) the Block hash (H$_i$), being Eq. 1.

$$H_i = SHA256(C + B + CT + DCS + E + H_{i-1}) \qquad (1)$$

Our Bodycam hardware consisted of a generic embedded device running Linux, capturing video at 15 fps, 640×480 continuous for 5 min. The format and length of S1 sessions is summarised in Table 1.

Table 1. Collected data from S1.

Event	Block count	S1 Block Avg kb	DCS Avg kb	Duration
E1	319	28.898	28.567	5 m:22 s
E2	324	28.568	28.237	5 m:28 s
E3	326	28.572	28.241	5 m:30 s

Scenario 1a (S1a). Normal Operation. The workflow is identical to S1, except the DCS is not submitted in real time. This data is backfilled once the camera has returned to base. The output can be derived on the data collected in S1 as *S1 Block Avg kb - DCS Avg kb*.

Scenario 2 (S2). Normal Operation. Given a video clip, locate and identify its blockchain data and verify the video integrity.

Given a known date and time, event code or operational identifier, blockchain queries are trivial, they are not covered here. For S2, searches were conducted in the reverse direction, given a clip of an arbitrary length, the blockchain is queried for the DCS data, using Pearson's correlation as our metric, our bespoke client tool produced both tabular and visual feedback on the clip's correlation to the blockchain stored DCS, grouped by keyframe. Through the use of client side object detection [11] granularity was further improved by grouping DCS correlation by object. We then calculated the Mean Deviation to provide an indicator of consistency of the comparison throughout the clip by object, these results are summarised in Table 2.

Table 2. Results of S2 client processing.

Event	Frame correlation mean	Frame mean deviation	Object correlation mean	Object mean deviation
E1	0.9989	0.0004	0.9996	0.0003
E2	0.9988	0.0005	0.9983	0.0013
E3	0.9994	0.00008	0.9977	0.0020

Scenario 2a (S2a). Abnormal Event. Perform the same procedure as S2, but with an altered video clip.

E1 video collected in S1 is clipped and colour tinted. When reprocessed the correlation score is much lower relative to known good samples. For example, the Mean Deviation of our example frame in Table 3 is .0105 (.9883 − .9778), higher than standard deviation for object level correlation of the sample, and much higher than the averages recorded in Table 2. A sample original and altered frame is shown for reference in Table 4.

Table 3. Analysis of the modified sample clip produced by S2a.

Event	Frame correlation	Frame mean deviation	Object correlation mean	Object mean deviation
E1	0.9913	0.0083	0.9883	0.0086

Table 4. Frame examples from an original and a modified video clip.

Original Video correlation for 'car' object .996	Modified Video correlation for 'car' object .9778

1.4   Results Discussion Points

Blockchain Transmission Efficiency. Table 1 provides a comparison between the DCS data field size, and the entire blockchain message including all described metadata fields and the AMQP (Advanced Message Queue Protocol) overhead, it is clear the S1a strategy provides an improvement of approximately 26 kilobytes per block (when transmitting uncompressed AMQP messages) by real time transmission of partial data. This comes at the expense of data being unavailable in the blockchain until it is uploaded (i.e., at the end of the officer's shift).

Video Identification and Integrity Analysis. Averages for the correlation of all three video segments were very high, (min .998), additionally the Average Deviation from Mean remained very low, not higher than .002, indicating consistent operation and verification of the video clip.

Analysing the correlation Mean of objects within the video and the Mean Deviation allows for more granular analysis. Recorded values also followed the pattern of the frame analysis (Table 2). It is important to note in this implementation of YOLO [11] objects detected in subsequent frames are not identified as the same real world object, therefore single objects appear and are evaluated as many times as they are detected within the clip.

For S2a, the resulting values in Table 3 show that modified objects can be detected by overall lower correlation average scores as well as higher than normal Standard Deviation of Mean values, this value however would be dependent on factors such as the length and number of objects detected, and the number of modified objects and the length of the sample clip.

1.5 Further Work

Of interest is the reduction of the DCS field size. Implementing zLib compression yields between 2:1–5:1 compression [12], and further to this additional strategies such as identification and storage of deltas only are currently being developed. When utilising the S1a partial upload strategy there is a risk that if the Bodycam fails to eventually upload the entire block, H_i cannot be recreated and the chain can no longer be verified, either against itself or against the Merkle root. Operational circumstances may create such a situation if the camera is damaged or lost in the field.

In order to implement the benefits shown in S1a the Merkle tree structure should be extended to support a two stage hash algorithm, allowing for recovery from the partial upload of blocks and the subsequent loss of destruction of the camera. Whilst not ideal this will at least provide an audit record, and so regardless of the workflow surrounding the management of video clips, the collection of recordings are immediately a public record.

Bodycams are almost always recording audio along with the video stream, currently there is no provision for audio data integrity protection. In much the same way as we have viewed watermarks as interchangeable, watermarking of audio streams would be similarly approached, linked to the same DLT infrastructure.

Where possible the system utilises infrastructure security features, such as transport SSL encryption provided by the Message Queue software. Whilst write access to the blockchain is currently controlled by secret key this does not address the potential for repudiation of blocks after they are committed. Therefore, subsequent versions of the camera software will support digital signing of the blocks on the camera.

Our system performs best when it can control the creation of keyframe data; although every effort has been made to implement a cross platform, hardware agnostic on-camera process, we have found inconsistency in some multimedia implementations on how keyframes are triggered and specified. Further work is required here, and it may be unavoidable that some customisation may be necessary to accommodate some system APIs.

1.6   Conclusion

Our software is designed to process large amounts of CCTV video data and produce statistical indications of integrity and abnormal operation. It is demonstrated here to another LEA requirement of cataloguing and verification of body worn video data. The Standard Deviation and Mean Deviation functions provide a method to process bulk data to detect anomalies of tampering, missing data or device malfunction. This method may not always be precise enough to conclusively determine tampering, but it is valuable as a triage method, and a method to recommend further analysis, especially for 3rd parties without access to original recordings, such as civil liberty groups. The system shown here is lightweight and vendor agnostic, allowing for implementation on a range of low powered collection devices and varying police workflows. Such a system would contribute to growing trust in police body worn surveillance systems and recognition of their potential to protect the interests of both civilians and policing officers alike.

References

1. Doyle, A., Lippert, R., Lyon, D.: Eyes Everywhere: The Global Growth of Camera Surveillance. Taylor & Francis Group, London (2012)
2. Goold, B.J.: Not just about privacy: police body-worn cameras and the costs of public area surveillance. Police Camera: Surveill. Priv. Accountability **2020**, 167–181 (2020)
3. Marx, G.T.: Introduction: The ayes have it - Should they? Police Body-worn Cameras (2021)
4. Blanchette, J.-F., Becker, S.: Bodycam footage as document: an exploratory analysis. In: Chowdhury, G., McLeod, J., Gillet, V., Willett, P. (eds.) iConference 2018. LNCS, vol. 10766, pp. 609–614. Springer, Cham (2018). https://doi.org/10.1007/978-3-319-78105-1_68
5. Police Body Cameras—American Civil Liberties Union. https://www.aclu.org/issues/privacy-technology/surveillance-technologies/police-body-cameras. Accessed 07 May 2021
6. EIP-20: ERC-20 Token Standard. https://eips.ethereum.org/EIPS/eip-20. Accessed 21 May 2021
7. Kerr, M., van Schyndel, R.: Adapting law enforcement frameworks to address the ethical problems of CCTV product propagation. IEEE Secur. Privacy **12**(4), 14–21 (2014)
8. Kerr, M., Han, F., Schyndel, R.V.: A blockchain implementation for the cataloguing of CCTV video evidence. In: Proceedings of AVSS 2018–2018 15th IEEE International Conference on Advanced Video and Signal-Based Surveillance (2019)
9. Chandrakar, N., Bagga, J.: Performance comparison of digital image watermarking techniques: a survey. Int. J. Comput. Appl. Technol. Res. **2**(2), 126–130 (2013)

10. Gstreamer. Gstreamer Project (2021). http://gstreamer.freedesktop.org. Accessed 24 May 2021
11. Redmon, J., Divvala, S., Girshick, R., Farhadi, A.: You only look once: unified, real-time object detection. In: Proceedings of the IEEE Computer Society Conference on Computer Vision and Pattern Recognition, vol. 2016-December, pp. 779–788 (2016)
12. Zlib Technical Details. https://zlib.net/zlib_tech.html. Accessed 24 May 2021

Road Rage Recognition System Based on Face Detection Emotion

Qingxin Xia$^{(\boxtimes)}$, Jiakang Li, and Aoqi Dong

North China Institute of Science and Technology, Hebei 065201, China
xiaqingxin@buaa.edu.cn.cn

Abstract. The drivers' anger caused by the influence of external environment leads to excessive aggressive driving behavior which brings great potential danger to traffic safety. This paper proposes a method using face recognition technology to design an emotional intelligence model of road rage with a high accuracy rate. Firstly, making a homemade emotion data set of road rage according to the definition of road rage and labeling the information of road rage in the data set. Secondly, using a sliding window combined with emotional intelligence scale to determine road rage emotion of drivers, so as to regulate driving behavior. Finally, the correctness and effectiveness of road anger emotional intelligence model were verified by the experimental scenes. It is of great practical significance to reduce the impact of road rage on road safety. Demos URL: https://b23.tv/CnMw6M.

Keywords: Face · Emotion · Road rage · Sliding window

1 Introduction

Emotional intelligence (EI), refers to the ability of individuals to monitor their own and others' moods and emotions, and to identify and use this information to guide their thoughts and behaviors [1]. Among the driving behaviors the driver's emotion is considered to be the most significant psychological factor that affects safe driving, the United States has been studied and concluded that nearly 94% of road safety traffic accidents are related to the driver's factors.

Road rage, as the name implies, is driving with anger and refers to aggressive or angry behavior by the driver of a car or other motor vehicle. On October 28, 2018, a bus crashed into the river at Wanzhou Yangtze River Second Bridge in Wanzhou District, Chongqing, killing 13 people and leaving two people missing [2]. The driver's road rage was the direct cause of the accident.

In today's rapid development of artificial intelligence, emotion recognition is an important method for machines to perceive humans and develop emotional intelligence, and the human face contains rich emotional information, so using an emotion recognition system based on face detection is the best choice for emotion recognition.

W. Xiang et al. (Eds.): BROADNETS 2021, LNICST 413, pp. 174–181, 2022.
https://doi.org/10.1007/978-3-030-93479-8_11

2 Related Work

The first studies on driver road rage identification were based on subjective survey methods with questionnaires and interviews. In 1994, Deffenbacher, L et al. [3] proposed the Driving Anger Scale, a method to determine the presence or absence of road rage by assessing driver performance through pre-defined content. Moriyama et al. from Tokyo Institute of Technology in Japan [4] screened the image information of angry, happy and calm facial expressions of drivers by using the method of labeled long-term change, and finally extracted facial features of multiple parts of drivers by using the method of separated facial information space, and carried out emotional classification.

Lei Hu et al. of Wuhan University of Technology [5] used a modified driving anger scale to analyze the behavioral characteristics of drivers' angry driving and its impact on drivers' physiological psychology and on traffic safety. Tang Ning [6] from Shanghai Jiaotong University and others based on the mood model established by psychology for emotions, and combined with relevant design content, further user research and scenario analysis of road rage were conducted and a set of interactive experimental models were established. Kobayashi et al. from the University of Tokyo in Japan, [7] extracted expression features based on feature points in three regions of the face, such as eyes, eyebrows and mouth, and built a neural network model accordingly to recognize six emotions such as happiness, sadness, anger, fear, disgust and surprise with an accuracy of 70%.

Azman, A et al. from Multimedia University Malaysia [8] used support vector machine and Viola-JonesHaar feature algorithm for real time detection of driver's facial expressions and alerted once the driver was detected to be angry for 3 s continuously. Yu Shenhao et al. [9] from Shandong University conducted an emotion elicitation experiment, collecting images and pulse signals from subjects, fusing face images and pulse features, and constructing a road rage emotion recognition model using Convolutional Neural Network and Softmax classifier, with an average recognition rate of 88.25%. Paweł Tarnowski et al. from Warsaw Polytechnic University [10] calculated the features of 3D face models. K-NN classifier and MLP neural network were used to classify the features, and seven emotional states based on facial expressions were identified.

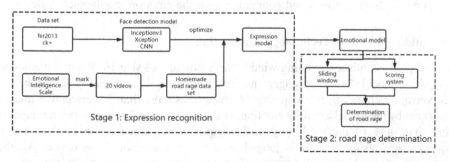

Fig. 1. Emotion recognition and road rage determination technology route

3 Methodology

This paper focuses on the problem of how to use face detection technology to identify emotions to achieve the road rage intelligence determination model, and the problem is broken down into two stages: recognition of driver expressions and determination of road rage status based on expression recognition results. As followed Fig. 1.

3.1 Labeling Data Set Using Emotional Intelligence Scale

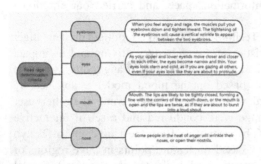

Fig. 2. Road rage determination criteria

The scale is based on the criteria for determining road rage mood, as shown in Fig. 2. The selected observers scored and labeled the measured data based on the characteristics of eyebrows, eyes, mouth and nose. Due to the lack of typical road rage datasets on the Internet, we selected 10 observers to annotate and analyze the driving videos (20 videos of 2 min each) and combined with the Emotional Intelligence Scale for the video set, divided into a training set and a test set for the related study.

3.2 Recognition from Expression to Emotion

Face expression recognition is already very mature [11]. So, this is not the focus of this paper's research. Based on the classical expression recognition algorithm, the home-made road rage data set is labeled by applying the emotional intelligence scale, and the expression model is trained and tested using the training and test sets, respectively, which construct the emotion recognition model. As the results can be presented: the bridge between expression and emotion is activated by expression pixels being labeled with emotion features, happy has strong correlation with eye and mouth related pixels, and angry has strong correlation with eyebrow, nose and mouth part pixels, so the effective recognition from expression detection to emotion can be achieved by extracting the feature points and combining with the emotion intelligence scale.

3.3 Sliding Window Technology Application

The program establishes a sliding window data structure of size 16. When the emotion recognition model detects an angry emotion, it deposits 1 in the array structure, and vice versa, it deposits 0. If a sequence of images has more than 3 consecutive images confirmed by the model as angry emotion, or the proportion of angry emotion images is more than 40% of the total images, the sequence is judged as an angry emotion sequence, and vice versa, it is judged as a non-angry emotion sequence. All the parameter settings here are the results of optimization after testing on training sets.

Figure 3 shows that there is partial data overlap in two adjacent image sequences, which can enhance the robustness of the driver road rage recognition method and make the determination more reasonable and accurate.

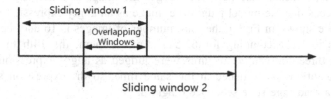

Fig. 3. Sliding window

3.4 Emotional Weighting Method to Determine Road Rage (Scoring Method)

According to the definition of emotions in psychology, human emotions can be divided into seven basic emotions: Angry, Disgust, Fear, Happy, Sad, Surprise and Neutral. And on the basis of the emotion recognition model, different emotions are given different weights. Finally, the road rage determination model is trained and optimized with the sliding window algorithm to achieve road rage determination.

4 System Design

4.1 Scenario Description

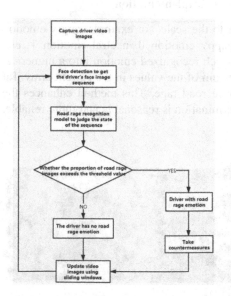

Fig. 4. The system design flow of this paper

Input: The driver acquires facial video images through the camera for data acquisition, as input to the facial expression recognition model, to driver emotion recognition, combined with emotion labeling using sliding window algorithm and emotional feature weight analysis method for road rage determination.

Output: Beep, music, or car seat vibration, etc.

Pre-processing: A total of 68 feature points are detected during face feature extraction and labeled in the graph. In addition, key parts such as eyebrows, eyes, nose, mouth, etc. are also extracted and labeled with scale criteria, which are finally input into our model to complete the emotion prediction. The system design flow of this paper is shown in Fig. 4.

4.2   Implementation of the Sliding Window Mechanism

When road rage emotion recognition is performed with this method on the face expression sequence in Fig. 5, the result vector obtained is [0,0,1,0,1,1,0,1,1,0,1,1, 0,1,1,1]. Where, 1 means that the model judges the image as a non-angry expression state and 0 means that the model judges the image as an angry expression state. In the image sequence shown in Fig. 5, the total number of images is 16 and the number of angry images is 10, accounting for 62.5%. Among them, the 14th to 16th facial expression of three consecutive pictures were judged as angry expression state. The above two conditions are satisfied at the same time, so the expression sequence is judged to be a road rage state sequence diagram.

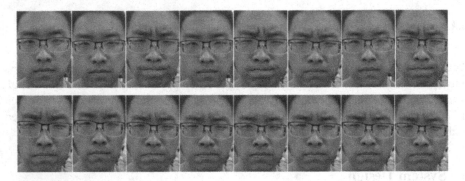

Fig. 5. Road rage state sequence diagram

4.3   Emotional Weighting Analysis Method Implementation

Each emotion identified is scored according to the scale, for example, angry emotion 10, surprised emotion 6, sad emotion 5, happy emotion 0, neutral emotion 1, etc. A sliding window is also created to convert each recognized emotion into a numerical value to be stored in an array. Calculates the sum of the values in the current array,if it reaches the threshold value, it is judged to be road rage. This method enhances the robustness of the determination, and the determination is reasonable and more reliable. The recognition effect is shown in Fig. 6.

Fig .6. Effect picture of road rage judgment.

In order to implement the model effects presentation, this paper chose to create a web application. The purpose of this platform is to provide an intuitive and easily accessible way to get a feel for the specific application of the road rage intelligence model.

5   Evaluation

5.1   Experimental Design

For how to translate the identified emotions into criteria for determining road rage by the emotional intelligence model, this study proposes three determination schemes, which are direct determination of anger, sliding window mechanism, and combination of sliding window and scoring system.

Firstly, 10 students made an artificial determination of the number of occurrences of road rage in 20 videos. The average value obtained was used as the standard value for the number of occurrences of road rage in each video.

The experiment was repeated three times independently for 20 videos using this scheme, and the data in the following table were obtained:

Table 1. Three times experiment independently for 20 videos.

Number of rounds	1	2	3	Average
1	11	10	11	11
2	12	11	10	11
3	13	12	13	13
4	12	12	11	12
5	12	13	12	12
6	6	5	5	5
7	14	14	14	14
8	22	23	21	22
9	8	8	7	8
10	16	17	18	16
11	5	6	6	6
12	2	1	2	2
13	7	8	8	8
14	17	17	18	17
15	11	11	11	11
16	15	16	14	15
17	8	9	10	9
18	8	8	8	8
19	9	10	9	9
20	11	10	11	11

5.2   Summary of the Comparison of the Three Schemes

The line and bar charts comparing the three scenarios with the standard values are shown in Fig. 7 and Fig. 8.

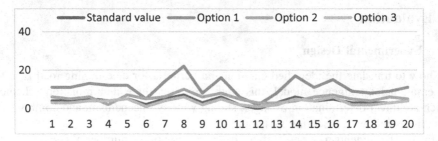

Fig. 7. Comparison line chart between the three schemes and standard values

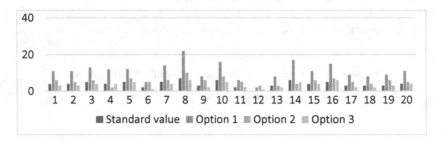

Fig. 8. A bar chart comparing the three schemes with the standard values

The line and bar charts clearly show that the determination results of scenario 3 (the model studied in this paper) fit the standard values very well and is the better scenario.

In addition, it is obvious from the data in the table that the data obtained in Option 1 are significantly higher compared to the standard data results. The solution's memory-lessness of expressions makes it more sensitive to each frame. The data obtained in Option 2 is more consistent with the standard data comparison results, but it is influenced by the accuracy of the emotion recognition model, and a small amount of experimental data will lead to an excessive influence factor of chance and robustness. Option 3 combines the application scale on the basis of Option 2, and the comparison between the obtained data and the real data shows that the determination scheme is most consistent with the real value than the first two schemes. Option 3 has a greater impact on the recognition rate when the simulated driver's expression changes in a smaller magnitude or has too many masked parts of the face, which further enhances the robustness of the experimental determination and makes the experimental data more reliable.

6   Conclusion

To address the problem of lack of representative training data sets for the determination of road rage, this paper constructs an emotional intelligence scale based on psycho-logical concepts, different weights are assigned to different identified emotions.

Exploring the determination of drivers' road rage based on a sliding window model, if there are more than three consecutive pictures of emotions recognized by face detection that are judged by the model as angry pictures, or if the proportion of angry pictures in the total window is more than 40%, then it is judged as road rage emotion, so that the experimental results are more robust. The problem of the size of the sliding window and the proportion of the window size occupied by the anger emotion is the key point to be explored and solved in the next experiment.

The model can be combined with intelligent driving assistance system, when the driver is identified as having road rage emotion, corresponding measures can be taken to make the driver's emotion reach a relatively safe and stable state, so as to reduce the impact of road rage emotion on traffic safety, which is of great practical significance to effectively protect the driver's life and property safety and maintain road safety.

Acknowledgements. This paper is respectively supported by basic science and technology business of central institutions of higher learning (NCIST funding) under No. 3142020018, and by Langfang science and technology project under No. 2021011025.

References

1. Salovey, P., Mayer, J.D.: Emotional intelligence. Imagination, Cognit. Pers. J. **9**(3), 185–211 (1990)
2. https://baike.baidu.com/item/10%C2%B728%E9%87%8D%E5%BA%86%E5%85%AC% E4%BA%A4%E5%9D%A0%E6%B1%9F%E4%BA%8B%E6%95%85/22995295?fr=al addin.
3. Deffenbacher, J.L., Oetting, E.R., Lynch, R.S.: Development of a driving anger scale. Psychol. Rep. **74**(1), 83–91 (1994)
4. Moriyama, T., Abdelaziz, K., Shimomura, N.: Face analysis is of aggressive moods in automobile driving using mutual subspace method. In: 2012 21st International Conference on Pattern Recognition(ICPR), pp. 2898–2901. IEEE (2012)
5. Lei, H.: Research on the Characteristics of Car Driving Behavior Under Anger and Its Impact on Traffic Safety. Wuhan University of Technology, Wuhan (2011)
6. Tang, N.: Design of recognition and regulation system of emotions-taking road rage as an example. In: Shanghai Jiaotong University, pp.10–12 (2018)
7. Kobayashi, H., Tange, K., Hara, F.: Real-time recognition of six basic facial expressions. J. Robot. Soc. Japan **14**(7), 994–1002 (1995)
8. Azman, A., et al.: Real time driver anger detection. In: International Conference on Information Science and Applications Conference 2018, Springer, Singapore (2018)
9. Shenhao, Y.: Research on Road Rage Emotion Recognition Based on Deep Learning and Information Fusion. Shandong University, Jinan (2018)
10. Tarnowski, P., Kołodziej, M., Majkowski, A. Rak, R.J.: Emotion recognition using facial expressions. Proc. Comput. Sci. **108**, 1175–1184 (2017). https://doi.org/10.1016/j.procs. 2017.05.025
11. Bahroun, S., Abed, R., Zagrouba, E.: KS-FQA: keyframe selection based on face quality assessment for efficient face recognition in video. IET Image Proc. **15**, 77–90 (2021)

A Drip Irrigation Remote Control System Using 5G-IoT Technology

Chen Xue$^{(\boxtimes)}$, Yong Feng, Fan Bai, and Tianyu Liu

Harbin Institute of Technology, Harbin, China
{xuechen,20S006030}@stu.hit.edu.cn, yfeng@hit.edu.cn

Abstract. Drip irrigation, a type of micro-irrigation system, has been applied in agriculture, forestry, and urban greening. In order to cut down the labor cost and improve agricultural efficiency, modern technology, such as communication methods, or computer science, has been used in drip irrigation for irrigating a wide area. The Internet of Things (IoT) used computing, intelligent mobiles, and mobile app to perform remote monitoring and control tasks. The 5G network is a new generation technology standard that is helpful to massive expand today's IoT technology. This paper proposes a frame structure for a drip irrigation remote control system (DIRCS) using 5G-IoT technology and mobile app. The system can be operated by people who are anywhere in the world using a mobile device. We utilize 5G-IoT technology to realize data storage and sharing in the platform. Moreover, we design layered software architecture to the presented IoT platform as an alternative technique to manage all the systems. Therefore, the drip irrigation system can be controlled remotely to overcome the previous problems like distance problem, range problem. The prototype demonstrates the effectiveness and efficiency of the design in the result.

Keywords: Remote drip irrigation control system · Internet of Things · 5G · Cloud server

1 Introduction

At present, agricultural technology is in an essential stage of transformation from traditional agricultural production management to modernization, and it still faces many challenges in agricultural science and technology to utilize new scientific methods effectively. Drip irrigation, which is a type of micro-irrigation system, has been used in agriculture, forestry, and urban greening. The goal of the irrigation is to place water directly into the root zone and make the minimum evaporation. The technology takes advantage of the potential in water and nutrients conservation by drip slowly into the soil roots. Drip irrigation systems consist of valves, pipes, tubing, and emitters which are used to distribute water.

Supported by the National Natural Science Foundation of China under Grant 61673132 and 62073095.

W. Xiang et al. (Eds.): BROADNETS 2021, LNICST 413, pp. 182–192, 2022.
https://doi.org/10.1007/978-3-030-93479-8_12

Drip irrigation is one of the fastest-growing irrigation technologies with the best water-saving effect in the world, compared with other irrigation systems, such as surface irrigation or sprinkler irrigation [1,2]. India has increased overall water productivity by 42% to 255% by shifting from conventional surface irrigation to drip irrigation, and the crops are banana, cotton, sugar cane and sweet potato [3].

With the requirement of agriculture production, agriculture now requires extensive land to produce. How to manage the environmental quality of soil for planting crop by using drip irrigation quickly and efficiently, researchers hold their huge interests towards the mixture of new technologies in irrigation. Thus, the researches on water usage reduction for drip irrigation based on new technologies have increased over the years [4,5]. The author proposed an innovative approach that estimates irrigation water used at the catchment scale based on satellite soil moisture data [6]. In [7], the author's images captured with a thermal imaging camera mounted on an unmanned aerial vehicle (UAV) were used to evaluate the water status of sugar beet plants in a plot with large spatial variability in terms of soil properties. The author proposed a drip irrigation system that can decide when to irrigate the farm by analyzing the environmental and soil conditions based on a fuzzy logic-based controller [8]. The author designed a irrigation system which use web-based software to remotely access and process the information gathered by all the stations and the irrigation controller [9]. The authors proposed an AREThOU5A platform with an IoT platform that is developed to perform intelligent irrigation practices and policies in water irrigation management of a perennial olive field [10].

As one of the most remarkable technologies of today, the IoT has been significantly indispensable for improving technology in agriculture and industry. About 28 billion intelligent devices by IoT technology are connected all over the world [11]. In the IoT, all interrelated digital devices have the computing capability to generate, consume, and process data with minimal human interaction. The IoT has been applied in many practical application, such as vehicles, transport and logistics, home automation, wearable technology, connected health, and appliances with remote monitoring capabilities [12]. With the increasing coupling and integration of IoT technology, cloud computing, and smart mobile phones, mobile app are increasingly used by people to perform remote monitoring and control tasks. Billions of IoT devices are connected by wireless communication technologies, such as 2G/3G/4G/5G, WiFi, Bluetooth, etc. Among them, 5G networks feature lower latency, higher capacity, and greater bandwidth [13,14]. The 5G networks are helpful to massive expand today's IoT technology, and boost IoT security, privacy, and other network challenges [15–17]. The author proposed the AREThOU5A project that aims to exploit the state-of-the-art technologies in the field of 5G-IoT as a means to promote rational use of water resources in agriculture [18].

In this paper, a novel remote irrigation control system using 5G-IoT technology is introduced. This paper aims to design the prototype which can be operated by people who are anywhere in the world using their smart phone. A novel layered architecture algorithm structure is proposed for remotely watering plants.

Therefore, the drip irrigation system can overcome the problems like distance problem, range problem. The remainder of this paper is organized as follows. Section 2 gives the detailed work about system of hardware structure. Section 3 introduce the work about system of software structure. In Sect. 4, results and discussion are given. Finally, a brief conclusion is presented in Sect. 5.

2   Platform of Remote Irrigation Control System

In this section, we discuss the details of the remote drip irrigation system, including its structure, subsystem, as well as algorithm method applied in MCU. Figure 1 displays a photograph of the DIRCS installed on a farm or field in laboratory environment, and the system is composed of four parts.

The first part is the drip irrigation system which can control by the terminal. All the data, such as the working status of the pump and valves, from sensors around the plants in farm is gathered and transferred by the controller via 5G networks. Moreover, it can evenly distribute water resources to the land-based on its requirement. The second part is cloud servers linking between the customer terminal and drip irrigation system, which help the system obtain data from the environment around the soil. This part utilizes MQTT protocol technology and 5G communication protocol. The third part is the 5G base station which connects other wireless devices to cloud servers. The last part is the terminal which shows the result of analyzing the current land experiment, such as soil moisture, and the user can execute the operation on the screen. All the data come and go through a 5G network, which can support massive irrigation systems management [19].

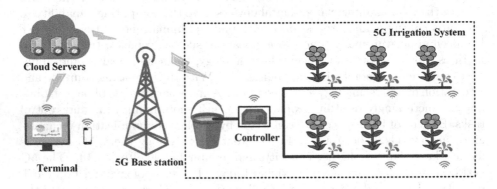

Fig. 1. Platform overview of the remote drip irrigation control system

2.1   Hardware Overview of Drip Irrigation System

The target of the hardware design is to realize the basic function of the drip irrigation system which can monitor and control the states of art by using cloud server technology efficiently. In the period of the construction for smart irrigation system, it needs to make use of the characteristics of 5G large capacity, realize the management of the large area of land as far as possible combined with IoT technology, so that a system is no longer an independent unit, but an efficient integration as a whole of linkage and information sharing. The design of the system is not only conductive to realize the real-time monitoring of state of farm, efficient management of farmer, environmental state, resource scheduling, real-time navigation and security alert, but also provide convenience for farmer and staff of farm. The drip irrigation platform consists of three parts: the perception module, the communication subsystem, and the user-interface subsystem. The appearance of DIRCS is shown in Fig. 2.

Fig. 2. System appearance of hardware

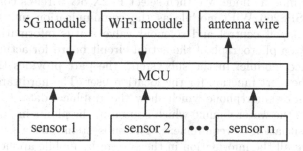

Fig. 3. Hardware structure of perception module

Perception module: The perception module is the essential component of all systems that can bring sensory information with some perception activities. It comprises current, voltage, temperature, and humidity sensors. These sensors provide helpful information to the controller for analyzing and managing all the plants in the land. In the subsystem, the part obtains the data from the sensor located around the plant. Figure 3 illustrates the hardware structure for the perception module of the proposed IoT platform. It consists of an antenna wire, an 5G module, an WiFi module, and multiple sensors. The module works as a sender of the electromagnetic radiation like 5G signal and WiFi signal which come from converting ambient information by sensors.

Connecting module: In the subsystem, the function of the part is like gateway which obtain the data from the previous module such as perception module, and transfer all the data to the cloud server or local processor by the WiFi network server or 5G network server. The system also can save all the data to the local server for quickly analyzing result. Therefore, the subsystem controls and routes all the information of the DIRCS. Figure 4 depicts the schematic diagram of the proposed communication subsystem circuit. It comprises of ESP8266 WiFi module, 5 V DC power source, and stm32f103c8t6 MCU.

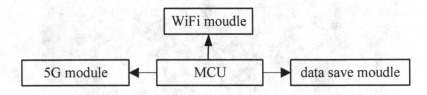

Fig. 4. Hardware structure of connecting subsystem

Actuator module: The actuator module is designed to control the work of field solenoid valves for pump. Figure 5 describes actual structure of actuator module. The subsystem comprise a driver circuit, a driver circuit, and a pump. stm32f103c8t6 single-chip microcomputer is been chosen as the processing unit of the actuator module node. We then select F02X 5G wireless communication module and ESP8266 WiFi module as the communication unit for realizing solenoid valve on/off control and solenoid valve status information feedback. Figure 6 displays a photograph of the actual circuit board for actuator module.

User-interface module: In the subsystem, the part provides the operation function and the alert function for the location user. The hardware of the subsystem is screen or smartphone which show the graphical data. Customers can directly manage the water volume which is used in the plants in farm according to the critical situation or requirement. The subsystem offer a friendly experience by showing all the information in the system by mobile application or web application, and use the MQTT protocol to communicate.

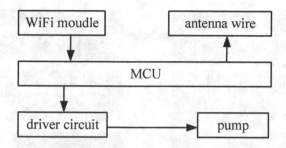

Fig. 5. Hardware structure of actuator module

Fig. 6. Actual circuit board of DIRCS

3 Software Layered Architecture Design

In this part, we put forward the software system structure of DIRCS in combination with 5G-IoT technology. The platform for irrigation management involves four-layer architecture, and Fig. 7 shows the structure of the platform software. This software platform is designed by the Java programming language and including web application and phone application.

Physical Layer (L1): Physical layer is the first layer of the software structure where all the physical connectivity of devices work in the hierarchy. Sensors gather and convert the data into binary bits, then transfer to the data link layer.

Data Link Layer (L2): Data link layer is defined as the second layer of the software Model. It converts bits data received from the physical layer, transfers them to the network layer, and stores some important and security data. This module also has permission for a dangerous environment.

Network Layer (L3): The network layer determines the physical path where the data should take, based on network conditions and service priority, and set several protocol functions operated within this layer. The layer also helps to

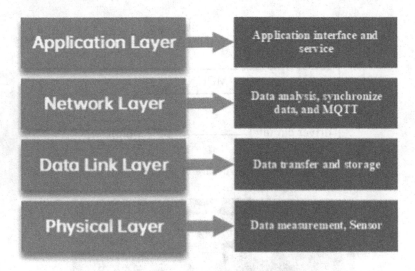

Fig. 7. The structure of DIRCS protocol stack

synchronize data between the user interface and server subsystem and obtain information from the provider. The main protocols involved in this layer are the MQTT and the TCP/IP.

Application Layer (L4): The last layer is the application layer which is directly related to user needs and operation. It provides a method or an interface for the consumer to access information on the network by using an app. It also supports services such as remote control, transfer, and share database.

3.1 Physical Layer Software Algorithms Design

The software algorithm design of the physic layer is designed based on the function of hardware in L1 layer. The design process of software algorithm in the layer is based on the function of the perception module and the actuator module, and the target of the software is mainly control the actuator and provide the information of the perception module. The actuator of the system is the pump which can be controlled automatically, and the driver switch automatically opens and closes to provide power for supporting pump drawing water based on the temperature and humidity sensor. Therefore, the proposed algorithm is shown in Table 1, and it can realize functions about remote controlling and observing the state of DIRCS in the first layer. Table 2 show the device reporting data protocol, and the protocol is applied in communication among modules. The protocol property is defined as the device attribute like ambient temperature. The protocol length is the byte length from the beginning of header to the check in the instruction. Status specifies whether data needs to be transparently transmitted.

Table 1. Monitoring and control algorithm for DIRCS in L1 layer.

Algorithm 1: Monitoring and Control Algorithm for DIRCS in L1 layer

Require: If plants need to water: open the pump and irrigate plants
Ensure: Real-time monitoring and good surrounding conditions
   1: Define WiFi Access Point Username
   2: Define MQTT server
   3: MCU.GPOI for Relay board
   4: H → Humidity   //From DHT-22
   5: T → Temperature   //From DHT-22
   6: T → Temperature Threshold value
   7: H_L → Humidity minimum Threshold value
   8: H_M → Humidity maximum Threshold value
   9: Initialize IoT   //Switching ON system at t=0
   10: MCU acquires the data (temperature, humidity)
      for each round **do**
         Get H and T
         if receive watering command **then**
         if H <H_M **then**
            Switch ON pump;
            Notify host in L4 layer Irrigation Complete!"
         else if H>H_L **then**
            Switch ON pump;
            Notify host in L4 layer plants need to water!"
         else
            Switch OFF pump
      end for
   22: Upload historical data to MQTT Server over WiFi or 5G
   23: Update status of sensors/actuators over WiFi or 5G
   24: Synchronize data to L4
   25: Control actuators remotely via L4 according to command
   25: Feedback actuators result to L4
   26: Update result in Cloud Server

3.2   Application Layer Software Algorithm Design

In the application layer, this layer's major feature is to provide specific services to the user and deliver the information from the physical layer. The customer can observe the standard operation data recorded in the MQTT cloud server, such as environmental temperature and state of remote pump through the Internet using the MQTT server. In contrast, the abnormal conditions are conveyed to the parents by triggering an alarm to take appropriate actions. We use stm32f103c8t6 as the central controlling unit, the same as the other development boards available, such as Ti DSP and Raspberry Pi. In these layer, application layer software algorithm is designed in two quick, built-in setting modes for users to realize the quick setting feature is proposed to help users operate this system.

Table 2. Device reporting data protocol

Instruction name	Instruction bytes	Instruction format
Header	1B	0xFF
Length	2B	0xFFFF
Property	2B	0xFFFF
Command	2B	0xFFFF
Flag	1B	0xFF
Action	2B	0xFFFF
Status	2B	0xFFFF
Check	2B	0xFFFF

Smart mode: In this mode, DIRCS will make a tradeoff between the payment and the energy consumption. In these situations, DIRCS will collect weather data from the weather information provider and make the most appropriate number of DIRCS work according to the farm environmental conditions. For example, when it's going to rain soon, the application layer will notify each module in advance to stop all DIRCSs working and then record the length of rain to calculate the next working time smartly. Moreover, the system reports all the things to the consumers, and the consumers can give orders according to the situation, which does not affect the consumer's other command.

Saving mode: In this mode, the highest priority of DIRCS is to save the total energy and water source. During daytime hours, these systems always work in the saving mode, and only several DIRCSs can work to meet the water needs of farm plants. The farm plants have to bear lower irrigation frequency in solar than normal mode. It will result in fewer days watering intervals. Under this mode, these working DIRCSs will participate in the low power mode as much as possible, and some parts of the system will turn off the power during the night.

4   Results and Validation

In the section, the result and validation of DIRCS are presented in detail. The first part is to test the prototype with the delay in downloading or uploading data from the DIRCS to the MQTT server. The process of uploading and downloading the data from the server has about a 1-s delay, but there is no time delay when using 5G connection type. Some results of the testing showed a slight time delay when the network is fluctuating, and it shows the reliability of the DIRCS highly depended on the strength of the connected network. In the second part, the test is conducted to verify the DIRCS from the application. As shown in Fig. 8, the MQTT server and customer interface in the phone app are synchronized and displayed on the screen, the microcontroller update all the data to cloud storage. In the interface, the customer can monitor the 5-days data for drip irrigation. Moreover, users can operate all the devices in the same app to control water

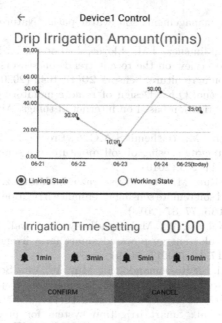

Fig. 8. Mobile application interface

volume precisely by pushing the button. The app provides all the operational data from all the devices for analyzing whether it is working correctly. The result from Fig. 8 shows that the prototype can provide accurate information about the recent water volume for five days to analyze irrigation efficiency.

5 Conclusion

In conclusion, we designed DIRCS prototype and fabricated it with a water pump, an MCU, a WiFi module, and a relay to test the proposed system. Then a new algorithm is proposed and applied in real situations to perform the monitoring and controlling irrigation tasks by MCU. In the process, MQTT technology and 5G-IoT data transmission technology have been utilized to transfer data and commands among the systems. The proposed technique can be widely used in agriculture due to its appealing simplicity and convenience.

References

1. Van der Kooij, S., Zwarteveen, M., Boesveld, H., Kuper, M.: The efficiency of drip irrigation unpacked. Agric. Water Manag. **123**, 103–110 (2013)
2. Badawy, A., El-Latif, A., Hefzy, M.M., Attia, A.: Effect of yeast extract and potassium humate on productivity and quality of potato (solanum tuberosum) under different regimes of drip irrigation system in newly reclaimed soils. Fayoum J. Agric. Res. Dev. **33**(1), 102–113 (2019)

3. Gleick, P.H.: Water management: soft water paths. Nature **418**(6896), 373–373 (2002)
4. Garca, L., Parra, L., Jimenez, J.M., Lloret, J., Lorenz, P.: IoT-based smart irrigation systems: an overview on the recent trends on sensors and IoT systems for irrigation in precision agriculture. Sensors **20**(4), 1042 (2020)
5. Liu, Y.C., Li, J.Q., Zuo, Q.K.: Design of remote monitoring and control system for agriculture drip irrigation based on internet of things. Autom. Instrum. **33**(4), 82–86 (2018)
6. Jalilvand, E., Tajrishy, M., Hashemi, S.A.G.Z., Brocca, L.: Quantification of irrigation water using remote sensing of soil moisture in a semi-arid region. Remote Sens. Environ. **231**, 111226 (2019)
7. Quebrajo, L., Perez-Ruiz, M., Prez-Urrestarazu, L., Martnez, G., Egea, G.: Linking thermal imaging and soil remote sensing to enhance irrigation management of sugar beet. Biosys. Eng. **165**, 77–87 (2018)
8. Al-Ali, A.R., Al Nabulsi, A., Mukhopadhyay, S., Awal, M.S., Fernandes, S., Ailabouni, K.: IoT-solar energy powered smart farm irrigation system. J. Electron. Sci. Technol. **17**(4), 100017 (2019)
9. Capraro, F., Tosetti, S., Rossomando, F., Mut, V., Vita Serman, F.: Web-based system for the remote monitoring and management of precision irrigation: a case study in an arid region of Argentina. Sensors **18**(11), 3847 (2018)
10. Boursianis, A.D., et al.: Smart irrigation system for precision agriculture-the AREThOU5A IoT platform. IEEE Sens. J. **21**, 17539–17547 (2020)
11. Mehta, A., Patel, S.: IoT based smart agriculture research opportunities and challenges. Int. J. Technol. Res. Eng. **4**, 541–543 (2016)
12. Kong, L., Khan, M.K., Wu, F., Chen, G., Zeng, P.: Millimeter-wave wireless communications for IoT-cloud supported autonomous vehicles: overview, design, and challenges. IEEE Commun. Mag. **55**(1), 62–68 (2017)
13. Yu, Z., Yu, J., Ran, X., Zhu, C.: A novel Koch and Sierpinski combined fractal antenna for 2G/3G/4G/5G/WLAN/navigation applications. Microw. Opt. Technol. Lett. **59**(9), 2147–2155 (2017)
14. Hua, Q., et al.: A novel compact quadruple-band indoor base station antenna for 2G/3G/4G/5G systems. IEEE Access **7**, 151350–151358 (2019)
15. Tewari, A., Gupta, B.B.: Security, privacy and trust of different layers in Internet-of-Things (IoTs) framework. Futur. Gener. Comput. Syst. **108**, 909–920 (2020)
16. Stergiou, C., Psannis, K.E., Gupta, B.B., Ishibashi, Y.: Security, privacy efficiency of sustainable cloud computing for big data IoT. Sustain. Comput. Inform. Syst. **19**, 174–184 (2018)
17. Shafique, K., Khawaja, B.A., Sabir, F., Qazi, S., Mustaqim, M.: Internet of Things (IoT) for next-generation smart systems: a review of current challenges, future trends and prospects for emerging 5G-IoT scenarios. IEEE Access **8**, 23022–23040 (2020)
18. Boursianis, A.D., et al.: Advancing rational exploitation of water irrigation using 5G-IoT capabilities: the AREThOU5A project. In: 2019 29th International Symposium on Power and Timing Modeling, Optimization and Simulation (PATMOS), pp. 127–132. IEEE, July 2019
19. Li, S., Da Xu, L., Zhao, S.: 5G internet of things: a survey. J. Ind. Inf. Integr. **10**, 1–9 (2018)

Multipath QUIC – Directions
of the Improvements

Michał Morawski[✉] [ORCID] and Michał Karbowańczyk [ORCID]

Lodz University of Technology, Lodz, Poland
{michal.morawski,michal.karbowanczyk}@p.lodz.pl

Abstract. The multipath transmission becomes the recognized alternative for traditional Quality of Service architectures. Recently, the multipath version of TCP protocol and its modern replacement – QUIC – has been proposed. The paper presents the dynamic properties of the data transfer between physical systems, engaging the multipath version of QUIC protocol (MPQUIC) which inherits the properties of its predecessors. The advantages and weaknesses of the transmission are emphasized and compared to the singlepath QUIC. While QUIC is designed to convey HTTP traffic, in the paper, general-purpose networking is investigated. Based on the measurements, the use recommendations are given together with the directions of improvements.

Keywords: Multipath QUIC · Congestion control · Head-of-line blocking

1 Introduction

The traditional way for dealing with network-related data transfer performance flaws is addressed to routers or switches configuration. The intermediate devices tamper packet orders and force drops according to rules defined in ISA [1] and DSA [2] architectures. Such an approach is mature and practical, but it has two serious drawbacks: it neglects the last/first mile link problems and is applicable in proprietary networks only. When using the public Internet, privileging some traffic over another is prohibited by law (network neutrality [3]). Today, the most vulnerable links are located at first/last mile (LTE, DSL, Wi-Fi, etc.). They are shared, prone to noise, congestion, and interferences. Thus, their throughput and delays fluctuate significantly. Furthermore, the network neutrality principle causes the traditional Quality of Service approaches to be hardly applicable for smartphones, IoT nodes, or even wirelessly connected laptops.

Instead of dealing with network and link layer solutions, recently, the transport protocols gain attraction. They are implemented at endpoints, so the modifications may be introduced irrespectively to service providers. Despite their continuous development [4], transport protocols are often considered ossified. Almost all the Internet transmissions are controlled by forty-year-old TCP and UDP protocols because the ubiquitous network devices (e.g., switches, routers, firewalls, load balancers) deal only with these Internet workhorses. Other protocols are restricted to specific environments. Recently, this ossification has been relaxed, and quantum leaps have emerged:

W. Xiang et al. (Eds.): BROADNETS 2021, LNICST 413, pp. 193–207, 2022.
https://doi.org/10.1007/978-3-030-93479-8_13

- *Multipath transmission*. Nowadays, when a new device is purchased, it is usually equipped with multiple network interfaces. Other ones may be easily added. Nevertheless, without enormous efforts, the user cannot engage them simultaneously, esp. when connecting to the same peer. The default interface is assigned statically, and even if the active path stalls or breaks, the client persistently tries to use the malfunctioned links, despite the availability of other options. If multiple communication paths are available, the simultaneous degradation of all possible ones is unlikely. Hence, when one path degenerates, the data transfer may be seamlessly shifted to other ones. While dispatching packets using different interfaces is straightforward, establishing transport sessions using old protocols is impossible. They identify a peer using its logical address, protocol, and port number. These entities are assigned to logical endpoints, so data originated from another interface of the same peer are rejected. Apart from peer identification, data transport needs to handle the data coherency and pace the transfer by adjusting it to fluctuations of available bandwidth. The recently developed multipath version of TCP (MPTCP) [5–7] allows for simultaneous transfer of data through different interfaces and paths and grants the establishing and tear down communication channel within a single logical connection.

- *Sending data in parallel*. TCP protocol has been designed for stream transfers, i.e., it correctly handles long, bulk data, e.g., a file transmission. Recently, many applications exchange relatively short but numerous, logically unrelated data – e.g., series of HTTP asynchronous requests and responses. If such programs employ classical TCP, they need either open as many separate TCP connections as necessary or multiplex logical streams within the single TCP flow. The first solution seems straightforward, but it requires many resources (memory and CPU) from both peers, especially if the transmission is encrypted, which is expected today. It requires additional code to permit identification and synchronization with the remaining transfers, as well. As explained in Sect. 3, multiplexing logical channels within a single TCP connection suffers from mutual blocking of parallel streams. This problem is incredibly intense for HTTP traffic. Therefore, Google has elaborated protocol Quick UDP Internet Connection – QUIC [8]. It discards the obsolete elements of TCP, but the algorithms governing the transfer are transplanted and adjusted. While developed with HTTP in mind, QUIC may be deployed in many other applications in general networking, IoT, or industrial data exchange.

Both MPTCP and QUIC may be perceived as improved in different directions versions of TCP. Indeed, they share with TCP most of the algorithms that govern the data flow. Consequently, the idea of merging MPTCP and QUIC has popped up. The Multipath QUIC (MPQUIC) has been developed [9] by the same team as MPTCP. It should inherit all the advantages of QUIC and MPTCP. In this paper, MPQUIC governed transmission is verified experimentally using public networks and real devices. It extends the initial evaluations [11–13] by investigating the dynamics and mutual interactions of particular streams. The strengths and weaknesses of the current implementation of MPQUIC are identified, and the research direction is proposed.

The rest of the article is organized as follows. In Sect. 2, the general issues of multipath communication are presented together with a short remainder of the

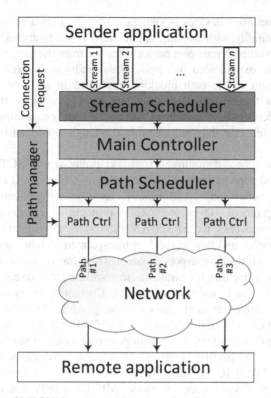

Fig. 1. Architecture of MPQUIC protocol. Elements taken from TCP are marked in green, from MPTCP – in yellow, from QUIC – in blue. (Color figure online)

state-of-the-art. In Sect. 3, the Head-of-Line blocking is explained as the most critical phenomenon impacting the multipath and multistream transmission. It allows introducing measures of transport efficiency. Next, in Sect. 4, the design of the physical setup is motivated and presented. Then, in Sect. 5, the results of the analysis of particular protocol modules are assessed. Finally, the observations are summarized in Sect. 6 and concluded in Sect. 7.

2 Multipath Transmission

Multipath transmission is the desirable feature recognized as an inexpensive way to increase transmission throughput. It is easily applicable at the link layer but not in the higher layers. Therefore, multiple attempts to design corresponding transport protocols have been taken up. The comprehensive survey concerning this topic can be found at [14]. Unfortunately, most of these solutions are not widely accepted due to challenges with their practical implementation. The common consensus for designing new network protocols requires providing the highest possible efficiency (high throughput, short delays) at the lowest possible cost (memory usage, CPU cycles used). Additionally, transparency to other layer protocols is desirable. It enforces compatibility with the installed network devices – switches, routers, firewalls, load balancers. In many cases, compatibility with existing applications is necessary as well.

In general, the multipath transport protocols suffer from the increase of the protocol delay (i.e., the delay experienced by applications) and uneven path loads [15]. This drawback is the result of the path blocking explained in the next section. Another deficiency concerns transmissions of short streams [16]. While the protocol stack algorithms make decisions in real-time without a clue concerning future transfer properties and requirements, they must be robust enough to efficiently handle any data transfer patterns.

The first widely accepted multipath transport protocol was SCTP [17]. Unfortunately, due to limited support from ubiquitous security devices, it is challenging to use SCTP for general networking. Additionally, appropriate applications need to be adjusted for this protocol. Therefore, SCTP protocol is currently widespread in telecommunication networks for SIGTRAN (SS7 over IP) signaling. Nevertheless, SCTP is still developed, and this research is transplanted to other solutions.

So far, the only multipath transport protocol which has received higher acceptance is MPTCP. Its design has met the enthusiastic response from researchers and is continuously improved, tuned, and complemented. Currently, in terms of general networking, its only competitor is the recently designed MPQUIC [9] protocol – an extended version of QUIC initially developed for HTTP traffic, but evaluating towards general-purpose applications [10]. Both multipath protocols are similar, but they differ in essential details, impacting their efficiency, as investigated in the paper. Both MPTCP and MPQUIC are fully transparent for network devices, although the default configuration of some firewalls blocks MPTCP. MPTCP is implemented in a kernel space, so it is transparent for the applications as well. Unfortunately, it is available only for Linux (partially, also for IOS and Android). MPQUIC must be included as a library by an application that requires more developers' efforts but breaks the dependency on an operating system.

The MPQUIC architecture (Fig. 1) reveals its similarity to previously developed protocols – QUIC, MPTCP, and legacy TCP. When an application requests a new connection, the *Path Manager* module is triggered. As in MPTCP, the module is responsible for the addition and removal of paths during the connection lifetime. Its activity is unrelated to data transfer. While for a single connection, the activity MPQUIC *Path Scheduler* is the same as in the MPTCP counterpart, then for the subsequent connections to the same peer, the behavior of the protocols is different. MPTCP repeats the process, but MPQUIC internally handles a new logical data stream. Instead of creating the new connection, MPQUIC employs *Stream Scheduler* initially developed for QUIC. By default, it runs under a round-robin policy, but the actual actions may be adjusted to particular needs [18–20]. Next, user data are handled by *Main Controller,* which shapes general flow properties. By default, it takes responsibility for transmission fairness, i.e., it restricts favoring multipath streams over single path ones. MPTCP uses LIA algorithm [6], and MPQUIC adjusted version of OLIA [21] – protocol elaborated initially for MPTCP. Next, data are split over currently available paths by *Path Scheduler*. By default, both multipath protocols use the path, which has the lowest delay and can acquire new data. However, the MPQUIC *Path Scheduler* is more flexible and may insert the frames belonging to different application streams into the same packet.

Many other strategies are developed, e.g., [22–25]. Nevertheless, *Path* and *Stream Schedulers* are unrelated and do not cooperate with each other.

After splitting a data stream, packets are transferred to the peer using *Path Controllers*. MPQUIC employs controllers similar to TCP [4]. Contrary to most TCP congestion control algorithms, it senses link bandwidth not based on drops as in TCP but based on an increase of packet delay. If it grows too much, congestion control leaves the slow-start phase. The linear-grow phase is pretty the same as in legacy TCP. As a result, MPQUIC experiences significantly fewer drops than (MP)TCP, especially in the initial phase.

For MPTCP, to provide compatibility with firewalls, the path controllers must follow the rules of singlepath TCP. The necessity of maintaining TCP-related flow control induces the separate TCP-like logic both at each *Path Controller* and at the *Main Controller*. MPQUIC is not obliged to obey such rules. From the point of view of firewalls, QUIC originated data are plain UDP datagrams. It allows for retransmission or even acknowledgment using a path different from the initially employed. The empowered version of SACK [26] is used for the acknowledgments, thus retrieving delayed or lost data do not impact dispatching other data.

All the controllers which are part of the protocols act independently. However, they interact with each other, with the network, and applications in a complex way, esp., if multiple parallel logical streams are transferred.

3   HoL Blocking Phenomenon

When transferring data from one peer to another, one assumes that the data belonging to different streams or conveyed using different paths do not interfere. Unfortunately, this reasoning is invalid. The data interact themselves through Head-of-Line blocking (HoL) phenomenon. There are two kinds of HoL blocking – path-related (PHoL, see Sect. 3.1) and stream-related (SHoL, see Sect. 3.2). Both of them increase protocol delay, especially when buffer-bloat (i.e., delay increase induced by filling buffers in interconnecting devices [27]) is present. Note, the impact of HoL depends on the activity of *Schedulers*, the *Path Controllers*, *Main Controller*, the applications, and the network state (Fig. 1).

3.1   Path-Related HoL Blocking

Let us consider packets conveying data from the same logical stream (Fig. 2). For some reason, the throughput on path 3 encounters throttling. Even though the data are transferred correctly using paths 1 (packets $x + 3$, $x + 4$) and 2, (packets $x + 5$, $x + 6$), the stream cannot be assembled coherently until segment $x + 2$ arrives. If it is, packets $x + 2$ up to $x + 6$ are instantaneously available to the user. However, if the receiver buffer is too short, the substreams conveyed using paths 1 and 2 must be suspended. A good quantitative measure of path-related HoL is the time of how long the given frame with data has been held in sender buffer waiting for the acknowledgment. This delay should be as low as the shortest SRTT (Smoothed Round Trip Time) read from path properties. The module responsible for the reduction of PHoL blocking is *Path Scheduler*.

3.2 Stream-Related HoL Blocking

Let us consider data conveying between the same peers, but logically different – e.g., file transfer together with interactive audio data and user keystrokes (Fig. 2). Bulk file transfer (most of the transferred data volume) has no special requirements. Audio data needs a constant bit rate, with the upper limit of delay, and keystrokes data are low

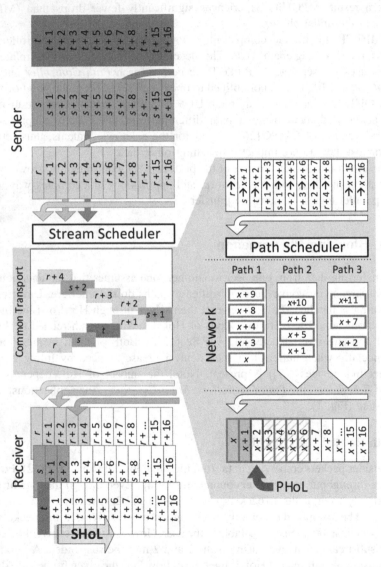

Fig. 2. Head of Line (HoL) blocking. r, s, t – number of frames for different logical streams. Stream-related HoL (SHoL) blocking: urgent stream t is blocked by streams r, s. Path-related HoL (PHoL) blocking: Single stream splits over three paths with different capabilities. x – transport offset. x is a mixture of streams r, s, t.

volume but urgent. Predominantly, only bulk data are present. If a user presses the key, the corresponding data are enqueued. They must wait until the previously sent low priority data are successfully delivered because the data order is fixed at the corresponding application activity.

Here, the quantitative measure of SHoL blocking phenomenon is the difference between the throughput of streams. For properly working transport, this value should be close to zero. The module responsible for the reduction of SHoL blocking is *Stream Scheduler*.

3.3 Protocol Efficiency

Due to the interaction of application logic, the network load, congestion control algorithms, schedulers activity (thus SHoL and PHoL blocking), the available paths are not fully used. The quantitative, popular measure of the protocol efficiency proposed in [28] is

$$
\varphi = \begin{cases} \frac{G - \max(c_i)}{\sum_{i=1}^{n} c_i - \max(c_i)}, & \text{if } G \geq \max(c_i), \\ \frac{G - \max(c_i)}{\max(c_i)}, & \text{otherwise,} \end{cases} \tag{1}
$$

where G is the throughput of multipath transmission, and c_i is the throughput of path i. $\varphi \in [-1, +1]$. If the measure reaches $+1$, then all the paths are fully engaged. If zero, then the multipath transmission has the same throughput as the fastest path. If $\varphi = -1$, the transmission stalls. Thus φ should never drop below zero, which indicates negative gain from multipath transport. Unfortunately, φ cannot be easily evaluated in a real environment in real-time. The throughput can be assessed *a posteriori*, as c_i = volume of data/transmission time. Thus c_i can be obtained only statistically. The paper is addressed to the assessment of dynamic properties of the transmission. Therefore (1) is redefined in the following way:

$$
\varphi(k) = \begin{cases} \frac{G(k) - \max(c_i(k))}{\sum_{i=1}^{n} c_i(k) - \max(c_i(k))}, & \text{if } G(k) \geq \max(c_i(k)), \\ \frac{G(k) - \max(c_i(k))}{\max(c_i(k))}, & \text{otherwise,} \end{cases} \tag{2}
$$

where k is the time instant of the subsequent frame departures. While evaluating (2), $c_i(k)$ is approximated by $c_i(k) \approx$ inflight data(k)/SRTT(k) and averaged from multiple runs of the single path transfer. The term "inflight data" refers to the amount of data already sent but not acknowledged yet. The evolution of the multipath efficiency – $\varphi(k)$ – allows for identifying weaknesses of the control algorithms.

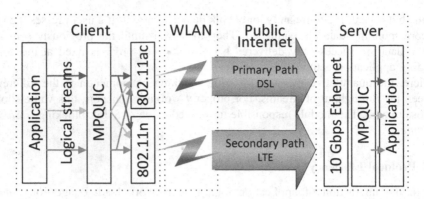

Fig. 3. Test setup. A multistream application employs MPQUIC protocol to send data using different paths. Different streams are marked with colors. The paths are established using different WLANs, and different providers of public Internet. The high performance infrastructure at last mile is shared among streams and paths.

4   Setup Design

In order to assess the dynamic properties of MPQUIC and compare them with QUIC, the test setup illustrated in Fig. 3 has been prepared. To make sure the application and operating system do not influence the transmission significantly, as a client, both inexpensive Raspberry Pi and Windows 10 based machines have been employed. The peer is run on a high-end server under Ubuntu Linux. Both client devices are equipped with two wireless communication interfaces. Next, data sent through the primary path encounter DSL as a likely bottleneck, and those sent through the secondary one – LTE. The segments sent through the DSL connection reach the destination in 8 hops, and those conveyed by LTE – in 11 hops. Initial RTTs during wee hours are 35–40 ms and 75–100 ms, respectively. The streams are generated using the dedicated application designed using DeConnick [9] code.

While the experiments involve real devices and public networks, it is impossible to receive precisely the same results in subsequent runs. Instead, the experiments have to be conducted ~30 times. For the presented assessments, the manually selected, in authors' opinion – most typical and frequently observed experiments are selected.

5   Results

The MPQUIC stack includes modules that interfere with each other. The experiments are planned to investigate the impact of particular parts of the protocol on the overall transmission properties. Hence, three scenarios are selected.

5.1 Path Controllers

When the only single communication path is allowed, then *Path Scheduler* is idle, together with the *Main Controller*. Additionally, if a single stream is conveyed, the *Stream Scheduler* is idle, as well. Thus, only *Path Controllers* impact the transfer. In fact, such transmission is similar to an ordinary TCP one. The comparison of QUIC (Cubic) and MPQUIC (OLIA) is illustrated in Fig. 4. QUIC is more aggressive than MPQUIC. It implies higher path delays but a greater throughput, as well. QUIC is vulnerable to series of drops starting ∼8 s (primary path) and ∼10 s (secondary path). It significantly increases the protocol delay – 5, 6 times more than in the case of less aggressive MPQUIC. However, if the application is not time-sensitive, then the impact of the drops on throughput is acceptable.

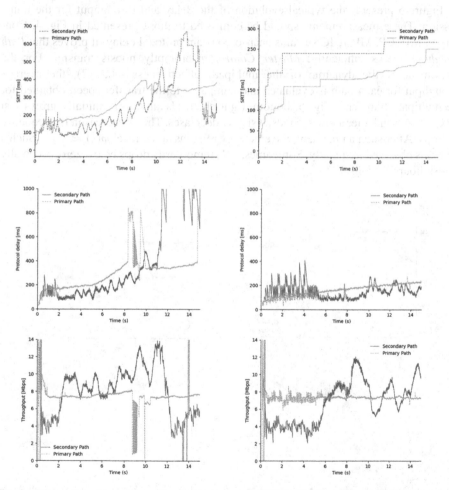

Fig. 4. Basic properties of the paths. Left: singlepath QUIC, Right: multipath QUIC where one path is active. Upper line: path perspective view (different vertical scale), middle line: protocol delay perspective view, bottom line: application perspective view.

Nevertheless, MPQUIC overperforms QUIC in terms of infrequent drops and short delays. Still, buffer bloat is present. It is exceptionally well visible on the primary path, where the constant throughput (~ 7.5 Mbps) accompanies the delay increase (35–220 ms). It is desirable to avoid this phenomenon, as in recently developed TCP congestion control algorithms (BBR [29], Wave [30]).

5.2 Master Controller and Path Scheduler

When more separate paths are available, then *Master Controller* (protocol fairness) and *Path Scheduler* (splitting process) impact the data transfer (Fig. 1). In the experiments, two uncoupled (without common bottleneck) paths are employed. Still, only one stream is conveyed, so *Stream Scheduler* does not influence the data transfer.

Figure 5 presents the typical evolution of the delay and throughput for the transmission. These measurements should be compared to those presented in Fig. 4. Contrary to MPTCP, MPQUIC sustains near-to-constant protocol delay. It proves that *Path Scheduler* works efficiently. *Master Controller* promptly boosts transfer. For the assessment of the dynamic of the multipath effectiveness $\varphi(k)$ (2), the average throughput for each path is evaluated and compared to the transfer speed obtained for the multipath transfer – Fig. 5, bottom, right chart. Usually, $\varphi(k)$ initially grows fast ($\varphi(k) \approx +1$), and after a few seconds, it slowly decreases. The direct reason is a sequence of drops. After such an incident, the efficiency remains at the level $\varphi(k) \approx +0.5$. Such a pattern is observed frequently. Sometimes, $\varphi(k)$ temporarily drops below zero, especially at rush hours.

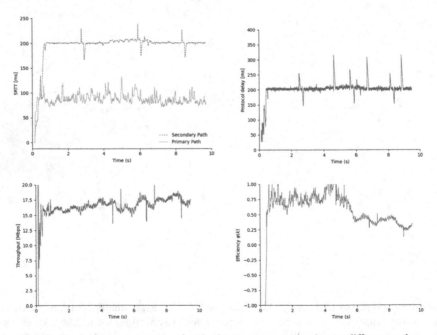

Fig. 5. Typical measurements of a single stream transmitted over different paths.

5.3   Stream Scheduler

The entire stack is evaluated in three subscenarios. In all of them, four streams are transmitted. Every new one starts two seconds after the previous one. From the point of view of previously started streams, the freshly added one is a disturbance. In the first subscenario, all the streams are transmitted continuously, with the best possible throughput. In the second one, stream 1 is a sequence of bursts (10 kB, every 100 ms). It illustrates a live media transmission, for example, voice or a game player activity. In the third subscenario, stream "1" is additionally privileged, i.e., the data from stream "1" are expedited as soon as they are available. The results of the measurements are presented in Fig. 6, each subscenario in subsequent rows.

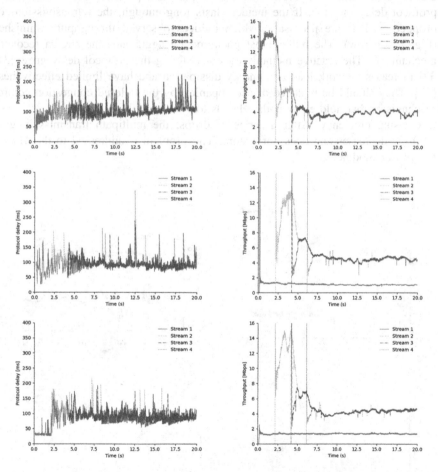

Fig. 6. Four streams transmitted using two paths scenario. Upper row: continuus transmission, middle row: short bursts for stream 1, bottom row: short bursts for priviledged stream 1.

In all cases, the disturbance introduced by a new stream transmission is quickly suppressed. However, the protocol does not obey the rules of priority correctly. Stream 1, despite is delayed like other streams, irrespectively from its priority, as an effect of buffer bloat vulnerability. If buffer bloat is present, *Stream Scheduler* has limited impact on transfer.

6 Result Assessment

The analysis of the protocol dynamics reveals problems that need to be solved:

- Buffer bloat vulnerability. The increase of path and protocol delay results in a protocol delay increase. If the incident lasts long enough, the retransmissions of dropped packets are necessary, which induces observed throughput diminishes (Fig. 7, top row). The buffer bloat phenomenon aggravates the stream recovery mechanisms. The reactive methods for constraining the protocol delay grow [31, 32] increases network load and energy dissipation and have limited effectiveness [33]. They should be replaced or accompanied by the tailored congestion control mechanisms that hold every path delay as low as possible.
- Decreasing efficiency. After a series of drops, the multipath transmission gain $\varphi(k)$ (2) decreases and does not restore. The problem is addressed to the *Master Controller* module.

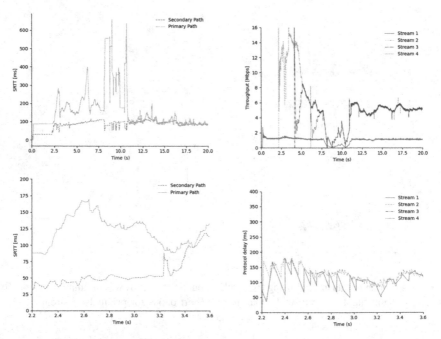

Fig. 7. Weaknesses of multipath transmission. Upper row: transmission throttling due to series of drops. Bottom row: oscillation of protocol delay due to path switching.

- *Stream Scheduler* and *Path Scheduler* are not cooperating with each other. For ordinary streams, the problem can be neglected. However, when MPQUIC is employed in real-time transmissions (e.g., unbuffered multimedia or interactive games), the delays should be constrained as high as possible. Even if *Stream Scheduler* privileges selected stream, *Path Scheduler* ignores this setting (Fig. 7, bottom row). Hence, stream delays oscillate among current path delay values. The efficient algorithm for assigning stream priority for *both* schedulers should be designed, not only for the *Stream Scheduler* [19].

7   Conclusions

The paper evaluates the dynamical properties of MPQUIC transmission in a natural network environment and using physical devices. MPQUIC protocol inherits the best advantages of its predecessors – multipath transmission, efficient congestion control, and streams decoupling. However, the protocol design is not closed, and the directions for further improvements are identified.

The necessity of implementing MPQUIC in an application is often considered a severe disadvantage compared to TCP or MPTCP. However, MPQUIC may be used in any operating system and device without restrictions introduced by firewalls, which sometimes tamper TCP options. Additionally, implementing new algorithms in the user space is more accessible than in the kernel space, as necessary for (MP)TCP. Therefore, the discovered weaknesses of MPQUIC should be solved promptly.

Acknowledgement. This work was supported in part by the National Science Centre, Poland, under Grant 2021/41/B/ST7/00108 "Robust control solutions for multi-channel networked flows".

References

1. Qadir, J., Ali, A., Yau, K.A., Sathiaseelan, A., Crowcroft, J.: Exploiting the power of multiplicity: a holistic survey of network-layer multipath. IEEE Commun. Surv. Tutor. **17** (4), 2176–2213 (2015). 4Q
2. Barreiros, M., Lundqvist, P.: QoS-Enabled Networks: Tools and Foundations. Wiley, Hoboken (2016)
3. Easley, R., Guo, H., Krämer, J.: From net neutrality to data neutrality. Inf. Syst. Res. **29**(2), 253–272 (2015)
4. Afanasyev, A., Tilley, N., Reiher, P., Kleinrock, L.: Host-to-host congestion control for TCP. IEEE Commun. Surv. Tutor. **12**(3), 304–342 (2010). 3Q
5. Ford, A., Raiciu, C., Handley, M., Bonaventure, O., Paasch, C.: TCP extensions for multipath operation with multiple addresses. RFC 8684 (2020)
6. Barré, S., Paasch, C., Bonaventure, O.: MultiPath TCP: From theory to practice. Technical report, Université Catholique de Louvain (2011)
7. Barré, S., Paasch, C.: MultiPath TCP – Linux kernel implementation. http://www.multipath-tcp.org
8. Langley, A., et al.: The QUIC transport protocol: design and internet-scale deployment. In: Proceedings of ACM SIGCOMM, New York, USA, pp. 183–196 (2017)

9. De Coninck, Q., Bonaventure, O.: Multipath QUIC: design and evaluation. In: Proceedings of 13th International Conference on emerging Networking EXperiments and Technologies (CoNEXT 2017), New York, NY, USA, pp. 160–166 (2017)

10. De Coninck, Q., Bonaventure, O.: Multiflow QUIC: a generic multipath transport protocol. IEEE Commun. Mag. **59**(5), 108–113 (2021)

11. Viernickel, T., Froemmgen, A., Rizk, A., Koldehofe, B., Steinmetz, R.: Multipath QUIC: a deployable multipath transport protocol. In: Proceedings of IEEE International Conference on Communications (ICC), Kansas City, MO, USA, pp. 1–7 (2018)

12. De Coninck, Q., Bonaventure, O.: MultipathTester: comparing MPTCP and MPQUIC in mobile environments. In: Proceedings of Network Traffic Measurement and Analysis Conference (TMA), Paris, France, pp. 221–226 (2019)

13. Vu, V.A., Walker, B.: On the latency of multipath-QUIC in real-time applications. In: 16th International Conference on Wireless and Mobile Computing, Networking and Communications (WiMob), pp. 1–7 (2020)

14. Li, M., et al.: Multipath transmission for the internet: a survey. IEEE Commun. Surv. Tut **18**(4), 2887–2925 (2016). Q4

15. Yedugundla, K., et al.: Is multipath transport suitable for latency sensitive traffic? Comput. Netw. **105**, 1–21 (2016)

16. Tang, W., Fu, Y., Dong, P., Yang, W., Yang, B., Xiong, N.: A MPTCP scheduler combined with congestion control for short flow delivery in signal transmission. IEEE Access **7**, 116195–116206 (2019)

17. Stewart, R. (ed.): Stream control transmission protocol. RFC 4960 (2007)

18. Wang, J., Gao, Y., Xu, C.: A multipath QUIC scheduler for mobile HTTP/2. In: Proceedings of 3rd Asia-Pacific Workshop on Networking 2019 (APNet 2019), New York, NY, USA, pp. 43–49 (2019)

19. Shi, X., Wang, L., Zhang, F., Zhou, B., Liu, Z.: PStream: priority-based stream scheduling for heterogeneous paths in multipath-QUIC. In: Proceedings of 29th International Conference on Computer Communications and Networks (ICCCN), Honolulu, HI, USA, pp. 1–8 (2020)

20. Chiariotti, F., Deshpande, A.A., Giordani, M., Antonakoglou, K., Mahmoodi, T., Zanella, A.: QUIC-EST: a QUIC-enabled scheduling and transmission scheme to maximize VoI with correlated data flows. IEEE Comm. Mag. **59**(4), 30–36 (2021)

21. Khalili, R., Gast, N., Popovic, M., Le Boudec, J.-Y.: MPTCP is not Pareto-optimal: performance issues and a possible solution. IEEE/ACM Trans. Netw. **21**(5), 1651–1665 (2013)

22. Paasch, C., Ferlin, S., Alay, O., Bonaventure, O.: Experimental evaluation of multipath TCP schedulers. In: Proceedings of on ACM SIGCOMM CSWS, pp. 27–32, Chicago, USA (2014)

23. Morawski, M., Ignaciuk, P.: Energy-efficient scheduler for MPTCP data transfer with independent and coupled channels. Comp. Commun. **132**, 56–64 (2018)

24. Hurtig, P., Grinnemo, K., Brunstrom, A., Ferlin, S., Alay, Ö., Kuhn, N.: Low-latency scheduling in MPTCP. IEEE/ACM Trans. Netw. **27**(1), 302–315 (2019)

25. Ferlin, S., Alay, Ö., Mehani, O., Boreli, R.: BLEST: blocking estimation-based MPTCP scheduler for heterogeneous networks. In: Proceedings of IFIP Networking Conference Workshops, pp. 431–439, Vienna, Austria (2016)

26. Floyd, S., et al.: An extension to the selective acknowledgement (SACK) option for TCP. RFC 2883 (2000)

27. Gettys, J.: Bufferbloat: dark buffers in the internet. IEEE Internet Comput. **15**(3), 96 (2011)

28. Kimura, B.Y.L., Lima, D.C.S.F., Villas, L.A., Loureiro, A.A.F.: Interpath contention in multipath TCP disjoint paths. IEEE/ACM Trans. Netw. **27**(4), 1387–1400 (2019)

29. Cardwell, N., Cheng, Y., Gunn, C.S., Yeganeh, S.H., Jacobson, V.: BBR: congestion-based congestion control. ACM Queue **14**(5), 20–53 (2016)
30. Abdelsalam, A., Luglio, M., Patriciello, N., Roseti, C., Zampognaro, F.: TCP wave over Linux: a disruptive alternative to the traditional TCP window approach. Comp. Netw. **184**, 1–14 (2021)
31. Ferlin, S., Kucera, S., Claussen, H., Alay, Ö.: MPTCP meets FEC: supporting latency-sensitive applications over heterogeneous networks. IEEE/ACM Trans. Netw. **26**(5), 2005–2018 (2018)
32. Michel, F., De Coninck, Q., Bonaventure, O.: QUIC-FEC: bringing the benefits of forward erasure correction to QUIC. In: Proceedings of IFIP Networking Conference, Warsaw, Poland, pp. 1–9 (2019)
33. Morawski, M., Ignaciuk, P.: A green multipath TCP framework for industrial internet of things applications. Comp. Netw **187**, 107831 (2021)

ARTI: One New Adaptive Elliptical Weighting Model Combining with the Tikhonov-ℓ_p-norm for Image Reconstruction

Chunhua Zhu[1,2,3](✉), Zhen Shi[1,2,3], and Weidong Yang[1,2,3]

[1] Key Laboratory of Grain Information Processing and Control,
Ministry of Education, Henan University of Technology,
Zhengzhou 450001, Henan, China
zhuchunhua@haut.edu.cn
[2] College of Information Science and Engineering, Henan University
of Technology, Zhengzhou 450001, Henan, China
[3] Henan Key Laboratory of Grain Photoelectric Detection and Control,
Henan University of Technology, Zhengzhou 450001, Henan, China

Abstract. To reconstruct the target-induced attenuation image keeping consistent with the observed measurement data, this paper explores the use of a new horizontal distance attenuation-based elliptical weighting model in building an attenuation image, where a horizontal distance attenuation factor and a vertical distance attenuation factor are introduced, respectively, which is able to clear the difference of the voxel weightings perpendicular to the line-of-sight (LOS) direction, as well as the difference of the voxel weightings parallel to the LOS direction. Compared with the existing model, the proposed model can additively reflect the occlusion effect of the radio frequency signal when the target is close to the transceiver nodes. Besides, the Tikhonov-ℓ_p-norm regularization is incorporated into the image reconstruction, which makes full use of the sparse ability of the ℓ_p-norm ($0 < p < 1$) to further reduce the noise interference. The experimental studies on indoor and outdoor scenarios with radio tomographic imaging are presented to validate the effectiveness of the proposed approach.

Keywords: Device-free localization · Radio tomographic imaging · Elliptical weighting model · ℓ_p-norm · Horizontal distance attenuation

1 Introduction

Radio tomographic imaging (RTI) technology can image the received signal strength (RSS) changes of wireless propagation within the wireless sensor networks (WSNs) area, where several mathematical models are applied to reconstruct images of moving targets in indoor and outdoor environments with low power and low cost [1]. In an RTI system, the elliptical weighting model has obtained widely application to derive the shadowing losses on links between many pairs of nodes in a wireless network, then image the attenuation of targets. The classical weighting model [2] was first proposed by Joey Wilson and Neal Patwari, which builds one ellipse by taking any two transceiver nodes as the elliptical focus; the voxel weightings within the ellipse are all equal

W. Xiang et al. (Eds.): BROADNETS 2021, LNICST 413, pp. 208–225, 2022.
https://doi.org/10.1007/978-3-030-93479-8_14

to one, and zero for the others, that is, the voxel weightings within the ellipse can't be distinguished. In 2014, Benjamin R. Hamilton proposed the inverse area elliptical model [3], which modeled the weight of each voxel as the reciprocal of the minimum ellipse area containing two sensor nodes and the voxel. The proposed model is able to distinguish the contribution of each voxel in the ellipse, and obtain greater positioning accuracy than other models. However, the higher computational complexity makes it impossible to apply in real time. In 2015, a const-eccentricity elliptical model was proposed in [4]. In the proposed model, the minor axis parameters of ellipse are positively correlated with link length, and images can be reconstructed with fewer voxels, thus noise interference is greatly reduced. But, how to determine the weightings inside the ellipse has not been considered. In 2019, an adaptive elliptical weighting model considering both the adjustment of ellipse coverage and the selection of voxel weighting was proposed in [6], and the indoor positioning and tracking experiments verify that the model can improve RTI performance. Besides, there are other elliptical models based on Fresnel diffraction theory, such as saddle surface model [12] and diffraction model [13, 14]. However, these models no longer define voxel weightings, but concern RSS changes, which can't be directly applied to the existing RTI systems.

Reviewing the existing research, for improving the image reconstruction quality and the positioning accuracy, the voxel weightings in one ellipse should be chosen to match the actual attenuation of the measurement data, besides, adjusting the range of the ellipse and selecting the optimal image reconstruction algorithm can deduce the interference of reconstructed images. In this paper, an innovative elliptical model is presented, which introduces an adaptive horizontal distance attenuation factor based on the adaptive elliptical model [6], so that the voxel weightings become a function of the horizontal distance and the vertical distance between the voxel and the transceiver nodes, thereby the new elliptical weighting model is able to better match the measurements.

Besides, a Tikhonov-ℓ_p-norm regularization is proposed to solve the ill-posed linear equations for imaging target position. The Tikhonov regularization is usually applied to transform the ill-posed problems into well-posed optimization problems [24], the target position can be estimated from Tikhonov regularized solution, but which is smoother resulting in inaccurate positioning. Actually, the target only occupies a few voxels in the whole monitoring area, which satisfies the sparsity of structure. Moreover, the compressive sensing (CS)-based solutions, such as the least absolute shrinkage and selection operator (LASSO) [25] and orthogonal matching pursuit (OMP) [5, 16], have been proven. However, compared with CS-based image reconstruction, Tikhonov regularized solution [17] can provide higher positioning accuracy. In 2019, Xu [7] proposed a novel regularized reconstruction method (referred to as Tikhonov-ℓ_1-norm regularization) with the objective function of linearly combining ℓ_1-norm and ℓ_2-norm regularization, which utilizes the correlation and sparsity of attenuated images, therefore improves the positioning accuracy and maintains the better imaging quality.

In fact, the optimization model under ℓ_1-norm sparse constraint needs more observation data to ensure the positioning accuracy in practical application, and there are several non-convex reconstruction models are proved to perform better than the ℓ_1-norm at low sampling rate [26], such as ℓ_0-norm and ℓ_p-norm. However, ℓ_0-norm-based optimization model is a mathematical non-deterministic polynomial (NP) problem.

Instead, ℓ_p-norm $(0 < p < 1)$ [23] can also promote the sparsity of the solution and avoid making the regular solution smoother. In this paper, the Tikhonov-ℓ_p-norm regularization will be explored in detail for image reconstruction in RTI system.

This paper is organized as follows: in Sect. 2, the principle of RTI and the proposed adaptive elliptical model are introduced. The ℓ_p-norm-based reconstruction method is presented in Sect. 3. The experiments in indoor and outdoor scenarios are given and analyzed in Sect. 4. Finally, the conclusion is presented in Sect. 5.

2   Radio Tomographic Imaging

2.1   Introduction of RTI

As illustrated in Fig. 1, there are L sensor nodes deployed around the monitor area, and the red ellipse represents the target. A communication link or LOS path is established between any two sensor nodes, and the total number of links can be denoted as $M = L(L-1)$. The monitor area is divided into N grids (referred to as voxels). When a target enters the monitor area, the RSS value will be changed as [8, 15]

$$\mathbf{y} = \mathbf{W}\mathbf{x} + \mathbf{n} \tag{1}$$

where $\mathbf{y} = [y_1, y_2, \ldots, y_M]^T \in \mathbf{R}^M$ denotes the RSS changes of all the links in the network, $\mathbf{W} = [\mathbf{w}_1, \mathbf{w}_2, \ldots, \mathbf{w}_M]^T \in \mathbf{R}^{M \times N}$ means the shadow weight matrix, $\mathbf{w}_i = [w_{i,1}, w_{i,2}, \ldots, w_{i,N}] \in \mathbf{R}^N$, $\mathbf{x} = [x_1, x_2, \ldots, x_N]^T \in \mathbf{R}^N$ is the signal fading value in the voxel, $\mathbf{n} = [n_1, n_2, \ldots, n_M]^T \in \mathbf{R}^M$ is the measurement noise vector.

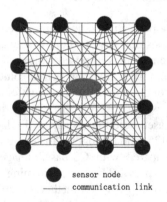

● sensor node
—— communication link

Fig. 1. RTI sensor node deployment.

When reconstructing a target image from measurement data, it needs to search for an optimal solution under the least-squared (LS) error:

$$\mathbf{x}_{LS} = \arg\min_{\mathbf{x}}\|\mathbf{W}\mathbf{x} - \mathbf{y}\|_2^2 \tag{2}$$

In RTI system, $\mathbf{W}$ is not full-rank, therefore, the LS solution of Eq. (2) will not be unique. In the classical RTI, the prior information of the attenuation signal $\mathbf{x}$ is added to the solution process as a constraint term, and the attenuation image can be reconstructed by Tikhonov regularization, the corresponding objective function is expressed as:

$$\min f(\mathbf{x}) = \|\mathbf{W}\mathbf{x} - \mathbf{y}\|_2^2 + \mu_1 \mathbf{x}^T \mathbf{C}^{-1}\mathbf{x} \tag{3}$$

where μ_1 is the Tikhonov regularization parameter [10]. $\mathbf{C}$ is the prior covariance matrix of $\mathbf{x}$, which can be approximately calculated as

$$[\mathbf{C}]_{lj} \approx \exp(-\frac{d_{lj}}{\delta}) \tag{4}$$

where d_{lj} is the distance from voxel l to voxel j, and δ is a "space constant" correlation parameter [1].

Setting the gradient of Eq. (3) to zero, the solution of Tikhonov regularization can be obtained:

$$\tilde{\mathbf{x}} = (\mathbf{W}^T\mathbf{W} + \mu_1 \mathbf{C}^{-1})^{-1}\mathbf{W}^T\mathbf{y} \tag{5}$$

here the target location is the voxels with the largest attenuation in the reconstructed image $\tilde{\mathbf{x}}$.

2.2 Elliptical Weighting Model Considering Horizontal Distance Attenuation

The weighting model can decide whether a voxel contributes to image reconstruction. Figure 2 shows the elliptical weighting model in the RTI system, where any two sensor nodes can be the foci of the ellipse, as Fig. 2(a) for the longest link.

In the classical weighting model [2] (referred to as Model 1), the parameter λ for adjusting the minor axis length of ellipse is a constant, which is obtained by experiments or estimated on-line [11]. If the voxel is within the ellipse, its weight is set to 1; otherwise, the weight is set to 0. In addition, as shown in link1 and link2 in Fig. 2(b), the link lengths may be different. Therefore, considering the influence of the link length on the weight, the weight inside the ellipse needs to be multiplied by the reciprocal of the square root of the link length:

$$w_{i,j} = \frac{1}{\sqrt{d_i}} \begin{cases} 1 & d_{ij}(1) + d_{ij}(2) < d_i + \lambda \\ 0 & otherwise \end{cases} \tag{6}$$

where d_i is the length of link i, and $d_{ij}(1)$, $d_{ij}(2)$ are the distances between voxel j and two sensor nodes, respectively.

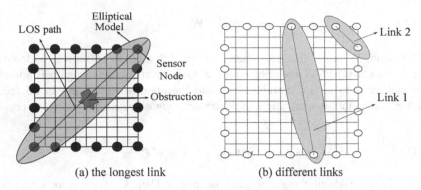

(a) the longest link   (b) different links

Fig. 2. The elliptical weighting model.

According to Eq. (6), λ is a fixed value for different d_i. Thereby, the shorter link length will lead to the bigger elliptical coverage which will introduce more measurement noise.

To solve the above problem, the const-eccentricity weight model (referred to as Model 2) is proposed in [4], which can be described as

$$w_{i,j} = \frac{1}{\sqrt{d_i}} \begin{cases} 1 & d_{ij}(1) + d_{ij}(2) < d_i + \frac{d_i}{d_{\max}}\lambda \\ 0 & otherwise \end{cases} \tag{7}$$

where $d_{\max}$ corresponds to the length of the longest link.

However, for Model 1 and Model 2, the attenuation contributions of different voxels in the same ellipse can't be distinguished, which leads to the mismatching between the weigh model and the measured data. For improving the positioning performance, an adaptive elliptical weight model (referred to as Model 3) is proposed in [6], which introduces one distance attenuation factor e^{-h} and the adaptive weighing value is defined as

$$w_{i,j} = \begin{cases} e^{-h} & d_{ij}(1) + d_{ij}(2) < d_i + \varphi\lambda \\ 0 & otherwise \end{cases} \tag{8}$$

where e is the base of the natural logarithm and h is the vertical distance from voxel j to the LOS path, and φ is a parameter adjusting the minor axis of ellipse adaptively:

$$\varphi = \frac{d_{\max}}{d_i} \tag{9}$$

According to Eq. (8), the weightings of voxels will change inversely with parameter h. For the shorter link, the coverage of the corresponding ellipse will become larger, and there is more valid measurement information for the following image reconstruction.

In fact, according to the attenuation characteristics of radio propagation, the voxel weight is not only related to the vertical distance from the voxel to the LOS path, but also related to the horizontal distance from the voxel to any two sensor nodes. The closer the voxel is to the sensor node, the greater the occlusion effect is on the node. Therefore, we can define the greater voxel weight to match the more RSS attenuation. Combined with the prior information $\mathbf{x}$, that is, the distribution of the attenuation map accords with the Gaussian process [18, 19], the horizontal and vertical distance attenuation factors can be expressed as exponential form, which are introduced into the proposed ellipse model (referred to as Model 4):

$$w_{i,j} = \begin{cases} e^{-h} * e^{-s} & d_{ij}(1) + d_{ij}(2) < d_i + \varphi\lambda \\ 0 & otherwise \end{cases} \tag{10}$$

where s is the normalized distance between the projection point of voxel j on the LOS path and any two sensor nodes.

$$\begin{aligned} s &= \min(l_1, l_2)/d_i \\ d_i &= l_1 + l_2 \end{aligned} \tag{11}$$

where l_1 and l_2 are the distances between the projection point of voxel j on the LOS path and two sensor nodes, respectively, as shown in Fig. 3.

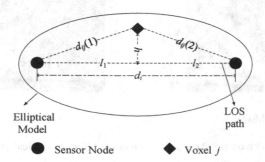

Fig. 3. Geometry of elliptical weighting model.

According to Eq. (10), our proposed model mainly includes two characteristics. Firstly, for the pixels in any two ellipses with different coverages, the corresponding pixel weighting can be distinguished despite of the same $\min(l_1, l_2)$ and h; secondly, for the pixels in one ellipse, those contribution reflecting path attenuation can be detailed to match the actual radio propagation.

Under the same link, the voxel weighting distribution of different ellipse model are shown in Fig. 4(a), Fig. 4(b), Fig. 4(c), Fig. 4(d), the color bar represents voxel weight, changing from 0–1. It can be seen that the weights of the voxels outside the ellipse are 0. In Fig. 4(a) and Fig. 4(b), the weights of all voxels are constant by Model

1 and Model 2 respectively. The weights of voxels by Model 3 only change in the vertical direction to the LOS path, that is, the weights of voxels are only related to the parameter h as Eq. (8). Besides, compared with Model 1, the other ellipse coverage can change with own adjustment parameters. In Model 4, the weights of voxels have the greater weights for the closer distance from the nodes, including the vertical direction and horizontal direction.

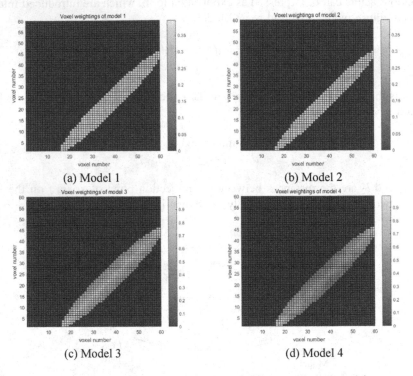

(a) Model 1   (b) Model 2

(c) Model 3   (d) Model 4

Fig. 4. Voxel weightings distribution of different elliptical models.

In order to evaluate the matching degree between the weighting model and measured data, the experiment of two WSN nodes is carried out as shown in Fig. 5(a), one target moves from $(-1.6, 0)$ to $(1.6, 0)$ along the LOS path and from $(0, -1.1)$ to $(0, 1.1)$ along the NLOS path as shown in Fig. 5(b). The collected RSS information in X and Y direction are shown, respectively, here the normalized RSS values have been fit to accessible curve. It can be seen that the attenuation trend is symmetrical round the origin of the axes as in Fig. 5(c) and Fig. 5(d), which is the center of link between two nodes, and X coordinate represents the horizontal direction of the communication link, Y coordinate represents the vertical direction of the communication link. From Fig. 5 (c), the RSS attenuation increases steadily when the target moves along LOS path from the center of link towards one node; and in the horizontal direction of the communication link of NLOS path, there is the worse RSS attenuation for the shorter vertical distance when the target moves near the center of the link. These worse RSS attenuations should correspond to the larger voxel weights, the proposed ellipse model (Model 4) can reflect the above RSS attenuation characteristics in RTI.

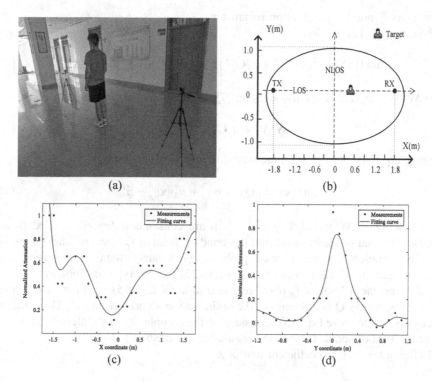

Fig. 5. The verification on the RSS attenuation characteristics in RTI. (a) the experiment scenario. (b) Illustration of the experimental setup. (c) RSS attenuation along the LOS path. (d) RSS attenuation along the NLOS path.

3 TIKHONOV-ℓ_p-norm-Based Image Reconstruction

Substituting Eq. (10) into Eq. (5), we can obtain the signal fading value of all voxels **x** in the monitoring area, then the Tikhonov regularization can solve the linear equations as Eq. (3) for imaging target position [24, 27, 28]. In several cases, there will inevitably appear artifacts and false targets in the reconstructed image because of the RSS measurement noise and calculation error of fading voxel weightings which will further deteriorate the quality of reconstructed image for the complex scenarios. Considering that the solution of the objective function as Eq. (3) satisfies the sparsity of structure, and combining the correlation among the fading voxels, the ℓ_p-norm($0 < p < 1$) is introduced as a sparse constraint to Eq. (3), then the new objective function can be obtained.

$$\min f(\mathbf{x}) = \|\mathbf{Wx} - \mathbf{y}\|^2 + \mu_1 \mathbf{x}^T \mathbf{C}^{-1} \mathbf{x} + \mu_2 \|\mathbf{x}\|_p^p \tag{12}$$

where μ_2 is ℓ_p-norm regularization parameter.

Sorting Eq. (12), we have

$$\min f(\mathbf{x}) = \mathbf{x}^T (\mathbf{W}^T \mathbf{W} + \mu_1 \mathbf{C}^{-1}) \mathbf{x} - 2\mathbf{x}^T \mathbf{W}^T \mathbf{y} + \mathbf{y}^T \mathbf{y} + \mu_2 \|\mathbf{x}\|_p^p \tag{13}$$

Since $\mathbf{W}^T \mathbf{W} + \mu_1 \mathbf{C}^{-1}$ is positive definite [7], the Cholesky decomposition is

$$\mathbf{W}^T \mathbf{W} + \mu_1 \mathbf{C}^{-1} = \mathbf{Q}^T \mathbf{Q} \tag{14}$$

Plugging Eq. (14) into Eq. (13), the objective function becomes

$$\min f(\mathbf{x}) = \|\mathbf{Qx} - \mathbf{b}\|^2 + \mu_2 \|\mathbf{x}\|_p^p + \Psi \tag{15}$$

where $\mathbf{b} = (\mathbf{Q}^T)^{-1} \mathbf{W}^T \mathbf{y}$ and $\Psi = \mathbf{y}^T \mathbf{y} - \mathbf{b}^T \mathbf{b}$ are constants independent of $\mathbf{x}$. In this case, Eq. (15) can be transformed into the standard form of ℓ_p-norm regularization, but which is a non-convex optimization problem. Fortunately, there exist several optimization algorithms based on the ℓ_p-norm [20–22] for this type of problem.

However, the Tikhonov-ℓ_p-norm regularization as Eq. (15) isn't the mixed norm [21], and the matrix $\mathbf{Q}$ is full rank, so the optimization algorithms in [20, 21] cannot be directly applied to solve Eq. (15). Considering the complexity of the algorithm, we can mirror the idea of sparse constrained regularization method [22].

Defining the weight coefficient matrix $\mathbf{A}$

$$\begin{aligned} \mathbf{A} &= \mathrm{diag}[a_1, \ldots, a_j, \ldots, a_N] \in \mathbf{R}^{N \times N} \\ a_j &= ((x_j^{k-1})^2 + \delta)^{-1+p/2} \end{aligned} \tag{16}$$

where x_j^{k-1} is obtained from the last iteration; δ is initialized to 1, k is the number of iterations. The solution of the kth iteration can be calculated as

$$\mathbf{x}^k = \Omega^k \mathbf{Q}^T (\mathbf{Q} \Omega^k \mathbf{Q}^T + \mu_2 \mathbf{I})^{-1} \mathbf{b} \tag{17}$$

where $\mathbf{I} \in \mathbf{R}^{N \times N}$ is identity matrix, Ω^k is the diagonal matrix.

$$\Omega^k = diag(1./\mathbf{A}) \tag{18}$$

The detailed iteration process is shown in Algorithm 1.

Algorithm 1 Iteration Process of Image Reconstruction

Input: Matrices $\mathbf{b}$, $\mathbf{Q}$; Parameters δ, p, μ_2; Initialize $\mathbf{x}^0 = \mathbf{Q} \backslash \mathbf{b}$, $k = 1$;

while $\delta \leq 10^{-6}$ **do**

   Construct the weight coefficient matrix $\mathbf{A}$ as

   for $j = 1:N$

$$a_j = ((x_j^{k-1})^2 + \delta)^{-1+p/2};$$

   end

   $\mathbf{A} = diag[a_1, a_2, ..., a_N]$;

   $\boldsymbol{\Omega}^k = diag(1./\mathbf{A})$;

   Update the matrix $\mathbf{x}^k$ as:

   $\mathbf{x}^k = \boldsymbol{\Omega}^k \mathbf{Q}^T (\mathbf{Q}\boldsymbol{\Omega}^k \mathbf{Q}^T + \mu_2 \mathbf{I})^{-1} \mathbf{b}$;

   if $\|\mathbf{x}^k - \mathbf{x}^{k-1}\|^2 \leq \sqrt{\delta}/100$ **then**

      $\delta = \delta/10$;

   end

   $k = k + 1$;

end

Output: Reconstructed Shadowing Image $\mathbf{x}^k$

---

4   Experimental Validation and Performance Analysis

4.1   Experiment Setup

To verify the effectiveness of the proposed algorithm, several experiments are carried out in outdoor and indoor scenarios as in Fig. 6(a) and Fig. 6(b), respectively, of which the monitoring area is a square of 4.5 m by 4.5 m in Fig. 6(a) and 6 m by 6 m in Fig. 6 (b). The relevant experiment parameters are listed in Table 1. In order to suppress the reflected signal, the flat directional antenna with horizontal beam width of 110° and vertical beam width of 30° are adapted, and the nodes are placed on the bracket with the height of 1m from ground. The nodes fully support the IEEE 802.15.4 protocol, and the maximum transmission power is 4.5 dBm, ensuring to cover the whole monitoring area. In order to measure RSS of all links quickly, a token-ring-like communication protocol [1] was adopted. When all nodes complete a round of signal transmission, RSS measurement information from all links is obtained.

(a) outdoor scenarios

(b) indoor scenarios

Fig. 6. Experimental scenarios.

Table 1. Experiment parameters.

	Node Spacing	Voxel Size	Node Number	N	λ
Indoor	1.5 m	0.1 m × 0.1 m	16	3600	0.05
Outdoor			12	2025	0.04

4.2   Positioning Performance Evaluation

For evaluating the positioning performance of different ellipse models and reconstruction methods, there are multiple index relevant to the image quality and positioning accuracy is adapted.

Defining the image quality σ_i^2 of the i-th target position is the difference between the normalized reconstructed image $\tilde{\mathbf{x}}_r$ and the true image $\mathbf{x}_i$,

$$\sigma_i^2 = \frac{\left\| \tilde{\mathbf{x}}_r - \mathbf{x}_i^2 \right\|}{N} \tag{19}$$

Here the true image $\mathbf{x}_i$ is modeled as a rectangle of 40 cm by 20 cm:

$$[\mathbf{x}_i]_j = \begin{cases} 1, & \textit{if the target occupies voxel } j \\ 0, & \textit{otherwise} \end{cases} \tag{20}$$

For N_T tested target positions, the average imaging quality and positioning accuracy respectively is:

$$\begin{aligned} RMSE_{(img)} &= \sqrt{\frac{1}{N_T} \sum_{k=1}^{N_T} \sigma_i^2} \\ RMSE_{(loc)} &= \sqrt{\frac{1}{N_T} \sum_{k=1}^{N_T} \left\| z_k - \tilde{z}_k \right\|^2} \end{aligned} \tag{21}$$

where $\tilde{z}_k$ and z_k represent the estimated value and real value of the k-th target position, respectively.

4.3 Performance Analysis of Different Ellipse Models

Assuming three outdoor target positions with (3.0 m, 3.0 m), (2.3 m, 2.3 m) and (1.5 m, 0.9 m), and adapting the Tikhonov reconstruction method, the reconstructed images by Model 1, Model 2, Model 3 and Model 4 respectively are shown as in Fig. 7. The brightest area is the target position, which is the worst attenuation voxel; and the energy concentration degree of the brightest area can embody the positioning performance. It can be seen from Fig. 7 that the proposed Model 4 can show higher energy concentration degree and the less artifact area for different target positions, mainly because of perfect matching between the Model 4 and the actual measured data.

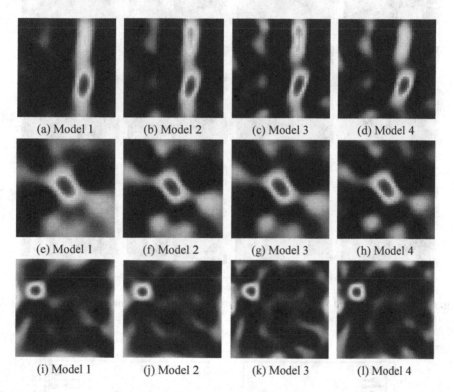

(a) Model 1   (b) Model 2   (c) Model 3   (d) Model 4

(e) Model 1   (f) Model 2   (g) Model 3   (h) Model 4

(i) Model 1   (j) Model 2   (k) Model 3   (l) Model 4

Fig. 7. The reconstructed image of different positions in outdoor scenarios. (a)–(d) position 1. (e)–(h) position 2. (i)–(l) position 3

In indoor scenarios, for positions (3.0 m, 4.8 m), (1.0 m, 1.2 m) and (4.8 m, 4.8 m), the reconstructed images are shown in Fig. 8. It can be seen that the positioning performance in indoor scenario is poorer than that in outdoor scenario, mainly rooting from indoor multipath effects.

The imaging quality and positioning error in different target positions also are provided as Fig. 9a and Fig. 9b, which is consistent to the conclusion from Fig. 7 and Fig. 8. The positioning and imaging results are listed in Table 2 lists. Compared with the other ellipse models, the imaging quality of Model 4 can be improved by about 15.2%, 9.9% and 3.7%, respectively; and the positioning accuracy of Model 4 increases by 31.8%, 19.9% and 9.8%, respectively.

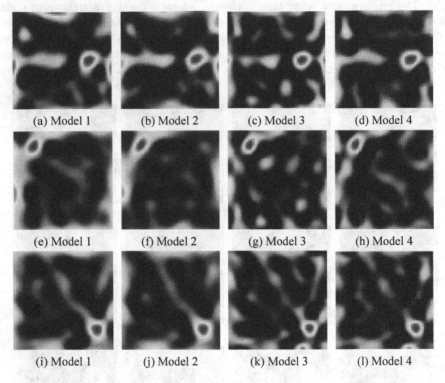

(a) Model 1   (b) Model 2   (c) Model 3   (d) Model 4

(e) Model 1   (f) Model 2   (g) Model 3   (h) Model 4

(i) Model 1   (j) Model 2   (k) Model 3   (l) Model 4

Fig. 8. The reconstructed image of different positions in indoor scenarios. (a)–(d) position 4. (e)–(h) position 5. (i)–(l) position 6.

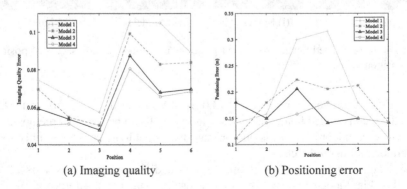

(a) Imaging quality   (b) Positioning error

Fig. 9. Positioning performance in different target positions.

Table 2. Positioning performance of different ellipse models.

		Model 1	Model 2	Model 3	Model 4
Imaging Quality	$RMSE_{(img)}$	0.3154	0.2969	0.2778	0.2676
	Median	0.2862	0.2762	0.2522	0.2418
	Standard Deviation	0.0355	0.0351	0.0272	0.0291
Positioning Accuracy (m)	$RMSE_{(loc)}$	0.2366	0.2013	0.1789	0.1613
	Median	0.1696	0.1937	0.1500	0.1458
	Standard Deviation	0.0859	0.0442	0.0261	0.0264

4.4 Comparative Analysis of Different Image Reconstruction

The proposed Model 4 is selected as the ellipse model in RTI, and positioning performance of the proposed Tikhonov-ℓ_p-norm-based image reconstruction is compared with the existing Tikhonov regularization [24, 27] and ℓ_1-norm regularization [7, 25, 29], respectively. The parameters of different image reconstruction methods are listed in Table 3, and the reconstructed images are shown in Fig. 10 for the outdoor scenarios and Fig. 11 for the indoor scenarios.

Table 3. Image regularization reconstruction parameters.

Parameter	Value	Description
μ_1	30	Tikhonov regularization [24, 27]
μ_2	2.2	ℓ_p-norm regularization
μ_3	20	ℓ_1-norm regularization [7, 25, 29]
p	0.4	Selection of norm p value

(a) Tikhonov   (b) Tikhonov-ℓ_1 (c) Tikhonov-ℓ_p

Fig. 10. Reconstruction results of position 1 in outdoor scenarios.

(a) Tikhonov   (b) Tikhonov-ℓ_1 (c) Tikhonov-ℓ_p

Fig. 11. Reconstruction results of position 4 in indoor scenarios.

Compared with Tikhonov regularization as Fig. 10(a) and Fig. 11(a), the Tikhonov-ℓ_1-norm and Tikhonov-ℓ_p-norm regularization can further reduce the artifacts in reconstructed image, mainly because of consideration the sparsity of the attenuated image, thereby the smaller attenuation components from noise and multipath interference will be suppressed in sparse reconstruction; for $0 < p < 1$, Tikhonov-ℓ_p-norm has the stronger ability of sparse reconstruction, resulting in the higher energy concentration and the less residual artifacts in the reconstructed images as Fig. 10(c) and Fig. 11(c). The corresponding imaging quality and positioning accuracy are shown in Table 4, and Fig. 12 for different target positions. From Table 4, the proposed RTI system can improve the average positioning accuracy (RMSE$_{(loc)}$) by 10.2% (compared to Tikhonov) and 5.0% (compared to Tikhonov-ℓ_1-norm); and the imaging error can reduce by 48.0% (compared to Tikhonov) and 19.1% (compared to Tikhonov-ℓ_1-norm). For different targets positions, the proposed Tikhonov-ℓ_p-norm regularization can also show its superiority over the existing reconstruction methods as Fig. 12.

Table 4. RMSE of different reconstruction methods.

		Tikhonov	Tikhonov-ℓ_1	Tikhonov-ℓ_p
Imaging Quality	RMSE$_{(img)}$	0.2676	0.1720	0.1391
	Median	0.2418	0.1609	0.1311
	Standard Deviation	0.0291	0.0228	0.0303
Positioning Accuracy (m)	RMSE$_{(loc)}$	0.1613	0.1526	0.1449
	Median	0.1458	0.1360	0.1323
	Standard Deviation	0.0264	0.0131	0.0179

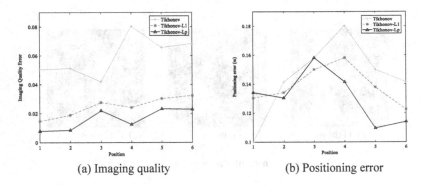

(a) Imaging quality   (b) Positioning error

Fig. 12. RTI performance curves of different reconstruction methods.

5   Conclusions

This study describes one new imaging model in RTI system, which mainly involves the following works: 1) the horizontal distance attenuation factor is firstly introduced to the adaptive elliptical model for computing the voxel contribution in monitoring area with higher sensitiveness on shadowing effects, 2) considering the sparsity, Tikhonov-ℓ_p-

norm-based image reconstruction ($0 < p < 1$) is combined into the imaging model, when the value of parameter p is smaller than 1, the regularization parameter μ_2 is far less than the existing Tikhonov regularization and ℓ_1-norm regularization, which will make the reconstructed image more sparse, thereby the proposed imaging model can provide the higher energy concentration of the target position and the less artifacts in reconstructed image. It should be noted that the optimal parameter p can only be decided by experiments in the proposed Tikhonov-ℓ_p-norm-based image reconstruction.

Author Contributions. Chunhua Zhu and Zhen Shi proposed the original idea and Qinwen Ji carried out the experiment. Chunhua Zhu and Zhen Shi wrote the paper. Zhen Shi supervised and reviewed the manuscript. All authors read and approved the final manuscript.

Funding. This research was financially supported by National Science Foundation of China (61871176): Research of Abnormal Grain Conditions Detection using Radio Tomographic Imaging based on Channel State Information; National Science Foundation of China (61901159): Research on Beamspace Channel Estimation in Massive MIMO Systems by Fusing Multi-Dimensional Characteristic Information; Applied research plan of key scientific research projects in Henan colleges and Universities (19A510011); Research of Abnormal Grain Conditions Detection Based on Radio Tomographic Imaging based on RSSI; Scientific Research Foundation Natural Science Project In Henan University of Technology (2018RCJH18): Research of Abnormal Grain Conditions Detection using Radio Tomographic Imaging based on Received Signal Strength Information; the Innovative Funds Plan of Henan University of Technology Plan (2020ZKCJ02): Data-Driven Intelligent Monitoring and Traceability Technique for Grain Reserves.

Conflicts of Interest. The authors declare no conflict of interest.

References

1. Wilson, J., Patwari, N.: Radio tomographic imaging with wireless networks. IEEE Trans. Mob. Comput. **9**(5), 621–632 (2010)
2. Wilson, J., Patwari, N.: Through walls: motion tracking using variance–based radio tomography networks. IEEE Trans. Mob. Comput. **10**(5), 612–621 (2011)
3. Hamilton, B.R., Ma, X., Baxley, R.J., Matechik, S.M.: Propagation modeling for radio frequency tomography in wireless networks. IEEE J. Sel. Top. Sig. Process. **8**(1), 55–65 (2014)
4. Tian, X., An, J., Wang, Z.: A const-eccentricity elliptical model in radio tomography imaging. J. Beijing Univ. Technol. **35**(07), 725–729 (2015)
5. Lei, Q., Zhang, H., Sun, H., Tang, L.: A new elliptical model for device-free localization. Sensors **16**(4), 1–12 (2016)
6. Zhu, C., Wang, J., Chen, Y.: ARTI (Adaptive Radio Tomographic Imaging): one new adaptive elliptical weighting model combining with tracking estimates. Sensors **19**(5), 1–12 (2019)
7. Xu, S., Liu, H., Gao, F., Wang, Z.: Compressive sensing based radio tomographic imaging with spatial diversity. Sensors **19**(3), 1–15 (2019)

8. Wang, M., Wang, Z., Bu, X., Ding, E.: An adaptive weighting algorithm for accurate radio tomographic image in the environment with multipath and WiFi interference. Int. J. Distrib. Sens. Netw. **13**(1), 1–11 (2017)

9. Zhu, C., Chen, Y.: Distance attenuation-based elliptical weighting model in radio tomography imaging. IEEE Access **6**, 34691–34695 (2018)

10. Ke, W., Zuo, H., Chen, M., Wang, Y.: Enhanced radio tomographic imaging method for device-free localization using a gradual-changing weight model. Progr. Electromagn. Res. M **82**, 39–48 (2019)

11. Kaltiokallio, O., Jantti, R., Patwari, N.: ARTI: an adaptive radio tomographic imaging system. IEEE Trans. Veh. Technol. **66**(8), 7302–7316 (2017)

12. Wang, J., Gao, Q., Pan, M., Zhang, X., Yu, Y., Wang, H.: Toward accurate device-free wireless localization with a saddle surface model. IEEE Trans. Veh. Technol. **65**(8), 6665–6677 (2016)

13. Wang, Z., Liu, H., Xu, S., Bu, X., An, J.: A diffraction measurement model and particle filter tracking method for RSS-based DFL. IEEE J. Sel. Areas Commun. **33**(11), 2391–2403 (2015)

14. Savazzi, S., Nicoli, M., Carminati, F., Riva, M.: A Bayesian approach to device-free localization: Modeling and experimental assessment. IEEE J. Sel. Top. Sig. Process. **8**(1), 16–29 (2014)

15. Wang, Z., Qin, L., Guo, X., Wang, G.: Dual-radio tomographic imaging with shadowing-measurement awareness. IEEE Trans. Instrum. Meas. **69**(7), 4453–4464 (2020)

16. Wang, J., et al.: E-HIPA: an energy-efficient framework for high-precision multi-target-adaptive device-free localization. IEEE Trans. Mob. Comput. **16**(3), 716–729 (2017)

17. Huang, K., Tan, S., Luo, Y., Guo, X., Wang, G.: Enhanced radio tomographic imaging with heterogeneous Bayesian compressive sensing. Pervasive Mob. Comput. **40**, 450–463 (2017)

18. Kaltiokallio, O., Bocca, M., Patwari, N.: Enhancing the accuracy of radio tomographic imaging using channel diversity. In: 2012 IEEE 9th International Conference on Mobile Ad-Hoc and Sensor Systems (MASS 2012), pp. 254–262. IEEE, Las Vegas (2012)

19. Bocca, M., Luong, A., Patwari, N., Schmid, T.: Dial it in: rotating RF sensors to enhance radio tomography. In: 2014 Eleventh Annual IEEE International Conference on Sensing, Communication, and Networking (SECON), pp. 600–608. IEEE, Singapore (2014)

20. Chartrand, R., Yin, W.: Iteratively reweighted algorithms for compressive sensing. In: 2008 IEEE International Conference on Acoustics, Speech and Signal Processing, pp. 3869–3872. IEEE, Las Vegas (2008)

21. Li, Z., Tang, J.: Unsupervised feature selection via nonnegative spectral analysis and redundancy control. IEEE Trans. Image Process. **24**(12), 5343–5355 (2015)

22. Chen, G., Chen, S.: Regularization method with ℓp-norm sparsity constraints for potential field data reconstruction. J. ZheJiang Univ. (Eng. Sci.) **48**(4), 748–756 (2014)

23. Zhang, T., Wu, H., Liu, Y., Peng, L., Yang, C., Peng, Z.: Infrared small target detection based on non-convex optimization with Lp-norm constraint. Remote Sens. **11**(5), 559 (2019)

24. Vogel, C.R.: Computational Methods for Inverse Problems. SIAM (2002)

25. Kanso, M.A., Rabbat, M.G.: Compressed RF tomography for wireless sensor networks: centralized and decentralized approaches. In: Krishnamachari, B., Suri, S., Heinzelman, W., Mitra, U. (eds.) DCOSS 2009. LNCS, vol. 5516, pp. 173–186. Springer, Heidelberg (2009). https://doi.org/10.1007/978-3-642-02085-8_13

26. Ma, M., Li, M., He, X., Liu, Y., Chen, X.: Research on ECT image reconstruction algorithm based on compression sensing and adaptive Lp norm. J. Mach. Tool Hydraulic Pressure **46**(12), 25–31 (2018)

27. Alippi, C., Bocca, M., Boracchi, G., Patwari, N., Rover, M.: RTI goes wild: radio tomographic imaging for outdoor people detection and localization. IEEE Trans. Mob. Comput. **15**(10), 2585–2598 (2015)
28. Denis, S., Berkvens, R., Ergeerts, G., Weyn, M.: Multi-frequency sub-1 GHz radio tomographic imaging in a complex indoor environment. In: 2017 International Conference on Indoor Positioning and Indoor Navigation (IPIN), pp. 1–8. IEEE, Sapporo, Japan (2017)
29. Cao, Z., Wang, Z., Fei, H., Guo, X., Wang, G.: Generative model based attenuation image recovery for device-free localization with radio tomographic imaging. Pervasive Mob. Comput. **66**, 1–13 (2020)
30. Ding, X., Choi, T. M., Tian, Y.: HRI: Hierarchic radio imaging-based device-free localization. IEEE Trans. Syst. Man Cybern. Syst. 1–14 (2020)

Calculation and Numerical Simulation of Building Integrated Photovoltaic System Based on BIM Technology

Yinghao Gan[1], Haoran Cai[2], Xiaofeng Liu[3], and Yanmin Wang[2(✉)]

[1] East University of Heilongjiang, Heilongjiang, Harbin, China
[2] Harbin Institute of Technology, Heilongjiang, Harbin, China
1180610805@stu.hit.edu.cn, wangyanmin@hit.edu.cn
[3] The Architectural Design and Research Institute of HIT, Heilongjiang, Harbin, China

Abstract. With the development of photovoltaic technology, the number of building integrated photovoltaic (BIPV) systems is increasing. Differing from the traditional design of BIPV systems based on the experience of experts, which suffers from high cost and non-maximum efficiency of equipment due to the information lack of buildings, this paper proposes a novel calculation approach based on building information modeling (BIM) technology. Taking a BIPV building located in Hainan, China as a example, the modelling process is given, which description is 1:1 to the real system. Besides, the geographic information attribute of Hainan and the thermal radiation of the building are considered, respectively. Numerical simulation validates the effectiveness of the proposed approach with advantages of high-accuracy and practicability.

Keywords: Smart building · Building Information Modeling (BIM) · Building Integrated Photovoltaic (BIPV) · Thermal analysis

1 Introduction

With the development of the whole society, the issue of energy consumption has become important. For the traditional fossil energy, it has been gradually exhausted. besides its use and discharge has caused serious environmental pollution, destroying the ecological balance, and further posing a serious threat to the life and health of human beings [1]. As an alternative solution, the building integrated photovoltaic (BIPV) technology has arisen to replace the traditional fossil energy by the solar energy. The advantages of BIPV lies on the savings of energy and cost due to the combination of the building and the photovoltaic systems [2]. On the one side, the building can provide enough area for the photovoltaic systems so that the support structure and transmission cost of the photovoltaic systems can be saved; while on the other side, the utilization of the distributed power generation system located in building can reduce the investment and maintenance cost of power. Therefore, BIPV technology has been attractive and the number of BIPV systems is increasing.

W. Xiang et al. (Eds.): BROADNETS 2021, LNICST 413, pp. 226–238, 2022.
https://doi.org/10.1007/978-3-030-93479-8_15

With the integration of photovoltaic architecture makes the building from the past independent power consumption to power generation complex, it can effectively reduce the energy consumption of the building, but also brings a series of new demands for the architectural design, i.e., architectural appearance, optimization deployment, photovoltaic building optimization, etc. However, it should be noted that, BIPV is a combination of photovoltaic modules and building materials (such as windows, building exterior walls, sun shading facilities, outer roofs, etc.) to form a new building material [1, 3]. Compared with the traditional photovoltaic architecture design method based on expert experience. The advantage of BIPV is that photovoltaic modules can not only generate photovoltaic power, but also play a role as building materials. For photovoltaic system, most photovoltaic modules are installed on the roof and wall, and are often affected by the building structure and external environment, and the complexity is not the same today [4]. The influence of the top edge and shape of the building on the photovoltaic array must be fully considered. The traditional method will be very complicated to face such problems.

For the BIPV system, the traditional methods are mostly on the basis of the experience of experts and ignore the connection between the building and the photovoltaic system [5]. On the one hand, if the photovoltaic system is introduced into the building, the photovoltaic module will change the appearance and structure of the building. Besides, the addition of photovoltaic will change the building from the original single power supply to multi power supply, and the electrical characteristics of the building will also change accordingly. On the other hand, due to the variety of architectural shapes, the installation of photovoltaic modules will be limited, and the photovoltaic modules can't play the maximum performance. Therefore, these factors should be considered in in the design of BIPV system [6, 7].

It is worth noticing that, some specific situations concerning the local climate and geologic conditions are also needed to be considered for the buildings. However, the research of BIPV systems often ignores these influences, leading to the degradation of accuracy [5]. Meanwhile, due to the existence of too many building information, it is difficult to cover all of these information. In order to solve the above problems, the building information modeling (BIM) technology has arisen [8]. By using BIM technology, the local geographic and meteorological information is introduced into the BIPV systems and further is used to analyze different conditions by changing the parameters. Therefore, the reliability of the electrical system can be guaranteed, and the optimal energy efficiency of the whole building system under any special circumstances can be realized.

BIM technology is a new technology in the construction industry in recent years. Revit is a BIM design software launched by Autodesk company. It is the most widely used in BIM market [5]. Many software companies have carried out the secondary development based on the platform of Revit. With the rapid development of BIM in the construction industry, BIM is more and more used in all stages of the whole construction life cycle. During the system design, the photovoltaic system and the building are both needed to be modelled by BIM software [9, 10]. However, although some professional software of distributed photovoltaic design as Pvsyst and Retscreen can provide the analysis functions related to photovoltaic, yet they can hardly support the application of BIM so that its shadow radiation analysis function is difficult to reflect the complex shape and environment of the building accurately.

In this paper, taking a hospital with BIPV system located in Hainan of China as an example, a novel calculation approach by combining BIM technology and the software Ecotect is proposed to realize the calculation and numerical simulation of BIPV systems. The structure of the paper is organized as follows. In Sect. 1, the modelling and parameter setting of the system is given; in Sect. 2, the solar model, shadow model and radiation model are established respectively for the solar radiation analysis. In Sect. 3, the numerical simulations concerning the thermal analysis, radiation, photovoltaic power generation are carried out. And the final conclusion of this paper is given in Sect. 4.

2 System Description and BIM Modelling

In this paper, we take a hospital with BIPV system located in Hainan of China as an example to investigate the calculation approach for its photovoltaic system. And the total construction area of this building is 51335.75 m^2. Figure 1 shows its 2D plane by AutoCAD software, which represents the traditional system description of this building. Innovatively, this paper introduces BIM technology to establish a 3D plane for this building, shown in Fig. 2. And the geographical characteristics of Hainan are directly considered and the thermal parameters of the building are shown in Table 1.

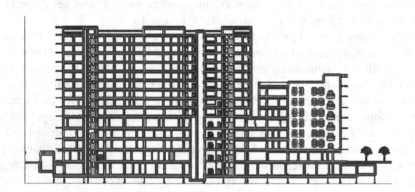

Fig. 1. Traditional 2D plane of the building based on AutoCAD

Table 1. Thermal parameter of the building

Texture	Number	Thermal conductivity
Crack resistant mortar	34	0.930
TF inorganic insulation mortar	22	0.030
Cement mortar	1	0.930
Aerated concrete block	30	0.240
Lime mortar	18	0.810

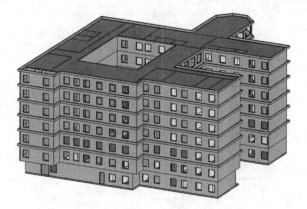

Fig. 2. 3D plane of the building based on BIM

Based on the thermal parameter of construction materials in Table 1, we further use Revit software to calculate its corresponding parameters, seen in Table 2. By combining the BIM model in Fig. 2 and the construction materials thermal parameter in Table 2, the Ecotect software is further introduced to simulate the geographical characteristics of Hainan. And the environmental humidity is set as 60%, the wind speed is set as 0.5 m/s, and the crowd density and clothing activities in the building are set as well for the accuracy of the simulation, seen in Fig. 3. And the parameter settings of the wall and window are given in Table 3 and Table 4.

Table 2. Revit calculation of thermal parameters

Function	Texture	Thickness(mm)
Structure 1	Crack resistant mortar	5.0
Structure 1	TF inorganic insulation mortar	20.0
Structure 1	Cement mortar	20.0
Structure 1	Aerated concrete block	200.0
Structure 1	Lime mortar	20.0

Table 3. Thermal parameter setting of the wall

Parameter	Data
U-Value (W/m²K)	1.552
Admittance (W/m²K)	4.220
Solar Absorption	0.428
Visible Transmittance	0
Thermal Decrement	0.41

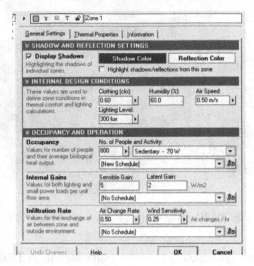

Fig. 3. Thermal parameter setting in Ecotect software

Table 4. Thermal parameter setting of the windows

Parameter	Data
U-Value (W/m^{2}K)	3.440
Admittance (W/m^{2}K)	2.800
Solar Absorption	0.403
Visible Transmittance	0.43
Thermal Decrement	-

3 Solar Radiation Analysis

3.1 Solar Model

In order to simulate the impact of climate environment on buildings, we first establish a solar motion model to calculate the shadow and solar radiation of photovoltaic system in Fig. 2. Declination, solar elevation angle and the azimuth of the sun are three key factors to be addressed in modeling. For the declination, it is the angle between the equatorial plane of the earth and the line connecting the sun and the center of the earth [11]. It is a phenomenon caused by the earth's orbit around the sun, which changes with time, with a cycle of years, reaching a maximum of 23.45° on June 22, the value reached −23.45° on December 22. For the solar elevation angle, it refers to the angle between the light of a certain place and the tangent line of the earth's surface connected with the earth's center. And for the azimuth of the sun, it refers to the angle between the sun's projection on the horizon plane and the local meridian. It is generally measured in a clockwise direction with the north direction of the target as the starting direction and the incident direction of the sun as the ending direction. Therefore, the declination angle δ, altitude angle α and azimuth angle φ_s can be calculated respectively as [12]

$$\delta = 23.45° \times \sin\left(360 \times \frac{284+n}{365}\right) \tag{1}$$

$$\alpha = \sin^{-1}(\sin\delta\sin\varphi + \cos\delta\cos\varphi\cos\tau) \tag{2}$$

$$\varphi_s = \cos^{-1}\left(\frac{\sin\alpha\cos\varphi - \cos\alpha\sin\varphi\cos\tau}{\cos\alpha}\right) \tag{3}$$

where n represents the accumulated day, φ is the local latitude, τ is the solar hour angle. When the sun's noon is zero, the clockwise direction is positive, while the counterclockwise direction is negative.

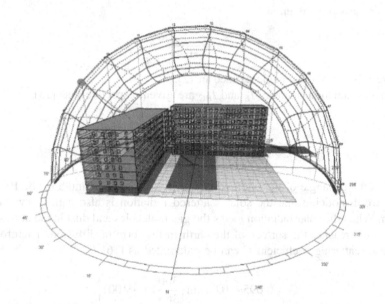

Fig. 4. Shadow analysis by Ecotect software

3.2 Shadow Model

Differing from the traditional shadow analysis such as instrumental measurement, theoretical formula approach, software simulation approach, which suffers from complex determination of the photovoltaic panel, this paper proposes a novel approach based on Ecotect software, shown in Fig. 4, which is simple and easy implementation. Based on the solar model in (1)–(3), the shadow analysis will be carried out by adding the solar meteorological data of a place in Hainan.

3.3   Radiation Model

In the following, we continue to establish a radiation model for the building in Fig. 2. Since the solar radiation energy received by objects on the surface is mainly composed of direct radiation, scattered radiation and reflected radiation, the direct solar radiation refers to the solar radiation that reaches the earth surface in the form of parallel light without changing the direction of radiation [13]. Therefore, the intensity of extraterrestrial solar radiation A can be calculated as [14]

$$A = 1160 + 75 \sin\left[\frac{360}{365}(n-275)\right] \tag{4}$$

The optical thickness coefficient k is given as

$$k = 0.7 + 0.035 \sin\left[\frac{360}{365}(n-100)\right] \tag{5}$$

The air mass m is given as

$$m = \frac{1}{\sin a} \tag{6}$$

where α is the altitude angle defined in (2).
The solar radiation intensity I_B and I_{BC} are given respectively as [15]

$$I_B = Ae^{-km} \tag{7}$$

$$I_{BC} = I_B \times (\cos\alpha\sin\beta\cos(\varphi_m-\varphi_s) + \sin\alpha\cos\beta) \tag{8}$$

where β is the tilt angle of the photovoltaic array, φ_m is the azimuth of the PV array.
It is worth noticing that the solar scattered radiation is also called sky scattered radiation. When the solar radiation meets the gas molecules and dust in the atmosphere, it scatters and reaches the surface of the earth in the form of diffusion. Therefore, the sky diffuse scattering coefficient C can be calculated as [16]

$$C = 0.095 + 0.04 \sin\left[\frac{360}{365}(n-100)\right] \tag{9}$$

By combining (7) and (9), the intensity of solar scattering radiation I_D can be calculated as

$$I_D = CI_B \tag{10}$$

And the solar scattered radiation intensity I_{DC} is given as [17]

$$I_{DC} = I_D\left(\frac{1-\cos\beta}{2}\right) \tag{11}$$

Solar reflected radiation refers to the solar radiation reflected by objects. Radiation usually accounts for a small proportion of the total radiation. Therefore, the solar reflected radiation intensity I_R can be calculated as [17]

$$I_R = \rho I_B (\sin \beta + C) \tag{12}$$

Where ρ Is the reflection coefficient of the object surface.

And the radiation intensity of horizontal solar reflection on inclined plane I_{RC} can be calculated as [18]

$$I_{RC} = I_R \left(\frac{1 - \cos \beta}{2} \right) \tag{13}$$

Based on the established solar model, shadow model and radiation model, the local meteorological data got by the Ecotect software can be introduced to the BIM model of the hospital in Fig. 2. By comparing with the traditional 2D plane of the building based on AutoCAD, the proposed approach based on BIM and Ecotect can improves the selection and placement of photovoltaic panels and the photoelectric efficiency.

4   Numerical Simulation

In order to test the proposed calculation approach based on BIM and Ecotect, we take the hospital located in Hainan as an example to realize its thermal analysis. In Fig. 5 and Fig. 6, the temperature change on the hottest day and coldest day of one year can be got by Ecotect software based on the local meteorological data of Hainan.

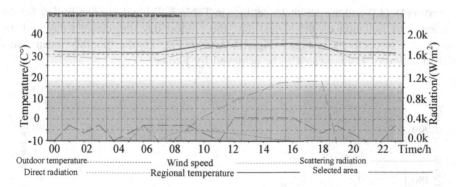

Fig. 5. Temperature change on the hottest day of the year

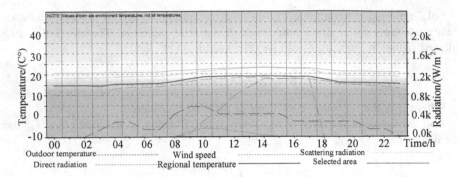

Fig. 6. Temperature change on the coldest day of the year

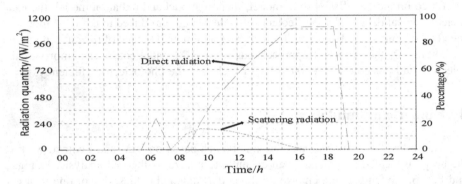

Fig. 7. Average solar radiation on the hottest day

From (4)–(13) and the parameter settings in Table 3, Table 4, we can further get the average solar radiation on the hottest day, the coldest day, the clearest day and the darkest day respectively in Fig. 7–Fig. 10. And in Fig. 11, the monthly mean direct solar radiation of Hainan can also be achieved by Ecotect.

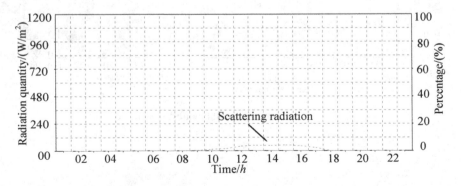

Fig. 8. Average solar radiation on the coldest day

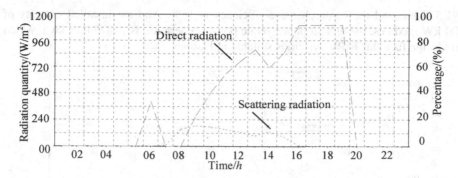

Fig. 9. Average solar radiation on the clearest day

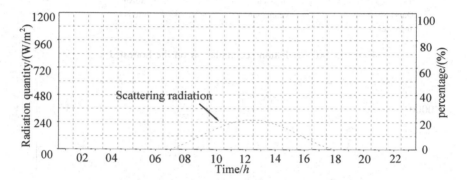

Fig. 10. Average solar radiation on the darkest day

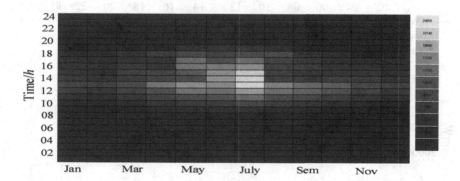

Fig. 11. Monthly mean direct solar radiation

Based on the above analysis of solar radiation data in Fig. 7–Fig. 11, we can get the amount of gain and loss of radiation, which is helpful for the calculation of photovoltaic power generation. And the solar radiation accumulation on the hottest day, coldest day, the day with the most abundant light and the radiation accumulation on the day with the least light of a year can be simulated in Fig. 12–Fig. 15. In conclusion, the solar radiation accumulations in different cases can be seen in Table 5, which are suitable for photovoltaic power generation. The total annual solar radiation per unit area is

991.575 kw, and the comprehensive efficiency is 15%. And the installed capacity of 100 kW modules, the annual photovoltaic power generation is 14873.625 kwh, which proves the fact that BIPV system is suitable in Hainan.

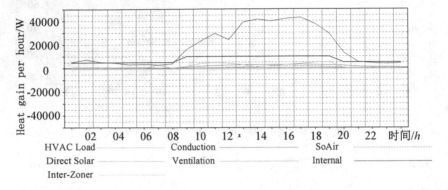

Fig. 12. Solar radiation accumulation on the hottest day

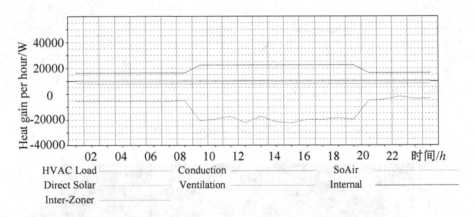

Fig. 13. Solar radiation accumulation on the hottest day

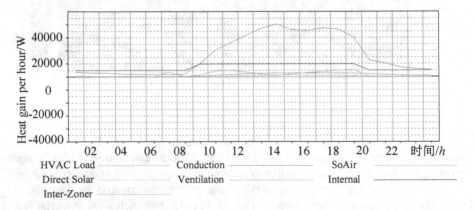

Fig. 14. Solar radiation accumulation on the hottest day

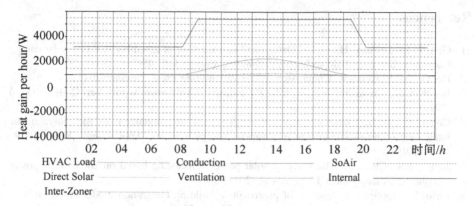

Fig. 15. Solar radiation accumulation on the hottest day

Table 5. Annual cumulative radiation data

	Avail	Average	Incident
Month	Wh/m^2	SHADE	Wh/m^2
January	92380	53%	41826
February	83595	52%	37185
March	117517	44%	62738
April	129005	41%	78718
May	173757	11%	124037
June	155111	0%	136761
July	199414	3%	165943
August	160981	30%	96198
September	138195	48%	84119
October	129062	45%	71468
November	87172	41%	54282
December	95216	49%	38263
Total	1563169		991575

5 Conclusion

In this paper, a novel calculation approach is proposed by BIPV systems. Differing from the traditional design based on 2D plane and experience of experts, the BIM technology and Ecotect are introduced so that 3D plane of the building and the local geographical characteristics. And taking a hospital in Hainan as an example, the numerical simulations are carried out to validate the proposed approach. Specially, the solar model, shadow model and radiation model have been established. It provides a reference for the application of photovoltaic power generation.

References

1. Guo, J., Li, J., Feng, H., Li, H.: Design and optimization of assembly building solar energy integration based on BIM technology. Building Energy Effi. **45**(06), 55–57 (2017)
2. He, G.: BIM Overview. China Architecture & Building Press, Beijing (2011)
3. Heechan, K.: China and overseas solar PV industry development report. Seri Q. **4**(1), 93–96 (2011)
4. Connolly, D.L.H., Mathiesen, B.V., et al.: A review of computer tools for analyzing the integration of renewable energy into various energy systems. Appl. Energy **87**(4), 1059–1108 (2010)
5. Jiang, Q.N., Chen, Z.: The study of solar power forecasting based on BP method power demand side management **13**(6), 21–24 (2011)
6. Zhao, L.: Application Research of photovoltaic building integration model based on BIM Technology. Railway Tech. Innov. (01), 55–57+60 (2017)
7. Li, D.Y.: Application of building information modeling (BIM) technology in housing construction. Value Eng. **35**(15), 146–148 (2016)
8. He, K., Gui, N., Qiu, Z.F., Pan, B.: An integrated design and analysis platform for BIPV based on BIM. Building Energy Effi. **44**(01), 26–32 (2016)
9. Xu, J.F., Bao, L.L., Ma, E.C., Xia, X.Y., Li, J.: Application technology of BIM-based prefabricated building system. J. Inf. Technol. Civil Eng. Archit. (2017)
10. Evins, R.: A review of computational optimization methods applied to sustainable building design. Renew. Sustain. Energy Rev. **22**, 230–245 (2013)
11. Wang, C., Wang, G.J.: Study of distribution rule of solar energy resources in Hainan. J. Hainan Normal Univ. **24**(02), 168–173 (2011)
12. Mühlbauer, M.: Smart building-integrated photovoltaics (BIPV) for Qatar, QScience Connect (2017)
13. Wang, L.J., Wang, J.S.: The radiometer on the inclined plane of solar panels with different installation methods. Acta Energiae Solaris Sinica **4**(06), 20–21 (2010)
14. Walker, L., Hofer, J., Schlueter, A.: High-resolution, parametric BIPV and electrical systems modeling and design. Appl. Energy (2019)
15. Wang, L., Wang, J.: Radiometer on inclined plane of solar panel with different installation methods Calculation. Solar Energy (6), 20–21 (2010)
16. Celik, B., Karatepe, E., Gokmen, N., et al.: A virtual reality study of surrounding obstacles on BIPV systems for estimation of long-term performance of partially shaded PV arrays. Renew. Energy **60**(5), 402–414 (2013)
17. Xu, H.J., Wang, H.C., Hu, J.H., et al.: Power flow calculation method based on Matpower. Internet of Things Technol. (1), 43–45 (2013)
18. Cheng, J.,Tang, X.L., Liang, A.J., Zhao, C.L.: Research on MPPT algorithm of PV array in partial shadow. Motor Control Appl. **48**(4) (2021)

Connected Autonomous Vehicle Platoon Control Through Multi-agent Deep Reinforcement Learning

Guangfei Xu[1,2], Bing Chen[3], Guangxian Li[4], and Xiangkun He[5(✉)]

[1] Shandong University of Technology, Zibo 255000, China
gfxu@sdut.edu.cn
[2] Liaocheng Academy of Agricultural Sciences, Liaocheng 252000, China
[3] Bentron Information Technology Co. Ltd., Shenzhen 518000, China
gaae@esoar.com.cn
[4] Guangxi University, Nanning 530000, China
[5] School of Mechanical and Aerospace Engineering, Nanyang Technological
University, Singapore 639798, Singapore

Abstract. The rise of the artificial intelligence (AI) brings golden opportunity to accelerate the development of the intelligent transportation system (ITS). The platoon control of connected autonomous vehicle (CAV) as the key technology exhibits superior for improving traffic system. However, there still exist some challenges in multi-objective platoon control and multi-agent interaction. Therefore, this paper proposed a connected autonomous vehicle latoon control approach with multi-agent deep reinforcement learning (MADRL). Finally, the results in stochastic mixed traffic flow based on SUMO (simulation of urban mobility) platform demonstrate that the proposed method is feasible, effective and advanced.

Keywords: Intelligent transportation system · Connected autonomous vehicle · Multi-objective platoon control · Multi-agent deep reinforcement learning

1 Introduction

In recent years, with the development of intelligent transportation system (ITS), people pay more attention to congestion, accident, fuel economy, et al. [1–3]. However, when vehicle flows running together, complex dynamic environment may make the running of vehicle flows hard to decide a target speed to deal with dynamic environment. It may be more difficult for vehicle flows satisfying all concerned objectives-high traffic efficient, energy, safe, and driving smoothness.

Single autonomous vehicle maybe relatively easy to obtain a proper speed to fulfil above mentioned aspects with artificial intelligent technology. It can be a important and effective way to solve multi-objectives problems in dynamic environment [4]. Deep learning (DL) as well as reinforcement learning (RL) are two main methods which are widespread adopted to make speed decision one after another [5]. Moreover, DL and RL make it easier to deal with the dynamic environment than other methods [6].

© ICST Institute for Computer Sciences, Social Informatics and Telecommunications Engineering 2022
Published by Springer Nature Switzerland AG 2022. All Rights Reserved
W. Xiang et al. (Eds.): BROADNETS 2021, LNICST 413, pp. 239–248, 2022.
https://doi.org/10.1007/978-3-030-93479-8_16

Lots of methods were proposed for single autonomous vehicle to obtain the proper speed. A rolling-horizon method can be effective to cope with complex trajectories [7]. However, proper speed which can be adequate to fulfill more objectives should be considered [8]. In the process of application of DL or RL, challenges may happen with policy prematurely converging to a local optimum. Therefore, research [9] considered PPO with entropy constraint to make the results better.

However, the learned speed may not suitable when put it into the convoy speed control. Namely, challenges also exist with how to determine a proper speed to make the whole convoy be high traffic efficient, safe and energy at the same time when facing with dynamic environment.

Therefore, the exploration of convoy speed control speed decision-making has become a hot spot. [10] designed different network to state a RL control method for CAVs to solve traffic congestion problem. And penetration rates are set with 2.5% which can be effective to have a better running flow. To improve the ability of RL control method, [11] setup four benchmarks to apply for different traffic problems.

Although multi-agents are concerned and applied in above researches, less attention is paid to multi-objectives emission of multi-agents in convoy speed control which make the convoy be put in a double squeeze.

As MADRL combines with both the advantage of deep neural network (DNN) and RL which can deal with large-scale dynamic information effectively when interacting with a dynamic environment.

Therefore, this paper proposes a connected autonomous vehicle platoon control through multi-agent DRL method. And the key contributions can be summarized as follows:

Firstly, a traffic control strategy is made using DRL with CAVs to deal with multi-objectives mission including high traffic efficient, safe and energy together on open road networks. It can balance various aspects for vehicle flow to achieve synthetically optimal state.

Secondly, it also be demonstrated that DRL can be adjusted to fulfil the requirement of convoy speed control. Namely, several traffic modes are formed which can be selected according to traffic situation.

The remainder of the article is organized as follows. Section 2 state the basic related knowledge of MADRL. Section 3 outlines the RL and multi-objective problem formulation for traffic efficient, safe and energy in open highway networks. Finally, Sect. 4 showed the simulation results of the proposed method.

2   Preliminaries

2.1   Markov Decision Processes

Markov Decision Processes (MDPs) is a description of transition from current state to next state. It is usually represented by a tuple: (S, A, R, P). Where, S means all the states of model including current state and next state, A is actions taken by model in the current state, R means the reward that the adopted A at the current state, P is the transition probability function [12].

2.2   Actor-Critic

Actor-Critic model is made up with the actor and critic model. The critic model updates through state-value function $V(s)$ and the action is evaluated by action-value function Q $(a|s)$. The actor model updates the critic model with the direction to make $V(s)$ higher [13].

2.3   Policy Gradient (PG)

PG method mainly considers the reward of the policy. The obtain of optimal policy is to use gradient descent [14]:

$$\bar{R} = E_t[\nabla_\theta \log \pi_\theta(a_t|s_t)\hat{A}_t],\tag{1}$$

where $\hat{A}_t$ is advantage function, π_θ is policy about parameter θ. And advantage function is written as follows:

$$\hat{A}_t = Q_{\pi_\theta}(s_t, a_t) - V_{\pi_\theta}(s_t),\tag{2}$$

To make the policy develop to the better way, a loss function is set as:

$$L(\theta) = E_t(\log \pi_\theta(a_t|s_t)A_t).\tag{3}$$

2.4   PPO

PPO is adequate to continuous state-action space. PPO usually has two developed forms: PPO-Penalty and PPO-Clip. The former is usually adopted for its simplified form. The purpose of PPO-Clip is to make the old and new policy similar when it is update [15].

PPO-Clip updates θ for the following equation:

$$\theta = \arg\max_\theta \mathop{E}_{s,a\,\pi_{\theta_{\text{old}}}} [L(s, a, \theta_{\text{old}}, \theta)].\tag{4}$$

Let $r_t(\theta) = \frac{\pi_\theta(a|s)}{\pi_{\theta_{\text{old}}}(a|s)}$ donates the probability ratio for the current policy and the old policy. To obtain the objective, loss function $L(s, a, \theta_{\text{old}}, \theta)$ can be described as:

$$L(s, a, \theta_{\text{old}}, \theta) = \min(r_t(\theta)\hat{A}_t, clip(r_t(\theta), 1 - \varepsilon, 1 + \varepsilon)A_t),\tag{5}$$

where ε is a hyperparameter.

Then an advantage function is set to evaluate the update effectiveness:

$$L_{\hat{A}_t} = -\sum_{t=1}^{T} \left(\sum_{t' > t} \gamma^{t'-t}\tau_{t'} - V_{\pi_\theta}(s_t)\right)^2,\tag{6}$$

where γ represents discount factor. $\tau_{t'}$ means the reward at time t'.

3   Experimental Setup

3.1   Flow: Working Environment

The research of this paper is based on Flow [16]. Flow is open source which can be easy access and expand. Flow supports custom modules and permits the research of complex environments, agents, metrics, and algorithms. Flow is built upon SUMO (Simulation of Urban Mobility) [17] which is used to set vehicle and traffic model, Ray RLlib [18] which is used to execute reinforcement learning [19], and OpenAI gym [20] which is used to go on the MDP.

3.2   Problem Setup

This article is concerned with multi-objectives optimization for multi-agent in convoy speed control. Moreover, how to make the whole convoy be high traffic efficient, safe, energy and driving smoothness at the same time when there are only proportionate connected autonomous vehicles controlled by DRL and the other vehicles are human-driven vehicles in the convoy. And the human-driven vehicles are driven by the Intelligent Driver Model (IDM) which is set based on rules in SUMO.

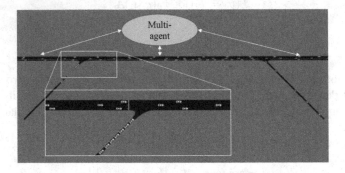

Fig. 1. Open highway network

3.3   Network Configuration

The setup of network can be seen in Fig. 1. It mainly includes a straight highway network and an on-ramp road to make the environment dynamic. The whole inflow rate and the on-ramp inflow rate are set as 4000 and 800 per hour, respectively. CAVs with a centralized controller are trained via MADRL to obtain multi-objectives. The length of main road, on ramp road and off ramp road are set as 1500 m, 250 m and 250 m, respectively. Meanwhile, lane number of them are set as 3, 1, 1, respectively.

3.4   Human-Driven Vehicles

The acceleration and deceleration of human-driven vehicles driven by IDM can be described as the following car following model:

$$
f(l_n, v_{fn}, v_n) = a\left[1 - \left(\frac{v_n}{v_0}\right)^{\delta} - \left(\frac{l^*(v_n, \Delta v_n)}{l_n}\right)^2\right]
\tag{7}
$$

where Δv_n is relative velocity with the preceding vehicle, denoted by:

$$
\Delta v_n = v_{fn} - v_n
\tag{8}
$$

where l^* is the desired headway of the vehicle which can be obtained by:

$$
l^*(v_n, \Delta v_n) = s_0 + \max\left(0, v_n T + \frac{v_n \Delta v_n}{2\sqrt{ab}}\right)
\tag{9}
$$

where s_0, v_0, T, δ, a, b are calibrated parameters to model highway traffic [21].

3.5   Autonomous Vehicles

In the convoy speed control, the CAVs are added with a certain percentage to influence the whole vehicle flow in the network. The CAVs can be seen as multi-agents whose actions (acceleration or deceleration in this paper) are sampled from DRL strategy considering multi-objectives including traffic efficient, safe and energy. The total inflow rate of the network is set as 4000 per hour and the inflow rate of autonomous vehicles is set 20% of total inflow.

3.6   Observations and Actions

The observation space of the learning agent is decided by the multi-objectives which consists of speed, acceleration, fuel consumption, distance between the autonomous vehicle and other vehicles in front and rear, respectively. To improve the training speed and obtained a better training effectiveness, all the observation vectors were normalized [22].

The action space consists of acceleration n of each autonomous vehicles n. Considering the real situation of vehicles, the acceleration can not be infinite. Therefore, the acceleration is clipped into the range $[-1, 1]$ in this paper.

3.7   Reward Designation

The speed control of CAVs should consider multi-objective tasks including traffic efficiency, fuel consumption, safety, driving smoothness at the same time. The designation of reward function can make the training result fulfill requirement.

(1) Traffic efficiency

Traffic efficiency is usually related to the speed of CAVs. And the speed of CAVs should not change sharply for the requirement of response time of all related CAVs. Therefore, a working efficiency reward function can be considered:

$$r_1 = \begin{cases} e^{-k_1 \cdot v_n} & v_{min} \leq |v_n| \leq v_{max} \\ -e^{-k_1 \cdot v_n} & v_n > v_{max} \\ -e^{-k_1 \cdot (v_n + v_{limit})} & v_n < v_{min} \end{cases}, \tag{10}$$

where v_{min} and v_{max} are the vehicle speed range respectively, v_{limit} is network speed limit, v_0 is the speed of CAVs, k_1 is a dynamically adjustable constant.

(2) Fuel consumption

Fuel consumption is considered in convoy control. The running convoy should be limited by the consumption as:

$$r_2 = e^{-k_2 \cdot Q_{cn}}, \tag{11}$$

where Q_{cn} is the fuel consumption of CAVs n, k_2 is a constant.

(3) Safety

When the CAVs are driving on road, Static or dynamic obstacles including surrounding vehicles, pedestrians, signal lights, et al. make it danger for CAVs. Therefore, a safety reward function can be set considering the distance between CAVs and others:

$$r_3 = -\frac{1}{\min(d_{fn}, d_{rn}) + 1}, \tag{12}$$

where d_f and d_r mean the distance between the CAVs and others in front and rear, respectively.

(4) Driving smoothness

Frequent acceleration and deceleration may make the convoy not smooth. Therefore, considering driving smoothness, the reward function can be set as:

$$r_4 = -1000 * |a_n| \tag{13}$$

where a_x and a_y mean the longitudinal and lateral acceleration, respectively.

(5) Multi-objectives

To make the training model be comprehensive in the above aspects, a multi-objective reward function can be obtained:

$$r = \frac{w_1}{\|w\|_1} r_1 + \frac{w_2}{\|w\|_1} r_2 + \frac{w_3}{\|w\|_1} r_3 + \frac{w_4}{\|w\|_1} r_4, \tag{14}$$

where w_i means the weights considering above four objectives, $w = [w_1 \quad w_2 \quad w_3 \quad w_4]$ is the weight vector.

The platoon speed matching the dynamic environment can be obtained by setting the proper value of the weight. The weight vector is set as: $w = [1 \quad 2 \quad 1 \quad 1]$.

3.8 Neural Network Designation

In this paper, we consider a four-layer neural network structure to train the model. The neural network mainly has an input layer, two hidden layers, and an output layer. The hidden layers include 128 neurons. The output is acceleration of CAVs. The states of both set CAVs agents include 8 dimensions which are shown in Table 1.

Table 1. The neural network input variables

	Variables	Input meaning	Unites
1	v_n	Speed of autonomous vehicle n	m/s
2	v_{fn}	Velocity of other vehicle in front	m/s
3	v_{rn}	Velocity of other vehicle in behind	m/s
4	d_{fn}	Distance with front vehicle	m
5	d_{rn}	Distance with behind vehicle	m
6	n_i	Lane numbers	
7	a_n	Longitudinal acceleration of autonomous vehicle n	m/s^2
8	Q_{cn}	Fuel consumption of autonomous vehicle n	

4 Simulation

To verify the effectiveness of the proposed connected autonomous vehicle latoon control approach with MADRL, a training is carried out in SUMO.

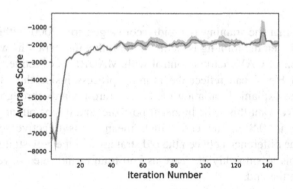

Fig. 2. Training results of connected autonomous vehicle latoon

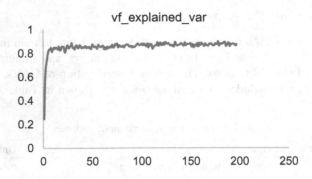

Fig. 3. vf_explained_var in the training

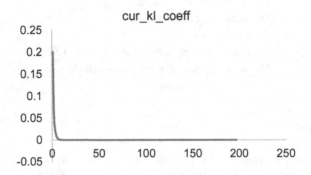

Fig. 4. cur_kl_coeff in the training

We can find that the training is rapidly converged to −2000 within 20 iterations from Fig. 2. And then the training is stable in the following iterations which means the whole designation of CAVs latoon control with MADRL is effective.

Figure 3 and Fig. 4 can reflect the training process inside the MADRL. vf_explained_var is the explained variation of those future rewards through the use of the value function. We want this to be higher if possible, and it tops out at 1; however, the results converge to 0.8 in the end which means it is effective to some extent. cur_kl_coeff is the difference between the old strategy and the new strategy at each time step. We want this to smoothly decrease as you train to indicate convergence. And it decreases to 0 in the end.

5   Conclusion

This paper presented a connected autonomous vehicle latoon control approach with multi-agent deep reinforcement learning (MADRL). In the designation of MADRL, multi-objectives are considered to achieve excellent comprehensive performance of latoon. The training results in stochastic mixed traffic flow based on SUMO platform represent that the proposed latoon control method is feasible, effective and advanced.

References

1. Liu, D., Wang, Y., Shen, Y.: Electric vehicle charging and discharging coordination on distribution network using multi-objective particle swarm optimization and fuzzy decision making. Energies **9**(3), 186 (2016)
2. Delgarm, N., Sajadi, B., Kowsary, F., et al.: Multi-objective optimization of the building energy performance: a simulation-based approach by means of particle swarm optimization (PSO). Appl. Energy **170**, 293–303 (2016)
3. Zhang, Y., Guo, L., Gao, B., Qu, T., Chen, H.: Deterministic promotion reinforcement learning applied to longitudinal velocity control for automated vehicles. IEEE Trans. Veh. Technol. **69**(1), 338–348 (2020). https://doi.org/10.1109/TVT.2019.2955959
4. Xu, G., et al.: Hierarchical speed control for autonomous electric vehicle through deep reinforcement learning and robust control. IET Control Theory Appl. 1–13 (2021). https://doi.org/10.1049/cth2.12211
5. Jardine, P.T.: A reinforcement learning approach to predictive control design: autonomous vehicle applications. Queen's University (Canada) (2018)
6. Hang, P., Lv, C., Huang, C., Cai, J., Hu, Z., Xing, Y.: An integrated framework of decision making and motion planning for autonomous vehicles considering social behaviors. Electr. Eng. Syst. Sci. 1–11 (2020)
7. Xu, J., Shu, H., Shao, Y.: Modeling of driver behavior on trajectory-speed decision making in minor traffic roadways with complex features. IEEE Trans. Intell. Transp. Syst. **20**(1), 41–53 (2019). https://doi.org/10.1109/TITS.2018.2800086
8. Liu, T., Wang, B., Cao, D., Tang, X., Yang, Y.: Integrated longitudinal speed decision-making and energy efficiency control for connected electrified vehicles. Electr. Eng. Syst. Sci. 1–11 (2020)
9. He, X., Fei, C., Liu, Y., Yang, K., Ji, X.: Multi-objective longitudinal decision-making for autonomous electric vehicle: a entropy-constrained reinforcement learning approach. In: 2020 IEEE 23rd International Conference on Intelligent Transportation Systems (ITSC), Rhodes, Greece, pp. 1–6 (2020). https://doi.org/10.1109/ITSC45102.2020.9294736
10. Kreidieh, A.R., Wu, C., Bayen, A.M.: Dissipating stop-and-go waves in closed and open networks via deep reinforcement learning. In: 2018 21st International Conference on Intelligent Transportation Systems (ITSC), pp. 1475–1480. IEEE, November 2018
11. Vinitsky, E., et al.: Benchmarks for reinforcement learning in mixed-autonomy traffic. In: Conference on Robot Learning, pp. 399–409. PMLR, October 2018
12. Achiam, J., Held, D., Tamar, A., Abbeel, P.: Constrained policy optimization. In: International Conference on Machine Learning, pp. 22–31. PMLR, July 2017
13. Bhatnagar, S., Sutton, R.S., Ghavamzadeh, M., Lee, M.: Natural actor-critic algorithms. Automatica **45**(11), 2471–2482 (2009)
14. Cao, X.R.: A basic formula for online policy gradient algorithms. IEEE Trans. Autom. Control **50**(5), 696–699 (2005)
15. Schulman, J., Wolski, F., Dhariwal, P., et al.: Proximal policy optimization algorithms. arXiv preprint arXiv:1707.06347 (2017)
16. Wu, C., Kreidieh, A.R., Parvate, K., Vinitsky, E., Bayen, A.M.: Flow: a modular learning framework for mixed autonomy traffic. IEEE Trans. Robot. (2021)
17. Krajzewicz, D., Erdmann, J., Behrisch, M., Bieker, L.: Recent development and applications of sumo-simulation of urban mobility. Int. J. Adv. Syst. Meas. **5**(3&4) (2012)
18. Duan, Y., Chen, X., Houthooft, R., Schulman, J., Abbeel, P.: Benchmarking deep reinforcement learning for continuous control. CoRR, vol. abs/1604.06778 (2016). http://arxiv.org/abs/1604.06778

19. Liang, E., et al.: Ray RLlib: a composable and scalable reinforcement learning library. arXiv preprint arXiv:1712.09381 (2017)
20. Brockman, G., et al.: OpenAI Gym. arXiv preprint arXiv:1606.01540 (2016)
21. Treiber, M., Kesting, A.: Trajectory and floating-car data. In: Treiber, M., Kesting, A. (eds.) Traffic Flow Dynamics, pp. 7–12. Springer, Heidelberg (2013). https://doi.org/10.1007/978-3-642-32460-4_2.
22. Xu, G., et al.: Hierarchical speed control for autonomous electric vehicle through deep reinforcement learning and robust control. IET Control Theory Appl. (2021)

5G-Enabled Smart Building: Technology and Challenge

Accurate Estimation on the State-of-Charge of Lithium-Ion Battery Packs

Mengying Chen[1](✉), Fengling Han[1], Long Shi[1], Yong Feng[2],
Chen Xue[2], and Chaojie Li[3]

[1] RMIT University, Melbourne, Australia
S3479314@student.rmit.edu.au
[2] Harbin Institute of Technology, Harbin, China
[3] UNSW, Sydney, Australia

Abstract. Lithium-ion batteries have been extensively used worldwide for energy storage and supply in electric vehicles and other devices. An accurate estimation of their state-of-charge (SoC) is essential to ensure their safety and protect them from the explosion caused by overcharge. Large amounts of training data are required for SoC estimation resulting in a great computational burden. Model-based observation method can effectively estimate battery SoC with a limited amount of data. This study applied a combined model, including a one-state hysteresis model and a resistor-capacitor (RC) model, to diminish the parameter estimation errors caused by the hysteresis phenomenon, increasing the estimation accuracy. The Luenberger observer was designed based on the hysteresis RC battery model and evaluated under dynamic stress test (DST) and federal urban driving schedule (FUDS). Our simulation results have shown that the hysteresis RC model has better performance in terms of SoC estimation accuracy using Luenberger observer. Additionally, after the investigation of communication technologies, 5G cellular network offers feasibility for real-time vehicle interaction.

Keywords: Luenberger observer · State-of-charge (SoC) estimation · Hysteresis resistor-capacitor model · Lithium-ion battery · Real-time vehicle interaction

1 Introduction

Lithium-ion (Li-ion) battery, as a promising technology with a long lifespan and high efficiency, has been generally employed as an energy storage device in electric vehicles (EV). Inside a battery pack, there are hundreds of Li-ion battery cells connected in series and parallel to deliver the desired output current and voltage [1]. However, Li-ion battery has potential safety hazard, such as explosion, when one or more of these battery cells overcharge. State-of-charge (SoC) is one of the most critical metrics in a battery management system (BMS) that indicates the current amount of energy stored in the battery. Compared with portable-electronic applications, EV applications require more accurate battery SoC estimation due to the high rate requirement and dynamic rate profiles, which incurs high data consumption and requires the trade-off between

W. Xiang et al. (Eds.): BROADNETS 2021, LNICST 413, pp. 251–262, 2022.
https://doi.org/10.1007/978-3-030-93479-8_17

estimation accuracy and response speed [2]. Nevertheless, most internal parameters of the battery, such as SoC, are hard to be observed after being manufactured. Battery SoC estimation is generally based on battery external characteristics, such as current, voltage, temperature, and etc.

The existing battery SoC estimation methods can be roughly classified into three categories, including the direct measurement methods, machine learning-based methods, and model-based methods. The direct measurement methods, such as the Coulomb counting method [3] and the open-circuit voltage method [4, 5], are used to quickly calculate the battery SoC. However, since these methods use open-loop control, the error will accumulate with time. Therefore, they are not accurate under dynamic working conditions. The machine learning approaches, for example, Artificial Neural network [6], fuzzy logic [7, 8], and support vector machine [9], regard a battery cell as a "black box" and establish the relationship between the inputs and outputs according to large amounts of training data [10]. Therefore, the quality and quantity of training data strongly influence the estimation accuracy. In addition, getting sufficient amount of data is time-consuming [10]. The model-based methods use a closed-loop observer to allow battery models to self-correct and tackle unexpected disturbance. Equivalent circuit models (ECMs) and electrochemical models (EMs) are commonly used to describe battery internal characteristics. The EMs are derived from the porous electrode and concentrated solution theories, describing the concentration and diffusion of Li-ions [11]. These models are more accurate but require large amount of computation. The ECMs use electrical circuit elements to describe the dynamic behaviours of a Li-ion battery. They are structurally simple and computationally efficient [12]. The hysteresis model usually combines with other types of model and depicts the battery hysteresis effects that are the discrepancy between the charge and discharge voltage under open-circuit conditions.

Among the model-based methods, the Kalman filter (KF) family and state observers are generally used algorithms for state estimation. The principle of an observer is to reconstruct system states from observations of its inputs and outputs [13]. The KF and the extended versions of KF, the extended Kalman filter (EKF) [14, 15] and unscented Kalman filter (UKF) [16, 17], are introduced to execute the battery SoC estimation. However, the EKF uses the linearization technique realized by applying Taylor series expansion with the assumption that the higher-order terms are negligible [18, 19]. This increases the estimation inaccuracy. Additionally, the Jacobian matrix used in this algorithm makes it difficult to compute [20]. The UKF applies a discrete-time filtering algorithm with Unscented Transform (UT) instead of the linearization technique [18, 19]. Thus, the accuracy and complexity of UKF is better than EKF as it can predicate states in a highly nonlinear system, and there is no need of a Jacobian matrix [19]. Nevertheless, this method suffers from poor robustness due to the uncertainty in modelling and disturbances in the system [19].

By adding a feedback term at the end of the state equation, the Luenberger observer is easily implemented. Since it is a close-loop observer, it is insensitive to parameter uncertainties, external disturbances and measurement noises. In [21, 22], Luenberger observers were designed to guarantee the nominal error convergence based on a reduced-order EM and a fractional-order model, respectively.

To the best of our knowledge, we are the first to investigate the performance of battery SoC estimation with and without considering the hysteresis phenomenon based on Luenberger observer. Firstly, taking the hysteresis into account, we established a hysteresis resistor-capacitor (RC) model that combines a hysteresis model [23] and an RC equivalent circuit model [1]. The Luenberger observer-based algorithm was used to evaluate the estimation performance of the hysteresis RC model. The system stability has been evaluated by using the Lyapunov method. Finally, we investigated the network capacity of the cellular network and Vehicular Ad hoc Networks (VANETs) applied in mobile vehicle environments, including the bandwidth, data rate, privacy and economy.

The rest of this paper was organized as follows: Sect. 2 introduced the principle of battery SoC and battery model. In Sect. 3, three Luenberger observers were applied to evaluate the hysteresis RC model. The experimental results were presented in Sect. 4. Finally, Sect. 5 analysed the network capacity for real-time vehicle interactions. Section 6 gave the conclusions.

2   Hysteresis Effect During Charging and Discharging of Rechargeable Batteries

Among model based battery SoC estimation methods, a precise battery model is essential to guarantee an accurate estimation. As previous discussion, equivalent circuit model has the advantage of simple structure and efficient computation. However, battery model establishment is still a big challenge due to the complex electrochemical reaction process. Adding the hysteresis will increase the modelling and battery SoC estimation accuracy. The zero-state hysteresis model and the one-state hysteresis are generally used in the literature. The zero-state hysteresis model simply assumes that the hysteresis voltage is a constant. However, this model is not adequate to simulate the behaviour of the battery under a dynamic environment because it cannot detect the slow transition of the hysteresis [24]. The one-state hysteresis model is designed to capture the change in the hysteresis value by adding a hysteresis state to the model [23]. Therefore, this research will utilize a combined model, including a hysteresis model and a RC equivalent circuit model.

2.1   State-of-Charge in Rechargeable Batteries

Battery state-of-charge (SoC) is one of the most important indicators that describes the residual capacity of a battery. SoC must be monitored for safety reason while charging the batteries. SoC denoted by Z can be defined as charges accumulated during the period from t_0 to t, which is formulated as follows:

$$Z(t) = Z(t_0) - \int_{t_0}^{t} I/C_n d\tau \tag{1}$$

$$\dot{Z}(t) = \frac{I}{C_n} \tag{2}$$

where I is input current; C_n is the capacity of the battery; $\dot{Z}$ is the changing rate of SoC.

An accurate estimation of SoC allows battery charging and discharging efficiently and could extend the battery life. However, it is also a challenge to find an effective method to measure battery SoC under dynamic operation conditions. Since the open-circuit voltage (OCV) is a known function of SoC, the battery SoC can be inferred from the OCV curve. Take INR 18650-20R battery [25] as an example, the relationship between OCV and SoC is shown in Fig. 1(a).

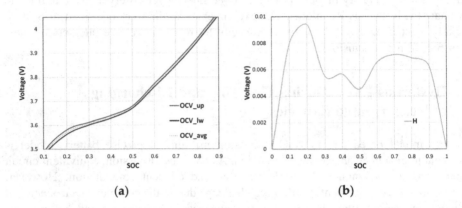

Fig. 1. (a) OCV curve of INR 18650-20R battery [25]; (b) maximum deviation from the OCV$_{\text{avg}}$ value.

2.2   Hysteresis Based Battery Model

Due to the hysteresis phenomenon in the physical systems, the OCV values in the state of charge and discharge are discrepant, as which are denoted as OCV_{up} and OCV_{lw}, respectively. The average value $OCV_{avg}(Z)$ can be expressed by:

$$OCV_{avg}(Z) = (OCV_{up} + OCV_{lw})/2 \tag{3}$$

The one-state hysteresis model [23] can be described as below:

$$\dot{V}_h = \left| \frac{I\gamma}{C_n} \right| [H(Z, \dot{Z}) - V_h] \tag{4}$$

where V_h is the hysteresis voltage that can be defined as a variable related to the SoC and time; γ is a positive constant and affects the rate of decay; $H(Z, \dot{Z})$ is a function that represents the maximum deviation from the OCV_{avg} value as a function of SoC and the rate of SoC, which can be demonstrated in Fig. 1(b) and Eq. (5):

$$H(Z,\dot{Z}) = (OCV_{up} - OCV_{lw})/2 \tag{5}$$

Therefore, the open-circuit voltage is given by:

$$V_{oc}(Z) = OCV_{avg}(Z) + sgn(I)V_h \tag{6}$$

where, $sgn(x)$ is a signum function allowing the equation to be stable for both charge and discharge [26]. By combining the hysteresis model [23] and a first-order resistor-capacitor (RC) ECM [1], the modified battery model becomes more accurate and can be described using several mathematical equations as follows, where V_t, V_{oc}, and V_p are three battery states representing the output terminal voltage, the open circuit voltage, and the polarization voltage respectively; $V_{oc}(Z)$ is known function of SoC and the relationship can be expressed by $\dot{Z} = k\dot{V}_{oc}$; k is the slop of V_{oc} function of SoC; R_t, R_p, C_p, and C_n are battery parameters indicating the Ohmic resistance, the diffusion resistance, the capacitor, and the capacity of the battery, which were identified using the Recursive Least Square (RLS) algorithm; I is the input current; and Δf is the model uncertainty.

$$\dot{V}_t = -a_1 V_t + a_1 V_{oc}(Z) + R_t \dot{I} + b_1 I \tag{7}$$

$$\dot{V}_{oc} = ka_2 V_t - ka_2 V_{oc}(Z) - ka_2 V_p \tag{8}$$

$$\dot{V}_p = -a_1 V_p + b_2 I + \Delta f \tag{9}$$

where $a_1 = 1/(R_p C_p)$; $a_2 = 1/(R_t C_n)$; $b_1 = k/C_n + 1/C_p + R_t/(R_p C_p)$; $b_2 = 1/C_p$.

The state equations correspond to Fig. 2, in which the hysteresis component consisting of hysteresis voltage and the average OCV is circled by a rectangle.

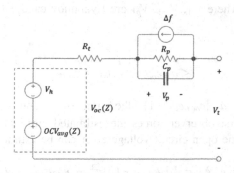

Fig. 2. Schematic diagram of the hysteresis RC equivalent circuit battery model.

3   Robust Battery SoC Estimation Using Luenberger Observer

After the battery model is established, the battery SoC can be estimated using observer-based methods. Among available methods, the Luenberger observer is insensitive to internal parameter uncertainties, external disturbances and measurement noises.

Based on the hysteresis RC model, three Luenberger observers can be designed for three battery states, including output voltage, open circuit voltage, and polarization voltage. In the battery case, the internal states are open circuit voltage and polarization voltage, while the external measurements are the input current and output voltage. Internal states can be estimated subsequently by calculating the observation error of output voltage:

$$\dot{\hat{V}}_t = -a_1 \hat{V}_t + a_1 \hat{V}_{oc}(Z) + R_t \dot{I} + b_1 I + L_t (V_t - \hat{V}_t) \tag{10}$$

$$\dot{\hat{V}}_{oc} = k a_2 \hat{V}_t - k a_2 \hat{V}_{oc}(Z) - k a_2 \hat{V}_p + L_{oc}(V_{oc} - \hat{V}_{oc}) \tag{11}$$

$$\dot{\hat{V}}_p = -a_1 \hat{V}_p + b_2 I + L_p (V_p - \hat{V}_p) \tag{12}$$

$$\hat{V}_{oc}(Z) = \widehat{OCV}_{avg}(Z) + sgn(I)\hat{V}_h \tag{13}$$

where $L_t, L_{oc},$ and L_p are constant feedback gains; and the estimated values are denoted by a "hat". Three observation errors can be defined as $e_t = V_t - \hat{V}_t$; $e_{oc} = V_{oc} - \hat{V}_{oc}$; and $e_p = V_p - \hat{V}_p$. Then, Eq. (10)–(13) can be rewritten as follows:

$$\dot{e}_t = -a_1 e_t + a_1 e_{oc} - L_t e_t \tag{14}$$

$$\dot{e}_{oc} = k a_2 e_t - k a_2 e_{oc} - k a_2 e_p - L_{oc} e_{oc} \tag{15}$$

$$\dot{e}_p = -a_1 e_p + \Delta f - L_p e_p \tag{16}$$

The Lyapunov candidate function can be chosen as $V_1 = 1/2 \cdot e^2$ to analyse the stability of the system, where V_{t1}, V_{oc1}, V_{p1} are Lyapunov candidate functions for three battery states:

$$\begin{aligned} \dot{V}_{t1} &= e_t \dot{e}_t = -a_1 e_t^2 + a_1 e_{oc} e_t - L_t e_t^2 \\ &\leq a_1 |e_{oc}||e_t| - (a_1 + L_t) e_t^2 \end{aligned} \tag{17}$$

When selecting $L_t > a_1(|e_{oc}/e_t| - 1)$, the sign of e and $\dot{e}$ is opposite. Thus, $\dot{V}_{t1} = e_t \dot{e}_t < 0$. The first observer forces the estimated terminal voltage towards the system output. Then the open circuit voltage error can be estimated as $e_{oc} \approx L_t e_t / a_1$.

$$\begin{aligned} \dot{V}_{oc1} &= e_{oc} \dot{e}_{oc} = k a_2 e_t e_{oc} - k a_2 e_{oc}^2 - k a_2 e_p e_{oc} - L_{oc} e_{oc}^2 \\ &\leq k a_2 (|e_t| - |e_p|)|e_{oc}| - (k a_2 + L_{oc}) e_{oc}^2 \end{aligned} \tag{18}$$

When selecting $L_{oc} > ka_2 [(|e_t| - |e_p|)/|e_{oc}| - 1]$, $\dot{V}_{oc1} = e_{oc}\dot{e}_{oc} < 0$. The second observer pushes the open circuit voltage error towards zero. Then the polarization voltage error can be estimated as $e_p \approx -L_{oc}e_{oc}/ka_2$.

$$\begin{aligned}
\dot{V}_{p1} &= e_p\dot{e}_p = -a_1e_p^2 + \Delta f e_p - L_p e_p^2 \\
&\leq |\Delta f||e_p| - (a_1 + L_p)e_p^2
\end{aligned} \tag{19}$$

When selecting $L_p > |\Delta f/e_p| - a_1$, $\dot{V}_{p1} = e_p\dot{e}_p < 0$. The third observer can force the polarization voltage error towards zero. After three estimated states converge to the real battery states, the battery SoC can be inferred from the OCV curve.

4   Results and Discussion

The Luenberger observer-based battery SoC estimation method discussed in this paper was evaluated using the experimental data provided by the Center for Advanced Life Cycle Engineering (CALCE) at the University of Maryland. Parameters of the battery sample under room temperature are given in Table 1.

Table 1. Parameters of the battery sample (INR 18650-20R) [25].

Characteristics/parameters	Name/values
Model type	LNMC/Graphite
Nominal capacity	2000 mAh
Nominal voltage	3.6 V
Charging cut-off voltage	4.2 V
Discharging cut-off voltage	2.5 V
Maximum current	22 A

4.1   Hysteresis Based Battery Model

The performance of battery SoC estimation has been tested by the dynamic street test (DST) and the federal urban driving schedule (FUDS) test. The DST simulates a dynamic discharge regime of an EV, which is a simplification of the real-life loading conditions of batteries [25]. The FUDS is more complex representing the power demands of an industry standard automobile [25]. Accurate battery SoC estimation is essential due to the high rate requirement and dynamic rate profiles [2]. Figure 3 gives the measured current and voltage of the sample battery under DST and FUDS, which will be used as input and output for real-time battery SoC estimation. It can be seen from Fig. 3 that the current variation range (the input) and the voltage variation trend (the output) of using DST and FUDS are the same. However, the FUDS presents high frequency and complex current and voltage profiles.

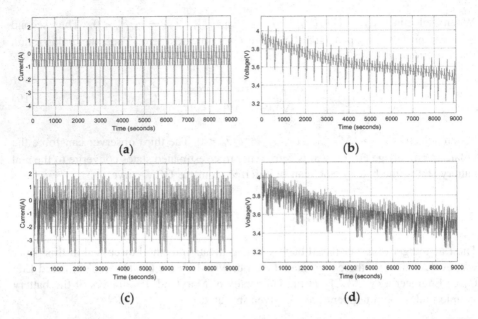

Fig. 3. Measured current and voltage of the battery sample: (a) measured current under DST; (b) measured voltage under DST; (c) measured current under FUDS; (d) measured voltage under FUDS.

4.2   Performance Evaluation Between Different Battery Models

The battery SoC has been estimated using Luenberger observers based on the hysteresis RC model (red dotted line) and the model without hysteresis terms (blue solid line) under the DST and FUDS test. The estimation results using Luenberger observers are illustrated in Fig. 4.

Figure 4(a) and Fig. 4(b) are the comparative results between estimated SoC and measured SoC, which has been zoomed from 3000 s to 5000 s. The simulation results were evaluated by the root mean square error (RMSE), which shows how close a fitted line consisting of estimates is to the measured data points [25]. The SoC estimation error is illustrated in Fig. 4(c) and Fig. 4(d).

It can be seen that the modified model (red line indicating) when considering the hysteresis effect is more close to the measured SoC (green solid line). Additionally, the FUDS results in a faster variation of battery SoC. Thus it has a high requirement in terms of response speed and system stability. The RMSEs based on the hysteresis RC model are 1.94% for DST and 1.95% for FUDS, while the RMSEs based on the model without hysteresis terms are 2.12% for DST and 2.07% for FUDS, respectively. It can be seen from Fig. 4 (a) and (b) that the estimated SoC can converge to the true values at about 1000 s.

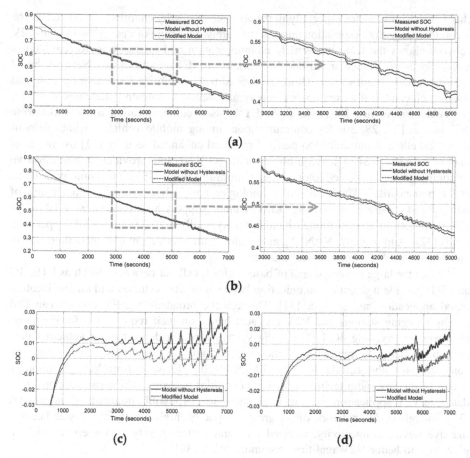

Fig. 4. Battery SoC estimation results using Luenberger observers: (a) SoC estimation results under DST; (b) SoC estimation results under FUDS; (c) SoC estimation error under DST; (d) SoC estimation error under FUDS.

Adding the hysteresis will increase the modelling and battery SoC estimation accuracy but also increase the computational complexity. By considering this, advanced technology such as 5G network may show a better future due to higher bandwidth consumption and higher date rate requirement.

5   Network Capacity for Real-Time Vehicle Interactions

Taking the advantage of bidirectional chargers, some EVs can supply or harvest energy to or from the grid. However, high penetration of EVs into the grid can bring challenges such as voltage instability, peak demand imbalance and power loss. [27] Vehicle-to-vehicle (V2V) charge sharing is considered as one of the most effective strategies to reduce the dependence on the power grid [28] and address the immediate charge needs of vehicles especially in the absence of nearby charging stations [29]. The accurate battery SoC estimation ensures the safety exchange of energy, while the V2V network allows the real-time vehicle communication and interactions. Recent studies mostly focus on Vehicular Ad hoc Networks (VANETs) and Cellular Network based communication frameworks. Those studies aim to minimize the charging cost and develop efficient and secure energy supply and demand matching strategies.

Vehicular Ad hoc Networks (VANETs) based communication frameworks were designed in [27, 28, 30] for communication among mobile vehicles, which demonstrates excellent communication performance and enhanced security [31] by means of road-side units (RSUs) and on-board units (OBUs) and provides a cost-effective solution with the Dedicated Short Range Communication (DSRC) technology or IEEE 802.11p standard. VANETs-based technologies have advantageous characteristics of privacy and economy. However, DSRC cannot support high data rates (1 Gbps) of V2V applications due to limited bandwidth (typically 10 MHz in 5.9 GHz spectrum band) [32]|. Additionally, VANETs may suffer from intermittent disconnections due to the short-range V2V communications [28].

Due to the large coverage area of base stations, cellular networks (such as LTE, 4G and 5G) provide a direct communication between nearby vehicles and enable location based application and services [31]. Through the broadcasting, EV owners can find nearby charging stations and V2V chargers based on their requirement for charging. However, the existing 4G-LTE cellular systems are not dedicated for vehicular data collection. Better communication incurs ever high cost and may lead to network congestion for other cellular services [27, 28]. Millimeter-wave (mmWave) technology is one of the key radio technologies in 5G cellular network, which can support high-date-rate V2V applications with its large bandwidths (possibly hundreds of megahertz) [33]. Therefore, 5G network offers greater capacity, higher data rate, lower latency, massive device connectivity, reduced cost and better Quality of Experience, which gives rise to better V2V real-time communication [34].

6 Conclusions

This paper aims to improve the state-of-charge (SoC) estimation accuracy by adding a hysteresis term into an RC equivalent circuit model that diminishes the parameter estimation errors caused by the hysteresis phenomenon. The validation test was carried out based on the hysteresis RC model and the model without the hysteresis terms under DST and FUDS, using Luenberger observers. Simulation results have shown that the Luenberger observer-based SoC estimation with the hysteresis RC model had better performance in terms of estimation accuracy comparing with the model without hysteresis terms. Additionally, 5G cellular network offers feasibility for real-time vehicle interaction. This paper is valuable for engineers in developing V2V energy and information sharing. Since EV applications requires both accurate SoC estimation and high convergence speed, future works will focus on methods that able to achieve both faster response speed and higher estimation accuracy. Moreover, reliable communication technologies will be investigated to allow V2V real-time communication.

References

1. Feng, Y.: Robust estimation for state-of-charge and state-of-health of lithium-ion batteries using integral-type terminal sliding-mode observers. IEEE Trans. Ind. Electron. **67**(5), 4013–4023 (2019)
2. Plett, G.: Extended Kalman filtering for battery management systems of LiPB-based HEV battery packs. J. Power Sources **134**(2), 262–276 (2004). https://doi.org/10.1016/j.jpowsour.2004.02.032
3. Aylor, J.H.: A battery state-of-charge indicator for electric wheelchairs. IEEE Trans. Ind. Electron. **39**(5), 398–409 (1992)
4. Xing, Y.: State of charge estimation of lithium-ion batteries using the open-circuit voltage at various ambient temperatures. Appl. Energy **113**, 106–115 (2014)
5. Barai, A.: A study of the open circuit voltage characterization technique and hysteresis assessment of lithium-ion cells. J. Power Sources **295**, 99–107 (2015)
6. Kang, L.: A new neural network model for the state-of-charge estimation in the battery degradation process. Appl. Energy **121**, 20–27 (2014)
7. Jiani, D., Zhitao, L.: A fuzzy logic-based model for Li-ion battery with SOC and temperature effect. In: 11th IEEE International Conference on Control & Automation (ICCA), pp. 1333–1338. IEEE (2014)
8. Salkind, A.J.: Determination of state-of-charge and state-of-health of batteries by fuzzy logic methodology. J. Power Sources **80**(1–2), 293–300 (1999)
9. Hu, X., Sun, F.: Fuzzy clustering based multi-model support vector regression state of charge estimator for lithium-ion battery of electric vehicle. In: International Conference on Intelligent Human-Machine Systems and Cybernetics 2009, vol. 1, pp. 392–396. IEEE (2009)
10. Lin, C.: Evaluation of electrochemical models based battery state-of-charge estimation approaches for electric vehicles. Appl. Energy **207**, 394–404 (2017)
11. Kemper, P.: Simplification of pseudo two dimensional battery model using dynamic profile of lithium concentration. J. Power Sources **286**, 510–525 (2015)
12. Zhang, C.: An improved model-based self-adaptive filter for online state-of-charge estimation of Li-ion batteries. Appl. Sci. **8**(11), 2084 (2018)
13. Ellis, G.: Observers in Control Systems: A Practical Guide. Elsevier (2002)
14. Luo, Y.: State of charge estimation method based on the extended Kalman filter algorithm with consideration of time-varying battery parameters. Int. J. Energy Res. **44**(13), 10538–10550 (2020)
15. Zheng, Y.: State-of-charge inconsistency estimation of lithium-ion battery pack using mean-difference model and extended Kalman filter. J. Power Sources **383**, 50–58 (2018)
16. Huang, C.: Robustness evaluation of extended and unscented Kalman filter for battery state of charge estimation. IEEE Access **6**, 27617–27628 (2018)
17. Nemounehkhah, B.: Comparison and evaluation of model-based state-of-charge estimation algorithms for a verified lithium-ion battery cell technology (2020)
18. Hannan, M.A.: A review of lithium-ion battery state of charge estimation and management system in electric vehicle applications: challenges and recommendations. Renew. Sustain. Energy Rev. **78**, 834–854 (2017)
19. Li, W.: Electrochemical model-based state estimation for lithium-ion batteries with adaptive unscented Kalman filter. J. Power Sources **476**, 228–534 (2020)
20. Zhang, F., Liu, G.: A battery state of charge estimation method using sliding mode observer. In: 7th world congress on intelligent control and automation 2008, pp. 989–994. IEEE (2008)

21. Du, J.: An adaptive sliding mode observer for lithium-ion battery state of charge and state of health estimation in electric vehicles. Control. Eng. Pract. **54**, 81–90 (2016)
22. Ning, B.: Adaptive sliding mode observers for lithium-ion battery state estimation based on parameters identified online. Energy **153**, 732–742 (2018)
23. Luenberger, D.G.: Observing the state of a linear system. IEEE Trans. Military Electron. **8** (2), 74–80 (1964)
24. Luenberger, D.: An introduction to observers. IEEE Trans. Autom. Control **16**(6), 596–602 (1971)
25. Dey, S.: Nonlinear robust observers for state-of-charge estimation of lithium-ion cells based on a reduced electrochemical model. IEEE Trans. Control Syst. Technol. **23**(5), 1935–1942 (2015)
26. Zou, C.: Nonlinear fractional-order estimator with guaranteed robustness and stability for lithium-ion batteries. IEEE Trans. Ind. Electron. **65**(7), 5951–5961 (2017)
27. Mastali, M.: Battery state of the charge estimation using Kalman filtering. J. Power Sources **239**, 294–307 (2013)
28. Li, Y.: A wavelet transform-adaptive unscented Kalman filter approach for state of charge estimation of LiFePo$_4$ battery. Int. J. Energy Res. **42**(2), 587–600 (2018)
29. Zheng, F.: Influence of different open circuit voltage tests on state of charge online estimation for lithium-ion batteries. Appl. Energy **183**, 513–525 (2016)
30. Kim, I.S.: Nonlinear state of charge estimator for hybrid electric vehicle battery. IEEE Trans. Power Electron. **23**(4), 2027–2034 (2008)

Fire Simulation and Optimal Evacuation Based on BIM Technology

Zhanzeng Li[1($\boxtimes$)], Yingying Li[2], Yang Ge[3], and Yanmin Wang[3]

[1] China Architectural Design and Research Group, Beijing, China
lizz@cadg.cn
[2] The Architectural Design and Research Institute of HIT, Heilongjiang,
Harbin, China
[3] Harbin Institute of Technology, Heilongjiang, Harbin, China
wangyanmin@hit.edu.cn

Abstract. In order to solve the problem of fire inducing and spread process with complex characteristics, this paper proposes a novel approach to realize fire dynamic simulation and evacuation optimization. Focusing on the inducing factors and spread, a fire source heat release rate and combustion model is established based on the technology of BIM and Pyrosim. And the evacuation settings and building environment are further concluded for the accurate dynamic simulation. For the evacuation optimization, the time of different evacuation path corresponding to specific evacuation exit is calculated and compared to achieve the optimal choice of the path in the case of building fire with complex environment.

Keywords: BIM · Pyrosim · Fire combustion · Evacuation optimization

1 Introduction

With the rapid development of social economy, coupled with the breakthrough of building technology, buildings are developing towards high-rise and large-scale, which bring a new challenge to fire safety. In the past five years, there were 142,3000 fires in China, causing 14,2000 casualties [1]. Since the 1990s, the number of building fires in China has accounted for more than 75% of the total number of fires, and the number of deaths and direct property losses caused by them account for 90% and 85% of them, respectively [2]. Building fire has brought great threat to personal safety and property safety, but also brings great challenges in fire safety research. Fire simulation and evacuation analysis are two key problems to be solved.

For the fire simulation, different models of fires have been established and the focuses are key data collection and impact analysis. In [3], a fire diffusion model of students' apartment was established using Pyrosim software to simulate the influence of automatic sprinkler system and windows on the fire layer temperature and smoke height. In [4], a 3D physical model of fire was established, and the spread process of fire smoke was simulated by the software of computational fluid dynamics (FDS). The distribution of high temperature smoke and visibility was studied, and the fire risk time of each fire scene was analyzed. In [5], the law of smoke spread in the process of fire

W. Xiang et al. (Eds.): BROADNETS 2021, LNICST 413, pp. 263–274, 2022.
https://doi.org/10.1007/978-3-030-93479-8_18

development was studied under the fire model in Pyrosim software, and relevant countermeasures and suggestions were proposed for the fire prevention and management of high-rise residential buildings. In [6], the influence of vehicle blockage on smoke flow mode and critical ventilation speed in tunnel fire was studied. In [7], a more practical CFD method was proposed to simulate the air flow in subway tunnels and stations by coupling the heat source in the station with the street level through the entrance and exit. However, the precision of the existing models is not high due to the complex spread characteristics of fire.

For the building emergency evacuation, most researchers focus on the evacuation scenario and efficiency analysis, which provides a theoretical basis for evacuation simulation and optimization. In [8], the evacuation simulation of a university teaching building was carried out based on pathfinder software and the relationship between the number of each floor. And the cumulative number of evacuees and the evacuation time in the daytime and night scenes of the university teaching building was also analyzed. In [9], the software of Pathfinder was used to simulate the emergency evacuation behavior of the crowd. And the room evacuation, floor evacuation and the evacuation of the whole building were also simulated. [10] changes the entrance and exit position and the width of stair flight respectively to simulate the evacuation situation at the entrance and exit of teaching building and the stairs of each floor under different scenes. [11] takes a circular atrium teaching building as the research object to study and analyze the smoke diffusion of the teaching building floor, and to obtain the best evacuation path and escape time of each floor after the fire. [12] studied a model for managing the movement of building occupants in case of fire emergency, which is more effective than the whole building strategy of full-stage building evacuation, partial building evacuation and local refuge. With the development of 5G technology and artificial intelligence, intelligent algorithm is applied in emergency evacuation. In [13], an improved k-medoids algorithm was proposed, which considered the influence of the relationship between individuals and the distance between individuals on the movement of people. In [14], the cellular automata method was used to establish a modified decision-making model under panic state based on field model, and the effect of panic on evacuation behavior was studied. However, the impact of fire environment and key data on evacuation is seldom studied.

Based on the above analysis, taking a school teaching building as an example, this paper proposes an advanced fire simulation and evacuation optimization approach. A fire combustion model combining BIM technology and fire simulation software is established, focusing on the complex spread characteristics of fire and the analysis and optimization of emergency evacuation. It provides suggestions for the fire drill and emergency evacuation of the school teaching building and can be extended to other large buildings.

2 Fire Combustion Modeling

2.1 Fire Parameters Calculation

Temperature and fire spread speed are two important elements in fire simulation [15, 16]. In order to get the temperature change around the fire source for the accurate situation of fire evacuation, we assume that the fire is caused by foam plastic burning substance and occurs in the chair of the teacher's office. And the heat release rate of the fire is exponentially increasing, i.e., there is

$$Q = at^2 \tag{1}$$

where t is the time of fire combustion (s), a is the fire growth coefficient (kw/s^2), Q is the heat release rate (kw).

Considering that the combustible material is foam plastic, the fire source is set as a fast fire. Table 1 gives the growth coefficient of heat release rate of different combustibles in fire and we take the coefficient of rapid fire of the fire growth coefficient, that is, $a = 0.04689$ kw/s^2. In order to simulate the real fire evacuation, the fire combustion time is first set as 250 s, which is calculated by (1). The heat release rate Q is 2930.63 kw, the integer can be set as 3000 kW. And we set the heat release rate to the combustion heat release rate at the beginning of the fire.

Table 1. Growth coefficient of heat release rate of combustible fire

Fire growth level	Typical combustibles	Fire growth factor (kw/s^2)
Slow fire	Common silicone rubber products	0.00293
Medium speed fire	Cotton and polyester cushion	0.01127
Fast fire	Mail bags, wooden brackets, foam plastics	0.04689
Super fast fire	Pool fire, fast burning furniture, light curtain	0.18781

Furthermore, the fire related parameters are set on Pyrosim software. Considering that the initial ignition source of the teaching building is set on the seat, the combustion area of the fire source is set as 1 m^2. The combustion reaction is a polyurethane combustion reaction. The material is heat conductive solid material and is defined as foam. The materials of other buildings in the space are defined as concrete, gypsum, Pinus ponderosa, steel and tile materials, according to Pyrosim software. The ambient temperature of the room is 20 °C, and the air flow rate is 0 m/s.

Based on the BIM building information model of teaching building, it is imported into Pyrosim software for fire simulation to get the following information concluded as the heat of fire combustion, combustion products, the change of fire temperature field, the gas flow phenomenon in fire space, fire spread and flame spread, the setting of spray device, the installation and monitoring of heat detector and the use conditions of smoke detector key information of sprinkler system start-up, fire extinguishing action and fire combustion change.

2.2 Evacuation Personnel and Environment Setting

Taking a teaching building as an example, two evacuation passageways with different directions are considered according to the relevant design specifications. When the roof height of the public area is lower than 6.0 m, the straight-line distance from all locations in the public area to the nearest evacuation exit should be less than the longest evacuation length of 40.0 m; When the average height in the area is not less than 20.0 m, it is 90.0 m; In other cases, it should not be greater than 60.0 m.

Considering the changes of the number of people in the teaching building during recess, school and after-school, the number of evacuees is set as 1700. Pyrosim software is used to set the evacuation personnel. Differing from the adoption of the traditional software of FDS and Evac, much unnecessary work can be avoided and the evacuation simulation of a five-story teaching building will be carried out.

3   Simulation and Analysis of Fire Combustion

Figure 1 shows the teaching building model established by BIM technology in this paper. The structure and data of building can be got. Figure 2 shows the room distribution on the first floor of the teaching building, and the other floors are similar. And the teachers' lounge is selected as a specific scene to simulate the fire combustion. A smoke sensor is placed at the door of the room to observe the change of smoke concentration and height with time. Here we assume that, the initial growth of the fire is rapid fire, and the fire growth factor is 0.04689. Referring to the technical specification for smoke control and extraction of teaching buildings, the heat release of places without spraying is 6 MW, $Q = 230$ kw.

Fig. 1. BIM model of the five-story building

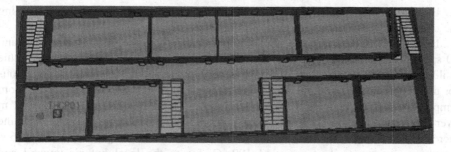

Fig. 2. Room distribution and setting of fire combustion

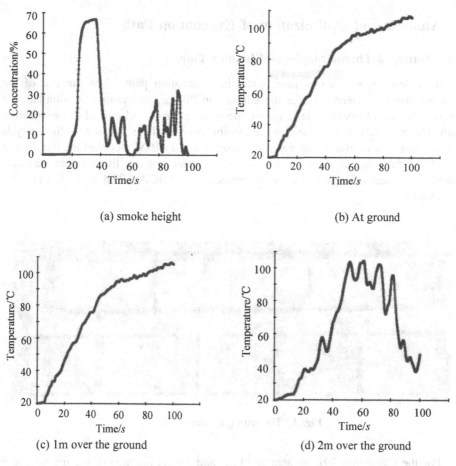

(a) smoke height

(b) At ground

(c) 1m over the ground

(d) 2m over the ground

Fig. 3. Temperature change in different positions

By combining the software of BIM and Pyrosim, the simulation results concerning the changes of temperature are given in Fig. 3(a)–(d).

In Fig. 3(a), it describes the smoke height change with the time. During 20 s and 40 s, the height of smoke is high to almost 70%, the people have time to run out of the building. After 50 s, the height of smoke is very low to about 30% and it is dangerous for the people in the building. As the fire happens, it spends about 53 s for the room temperature to 100 °C in Fig. 3(b), while in Fig. 3(c), the time for the position of 1 m over the ground is about 71 s. However, it should be noted in Fig. 3(d) that, with the increase of the height, the time for the position of 2 m over the ground is about 76 s, but the temperature vibrates around 100 °C due to the local hot air upward and downward.

4 Analysis and Optimization of Evacuation Path

4.1 Setting of Thermocouples and Ignition Point

In the following, we further investigate the evacuation path when the fire of the building happens. Here we take the Classroom 201 as an example to simulate the ignition point and assume the stairs are the only entrance and exit of the evacuation path. The information of temperature and visibility of smoke is selected for the analysis and optimization of evacuation path. In the second-story BIM model of the building in Fig. 4, we can see that there are four stairs. In order measure the temperature accurately, 29 thermocouples are used, named as THCP01-THCP16, LAYER01-LAYER13.

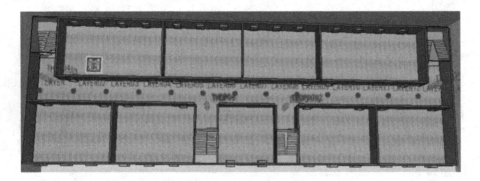

Fig. 4. The setting of thermocouples

For the Classroom 201, its area is 70 m^2 and we set the area of the fire source is 4 m^2. According to the fire load in the building, we assume that the initial growth of the fire is ultra fast fire, the fire growth factor is 0.1878; the heat release of the office without spray is 6 MW, $Q = 230$ kW, and the time from fire to effective combustion is 178 s.

4.2 Simulations

Based on the setting of Fig. 4, we use the software of Pyrosim to simulate the fire combustion concerning the flue gas and these evacuation paths, i.e., left staircase, middle-left staircase, middle-right staircase and right staircase.

(1) **Spreading process of flue gas**

In order to test the spreading process of flue gas, the thermocouples in Fig. 4 are used. And the height of the judgment point of flue gas sets 1.8 m. The simulations are given in Fig. 5(a)–(d).

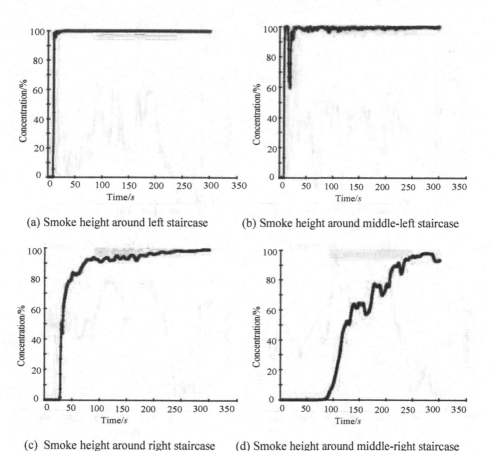

(a) Smoke height around left staircase   (b) Smoke height around middle-left staircase

(c) Smoke height around right staircase   (d) Smoke height around middle-right staircase

Fig. 5. Simulation results of flue gas

Taking 1.8 m as a smoke hazard height determination point, Fig. 5(a)–(d) illustrate the spreading process of the four evacuation paths, i.e., left staircase, middle-left staircase, right staircase and middle-right staircase. The time of smoke reaching the 1.8 m hazard height of the four cases can be got from simulations as 10 s, 25 s, 250 s and 300 s, respectively, which is important for the people to have enough time to escape the building after the fire happens.

(2) **Temperature change around the left staircase**

Focused on the temperature change at left staircase, it is important for the people to escape from this exit. In the following, four cases of the temperature change are considered, i.e., around the ground, 1 m over the ground, 2 m over the ground and 3 m over the ground. As the increase of the height, it is a fact that, the temperature will increase due to the local hot air upward. Meanwhile, as the increase of the time, the temperature oscillation will get slow.

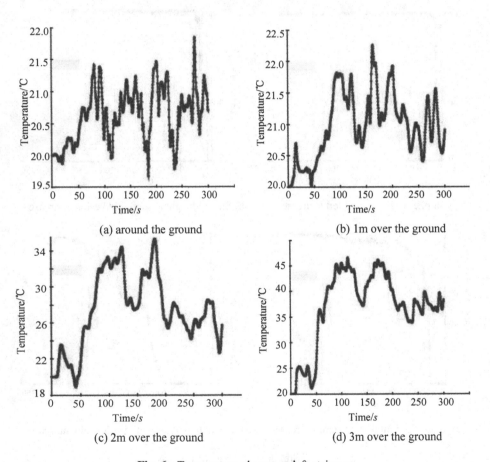

(a) around the ground

(b) 1m over the ground

(c) 2m over the ground

(d) 3m over the ground

Fig. 6. Temperature change at left staircase

(3) **Temperature change around the middle-left staircase**

Similarly, the temperature change at the middle-left staircase is investigated and given in Fig. 7. Still the four positions around the ground, 1 m over the ground, 2 m over the ground and 3 m over the ground are considered. The same conclusion can be got as that of Fig. 6.

In the following, simulations of the left two cases concerning the temperature changes around the middle-right staircase and the right staircase are given briefly (Figs. 8 and 9).

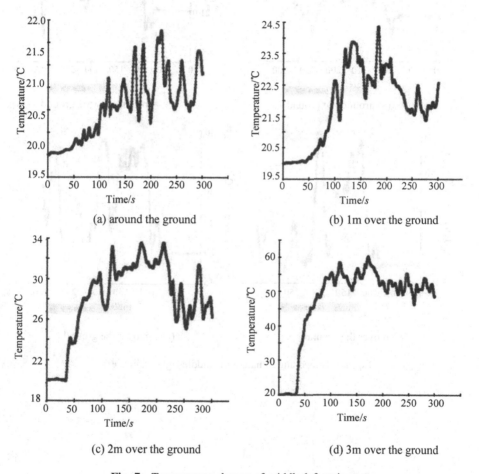

Fig. 7. Temperature change of middle-left staircase

(4) Temperature change around the middle-right staircase

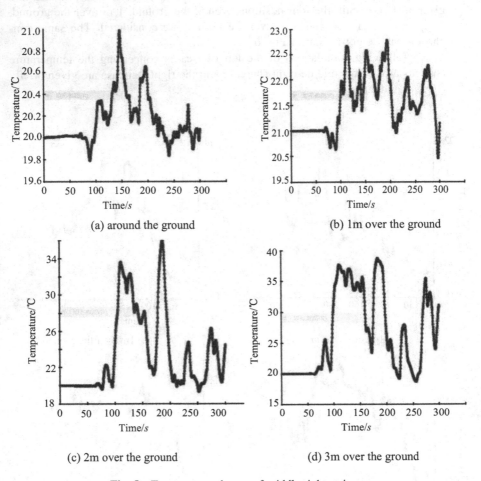

(a) around the ground

(b) 1m over the ground

(c) 2m over the ground

(d) 3m over the ground

Fig. 8. Temperature change of middle-right staircase

(5) Temperature change around the right staircase

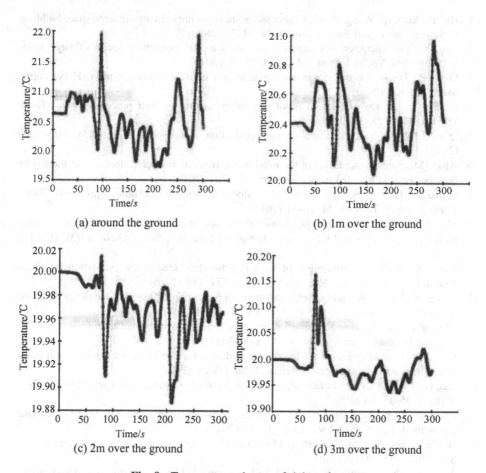

Fig. 9. Temperature change of right staircase

5   Conclusion

In this paper, a novel approach concerning the dynamic simulation of fire combustion and evacuation optimization is proposed based on the technology of BIM and Pyrosim. Taking a five-story teaching building as an example, the temperature and smoke height are two key factors affecting the evacuation of the people in the building. Therefore, the two parameters are investigated around every entrance and exit under typical fire place by setting different thermocouples. It also guides the optimal choice of evacuation paths for the people in the building.

274   Z. Li et al.

References

1. Hu, Y., Xiao, Q., Wang, H., Li, J.: simulation study on fire scenarios in large space building. J. Beijing Univ. Civil Eng. Archit. **36**(2), 74–79 (2020)
2. Cao, Y.: Fire characteristics and performance-basedfire protection design of large space buildings. Fire Technol. Prod. Inf. **24**(1), 23–26 (2016)
3. Ding, P.: Discussion on comprehensive treatment of dust in cement plant. Hebei Agric. Mach. **12**, 121 (2020)
4. Li, D., Xu, S.: Dust explosion proof and safety control in flour processing plant. Grain Process. **44**(5), 28–30 (2019)
5. Qian, Z., Wang, Y.: IOT technology and application. Acta Electron. Sin. **40**(5), 1023–1029 (2012)
6. Altay, M., Surmen, A.: Effect of the relative positions of vehicular blockage on the smoke flow behavior in a scaled tunnel. Fuel **25**, 694–701 (2019)
7. Fernando, E.C., Greg, B., Rainald, L.: Modeling subway air flow using CFD. Tunn. Undergr. Space Technol. **24**, 20–31 (2014)
8. Ma, H., Ma, Y.: Research on optimization simulation of evacuation on strategy for teaching buildings in colleges and universities. J. North China Inst. Sci. Technol. **17**(3), 105–110 (2020)
9. Fang, X., Yang, Z.: Simulation of high rise building emergency evacuation based on Pathfinder. J. Bohai Univ. Nat. Sci. Ed. **37**(2), 177–183 (2016)
10. Wang, Z., Li, Y.: A study on exit and stairs optimization of teaching buildings based on pathfinder simulation. Saf. Secur. **41**(4), 15–21 (2020)
11. Shen, B., Song, X., Liu, X.: Study on fire smoke flow law and evacuation time of annular teaching building. Shanxi Arch. **47**(1), 1–4 (2021)
12. Groner, N.E.: A decision model for recommending which building occupants should move where during fire emergencies. Fire Saf. J. **80**, 20–29 (2016)
13. Liu, G., Liu, H., Lv, L.: Relationship-integrated crowds simulation. J. Chin. Comput. Syst. **37**(8), 1735–1740 (2016)
14. Chen, C., Tong, Y.: Study on crowd evacuation model under panic state based on cellular automata. J. Saf. Sci. Technol. **15**(6), 12–17 (2019)
15. Bergh, F., Engelbrecht, A.: A study of particle swarm optimization particle trajectories. Inf. Sci. **176**(8), 937–971 (2016)
16. Xiao, Y.: The theoretical basis of CFAST fire model. Fire Tech. Prod. Inf. **25**(3), 90–92 (2018)

Discrete Sliding Mode Control of PMSM with Network Transmission

Xin Hui[1], Yingying Li[2], Jian Cui[1], Mingyang Yang[1],
and Yanmin Wang[1(✉)]

[1] Harbin Institute of Technology, Harbin, Heilongjiang, China
20S006104@stu.hit.edu.cn, wangyanmin@hit.edu.cn
[2] The Architectural Design and Research Institute of HIT,
Harbin, Heilongjiang, China

Abstract. In this paper, a novel discrete full-order terminal sliding mode (FTSM) control approach is proposed for a permanent magnet synchronous motor (PMSM) working in network transmission environment. By utilizing the vector control technology, the decoupled model of PMSM with the structure of double closed loop can be deduced. The discretization influence of network transmission is specially investigated by comparing the control performances in continuous domain and discrete domain, following the guaranteed stability condition when working in network transmission environment. In order to simulate the network transmission environment, a test platform based on OPC technology is established. Simulations validate the proposed approach.

Keywords: Network transmission · Permanent magnet synchronous motor · Sliding mode control · OPC technology

1 Introduction

In recent years, the computer technology, network communication technology and control technology have been developed rapidly. Specially with the emergence and wide application of distributed control system, field bus control system and industrial Ethernet control system, which indicates that the network is becoming a new characteristic of control systems, including the permanent magnet synchronous motor (PMSM) [1]. The introduction of network transmission into the traditional control systems with peer to peer communication will bring benefits of structure networking and the intelligence of the controlled nodes [2]. Therefore, the research topic concerning the networked control systems (NCS) has become a hotspot. According to the 2010 market research report of Cisco Systems, the number of industrial Ethernet nodes throughout the world is about 300,000,000 [3].

Compared with the traditional PID and other conventional control approaches, sliding mode (SM) control has become a new control type due to its strong robustness, excellent dynamic and static control characteristics [4]. At present, there are two kinds approaches often used in the control of PMSM, i.e., linear sliding mode (LSM) and

W. Xiang et al. (Eds.): BROADNETS 2021, LNICST 413, pp. 275–284, 2022.
https://doi.org/10.1007/978-3-030-93479-8_19

terminal sliding mode (TSM) which eliminate some undesired drawbacks such as high-frequency chattering and control singularity. Recently, a novel full-order TSM control approach is proposed due to its global control continuity [5]. Its idea is on the basis of high-order sliding mode (HOSM) to solve the chattering problem, while the control singularity can be avoided due to the introduction of special fractional power term [6].

At the same time, with the rapid development of digital technology and the increasing emergence of programmed microprocessor hardware applied in PMSM control systems, the discretization of SM controller has been given increasing amount of attention [7, 8]. In general, the discretization of SM controller includes two steps: designing an appropriate algorithm for the controlled systems in continuous-time domain on the basis of the expected dynamic and static performances; and further making an analog-to-digital (AD) transformation for the corresponding digital controller approximating to the original continuous-time counterpart [9, 10]. Although it is known that the smaller the sampling time is, the better the control performance of the discrete system will be, while it should be noted that although the sampling time is sufficiently small, the control performance of the digital controller is lower than the analog controller's. Therefore, how to select the sampling time and SM parameter is an important issue to be addressed for the control of PMSM systems.

In this paper, a novel full-order terminal SM approach is proposed for the network controlled PMSM system with consideration of the time-delay of communication characteristics. The structure of the paper is organized as follows. In Sect. 2, the modelling and controller design based on the full-order sliding mode control is given for PMSM control system in continuous domain, following its discretization and guaranteed stability in Sect. 3. And finally the simulation and conclusion are given in Sect. 4 and Sect. 5, respectively.

2   System Description in Continuous Domain

For the PMSM system in dq-axes, we assume the magnetic circuit is unsaturated, the space magnetic field is sine wave, eddy current and magnetic hysteresis loss can be excluded. Therefore, the equations of PMSM can be got as [11]

$$\begin{cases} \dot{i}_d = -\frac{R_s}{L} i_d + p\omega i_q + \frac{u_d}{L} \\ \dot{i}_q = -p\omega i_d - \frac{R_s}{L} i_q - \frac{p\psi_f}{L}\omega + \frac{u_q}{L} \\ \dot{\omega} = \frac{3p\psi_f}{2J} i_q - \frac{B}{J}\omega - \frac{T_L}{J} \end{cases} \tag{1}$$

where, i_d, i_q are dq-axes stator currents; u_d, u_q are dq-axes stator voltages; L is the equivalent inductance of winding; R_s is the stator resistance; p is number of motor pole pairs; ψ_f is magnetic potential generated by permanent magnet; ω is motor's mechanical angular velocity; T_L is load torque; J is total inertia of rotor and load; B is friction coefficient.

In order to remove the couplings in (1), the vector control method [12] is introduced in this paper. The double closed-loop controller of PMSM is designed on the basics of full-order TSM approach, and the system diagram is given in Fig. 1, where the outer loop is a speed loop, and the inner current loop is decoupled into two independent controllers based on $i_d = 0$.

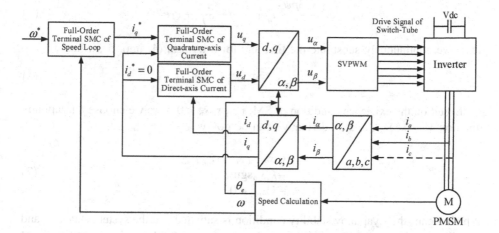

Fig. 1. System control scheme with double closed-loop structure

2.1 Design of Speed Controller

Here we define the speed tracking error $e_\omega = \omega^* - \omega$, where ω^* is the desired speed. And from (1), the first derivatives of e_ω can be obtained as

$$\dot{e}_\omega = \dot{\omega}^* - \frac{3p\psi_f}{2J}i_q^* + \frac{B}{J}\omega + \frac{T_L}{J} \tag{2}$$

The control objective is to make the speed error e_ω converge to zero. And the design process of full-order TSM controller is described as follows.

Step 1: A TSM sliding surface is designed as

$$s_\omega = \dot{e}_\omega + c_1 e_\omega^{p_1/q_1} \tag{3}$$

where the design parameter $c_1 > 0$, p_1 and q_1 are integers with $0 < p_1/q_1 < 1$.

Step 2: Based on the equivalent control of SM [13], here we design the control low i_q^* as

$$\begin{cases} i_q^* = \frac{2J}{3p\psi_f}\left(i_{qeq}^* + i_{qn}^*\right) \\ i_{qn}^* = k_1 \int \mathrm{sgn}(s_\omega) \\ i_{qeq}^* = \dot{\omega}^* + \frac{B}{J}\omega + \frac{T_L}{J} + c_1 e_\omega^{p_1/q_1} \end{cases} \tag{4}$$

Where i_{qeq}^* is the equivalent control term to drive the system to reach and stay on the sliding surface; i_{qn}^* is the switching control term to overcome the influence of external disturbance and internal parameter disturbance; $k_1 > 0$.

Step 3: Ignoring the influence of system parameters disturbance and external disturbance temporarily, and substituting (2) into (3), it yields

$$S_\omega = \dot\omega^* - \frac{3p\psi_f}{2J}i_q^* + \frac{B}{J}\omega + \frac{T_L}{J} + c_1 e_\omega^{p_1/q_1} \tag{5}$$

Then we continuously substitute the first and third term in (4) into (5), it has

$$S_\omega = -i_{qn} \tag{6}$$

Based on the existence condition of SM, i.e., $s_w \dot s_w < 0$, here we choose a Lyapunov
function $V = 0.5 S_\omega^2$, and its derivative can be got as

$$\begin{aligned} &= s_\omega \dot s_\omega = s_\omega(-\dot i_{qn}^*) \\ \dot V &= -k_1 s_\omega \mathrm{sgn}(s_\omega) \\ &= -k|s_\omega| < 0 \end{aligned} \tag{7}$$

Which means the Lyapunov stability condition is satisfied and the system states e_ω and
$\dot e_\omega$ will converge to zero in a finite time. And after that, the dynamic characteristics of
the PMSM system can be described as

$$S_\omega = \dot e_\omega + c_1 e_\omega^{p_1/q_1} = 0 \tag{8}$$

Here we assume $e_\omega(0) \neq 0$ is the initial value of the variable e_ω. Therefore from
(8), the convergence time from $e_\omega(0)$ to $e_\omega(t_s) = 0$ can be calculated as

$$t_s = -\frac{1}{c_1} \int_{e_\omega(0)}^0 \frac{de_\omega}{e_\omega^{p_1/q_1}} = \frac{|e_\omega(0)|}{c_1(1 - p_1/q_1)} \tag{9}$$

2.2   Design of Current Controller

For the current loop in Fig. 1, it includes two independent controllers. As the full-order
TSM controller design of the speed loop, we define current error variable $e_d = i_d^* - i_d$.
From (1), the corresponding error system of the d-axis current can be described as

$$\dot e_d = -p\omega i_q + \frac{R_s}{L}i_d - \frac{u_d}{L} \tag{10}$$

And the controller can be designed as

$$\begin{cases} s_d = \dot e_d + c_2 e_d^{p_2/q_2} \\ u_d = L(u_{deq} + u_{dn}) \\ u_{deq} = -p\omega i_q + \frac{R_s}{L}i_d + c_2 e_d^{p_2/q_2} \\ u_{dn} = k_2 \int \mathrm{sgn}(s_d) \end{cases} \tag{11}$$

where s_d is the designed sliding surface; $c_2 > 0$, p_2 and q_2 are integers with $0 < p_2/$ $q_2 < 1$; u_{deq} and u_{dn} are the equivalent control and switching control of u_d respectively, $k_2 > 0$.

For the q-axis current, we define its current error variable $e_q = i_q{}^* - i_q$. From (1), the direct axis current error system can be deduced as

$$\dot{e}_q = \dot{i}_q^* + p\omega i_d + \frac{R_s}{L}i_q + \frac{p\psi_f}{L}\omega - \frac{u_q}{L} \tag{12}$$

And based on the full-order TSM approach, the corresponding controller can be designed as

$$\begin{cases} s_q = \dot{e}_q + c_3 e_q^{p_3/q_3} \\ u_q = L(u_{qeq} + u_{qn}) \\ u_{qeq} = \dot{i}_q^* + p\omega i_d + \frac{R_s}{L}i_q + \frac{p\psi_f}{L}\omega + c_3 e_q^{p_3/q_3} \\ u_{qn} = k_3 \int \mathrm{sgn}(s_q) \end{cases} \tag{13}$$

where, $c_3 > 0$; p_3 and q_3 are integers, and $0 < p_3/q_3 < 1$; u_{qeq} and u_{qn} are the equivalent control and switching control of u_q respectively, $k_3 > 0$.

3 System Discretization Based on Zero-Order Holder

In order to test the influence of network transmission, the zero-order holder is adopted to simulate the system discretization. Here we take the speed loop as an example to illustrate the process. In order to simplify the explanation, we define variables

$$\begin{cases} \alpha = \frac{-3p\psi_f}{2J} \\ b = \frac{B}{J} \\ p = \dot{\omega}^* + \frac{T_L}{J} \end{cases} \tag{14}$$

By substituting (14) into (2), the speed error system can be changed as

$$\dot{e}_\omega = \alpha i_q^* + b\omega + p \tag{15}$$

By adopting zero-order holder, the discretization of the system (15) can be expressed as

$$e_\omega(k+1) = \Phi\omega(k) + \Gamma i_q^*(k) + p \int_0^h e^{\alpha\tau} d\tau \tag{16}$$

where h is the sampling period, and the variables

$$\begin{cases} \Phi = e^{\alpha T} \\ \Gamma = b \int_0^h e^{\alpha \tau} d\tau \end{cases}$$

with

$$\begin{cases} e^{\alpha h} = I + \alpha h + \frac{\alpha^2 h^2}{2!} + O(h^3) \\ \int_0^h e^{\alpha \tau} d\tau = hI + \frac{h^2 \alpha}{2!} + O(h^3) \end{cases} \tag{17}$$

Correspondingly, the sliding surface in (3) and the full-order TSM controller in (4) can be discretized respectively as

$$s_\omega(k) = \frac{e_\omega(k) - e_\omega(k-1)}{h} + C_1 e_\omega(k)^{\frac{p_1}{q_1}} \tag{18}$$

$$\begin{cases} i_q^*(k) = \frac{2J}{3p\psi_f} \left(i_{qeq}^*(k) + i_{qn}^*(k) \right) \\ i_{qn}^*(k) = i_{qn}^*(k-1) + hk_1 \text{sgn}(s_w(k)) \\ i_{qeq}^*(k) = \frac{w^*(k) - w^*(k-1)}{h} + \frac{B}{J} w(k) + \frac{T_L}{J} + C_1 e_w(k)^{\frac{p_1}{q_1}} \end{cases} \tag{19}$$

In order to guarantee the system stability after discretization, the discrete SMC stability condition $s_w^2(k+1) < s_w^2(k)$ should be satisfied. Therefore, it has

$$\left| \frac{e^{\alpha h}\omega(k) + b \int_0^h e^{\alpha \tau} d\tau \left(\frac{-1}{\alpha} \left(i_{qn}^*(k-1) + hk_1 \text{sgn}(s_\omega(k)) + C_1 e_\omega(k)^{\frac{p_1}{q_1}} + p(k) + b\omega(k))\right) + p \int_0^h e^{\alpha \tau} d\tau - e_\omega(k)}{h} \right.$$

$$\left. + C_1 \left(b \int_0^h e^{\alpha \tau} d\tau \left(\frac{-1}{\alpha} \left(i_{qn}^*(k-1) + hk_1 \text{sgn}(s_\omega(k)) + C_1 e_\omega(k)^{\frac{p_1}{q_1}} + p(k) + b\omega(k))\right) + p \int_0^h e^{\alpha \tau} d\tau \right)^{\frac{p_1}{q_1}} \right|$$

$$< \left| \frac{e_\omega(k) - e_\omega(k-1)}{h} + C_1 e_\omega(k)^{\frac{p_1}{q_1}} \right| \tag{20}$$

Similarly, for the d-axis current controller in (11) and q-axis current controller in (13), their discretization can be deduced respectively as

$$\begin{cases} s_d(k) = \frac{e_d(k) - e_d(k-1)}{h} + c_2 e_d(k)^{p_2/q_2} \\ u_d(k) = L(u_{deq}(k) + u_{dn}(k)) \\ u_{deq}(k) = -p\omega i_q(k) + \frac{R_s}{L} i_d(k) + c_2 e_d(k)^{p_2/q_2} \\ u_{dn}(k) = u_{dn}(k-1) + hk_2 \text{sgn}(s_d(k)) \end{cases} \tag{21}$$

$$\begin{cases} s_q(k) = \frac{e_q(k) - e_q(k-1)}{h} + c_3 e_q(k)^{p_3/q_3} \\ u_q(k) = L(u_{qeq}(k) + u_{qn}(k)) \\ u_{qeq}(k) = \frac{i_q^*(k) - i_q^*(k-1)}{h} + p\omega i_d(k) + \frac{R_s}{L} i_q(k) + \frac{p\psi_f}{L} \omega(k) + c_3 e_q(k)^{p_3/q_3} \\ u_{dn}(k) = u_{dn}(k-1) + hk_3 \text{sgn}(s_q(k)) \end{cases} \tag{22}$$

4 Simulation and Experiment

In order to validate the proposed the double closed-loop full-order TSM control approach and the discretization influence of of network transmission on the system, the PMSM parameters are chosen as: the rated speed n_e = 3000 r/min, phase resistance R_s = 2.26 Ω, polar logarithm p_n = 4, permanent magnet flux ψ_f = 0.0103 Wb, winding equivalent inductance L = 1.31 mH, moment of inertia J = 0.00009 kg m^2, friction coefficient B = 0.00005 N m s, load torque is 0, given the rotating speed ω^* = 100 rad/s, the current limit is 6 A. In the following, the simulation and experiment are given respectively.

4.1 Simulation Results

In order to validate the proposed full-order TSM approach applied in PMSM with double closed-loop structure in Fig. 1, the parameters of speed controller in (3) and (4) are chosen as: p_1 = 3, q_1 = 5, c_1 = 100, k_1 = 200000; the parameters of d-axis current controller in (11) are chosen as p_2 = 3, q_2 = 5, c_2 = 10, k_2 = 10; and the parameters of d-axis current controller in (13) are chosen as p_3 = 3, q_3 = 5, c_3 = 10, k_3 = 10. In continuous domain, we compare the proposed full-order TSM control approach with the traditional PID control, and the comparative simulations are given in Fig. 2(a)–(e).

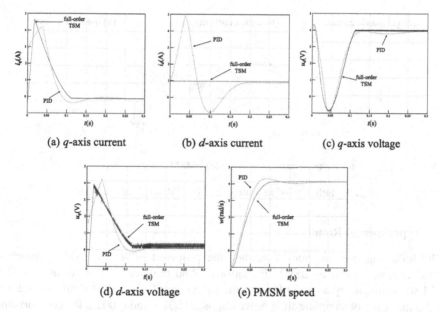

(a) q-axis current   (b) d-axis current   (c) q-axis voltage

(d) d-axis voltage   (e) PMSM speed

Fig. 2. Simulation comparisons of full-order TSM and PID

From the comparative simulations in Fig. 2, we can see that, the control performance of PMSM under the control of full-order TSM approach is better than the traditional PID control at fast speed and high accuracy. Furthermore, we test the discretization influence of network transmission. And the sampling period h are chosen as 0.001 s, 0.003 s and 0.005 s for comparison. The simulations are given in Fig. 3(a)–(e) and Table 1.

Table 1. Output results of speed with different sampling period h

Sampling period h (s)	Rise time (ms)	Maximum speed ω (rad/s)	Relative steady state error
0.001	54	100.56	0.04%
0.003	51	101.06	0.41%
0.005	50	101.64	1.33%

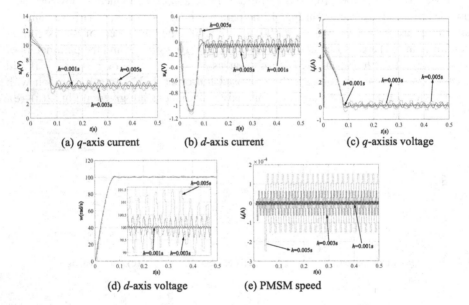

(a) q-axis current   (b) d-axis current   (c) q-axisis voltage

(d) d-axis voltage   (e) PMSM speed

Fig. 3. Influence of sampling time on PMSM control system

4.2   Experimental Results

In the following, we continue to validate the proposed full-order TSM approach in PMSM control system by dSPACE platform. And the step size is set as 0.0001 s, PWM wave frequency as 2500 Hz and the given speed $n^* = 2000$ r/min. In order to test the influence of sampling time h, we choose 0.001 s and 0.002 s for comparisons. And the experimental results are shown in Fig. 4(a)–(b) and Table 2.

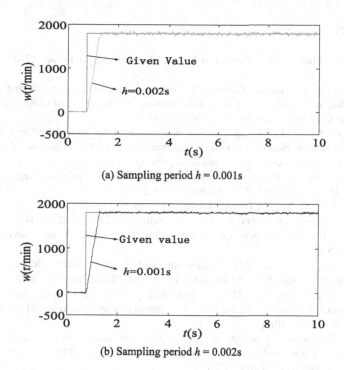

(a) Sampling period $h = 0.001$s

(b) Sampling period $h = 0.002$s

Fig. 4. Comparisons of motor speed with different sampling times

Table 2. Comparison of motor speed with different sampling periods

Sampling period h (s)	Rise time (ms)	Maximum speed ω (rad/s)	Relative steady state error
0.001	0.46	46	2.32%
0.002	0.47	88	4.39%

5 Conclusion

In this paper, a novel full-order TSM approach is proposed for the control of PMSM working in network transmission environment. In order to remove the model coupling, the vector control approach is utilized and correspondingly, the system is decomposed into two closed loops. Specially, the discretization influence of network transmission is investigated by comparing the control performances in continuous domain and discrete domain. And the guaranteed stability condition after the system discretization is deduced. The comparative simulations and experiment results validate the proposed approach.

References

1. Vadim, I.U.: Sliding Mode Control in Electro-Mechanical System, pp. 17–40. CRC Press (2009)
2. Capisani, L.M., Ferrara, A., Garonzi, A.: Robust interaction control via first and second order sliding modes of planar robotic manipulators. In: Decision and Control (CDC), 2010 49th IEEE Conference, pp. 16–18 (2010)
3. Pang, H.P., Liu, C.J., Liu, Z.: Sliding mode control for time-delay systems with its application to networked control systems. In: Proceedings of the International Conference on Intelligent Systems Design and Applications, pp. 182–197 (2006)
4. Utkin, V.I.: Sliding Modes in Control and Optimization. Springer, Berlin, Heidelberg (1992). https://doi.org/10.1007/978-3-642-84379-2
5. Feng, Y., Bao, S., Yu, X.: Inverse dynamics nonsingular terminal sliding mode control of two-link flexible manipulators. Int. J. Robot. Autom. **19**(2), 91–102 (2004)
6. Levant, A.: Homogeneity approach to high-order sliding mode design. Automatica **41**(5), 823–830 (2005)
7. Ma, H.F., Wu, J.H., Xiong, Z.H.: Discrete -time sliding -mode control with improved quasi - sliding -mode domain. IEEE Trans. Ind. Electron. **63**(10), 6292–6304 (2016)
8. Nguyen, D.T., Quang, P.H.: Discrete -time sliding mode control with state bounding for linear systems with time -varying delay and unmatched disturbances. IET Control Theory Appl. **11**(9), 1700–1708 (2015)
9. Maity, S.: Dynamics and stability issues of a discretized sliding – mode controlled DC – DC buck converter governed by fixed – event – time switching. IEEE Trans. Circuits Syst. I Regul. Pap. **60**(6), 1657–1669 (2013)
10. Enric, V.I., Adria, M.P., Roberto, G.: Direct digital design of a sliding mode – based control of a PWM synchronous buck converter. IET Power Electron. **13**(10), 1714–1720 (2017)
11. Feng, Y., Zheng, J., Yu, X., Truong, N.V.: Hybrid terminal sliding mode observer design method for a permanent magnet synchronous motor control system. IEEE Trans. Ind. Electron. **56**(9), 3424–3431 (2009)
12. Zhang, W., Ying, Z.-F., Zhang, X.-D.: Vector control method for induction motor of electric vehicle under the constraint of battery output power. advanced science and industry research center. In:Proceedings of 2019 International Conference on Artificial Intelligence, Control and Automation Engineering (AICAE 2019). Advanced Science and Industry Research Center: Science and Engineering Research Center, vol. 6 (2019)
13. Yang, M., Niu, L., Xu, D.G.: Antiwindup design for the speed loop PI controller of a PMSM servo system. Turkish J. Electr. Eng. Comput. Sci. **21**, 1318–1327 (2013)
14. Sun, S., Xie, L., Xiao, W.: Optimal full-order filtering for discrete-time systems with random measurement delays and multiple packet dropouts. J. Control Theory Appl. **8**(1), 105–110 (2010)
15. Behera, A.K., Bandyopadhyay, B.: Steady – state behaviour of discretized terminal sliding mode. Automatica **54**, 176–181 (2015)
16. Xu, Q.S.: Enhanced discrete -time sliding mode strategy with application to piezoelectric actuator control. IET Control Theory Appl. **18**(7), 2153–2163 (2013)

Smart Medical and Nursing Platform Based on 5G Technology

Xiaofeng Liu[1]($\boxtimes$), Ning Li[1], Yuchen Liu[2], and Yujia He[2]

[1] The Architectural Design and Research Institute of HIT,
Heilongjiang, Harbin, China
[2] Harbin Institute of Technology, Heilongjiang, Harbin, China

Abstract. In order to solve the problem of aging population and to relieve the massive impact on the pension service system, a design scheme of smart medical and nursing platform based on 5G technology is proposed. The model of participants and services related to the medical and nursing systems are established. Based on the information flow in the process of service, the intelligent vital signs monitoring system, pension service management system and decision-making system are introduced into the design of the smart medical and nursing platform. Specially, by utilizing 5G technology, the health information of the elderly, disease early warning and implementation of pension scheme are guaranteed by the perception layer, network layer and application layer, respectively. The proposed scheme can benefit the elderly health records, personalized pension plan, telemedicine diagnosis, etc.

Keywords: 5G technology · Smart building · Smart medicine · Aging issue

1 Introduction

Family planning policy has effectively controlled the growth rate of China's population, but it has also brought the problem of population aging. China has entered an aging society in 2000 and it is estimated that the elderly over 60 will be more than 25% of the total population by 2030. This proportion will increase with the time, which means that the aging problem will be more serious in the future [1]. At present, home-based care is still the main mode of care for the aged in China, and with the increase of the elderly population, "421" type of "inverted pyramid" pension model is more common, which undoubtedly increases the burden of young people [2].

With the development of society and the improvement of medical technology, people's average life expectancy continues to extend, and with the increase of age, the probability of the elderly is also increasing, so the conventional home-based care has disadvantages, and now the increasing work pressure of young people makes them have less time to take care of the elderly, which makes it difficult to find accidents in time, resulting in unexpected consequences [3]. At the same time, the service level of the current social pension institutions is uneven, and the fees of the better pension institutions are mostly higher, while the facilities of the institutions with lower prices are not complete, and the service level is low [4]. So most of the elderly are not willing to spend their old age in the pension center. In order to provide a better pension

W. Xiang et al. (Eds.): BROADNETS 2021, LNICST 413, pp. 285–295, 2022.
https://doi.org/10.1007/978-3-030-93479-8_20

environment for the elderly, the Ministry of industry and information technology, the Ministry of civil affairs and other departments have put forward the action plan for the development of smart and healthy pension industry, which uses the existing Internet technology to build a pension community with the functions of nursing home and hospital for the elderly, and realizes the pension mode of combining medical care with pension [5]. At the same time, it can provide better care and service for the elderly through the internet platform health management and spiritual care [6].

The application and promotion of internet in medical and nursing services partly depends on the transmission rate and reliability. With the appearance of 5G network, tele-medicine becomes possible. Compared with 4G, 5G takes full account of the connection requirements between people and things, things and things, and pays more attention to performance indicators such as speed, delay, connection density, etc. [7]. The transmission rate is increased by 10–100 times, and the transmission delay is greatly reduced. Conventional equipment has only 1 ms delay time [8]. The application of 5G high-speed rate and low delay in elderly care can greatly reduce the waste of medical resources, and provide 24-h comprehensive medical care, medical diagnosis and remote control for the elderly [9–11].

Based on 5G network technology, this paper proposes a pension mode of regional sharing medical and nursing combination. Starting from the needs of the elderly, we build a pension model that is in line with the combination of medical care and pension. And then, according to the information flow of the service mode, the implementation process is analyzed, and a reasonable and new service architecture is designed. Finally, 5G technology is used to build the medical care management platform, and the construction scheme of each layer network is given to realize the functions of intelligent nursing, medical diagnosis and service platform management.

2   Design of Old-Age Service Mode Combining Medical Care and Nursing

At present, China's pension service resources are relatively lacking and the distribution of resources is unbalanced, and the service level of pension institutions is uneven, there is no better charging standard, resulting in the majority of the elderly are still home-based care. In order to solve this problem, the new mode of medical and pension service is shown in Fig. 1. Through the construction of a reasonable service supervision platform, we can not only standardize the pension industry, but also optimize the allocation of pension resources, and provide high-quality services for the elderly with limited pension resources [12, 13].

Differing from the traditional medical and pension service institutions, this paper advocates the elderly service market as the leading, through the current existing market demand, integration of pension resources, improve the medical and pension service industry, so as to make it competitive and dynamic. According to the pattern analysis, can be combined by building the medical raise pension service platform, the elderly can choose or pension institution endowment in the home, the elderly and their families,

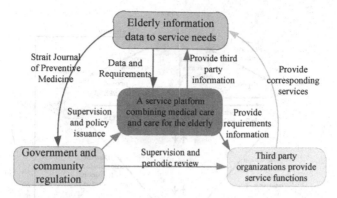

Fig. 1. A service platform combining medical care and nursing care

management and service providers to participate, to ensure effective communication between, ensure quality of pension services, and effective supervision of the implementation services market [14].

Through this platform, children and the elderly can check the health status of their parents through APP, telephone consultation and other ways, and can choose effective medical care or medical diagnosis for the elderly according to relevant data. It should be noted that in order to protect the personal information of the elderly from disclosure, the health data platform for the elderly has no right to view and call. At the same time, children can also choose housekeeping services, care services, nutrition catering and other services for their elders through the platform, which can greatly reduce the burden of children and maintain social stability. Third-party institutions, after passing the review of the platform, can log into the platform in the form of a unit and provide relevant old-age care services, such as housekeeping services and medical services. However, government departments can supervise third-party institutions through the information already available in the database, and implement a points-based system [15]. Institutions that have received more complaints are not allowed to log on to the platform. At the same time, the annual general examination system is adopted, so that institutions with substandard service level and institutions with safety risks can withdraw from the platform, so as to realize effective supervision of service and protect the vital interests of the elderly. If the elderly have an accident, the medical equipment carried by the elderly can immediately alarm the platform, urgently call the nearby medical resources, provide medical assistance to the elderly according to the registration information, and at the same time, the platform will notify the children through the APP in an emergency. The business operation mode of the platform is shown in Fig. 2.

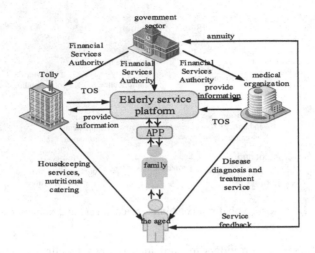

Fig. 2. The way of operating

3 Medical Care Model Framework Design

3.1 Flow of Service Information

In order to realize the model of intelligent medical care for the aged, it is necessary to acquire, process and analyze data quickly and accurately, and ensure that the information collection, processing and feedback are correct and effective. With the rapid development of the Internet, cloud computing, intelligent information acquisition platform, 5G communication and other technologies, the intelligent medical and nursing mode has the foundation to realize the combination of medical and nursing mode from small families and apartments to large communities and nursing homes.

In order to make the elderly service platform run efficiently, it is necessary to determine the specific flow process of service information, so as to collect, process and analyze service information reasonably. First is information collection, because the old man belongs to individual privacy information, so information collection should be led by the government departments, multi-sectoral cooperation, using the Internet, 5G technology integration in a safe environment health and pension service resources, gathering the elderly health information related to the pension service and the information of all participants. Then the collected data of the elderly are analyzed and compared with the data in the database to generate a health log. Finally, according to the analysis results, appropriate quality services are formulated for the elderly to make them satisfied, so as to improve the elderly's nursing experience, let their children rest assured, and reduce their burden.

In the established database, the information of all participants in the service mode is stored in the cloud server in the form of registration by government departments, collection by medical institutions, Internet of Things device records and electronic health records. At the same time, multiple service sub-platforms such as housekeeping service, medical and health service and catering service are supported. According to the elderly's personal needs, living habits, health status, past medical history, diagnosis and treatment, family medical history, present medical history, physical examination results and the occurrence, development, treatment and prognosis of the disease, the system management personnel will feed back the processed information to each sub-platform. Based on their own advantages, each sub-platform develops satisfactory services for the elderly according to their needs, and finally sends the service information to the service provider (personnel and institutions), the elderly and their relatives respectively through mobile APP, official website and wearable devices. Furthermore, the elderly can enjoy daily services such as caring care, housekeeping cleaning, health lectures, disease prevention, disease diagnosis and treatment, regular physical examination, nutrition and catering, rescue for serious diseases, psychological counseling and index monitoring. Figure 3 shows the transmission direction and data processing mode of the service information of the intelligent medical and nursing platform, so as to ensure the efficient collection and processing of information and provide high-quality services for the elderly.

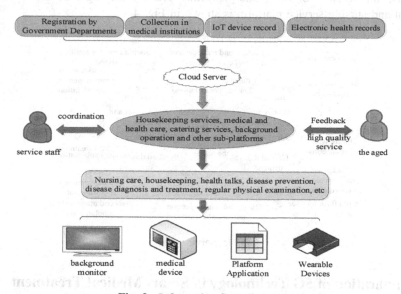

Fig. 3. Information flow diagram

3.2 Logic Design of Medical and Nursing Service Platform

As a result of current endowment resources is still very limited, so you need to maximum efficiency to use the existing service resources, so need to integrate reasonably the resources platform, the platform inside the service personnel in accordance with the professional and technical group, coordination and cooperation to improve the pension service, design service logic, pension service process was optimized by using advanced optimization, rational utilization of resources endowment. According to the characteristics of information flow, the service platform is divided into health consultation sub-platform, medical diagnosis and treatment service sub-platform, user nursing sub-platform, housekeeping and nursing sub-platform, background management and coordination service sub-platform and elderly meal matching service sub-platform, so that the elderly can choose relevant services according to their actual needs.

The platform takes the needs of the elderly as the service direction and provides corresponding services by using the divided sub-platforms. Through health consulting platform provide consultation service for health, when health problems may come up, can further complete medical diagnosis and treatment by a medical treatment service platform service function, through the two platforms, can satisfy the elderly body care, mental health counseling and medical consultation and so on demand, for the elderly to provide more convenient, more comprehensive medical services; Through the elderly meal matching service sub-platform, the daily healthy diet needs of the elderly can be realized. At the same time, all information and service contents can be sorted out through the backstage management and coordination service sub-platform, so as to realize disease prevention, customize more reasonable services for the elderly, and supervise the services of other sub-platforms. The service logic of the intelligent medical and nursing service platform is shown in Fig. 4.

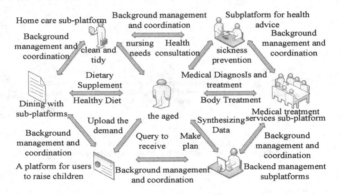

Fig. 4. Service logic

4   Application of 5G Technology in Smart Medical Treatment

The old-age service platform combining medical care cannot be separated from the support of medical institutions, and the old-age service is mainly limited by the shortage of medical resources. In order to solve the impact of medical resources on elderly care services, 5G technology has advantages such as high rate, low delay and large capacity, which can realize the Internet of Things of medical devices, provide technical and infrastructure support for tele-medicine, and alleviate the imbalance of medical resources.

5G is the fifth generation of mobile phone mobile communication standard, also known as the fifth generation of mobile communication technology. Compared with the previous generation of mobile communication technology, 5G has the characteristics of fast transmission rate, low delay and high connection density. Its enhanced mobile bandwidth has an experience rate of 100M bit/s, and the peak rate is more than 1G bit/s. It is suitable for high-definition video business, 2K/4K video, VR/AR and other aspects, which lays a foundation for the realization of telemedicine medical detection and care, medical diagnosis and guidance, remote control and other functions, and provides the possibility for the intelligent development of the medical industry. With the help of the ubiquitous 5G high-speed Internet, vigorously developing smart mobile medical services will be an effective way to solve the pain points of the current medical industry [5]. Based on 5G wireless network, smart mobile medical services can connect patients and doctors in different Spaces closely, so as to ease the problem of seeing a doctor and improve people's health.

The use of 5G can improve the scope of high-precision medical equipment detection, disease data analysis, remote clinical diagnosis and other services. In the field of medical testing and nursing service, data of medical monitoring and nursing equipment need to be collected. 5G technology can monitor these devices constantly for a long time, making the obtained data timely and accurate. In order to facilitate the monitoring of various indicators of patients, patients are usually equipped with portable monitoring devices and mobile terminals, etc., and the patient's health status, physical condition and location information is transmitted, processed and alerted by 5G technology. These can monitoring services for the elderly, seriously ill patients, the newborn, patients with chronic diseases, such as the provision of real-time, remote monitoring, health not remind, disease prevention, such as service, gathering data related to the patients, the disease killed in the initial stage, have the effect of prevention and treatment, safeguarding the health of patients, improve the level of medical treatment, as shown in Fig. 5.

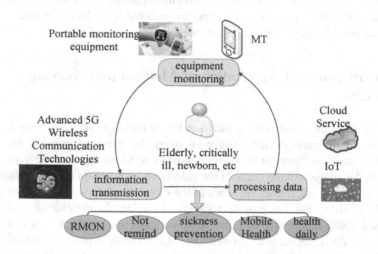

Fig. 5. Medical monitoring and nursing application architecture diagram

During the construction of smart hospital, it need to integrate a large number of medical resources, make use of the characteristics of 5G large capacity, realize the interconnection of hospital equipment as far as possible and build local network in the hospital, so that the hospital is no longer an independent low efficiency mode of resource sharing, but an efficient mode of linkage and medical information sharing, and reduce unnecessary waste of time. Besides from providing convenience for patients and doctors, it is conducive to the harmonious development of doctor-patient relationship, and to realize the real-time monitoring of patients' disease indicators, efficient management of medical staff, hospital asset management and equipment maintenance, medical resource scheduling, real-time navigation and security services.

However, 5G technology is still in development and its combination with medical treatment is full of many possibilities, which is worth exploring. At present, the intelligent construction of the medical industry has a long way to go. Mobile medical services, tele-medicine, precision equipment medical, big data comparison and other services have not yet been popularized, and the society needs a process of transition and adaptation to accept the changes brought by smart medicine gradually. At the same time, the promotion of smart medicine will inevitably lead to a series of new problems, and the implementation of specific policies is also related to the local actual situation. Smart medicine is not outside the law, and the relevant departments of smart medicine should improve the corresponding laws and regulations. When the early technology is not mature, we should adopt strict qualification approval mechanism for institutions with intelligent medical services, standardize medical diagnosis and treatment behavior, establish and properly keep patients' medical records, and reasonably solve doctor-patient disputes. At the same time, in order to ensure that patients' personal information and medical technology are not leaked, relevant departments need to supervise and provide security.

If intelligent medical care is popularized, the medical care service platform will be easier to realize. Through the sharing of information resources of various platforms, the elderly can get better mobile medical services, making it no longer difficult to see a doctor, and provide health protection for them.

5 Construction and Application of Medical and Nursing Platform

The intelligent medical and nursing platform based on 5G technology provides a new model for elderly care services. Differing from the previous pension model, the intelligent pension platform provides personalized services for the elderly pays more attention to the analysis of the needs of the elderly and it relies on the computing power of the big data platform, refines the needs of the elderly, and serves a variety of pension needs. The platform can also provide a variety of choices for the elderly, whether it is home-based care, community care, institutional care, the platform can monitor the indicators of the elderly, and through the 5G network real-time transmission of information and data, platform analysis data timely protection of the elderly. Intelligent platform enables the elderly to enjoy the maximum pension resources, secure pension services, optimize the allocation of social resources, and promote the development of pension service related industries. Therefore, it is particularly important to build an intelligent, digital, diversified, networked and information-based medical and pension platform.

The core of the intelligent medical and nursing platform is to serve the elderly. The most basic thing is to provide the elderly with nursing homes, so that the elderly can live comfortably. Combined with the situation of the residence, the intelligent medical and nursing service can be accessed. The second is to provide supporting service-oriented equipment for the elderly and optimize the control process to provide convenience for the elderly life. Finally, the combination of 5G, cloud platform and other technologies will organically integrate all kinds of resources through continuous collection, analysis, processing, and improvement of data in the database. The application of intelligent pension system is shown in Fig. 6.

The intelligent medical and nursing platform based on 5G technology is built from three levels, the perception layer, the network layer and the application layer. In the sensing layer, wearable devices and monitoring devices are used to collect the information of the elderly, as well as the information of all participants, forming a sound health monitoring, disease early warning and elderly care service system. 5G technology ensures the timeliness of uploaded data, with little interference from the outside world, and stable synchronization of data on the transmission belt. The network layer uses 5G, Internet of Things and cloud platform to realize the analysis, sorting and optimization of the collected data and to build the elderly service database, accurately call the elderly care resources, and transfer the service information to the terminal device to promote the development of the elderly health records, personalized pension plan, tele-medicine diagnosis, etc. The application layer is responsible for the specific implementation of the pension plan formulated by the smart pension platform. 5G transmits data without delay, provides real-time feedback on users' needs and service feelings, and provides services such as health consultation, disease diagnosis and treatment, housework arrangement, meal matching and so on for the elderly. The framework of the system is shown in Fig. 7.

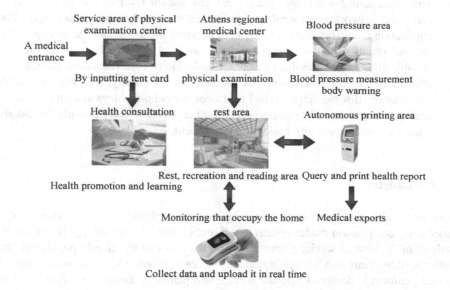

Fig. 6. Intelligent pension system application

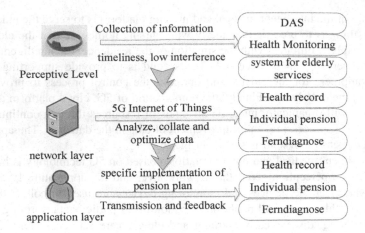

Fig. 7. The framework of smart pension system

(1) Perception layer is the basic structure of intelligent medical and nursing system. Its main function is to collect and transmit data, so as to realize the real-time monitoring and automatic management of data for the elderly. In the smart pension system, the needs of the elderly should be fully considered, and the health records of the elderly should be improved through the collected data.

(2) The network layer is the transition layer of the intelligent medical and nursing system. It analyzes, sorts and filters the data collected by various devices and uploaded by service institutions. It can transmit and feed back data through wireless network, Bluetooth, 5G and other technologies. It can process and analyze data by 5G, Internet of things, cloud platform and manage and supervise the platform.

(3) The application layer is the specific implementation layer of intelligent medical care. The network layer sends the processed data to the application layer. The application layer formulates elderly care services for the elderly according to the internal situation of the building and the needs of the elderly, realizes the reasonable allocation of medical resources and elderly care resources, provides an efficient and comfortable living environment for the elderly, and provides health consultation, disease diagnosis and treatment, household chores and other services Dining collocation, safety inspection and other services really provide the elderly with a living and security building environment.

6 Conclusion

In order to alleviate the problem of the lack of medical and pension resources, this paper designs a pension model system based on 5G network technology. Based on the analysis of the flow of service information and the needs of the elderly population, the platform architecture and service logic analysis are realized. The medical and nursing service platform is designed, and the service sub platforms are reasonably divided to improve the operation efficiency. With the advantages of 5G technology, the combination of medical and nursing and the allocation of pension resources can be optimized. Finally, the construction scheme of each layer network is given to realize the functions of intelligent nursing, medical diagnosis and service platform management. Through the medical care service platform, we can provide high-quality services for the elderly at home with limited pension resources, so that the elderly can enjoy their old age and reduce the burden of their children.

References

1. Yang, B.: Research on the construction of intelligent healthcare community under the background of smart city development. Constr. Sci. Technol. **408**, 41–44 (2020)
2. Sheng, Y., Peng, H., Feng, I.: Intelligent medical application based on 5G mobile network. Des. Technol. Posts Telecommun. (07), 1–5 (2019)
3. Chen, J.: Research on the mode of smart community elderly-care services under the background of "Internet Plus." Intell. Comput. Appl. **10**(02), 307–311 (2020)
4. Mei, L.: The design and implementation of cloud service platform for medical & health care combined with pension. Modern Inf. Technol. **03**(21), 19–21 (2019)
5. Liu, L., Liu, Y., He, J., Chen, Z.: Design and implementation of mobile intelligent rehabilitation management system. J. Med. Inform. **40**(12), 23–26 (2019)
6. Wu, L., Yao, Y., Zhang, F., Li, C., Chen, Y., Hou, J.: A discussion on the new model of "Combination of Medical Care and Nursing Care" wisdom pension in Heilongjiang Province based on "Internet+." China Health Ind. **17**(19), 145–147 (2020)
7. Wu, Y., Li, L., Zhang, S., Wang, T.: Mobile emergency hospital design under wisdom medical assistance mode. Architectural J. **20**, 111–116 (2019)
8. Chen, Y., Mei, H.: Research on intelligent pension building system based on IOT technology-talking Japan as an example. Architectural J. **22**, 50–56 (2020)
9. Huo, D., Bai, X.: Application of future 5G in smart buildings. Electr. Technol. Intell. Build. **14**(01), 41–43 (2020)
10. Li, Y., Cheng, L.: Primary exploration of innovative model of smart medical care for the aged in China. Mod. Hosp. Manag. **13**(06), 18–21 (2015)
11. Wu, X., Wu, Y., Huang, X., Liao, S.: Study on the optimization of health management model for the elderly in urban communities under the background of smart medical treatment. China Med. Herald **17**(33), 194–197 (2020)
12. Zhu, X.: A survey on application of artificial intelligence for intelligent healthcare. Unmanned Syst. Technol. **3**(03), 25–31 (2020)
13. Wang, C., Sheng, Z., Sun, X.: A theoretical framework of elderly users' demand for smart senior care and health care. Theory Exploring **43**(11), 71–78 (2020)
14. Fang, Y.: Discussion on elderly-oriented electrical design for medical and nursing buildings. Build. Electr. **39**(07), 23–26 (2020)
15. Shu, J., Zhang, X.: Research on the status quo of artificial intelligence in institutional pension under the background of "Internet+." Intell. Comput. Appl. **10**(04), 267–268 (2020)

Time-Domain Predictable Trajectory Planning for Autonomous Driving Based on Internet of Vehicles

Qiuxin Song[1], Zonghao Li[1], Haolin Li[2], Niaona Zhang[1(✉)], and Jiasen Xu[1]

[1] Changchun University of Technology, Jilin 130012, China
[2] State Grid Baishan Power Supply Company, Jilin 134300, China

Abstract. For the polynomial lane change method, the lane change trajectory is planned only at the initial time, and it cannot cope with the problem that other traffic participants enter the driving environment during the lane change process. This paper decomposes the polynomial lane change method into lateral displacement planning and longitudinal velocity planning. The Pontryagin minimum principle is used to solve the optimal lane change duration meeting the requirements of different driving conditions, and the polynomial method is used to plan the lateral displacement trajectory. In the longitudinal direction, the variable acceleration motion equation is used to describe the trajectory, so as to establish a prediction model, the real-time driving environment information is obtained through the internet of vehicles to realize the speed rolling optimization, the trajectory dynamic planning is carried out during the driving process, and the slack variable is introduced to solve the problem that the vehicle suddenly increases speed beyond the constraint range. Through Matlab/Simulink and Prescan co-simulation verification, the trajectory planned in this paper not only meets the requirements of comfort and lane change efficiency, but also has better avoidance capabilities for other traffic participants and is easy to follow in real vehicles.

Keywords: Quintic polynomial · Path planning · Model predictive control · Internet of Vehicles

1 Introduction

In recent years, lane change of autonomous driving has become a hot research topic for scholars at domestic and foreign [1]. The development of 5G communication technology has greatly improved the communication ability between vehicles and the surrounding traffic environment [2], thus enabling vehicles to better cope with the complex driving environment and providing a great guarantee for vehicles to plan a safe and efficient lane change trajectory in real time.

The work was supported in part by the National Natural Science Foundation of China U1864206, in part by the National key research and development plan of China under Grant 2017YFB0103600 and 2017YFB0103700, in part by the Science and Technology Development Plan of Jilin Province under Grant 2019C040-5 and 20180519014JH.

W. Xiang et al. (Eds.): BROADNETS 2021, LNICST 413, pp. 296–303, 2022.
https://doi.org/10.1007/978-3-030-93479-8_21

Curve-fitting path planning method is often used in the field of intelligent vehicles [3]. By giving the vehicle starting point and ending point, a trajectory with continuous curvature, satisfying comfort and dynamic constraints is generated [4]. Among them, arcs, Bessel curves and polynomial functions are commonly used [5]. Literature [6] realized trajectory planning by using geometric features of circular arc curve, but curvature discontinuity would appear at the end of circular arc, which would affect the stability of the car body. In Literature [7], Bezier curve is used for path planning, and the obstacle avoidance function is realized on electric vehicles. However, it is difficult to select control points for path planning based on Bezier curve. In contrast, for polynomial functions, these problems can be reduced by adjusting the order of the polynomial to achieve the desired performance. Literature [8] proposes a quintic polynomial automatic lane change model, and analyzes the key variables that affect the performance of lane change, thus generating the optimal lane change trajectory. However, only the state information of the starting and ending points is considered.

Combining the above problems, this paper considers that the planned trajectory satisfies performance indicators such as comfort, safety, lane change efficiency, etc., and uses the Pontryagin principle of minimum to solve the lateral displacement corresponding to the optimal lane change duration. Through the model predictive control method, the longitudinal speed is optimized by rolling to cope with the situation of other traffic participants in the driving process, so as to achieve dynamic path planning. Matlab/Simulink and Prescan co-simulation were used to verify the two driving conditions of free lane change and active lane change by traffic participants.

2 Trajectory Planning

In this paper, the current state (position, speed, acceleration) of the lane change vehicle, environmental information and the state of other traffic participants are collected through the Internet of Vehicles and sensors that include 5G communication technology. During lane change, the vehicle is driving on the road in a longitudinal variable acceleration motion. In order to ensure that the lateral displacement is continuous and the curvature is smooth during the lane change process, a quintic polynomial is used to describe the lateral displacement trajectory. Combining the initial state displacement, velocity and acceleration of the lateral movement are all zero, the end state velocity and acceleration are zero, and the end displacement is the distance between the center lines of the two lanes, and the lane change trajectory model is obtained as:

$$\begin{cases} x(t) = x_{t_0} + v_{x_{t_0}} t + \frac{1}{2} a_{x_t} t^2 \\ y(t) = \frac{6y_{t_f}}{t_f^5} t^5 - \frac{15y_{t_f}}{t_f^4} t^4 + \frac{10y_{t_f}}{t_f^3} t^3 \end{cases} \tag{1}$$

Where, $x(t)$, x_{t_0}, $v_{x_{t_0}}$, a_{x_t} respectively represent the displacement at time t, the displacement at initial time, the initial velocity and the acceleration at time t in longitudinal motion; $y(t)$ is the lateral displacement at the end of lane change. t, t_f are lane change time and lane change duration respectively.

Trajectory planning meets the needs of comfort, safety, and efficiency. Among them, comfort is characterized by $|a_x| \leq a_{x_{\max}} (a_{x_{\max}} = 0.4g), |a_y| \leq a_{y_{\max}} (a_{y_{\max}} = 0.4g)$; efficiency is characterized by $0 \leq t \leq t_f (t_f \leq 5)$; and safety is characterized by $0 < y(t) < y_{t_f} (0 < t < t_f), 0 < v_x(t) < v_{x_{\max}} (0 < t < t_f)$.

According to the lane change trajectory model, the lateral trajectory is determined by the duration of the lane change and the end lateral displacement. The terminal lateral displacement is determined by the distance between the centerlines of the two lanes, and the lane width is 3.75 m according to the international standard [9]. The lane change duration is often set by empirical values, which is uncertain [10]. In this paper, combining the lateral boundary conditions and comfort requirements, the lane change duration should be greater than 2.35 s, and the lane change duration is a variable. Taking safety, comfort and lane change efficiency as the objective function, establish a lateral trajectory optimization model:

$$\min C = w_j \frac{1}{t_f} \int_0^{t_f} j_y^2 dt + w_t t_f$$
$$s.t. \left\{ 0 \leq y(t) \leq 3.75, |a_y| \leq a_{y_{\max}} (a_{y_{\max}} = 0.4g), 2.35 \leq t \leq 5 \right. \tag{2}$$

Where ω_j, ω_t represents the weight; j_y is the lateral jerk, which represents the rate of change of acceleration, obtained by taking the third derivative of lateral displacement.

The objective function is solved by Pontryagin's minimum principle [11, 12], and the optimal lane change duration is substituted into the lateral trajectory function.

3   Longitudinal Speed Rolling Optimization

In the process of lane change, due to the use of 5G communication technology, vehicles can receive and send information about the surrounding environment in real time. When other traffic participants are involved and may cause a collision, the lane change vehicles adjust the current planned path by rolling optimization of longitudinal speed.

This article quotes the double integrator in the literature [13] to derive the Eq. (1) longitudinal equation as the longitudinal motion model:

$$\begin{cases} x_t = x_0 + v_{x_{t_0}} t + \frac{1}{2} a_{x_t} t^2 \\ v_{x_t} = v_{x_{t_0}} + a_{x_t} t \end{cases} \tag{3}$$

Where, x_t represents the longitudinal displacement of the vehicle at time t; v_{x_t} represents the longitudinal velocity at time t.

The method discretization is carried out by the Taylor formula method, so that $a_x(k) = a_x(k-1) + \Delta a_x(k-1)$ obtains the discretization model:

$$\begin{aligned} x(k+1) &= x(k) + v_x(k) \cdot H + \frac{1}{2} a_x(k-1) \cdot H^2 + \frac{1}{2} \Delta a_x(k-1) \cdot H^2 \\ v_x(k+1) &= v_x(k) + a_x(k-1) \cdot H + \Delta a_x(k-1) \cdot H \\ a_x(k) &= a_x(k-1) + \Delta a_x(k-1) \end{aligned} \tag{4}$$

Where, $H = 0.01$ s is the sampling interval; x, v_x, a_x is the state quantity, Δa_x is the control input quantity, and $\Delta a_x(k-1)$ represents the incremental longitudinal acceleration of the vehicle at the moment $k-1$.

Equation (4) is transformed into matrix form, and the prediction model in this paper is described as follows:

$$X = T_x\Delta A + B_x, V = T_v\Delta A + B_v, A = T_a\Delta A + B_a \tag{5}$$

Where, the state matrices X, V, A and control input matrix ΔA are as follows:

$$X = [x(k+1) \quad x(k+2) \quad \cdots \quad x(k+p)]^T_{1\times p}$$
$$V = [v_x(k+1) \quad v_x(k+2) \quad \cdots \quad v_x(k+p)]^T_{1\times p}$$
$$A = [a_x(k-1) \quad a_x(k) \quad \cdots \quad v_x(k+p-2)]^T_{1\times p}$$
$$\Delta A = [\Delta a_x(k-1) \quad \Delta a_x(k) \quad \cdots \quad \Delta v_x(k+p-2)]^T_{1\times p}$$

The control input matrix ΔA and its coefficient matrix T_x, T_v, T_a are:

$$T_x = \begin{bmatrix} \frac{H^2}{2} & 0 & \cdots & 0 \\ 2H^2 & \frac{H^2}{2} & \cdots & 0 \\ \vdots & \vdots & \ddots & \vdots \\ \frac{p^2H^2}{2} & \frac{(p-1)^2H^2}{2} & \cdots & \frac{H^2}{2} \end{bmatrix}_{p\times p} \quad T_v = \begin{bmatrix} H & 0 & \cdots & 0 \\ 2H & H & \cdots & 0 \\ \vdots & \vdots & \ddots & \vdots \\ pH & (p-1)H & \cdots & H \end{bmatrix}_{p\times p}$$

$$T_a = \begin{bmatrix} 1 & 0 & \cdots & 0 \\ 1 & 1 & \cdots & 0 \\ \vdots & \vdots & \ddots & 0 \\ 1 & 1 & \cdots & 1 \end{bmatrix}_{p\times p}$$

The other parameter matrices are:

$$B_p = \begin{bmatrix} p_x(k) \\ p_x(k) \\ \vdots \\ p_x(k) \end{bmatrix}_{p\times 1} + \begin{bmatrix} Hv_x(k) \\ 2Hv_x(k) \\ \vdots \\ pHv_x(k) \end{bmatrix}_{p\times 1} + \begin{bmatrix} \frac{1}{2}H^2a_x(k-1) \\ 2H^2a_x(k-1) \\ \vdots \\ \frac{p^2}{2}H^2a_x(k-1) \end{bmatrix}_{p\times 1}$$

$$B_v = \begin{bmatrix} v_x(k) \\ v_x(k) \\ \vdots \\ v_x(k) \end{bmatrix}_{p\times 1} + \begin{bmatrix} Ha_x(k-1) \\ 2Ha_x(k-1) \\ \vdots \\ pHa_x(k-1) \end{bmatrix}_{p\times 1} \quad B_a = \begin{bmatrix} a_x(k-1) \\ a_x(k-1) \\ \vdots \\ a_x(k-1) \end{bmatrix}_{p\times 1}$$

In this paper, the relative minimum safety distance of the workshop is set to 2 m. During the lane change process, when other traffic participants enter, the area outside this area is a safe driving area. During the dynamic trajectory planning, the lane change vehicle must drive strictly at The safe driving area is the target, and the trajectory curve is smooth during the lane change. In view of the possible problem that the acceleration exceeds the maximum acceleration constraint caused by the sudden increase in the lane change, the slack variable S is introduced in this paper, and the slack variable S is introduced to solve the problem while slack The minimum variable is the goal; at the end of the lane change, the vehicle is driven at a constant speed in the target lane, so the speed is set as the speed of the target lane, and the acceleration at the end is 0. Considering the above conditions, the following objective function is designed:

$$\min_{\Delta A, S} \omega_1(X - X_f)^T(X - X_f) + \omega_2(V - V_f)^T(V - V_f) + \omega_3 A^T A + \omega_4 \Delta A^T \Delta A + \omega_5 S^T S$$

$$(6)$$

Where, X_f, V_f, S represent the displacement matrix and velocity matrix at the end time and the slack variable matrix respectively; $\omega_1, \omega_2, \omega_3, \omega_4, \omega_5$ represents the weight and $X_f = (x_f \quad \cdots \quad x_f)_{1 \times p}^T, V_f = (v_f \quad \cdots \quad v_f)_{1 \times p}^T, S = (s_1 \quad s_2 \quad \cdots \quad s_p)_{1 \times p}^T.$

The combined performance index optimization problem is subject to the following constraints:

$$X_{min} < X < X_{max}, V_{x_{min}} < V_x < V_{x_{max}}, A_{x_{min}} < A_x < A_{x_{max}} \qquad (7)$$

For each step, the control input is the optimal solution obtained from the quadratic programming problem, and its first value is applied to the system, that is:

$$\Delta a^*(k) = (1 \quad 0 \quad 0 \quad \cdots \quad 0)_{1 \times k} \Delta A^*(k) \qquad (8)$$

4   Simulation Analysis

This paper uses Matlab/Simulink to write the path planning algorithm program; In the prescan, a 300 m long, 3.75 m wide two-car straight lane in the same direction was established. The phantom vehicle without dynamic performance was taken as the ideal trajectory to verify the effectiveness of the algorithm. At the same time, a 2-DOF vehicle with a driver model was added to verify the tracking ability of the planned trajectory. All vehicles in the environment are equipped with radar and Internet of vehicles with 5G communications technology.

When lane change is free, as shown in Fig. 1, the optimal lane change duration is 5 s, the lateral displacement is 3.75 m, and the longitudinal displacement is 154.77 m, and the lane change trajectory is continuous and smooth. The longitudinal velocity was increased from 28 m/s to 32 m/s. During the lane change process, the longitudinal

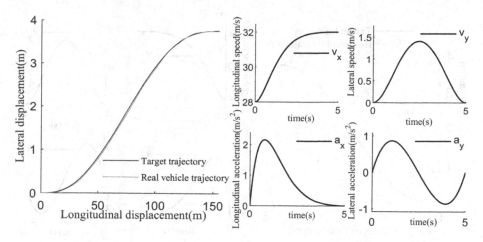

Fig. 1. Free lane change track and motion parameter diagram

velocity curve did not fluctuate repeatedly, which would not bring longitudinal compression force to passengers. The maximum lateral acceleration is 0.87 m/s^2, and the longitudinal acceleration is less than 0.4 g, which fully meets the requirements of comfort. Blue represents the 2-DOF vehicle trajectory, which is basically consistent with the target trajectory, indicating that the target trajectory is easy to follow.

When avoiding obstacles and changing lanes, this article mainly considers the collision between the vehicle in front of the current lane and the vehicle behind the target lane. In the scenario in Fig. 2, the initial distance between the vehicle in front of the current lane and the vehicle is 7.8 m, and the distance between the vehicle behind the target lane and the vehicle is 7.2 m. and the optimal lane change duration is calculated to be 3 s. All parameters meet the performance index requirements, and the trajectory is continuous and smooth without collision. The green trajectory is the trajectory of the vehicle with 2 degrees of freedom. It can be observed that the error with the target trajectory is small, which verifies that the trajectory is easy to follow.

Figure 3 is measured by the Internet of Vehicles and radar containing 5G communication technology. From the beginning of the lane change to 1.42 s, the relative distance between the lane change vehicle and the two vehicles is continuously decreasing, and the lane change vehicle drives out of the current lane in 1.42 s relative to the preceding vehicle. The distance becomes zero. Prior to this, the minimum driving relative distance between the two vehicles was 2.4 m. After 2.3 s, the speed of the lane change vehicle was close, and the relative distance of 2.97 m was always maintained with the vehicle behind the target lane.

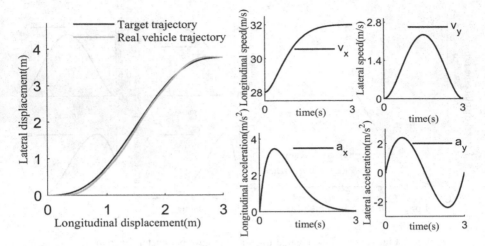

Fig. 2. Obstacle avoidance and lane change trajectory and motion parameter diagram

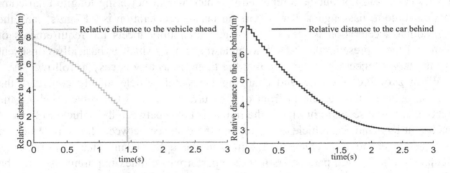

Fig. 3. Relative distance to other traffic participants in two lanes

5 Conclusion

This paper aims at the quintic polynomial lane change method, which cannot cope with the problem of other traffic participants entering during the lane change process. Combined with the horizontal two-point boundary conditions, the unknown coefficients of the horizontal quintic polynomial are solved to establish a lane change trajectory model. The Pontryagin minimum principle is used to find the optimal lane change duration, and the acceleration change in the next 5 s is predicted at the current moment through the prediction model, and the first set of values is applied to the next sampling interval for rolling optimization. Using Matlab/Simulink to program the algorithm, two lane change driving conditions are established in prescan for co-simulation. The results show that the algorithm planned in this paper guarantees the safety of the vehicle under the premise of comfort and lane change efficiency. Other vehicles entering during the lane change have good evasion capabilities. The addition of a 2-degree-of-freedom vehicle model verifies that the planned trajectory is easy to follow in the two working conditions.

References

1. Umberto, M., Shilp, D., Saber, F., et al.: Towards connected autonomous driving: review of use-cases. Veh. Syst. Dyn. 1–36 (2018)
2. Zhang, X., Xia, B., Zhang, F.: Multi-objective planning of high-speed lane change trajectory based on V2V. J. Jiangsu Univ. (Nat. Sci. Edn) **41**(2), 131–137 (2020)
3. Zhang, T.: Research on intelligent vehicle lane change method based on Internet of Vehicles Information. Jiangsu University (2019)
4. Wang, B.: Risk assessment and trajector planning for obstacle-avoidance of intelligent vehicle. Autom. Technol. **06**, 32–37 (2018)
5. Meng, J.: Research on vehicle active lane change trajectory planning and tracking control. Hefei University of Technology (2020)
6. Horst, J., Barbera, A.: Trajectory generation for an on-road autonomous vehicle. In: Defense and Security Symposium. International Society for Optics and Photonics, p. 62302J (2006)
7. Yang, K., Sukkarieh, S.: Real-time continuous curvature path planning of UAVs in cluttered environments. In: Proceeding of the 5th International Symposium on Mechatronics and its Applications, Amman, Jordan (2008)
8. Ding, Y., Zhuang, W., Wang, L., et al.: Safe and optimal lane-change path planning for automated driving. Proc. Inst. Mech. Eng. Part D J. Autom. Eng. **225**, 095440702091373 (2020)
9. Luo, Y., Yong, X., Cao, K., et al.: A dynamic automated lane change maneuver based on vehicle-to-vehicle communication. Transp. Res. Part C **62**, 87–102 (2016)
10. Li, C.: Research on automatic lane change of intelligent vehicle in expressway environment. Chang'an University (2019)
11. Mueller, M.W., Hehn, M., Dandrea, R.: A Computationally efficient motion primitive for quadrocopter trajectory generation. IEEE Trans. Rob. **31**(6), 1294–1310 (2017)
12. Berstekas, D.P.: Dynamic programming and optimal control. Athena Sci. (1995)
13. Wang, Y., Liu, Z., Zuo, Z., et al.: Trajectory planning and safety assessment of autonomous vehicles based on motion prediction and model predictive control. IEEE Trans. Veh. Technol. **68**(99), 8546–8556 (2019)

5G: The Advances in Industry

Rate-Compatible Shortened Polar Codes Based on RM Code-Aided

Chunjie Li[1,2], Haiqiang Chen[1,2(✉)], Zelin Wang[1,2], Youming Sun[1,2], and Xiangcheng Li[1,2]

[1] School of Computer, Electronics and Information, Guangxi University, Nanning 530004, People's Republic of China
haiqiang@gxu.edu.cn
[2] Guangxi Key Laboratory of Multimedia Communications and Network Technology, Guangxi University, Nanning 530004, People's Republic of China

Abstract. The minimum Hamming distance is not considered for the traditional rate-compatible shortened polar (RCSP) codes, which may cause performance degradations. In this paper we propose a hybrid algorithm to construct RCSP codes based on Reed-Muller (RM) code-aided. The shortened bits and pre-frozen bits are jointly designed by the row weight property of the common generator matrix G_N for the RM/Polar code. First, the selected shortened bits are guaranteed to be uniquely depended upon the pre-frozen bits, which makes them completely be known by the decoder. Second, the proposed construction method is designed in such way, so that the minimum row weight of G_N can be maximized. More specifically, when multiple candidate positions satisfy the conditions (weight-1 column constraint), those rows having less weights are deleted to form the shortened/pre-frozen bits, which can reduce the number of rows with small weight and naturally, make the resulting RCSP codes have larger minimum Hamming distance in average. Simulation results show that the proposed RCSP codes perform better than the traditional shortened codes at low code rates. While at high code rates, the proposed RCSP codes can achieve better performance than that of the quasi uniform punctured (QUP) polar codes, especially at large signal-to-noise ratio (SNR) region. The proposed RCSP codes can find applications in future communications, such as the beyond 5th generation (B5G) and 6th generation (6G) systems.

Keywords: Polar codes · Rate-compatible · Reed-Muller codes · Hamming distance · Shortening

1 Introduction

Polar codes are the first family of codes which have been proven to achieve the capacity of any symmetric binary-input discrete memoryless channel (B-DMC) [1]. Polar codes have good structural characteristics and low encoding

This work was supported by NSF of China (No. 61761006, 61961004) and NSF of Guangxi (No. 2017GXNSFAA198263, 2017GXNSFAA198276, 2018GXNSFAA138079).

and decoding complexity. At the end of 2016, polar codes were selected as the candidate coding scheme for the 5G mobile communications, and were finally adopted as the coding standard for the uplink/downlink channel control [2].

However, the length of polar codes are limited to powers of 2 due to the original Kronecker power construction, which restricts their flexible applications in practice. Polar codes with arbitrary lengths and rates can be mainly obtained by puncturing, shortening and repetition, resulting the rate-compatible polar codes. These rate-compatible schemes are also recommended in 5G NR [3].

Punctured polar codes are first proposed in [4], where random puncturing and stopping-tree puncturing were both analysed and compared. Niu et $al.$ proposed an efficient puncturing scheme [5], in which the puncturing positions are designed to be quasi-uniform distribution after bit-reversal permutation, thus called the quasi-uniform puncturing (QUP). The QUP has better row weight property than random puncturing and can achieve excellent decoding performances, especially at low code rates. The traditional shortening scheme was discussed in [6], where a simple shortening method was given. The last N_p coded bits, whose values are completely determined by the pre-frozen bits, are shortened to form the rate-compatible shortened polar (RCSP) codes.

It is shown that the minimum Hamming distance has a significant impact on error performance of polar codes. Thus, constructing polar codes with large minimum Hamming distance to improve decoding performance becomes possible. Similar work can be seen in [7], where the minimum Hamming distance is increased by joint optimization of the shortening pattern and the set of frozen symbols. Li et $al.$ proposed the RM-Polar codes, which have much better distance property than polar codes and thus show better performance [8].

However, neither of the QUP scheme and the traditional shortening scheme consider the distance property in their construction and this may cause potential performance degradations. Actually, polar codes can be seen as a generalization of RM codes [9,10] and they share a common generator matrix [11]. This enable us to jointly optimize the distance property of the RCSP codes under row weight constraint of RM codes. Motivated by this, we propose a hybrid algorithm to construct the rate-compatible shortened polar codes by combining with the RM-rule constraint. The proposed algorithm maintains the superiority of the traditional shortened polar codes, $i.e.$, the shortened bits are designed to be completely known by the decoder thus the corresponding log-likelihood ratios (LLRs) can be set to infinity (or minus infinity) to ensure the decoding performance. To further improve the performance, a distance-greedy construction method is proposed to maximize the minimum row weight of G_N.

More specifically, those rows having less weights are first deleted during code construction to form the shortened/frozen bits, which can reduce the number of rows with small weight. Consequently, the constructed RCSP codes will have larger minimum Hamming distance in average. Simulation results show that the proposed RCSP codes have better frame error rate (FER) performance than the traditional shortened polar codes at low code rate. While at high code rate, the proposed RCSP codes outperform the QUP codes, especially at large signal-to-noise ratio (SNR) region.

The rest of this paper is organized as follows. In Sect. 2, we provide a short background on polar codes and RM codes, and introduce the RCSP codes construction system model. Section 3 gives a brief introduction to the traditional shortening method, then propose the RM code-aided hybrid RCSP algorithm. Section 4 gives the row property analysis of generator matrix and the simulation results. Section 5 concludes the paper.

2   Background

2.1   RM Codes

This subsection uses the Kronecker construction method to describe RM codes. Since RM code is a linear block code, which can be constructed by a generator matrix. Let $RM(n, n)$ denote the nth order RM code, and let $\mathbf{G}_N$ be the N-dimension generator matrix with $N = 2^n$, which can be defined as

$$\mathbf{G}_N = \mathbf{F}^{\otimes n} \tag{1}$$

where $\mathbf{F} = \begin{bmatrix} 1 & 0 \\ 1 & 1 \end{bmatrix}$, $\mathbf{F}^{\otimes n}$ is the nth Kronecker power of $\mathbf{F}$. The rth order RM code $RM(n, r)$ can then be defined as the linear code with a sub-matrix of $\mathbf{G}_N$, which is obtained by selecting rows of $\mathbf{G}_N$ with Hamming weights $\geq 2^{n-r}$.

The row weight of the generator matrix $\mathbf{G}_N$ has the following constraint with the row index. Let i denote an integer, $i \in \{0, 1, \cdots, N - 1\}$, and $\pi(i) = (b_{n-1}b_{n-2}\cdots b_1 b_0)$ is the binary representation of i over n bits. Let $w_t(i)$ represent the Hamming weight of $\pi(i)$. The Hamming weight of ith row can be calculated by $w_r(i) = 2^{w_t(i)}$.

Since the RM code is a linear code, each row of the generator matrix can be regarded as a legal codeword. Therefore, the minimum row weight of the generator matrix corresponds to the minimum Hamming distance of the RM code. Actually, an RM code is equivalent to a special polar code which has the maximum row weight constraint. For example, an rth order RM code $RM(n, r)$ is equivalently a polar code with the frozen set $\mathcal{A}^c$ that satisfies the distance constraint $\mathcal{A}^c = \{i|w_r(i) < 2^{n-r}\}$. With this constraint, the minimum Hamming distance of the polar code is $d_{min} = \min\{w_r(i)|i \in \mathcal{A}\}$, where $\mathcal{A}$ is the complementary set of $\mathcal{A}^c$, called the information set.

2.2   Polar Codes

Given a B-DMC $W : \mathcal{X} \rightarrow \mathcal{Y}$, where $\mathcal{X} \in \{0, 1\}$ and $\mathcal{Y}$ denote the input and output alphabet, respectively. The channel transition probabilities can be defined as $W(y|x)$, $y \in \mathcal{Y}$, $x \in \mathcal{X}$. Let a_0^{N-1} denote a row vector $(a_0 \cdots a_{N-1})$, and $a_i^j = (a_i \cdots a_j)$ denote a subvector, $0 \leq i \leq j \leq N - 1$. After channel combining and splitting operation on N independent uses of W, we get N successive uses of synthesized binary input channels $W_N^{(i)}$, $i \in \{0, 1, \cdots, N-1\}$, which can be defined by the transition probabilities as follows:

$$W_N^{(i)}(y_0^{N-1}, u_0^{i-1}|u_i) = \sum_{u_{i+1}^{N-1} \in \mathcal{X}^{N-i-1}} \frac{1}{2^{N-1}} W_N(y_0^{N-1}|u_0^{N-1}). \tag{2}$$

The N independent subchannels can be divided into two parts. One part of channels with capacity tends to be 1, called "noiseless channel", and the other part of channels with capacity tends to be 0, called "full noise channel". The reliability of each subchannel can be computed by using the Bhattacharyya parameter [1], density evolution (DE) [12], Gaussian approximation (GA) [13] or polarization weight [14]. The K most reliable subchannels with indices in $\mathcal{A}$ carry information bits and the rest subchannels in $\mathcal{A}^c$ are set to be fixed values, such as all zeros. For an (N, K) polar code with K message bits and N coded bits, the encoding process can be defined as

$$c_0^{N-1} = u_0^{N-1}\mathbf{G}_N, \tag{3}$$

where $u_0^{N-1} = (u_0, u_1, \cdots, u_{N-1})$ is the source information vector and $c_0^{N-1} = (c_0, c_1, \cdots, c_{N-1})$ is the polar codeword.

As mentioned above, polar codes can be seen as a generalization of RM codes and both of them are defined by the same generator matrix $\mathbf{G}_N$. However, they select the information bits according to different constraints. In particular, the Hamming distance is considered in the RM codes construction, which can be exploited to optimize the proposed RCSP codes in this paper.

2.3   System Model

The system model of the proposed RCSP codes construction is depicted in Fig. 1. In the transmitter, a K-bit information block is input into the polar encoder. After polar encoding, we get the N-bit polar codeword. To match arbitrary code length, the output polar code needs to be adjusted by shortening some bits from the N-bit encoded block, resulting in the M-bit RCSP codes. Then the RCSP codes with length-M is fed into the channel. In the receiver, we perform the opposite operation to get the corresponding estimated bits. Note that, the proposed RCSP codes are jointly designed with the encoding unit. The row weight constraint of RM code is employed to maximize the Hamming distance in the code construction. This is quite different from the traditional shortening scheme.

3   RM Code-Aided RCSP Codes

3.1   The Shortening Construction

Let $\mathbf{g}_j$ denote jth column vector of the generator matrix $\mathbf{G}_N$, where $j = 0, 1, \cdots, N-1$. Let $Q(\mathbf{g}_j)$ denote the index set of the "1" positions in $\mathbf{g}_j$. The vector $\mathbf{p} = (p_0, p_1, \cdots, p_{N-1})$ is the shortening pattern with $p_i \in \{0, 1\}$ and the

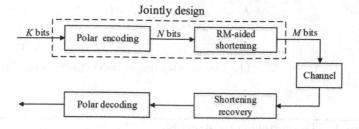

Fig. 1. The system model.

index $i = 0, 1, \cdots, N-1$, where the 1s imply the shortened positions. The index set of shortened positions can be represented as $Q(\mathbf{p})$. Let c_j be a code bit of c_0^{N-1}, which can be defined as follows:

$$c_j = \sum_{i \in Q(\mathbf{g}_j)} \oplus u_i. \tag{4}$$

Assume that c_j is selected as a shortened bit, then all the elements $i \in Q(\mathbf{g}_j)$ are designated to be the frozen bits. This is the key step to ensure that c_j is completely determined by the frozen bits, thus is known by the decoder. Define the pre-frozen set $\mathcal{A}_S^c$ as follows:

$$\mathcal{A}_S^c = \bigcup_{j \in Q(\mathbf{p})} Q(\mathbf{g}_j). \tag{5}$$

Note that the frozen positions in $\mathcal{A}_S^c$ are only determined by the shortening pattern, but not the sub-channel reliabilities. In order to minimize the number of pre-frozen bits, *i.e.*, the cardinality of $\mathcal{A}_S^c$, the *weight-1 first* criterion is introduced in [6]. Equivalently, the following equation should be satisfied,

$$|Q(\mathbf{g}_j)| = 1, \tag{6}$$

where $j \in Q(\mathbf{p})$. This implies that the shortening positions are always selected from the index of columns with weight-1. With this constraint, the number of shortened bits is exactly the pre-frozen bits, *i.e.*, $N_p = |\mathcal{A}_S^c|$. The pre-frozen set $|\mathcal{A}_S^c|$ with minimum cardinality can be determined by the following construction algorithm by N_p step. Let $\mathcal{A}_S^{c(k)}$ be the temporary set at the k-step, with $\mathcal{A}_S^{c(0)} = \emptyset$. Let $Q(\mathbf{p}^{(k)})$ be the corresponding shortening set at the k-step, with $Q(\mathbf{p}^{(0)}) = \emptyset$. Let $f^{(k)}$ be the selected pre-frozen bit at the k-step, then these two sets can be computed by

$$\mathcal{A}_S^{c(k)} = \mathcal{A}_S^{c(k-1)} \bigcup f^{(k)}, \tag{7}$$

and

$$Q(\mathbf{p}^{(k)}) = Q(\mathbf{p}^{(k-1)}) \bigcup f^{(k)}, \tag{8}$$

where $1 \leq k \leq N_p$. The pre-frozen bit $f^{(k)}$ can be selected from the temporary weight-1 set $\mathcal{W}^{(k)}$, which is determined by the pre-frozen construction function as follows:

$$\mathcal{W}^{(k)} = \underset{j' \in \mathcal{N}^{(k)}}{\arg} |Q(\mathbf{g}_{j'})| = 1, \tag{9}$$

where $\mathcal{N}^{(k)}$ is the index set after shortening, with $\mathcal{N}^{(k)} = \mathcal{N}^{(k-1)} - \mathcal{A}_S^{c(k-1)}$ and $\mathcal{N}^{(0)} = \{0, 1, \cdots, N-1\}$. The shortening construction algorithm can be described as follows.

Algorithm 1. The shortening construction

1: Given the required shortened code length M, the mother code length $N = 2^{\lceil \log_2 M \rceil}$, the generator matrix $\mathbf{G}_N$ and the number of shortening bits $N_p = N - M$
2: **Initialization:** $\mathcal{N}^{(0)} = \{0, 1, \cdots, N-1\}$, $\mathcal{A}_S^{c(0)} = \emptyset$
3: **for** $k = 1 : N_p$ **do**
4: Update $\mathcal{N}^{(k)} = \mathcal{N}^{(k-1)} - \mathcal{A}_S^{c(k-1)}$
5: Compute $\mathcal{W}^{(k)}$ according to (9)
6: Select the k-th pre-frozen bit $f^{(k)}$ from $\mathcal{W}^{(k)}$
7: Compute $Q(\mathbf{p}^{(k)})$ according to (8)
8: Compute $\mathcal{A}_S^{c(k)}$ according to (7)
9: **end for**

Remarks 1: In each step, only one bit is allowed to be selected from $\mathcal{W}^{(k)}$. However, the cardinality of $\mathcal{W}^{(k)}$ is greater than 1 in most case, which means there exist more than one possible scheme to pick out $f^{(k)}$. Specifically, if we modify the pre-frozen construction function as

$$\mathcal{W}^{*(k)} = \max \underset{j' \in \mathcal{N}^{(k)}}{\arg} |Q(\mathbf{g}_{j'})| = 1, \tag{10}$$

then the Algorithm 1 is equivalent to the shortening scheme presented in [6], where the last successive N_p indices are designated as the shortened bits and thus the pre-frozen bit positions.

Example 1: Consider a shortened polar code with $M = 6$, then we have $N = 8$ and $N_p = N - M = 2$, and the generator matrix is $\mathbf{G}_8 = \mathbf{F}^{\otimes 3}$. Figure 2 shows the shortening construction process with the pre-frozen construction function defined in (10). There are 2 steps to perform the construction. At the first step, only the last column $\mathbf{g}_7$ satisfies the weight-1 constraint. Thus we have $\mathcal{W}^{(1)} = \{7\}$ and $f^{(1)} = 7$. Obviously, $\mathbf{p}^{(1)} = (00000001)$ and $Q(\mathbf{p}^{(1)}) = \{7\}$, $\mathcal{A}_S^{c(1)} = \{7\}$, as shown in Fig. 2(a). It can be seen that the column 7 and row 7 are deleted from $\mathbf{G}_8$. At the second step, there exist 3 columns, $\mathbf{g}_3, \mathbf{g}_5, \mathbf{g}_6$ satisfy the weight-1 constraint. According to (10), only the maximum index 6 is selected, $i.e.$, $\mathcal{W}^{(2)} = \{6\}$ and thus $f^{(2)} = 6$. Similarly, $\mathbf{p}^{(2)} = (00000011)$ and $Q(\mathbf{p}^{(2)}) = \{6, 7\}$, $\mathcal{A}_S^{c(2)} = \{6, 7\}$, as shown in Fig. 2(b). At this step, column 6 and row 6 are deleted from $\mathbf{G}_8$.

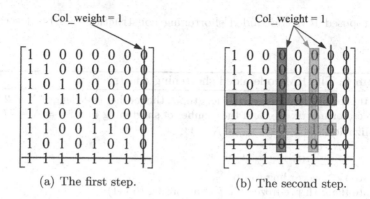

(a) The first step.   (b) The second step.

Fig. 2. Shortening construction of Example 1.

3.2 RM Code-Aided Shortening Algorithm

As discussed in the previous subsection, the pre-frozen construction function $\mathcal{W}^{(k)}$ is of importance, since the pre-frozen bit is determined by this function. To guarantee the minimum number of the pre-frozen bits, it is required that $|\mathcal{A}_S^{c(N_p)}| = |Q(\mathbf{p}^{(N_p)})| = N_p$. Therefore, the weight-1 constraint is introduced for the pre-frozen construction function, as shown in (9). However, there exist more than one column with weight-1 at the k step when $k > 1$, implying that the cardinality $|\mathcal{W}^{(k)}| > 1$ thus $f^{(k)}$ may have different construction schemes. Although the scheme according to (10) has a simple shortening pattern, the construction does not take the Hamming distance into account, which may cause performance degradation.

In this subsection, we propose a distance-greedy shortening scheme with the help of RM codes, called RM code-aided shortening construction scheme. Since polar code is the linear block code obtained by the generator matrix G_N, the minimum Hamming distance is then depended on the minimum row weight of G_N. Moreover, polar codes are essentially a generalization of RM codes, and they share a common generator matrix G_N. We can jointly optimize the distance property of the RCSP codes under the row weight constraint of RM codes.

Let t be an element of $\mathcal{W}^{(k)}$ at the k step, which is also a candidate for $f^{(k)}$. According to the row weight property of RM code, different index t shows different weight for the t-row of G_N. In order to maximize the Hamming distance, the row having the minimum weight at each construction step is deleted first. Thus, the pre-frozen bit $f^{(k)}$ at the k step can be computed by

$$f^{(k)} = \min_{t \in \mathcal{W}^{(k)}} \arg \min w_r(t). \tag{11}$$

Equation (11) indicates that, the selected index t from the candidates corresponds to the t-row of G_N with minimum row weight. In other words, the shortened bit is selected to maximize the row weight of generator matrix and thus the Hamming distance of the resulting RCSP codes can be improved.

The proposed RM code-aided shortening construction can be described as follows.

Algorithm 2. The RM code-aided shortening construction

1: Given the required shortened code length M, the mother code length $N = 2^{\lceil \log_2 M \rceil}$, the generator matrix $\mathbf{G}_N$ and the number of shortening bits $N_p = N - M$
2: **Initialization:** $\mathcal{N}^{(0)} = \{0, 1, \cdots, N - 1\}$, $\mathcal{A}_S^{c(0)} = \emptyset$
3: **for** $k = 1 : N_p$ **do**
4:   Update $\mathcal{N}^{(k)} = \mathcal{N}^{(k-1)} - \mathcal{A}_S^{c(k-1)}$
5:   Compute $\mathcal{W}^{(k)}$ according to (9)
6:   Compute the k-th pre-frozen bit $f^{(k)}$ according to (11)
7:   Compute $Q(\mathbf{p}^{(k)})$ according to (8)
8:   Compute $\mathcal{A}_S^{c(k)}$ according to (7)
9: **end for**

Remarks 2: Different from the Algorithm 1, the proposed construction algorithm is designed to be distance-greedy. When the candidates in $\mathcal{W}^{(k)}$ are greater than 1, we choose the one which has the minimum weight. Note that, if the index t produces the same minimum row weight $w_r(t)$, then the minimum index is selected, implying the uppermost row will be deleted.

Example 2: We construct shortened codes with code length $M = 12$, then we have $N = 16$ and $N_p = 4$, and the generator matrix is $\mathbf{G}_{16} = \mathbf{F}^{\otimes 4}$. Figure 3 shows the process of shortening construction with the pre-frozen construction function defined in (9) and $f^{(k)}$ defined in (11). We have four steps to construct the shortened code. At the first step, only the last column $\mathbf{g}_{15}$ satisfies the weight-1 constraint. Thus we have $\mathcal{W}^{(1)} = \{15\}$ and $f^{(1)} = 15$. Obviously, $\mathbf{p}^{(1)} = (0000000000000001)$ and $Q(\mathbf{p}^{(1)}) = \{15\}$, $\mathcal{A}_S^{c(1)} = \{15\}$, as shown in Fig. 3(a). It can be seen that the column 15 and row 15 are deleted from $\mathbf{G}_{16}$. At the second step, there exist 4 columns, $\mathbf{g}_7, \mathbf{g}_{11}, \mathbf{g}_{13}, \mathbf{g}_{14}$ satisfy the weight-1 constraint. According to (9) and (11), we have $\mathcal{W}^{(2)} = \{7, 11, 13, 14\}$ and thus $f^{(2)} = 7$. Similarly, $\mathbf{p}^{(2)} = (0000000100000001)$ and $Q(\mathbf{p}^{(2)}) = \{7, 15\}$, $\mathcal{A}_S^{c(2)} = \{7, 15\}$, as shown in Fig. 3(b). At this step, column 7 and row 7 are deleted from $\mathbf{G}_{16}$. The third step is shown in Fig. 3(c). There are 3 columns, $\mathbf{g}_{11}, \mathbf{g}_{13}, \mathbf{g}_{14}$ satisfy the weight-1 constraint. Accordingly, we have $\mathcal{W}^{(3)} = \{11, 13, 14\}$ and thus $f^{(3)} = 11$. Then, $\mathbf{p}^{(3)} = (0000000100010001)$ and $Q(\mathbf{p}^{(3)}) = \{7, 11, 15\}$, $\mathcal{A}_S^{c(3)} = \{7, 11, 15\}$. At this step, column 11 and row 11 are deleted from $\mathbf{G}_{16}$. At the fourth step, there exist 3 columns, $\mathbf{g}_3, \mathbf{g}_{13}, \mathbf{g}_{14}$ satisfy the weight-1 constraint. Thus, we have $\mathcal{W}^{(4)} = \{3, 13, 14\}$ and $f^{(4)} = 3$. Similarly, $\mathbf{p}^{(4)} = (0001000100010001)$ and $Q(\mathbf{p}^{(4)}) = \{3, 7, 11, 15\}$, $\mathcal{A}_S^{c(4)} = \{3, 7, 11, 15\}$, as shown in Fig. 3(d). At this step, column 3 and row 3 are deleted from $\mathbf{G}_{16}$. Finally, the RCSP code jointly designed by the pre-frozen set $\mathcal{A}_S^c = \{3, 7, 11, 15\}$ and the shortened pattern $\mathbf{p} = (0001000100010001)$ is constructed.

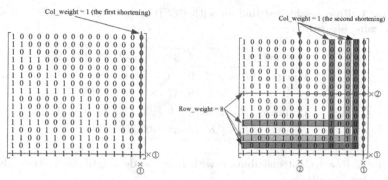

(a) Delete the last column and row

(b) Delete the uppermost row and the corresponding weight-1 column

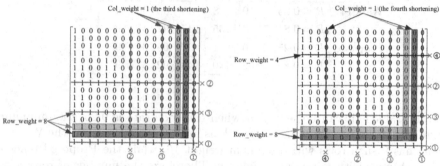

(c) Delete the uppermost row and the corresponding weight-1 column

(d) Delete the row with the minimum weight and the corresponding weight-1 column

Fig. 3. RM code-aided shortening construction of Example 2.

4 Simulation Results

4.1 Row Weight Property

As described above, the minimum Hamming distance of a polar code can be obtained by the minimum row weight of G_N. Therefore, the Hamming distance of the resulted RCSP code could be known by the row weight property of G_N after being shortened and frozen. In this subsection, we analyze and compare the row weight distribution with the shortening scheme in [6] (marked by Wang14) and the proposed RM code-aided shortening construction scheme (marked by Proposed). The row weight distribution with different code lengths and code rates are considered.

Table 1 shows the row weight distribution of the polar code with $N = 512$, $M = 312$, $N_p = N - M = 200$, $R = 0.25$ and 0.8, respectively. Table 2 corresponds to the code with $N = 1024$, $M = 600$, $N_p = N - M = 424$, $R = 0.25$ and 0.8, respectively.

Table 1. Row weight distribution with RCSP code length $M = 312$ under different shortening algorithms

Row weight		4	8	16	32	64	128	256
Wang14	$R = 0.25$	0	0	9	32	28	8	1
	$R = 0.8$	8	47	87	68	31	8	1
Proposed	$R = 0.25$	0	0	3	37	29	8	1
	$R = 0.8$	3	51	88	68	31	8	1

Table 2. Row weight distribution with RCSP code length $M = 600$ under different shortening algorithms

Row weight		4	8	16	32	64	128	256	512
Wang14	$R = 0.25$	0	0	8	38	58	36	9	1
	$R = 0.8$	7	52	135	147	92	37	9	1
Proposed	$R = 0.25$	0	0	1	37	66	36	9	1
	$R = 0.8$	1	52	140	148	92	37	9	1

From Table 1, it can be seen that when the code rate is 0.25, the minimum row weight of the two shortening algorithms are both 16. However, the Wang14 scheme has 9 such rows with minimum weight 16, while the Proposed scheme has 3 such rows with minimum weight 16. Therefore, the number of rows with minimum weight of the proposed algorithm is less than that of the Wang14, which implies that the Hamming distance among the RCSP codewords can be improved in average. When the code rate changes to 0.8, we have the similar observations. That is, the number of rows with minimum weight (say, 4 in this case) of the proposed algorithm is still less than that of the Wang14 scheme, which shows a better distance property in average. As shown in Table 2, the code length now changes to $N = 1024$. Similarly, for the two code rates, the number of rows with minimum weight of the Proposed scheme are both less than that of the Wang14 scheme.

In summary, the Proposed algorithm can reduce the number of rows with minimum weight and thus can improve the Hamming distance property of the constructed RCSP codes in average. The improvement of the minimum Hamming distance may have a positive impact on the decoding performance, as shown in the performance analysis in the next subsection.

4.2 Decoding Performances

In this subsection, we compare the frame error rate (FER) performance of the proposed RM-aided shortening construction scheme (Proposed), the Wang14 [6] and the QUP [5] schemes under different code rates and different code lengths. In the simulations, the GA method is used for the channel reliability estimation and the SC decoding is performed. The additive white Gaussian noise (AWGN) channel with binary phase-shift keying (BPSK) modulation is considered. The total number of simulation frames is 10^7, and the maximum number of error frames is 200. When the simulation reaches the total number of frames or reaches the maximum number of error frames, the simulation is stopped.

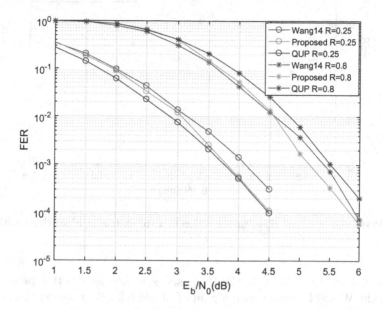

Fig. 4. Performance comparison under different rate matching algorithms with $M = 312$

Figure 4 shows the performances of the RCSP codes with the length $M = 312$ and mother code length $N = 512$. The code rates are set to be $R = 0.25$ and 0.8, respectively. We have the following observations.

- When the code rate is 0.25, the Proposed scheme has a significant performance gain compared with the Wang14 scheme. For example, at the FER $= 10^{-3}$, there is a gain of about 0.3 dB.
- Compared with the QUP scheme, the Proposed scheme shows a slightly performance degradation at low SNR region. However, the performance gap becomes smaller with the increasing of the SNR and can be ignored at high SNR region.
- For the code rate $R = 0.8$, the Proposed scheme performs as well as the Wang14 scheme but has a better FER performance than that of the QUP scheme. For example, when the FER is 10^{-3}, it has a performance gain about 0.35 dB compared with the QUP scheme.

In Fig. 5, we show the performances of the RCSP codes with the length $M = 600$ and mother code length $N = 1024$. The code rates are set to be $R = 0.25$ and 0.8, respectively. We have a similar observation as expected.

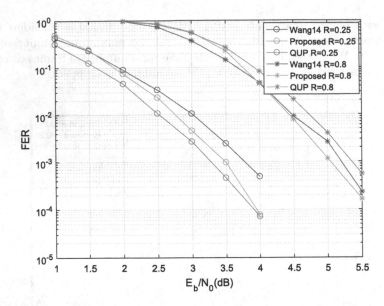

Fig. 5. Performance comparison under different rate matching algorithms with $M = 600$

- When the code rate is 0.25, the Proposed scheme has a better performance than the Wang14 scheme with a gain of about 0.3 dB at the FER = 10^{-3}.
- The QUP scheme performs better that the Proposed scheme at low SNR region, but the performance gap can be ignored at high SNR region.
- When the code rate is 0.8, the Proposed scheme has a comparable performance of the Wang14 scheme, but achieves a performance gain about 0.35 dB of the QUP scheme at the FER = 10^{-3}.

5   Conclusion

In this paper, we have proposed a hybrid algorithm to construct the rate-compatible shortened polar code by combining with the RM-rule constraint. First, the shortened bits are designed to be completely known by the decoder and thus the corresponding log-likelihood ratios (LLRs) can be set to infinity (or minus infinity) to guarantee the decoding performance. Second, a distance-greedy construction method is proposed to further improve the performance. When multiple candidate positions satisfy the weight-1 column constraint, we tend to choose the rows having less weights to form the shortened/pre-frozen bits. In this way, the generator matrix of the shortened code can be constructed with row weight as large as possible. The row weight distributions of generator matrix show that the Proposed scheme has less rows with minimum weight, which makes the Hamming distance of the constructed RCSP codes be larger in average. Simulation results show that the Proposed scheme can achieve performance gains at different levels when compared with the Wang14 scheme and the QUP scheme.

References

1. Arikan, E.: Channel polarization: a method for constructing capacity-achieving codes for symmetric binary-input memoryless channels. IEEE Trans. Inf. Theory **55**(7), 3051–3073 (2009)
2. 3GPP. Multiplexing and Channel Coding: 3GPP 38.212 vol. 15.1.0 [S] (2018)
3. Multiplexing and Channel Coding [S], document 3GPP TS38. 212 V15. 0.0 (2017)
4. Eslami, A., Pishro-Nik, H.: A practical approach to polar codes. In: 2011 IEEE International Symposium on Information Theory Proceedings, St. Petersburg, Russia, pp. 16–20. IEEE (2011)
5. Niu, K., Chen, K., Lin, J.: Beyond turbo codes: rate-compatible punctured polar codes. In: 2013 IEEE International Conference on Communications, Budapest, Hungary, pp. 3423–3427. IEEE (2013)
6. Wang, R., Liu, R.: A novel puncturing scheme for polar codes. IEEE Commun. Lett. **18**(12), 2081–2084 (2014)
7. Miloslavskaya, V.: Shortened polar codes. IEEE Trans. Inf. Theory **61**(9), 4852–4865 (2015)
8. Li, B., Shen, H., Tse, D.: A RM-Polar codes. arXiv preprint arXiv:1407.5483 (2014)
9. Muller, E.D.: Application of Boolean algebra to switching circuit design and to error detection. Trans. I.R.E. Prof. Group Electron. Comput. **EC-3**(3), 6–12 (1954)
10. Reed, I.: A class of multiple-error-correcting codes and the decoding scheme. Trans. IRE Prof. Group Inf. Theory **4**(4), 438–449 (1954)
11. Arikan, E.: A survey of reed-muller codes from polar coding perspective. In: 2010 IEEE Information Theory Workshop on Information Theory, Cairo, Egypt, pp. 1–5. IEEE (2010)
12. Mori, R., Tanaka, T.: Performance of polar codes with the construction using density evolution. IEEE Commun. Lett. **13**(7), 519–521 (2009)
13. Trifonov, P.: Efficient design and decoding of polar codes. IEEE Trans. Commun. **60**(11), 3221–3227 (2012)
14. He, G.: β-expansion: a theoretical framework for fast and recursive construction of polar codes. In: 2017 IEEE Global Communications Conference, Singapore, pp. 1–6. IEEE (2017)

Research on Wheat Impurity Image Recognition Based on Convolutional Neural Network

Chunhua Zhu[1,2,3(✉)] and Tiantian Miao[1,2,3]

[1] Key Laboratory of Grain Information Processing and Control, Ministry of Education, Henan University of Technology, Zhengzhou 450001, Henan, China
zhuchunhua@haut.edu.cn
[2] College of Information Science and Engineering, Henan University of Technology, Zhengzhou 450001, Henan, China
[3] Henan Key Laboratory of Grain Photoelectric Detection and Control, Henan University of Technology, Zhengzhou 450001, Henan, China

Abstract. The doping rate is one of the important indexes to evaluate the quality grade and price of wheat. In order to accurately and quickly recognize impurities (wheat husk) in wheat grains, images of doped wheat were collected and Convolutional Neural Network (CNN) was used to realize the classification and recognition of grains and impurities in wheat grains. In this study, image segmentation and image enhancement were used to preprocess the acquired images to establish the image database of wheat grains and impurities. According to the characteristics of image data, the classic CNN, VGGNet and ResNet network models for wheat impurity images recognition were established. Simulation analysis shows that, compared with the classical CNN and VGGNet network models, the ResNet network model has the best recognition performance. The recognition accuracy of the test set is 96.94%, the recognition time is 5.60 ms.

Keywords: Convolutional neural network · Wheat grains · Impurities

1 Introduction

Wheat is one of the main food crops in China and also an important export product. According to China's wheat national standard [1], doping rate is one of the important indicators for evaluating wheat quality grade and price during wheat purchase and market circulation. At present, wheat impurity detection methods mainly include electric screening method, hand screening method [2], sensory detection method [3], and image detection method [4]. Electric screen method and hand screen method can not meet the requirements of rapid field detection because of the long detection time. Artificial sensory detection is easily mixed with subjective factors, which brings great uncertainty to wheat quality grading. In the aspect of image detection, researchers have studied wheat impurity recognition by using linear discriminant analysis model [5, 6], artificial neural network [7, 8] and other technologies, and achieved good recognition effect. However, the calculation process of this kind of method is relatively

W. Xiang et al. (Eds.): BROADNETS 2021, LNICST 413, pp. 320–328, 2022.
https://doi.org/10.1007/978-3-030-93479-8_23

complicated, and the algorithm performance depends on the extracted input data features, which cannot meet the needs of actual image detection.

In recent years, deep learning has become a research hotspot in the field of image recognition. Deep learning technology represented by convolutional neural network has been applied to many aspects of the agricultural field [9–15]. Convolutional neural network can directly recognize the original image, avoiding the complex process of artificial feature design, selection, optimization and so on, and can well meet the needs of real-time detection. Therefore, in this paper, three convolutional neural network models, including classic CNN, VGGNet and ResNet, are adopted to realize the recognition of impurities in adulterated wheat. Through the establishment of wheat grains and impurities image database, model optimization design and recognition effect evaluation, the convolutional neural network with the best detection effect in the recognition of wheat impurity image is discussed.

2 Image Acquisition and Preprocessing

2.1 Image Acquisition

In this paper, the impurities in wheat grains was taken as the detection target, and the materials used in the experiment were from Xinglong National Grain Reserve Bank in Zhengzhou, Henan Province. Because the size and shape of wheat husk are different greatly, so the wheat husk with similar wheat grains size and shape is selected as the experimental material manually.

The background of image acquisition is black light-absorbing flocking background cloth, and the acquisition equipment is Sony camera (ILCE-7RM2 model, 42.4 million effective pixels). Wheat grains and impurities were randomly placed in a distribution of 10×10, as shown in Fig. 1. Among them, wheat grains and impurities were collected 3000 grains respectively.

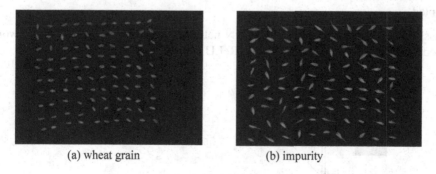

(a) wheat grain   (b) impurity

Fig. 1. Image acquisition sample.

2.2   Image Preprocessing

Image preprocessing is divided into three parts: multi-grain segmentation, size unification and data expansion, as shown in Fig. 2. First, the collected images are converted into grayscale images. Then, Graythresh function is used to find the optimal threshold to transform the grayscale image into a binary image. Finally, multi-grain images were segmented into single grain images by using the minimum outer rectangle method. The size of single grain image obtained by the minimum outer rectangle method is different, so it is necessary to unify the size of single grain image. In this study, the image size was unified as 32×32. Due to the small amount of image data collected, the images with the same size were left rotated 90° and 180° respectively. After image processing, 18000 image sample sets were obtained, including 9000 wheat grain images and 9000 impurity images respectively.

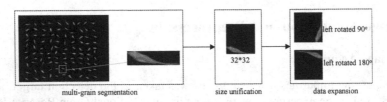

Fig. 2.   Image preprocessing.

3   The System Model

3.1   Convolutional Neural Network Structure

In order to meet the requirements of real-time detection of adulterated wheat and considering the size of the sample in the image database established in this paper, a modified convolutional neural network structure suitable for this experiment was adopted.

Classic CNN Network. The classic CNN network is shown in Fig. 3. This network introduced the activation function layer ReLU on the basis of LeNet-5 network.

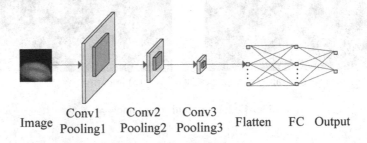

Fig. 3.   Classic CNN network.

In Fig. 3, the classic CNN network structure has a total of 9 layers, including 3 convolution layers, 3 pooling layers, 1 Flatten layer, 1 full connection layer, and 1 output layer. After each convolution layer, there is a ReLU activation layer. The role of convolution layer is mainly to extract the features from the input image. The convolution kernel size of convolutional layer Conv1 is 5 * 5, and the step size is 1. The size of the feature graph of the image after the convolution operation of Conv1 is 32 × 32. The convolution kernel size and step size of convolutional layer Conv2 and Conv3 are the same as those of convolutional layer Conv1. The pooling layer adopts the maximum pooling to perform the down-sampling operation on the feature map. The size of Pooling1 is 2 * 2, and the step size is 2. The size of the feature graph obtained by sampling under Pooling1 of the pooling layer is 16 × 16. Pooling2 and Pooling3 have the same size of pooling region and step size as Pooling1. Flatten is often used in the transition from the convolutional layer to the fully connection layer, which acts as a one-dimensional input. The function of the full connection layer is to make full connections between each neuron in the layer and all neurons in the upper layer. The output dimension sizes of the network convolution layer, Flatten layer and full connection layer are 32, 64, 128, 2048 and 2 respectively.

VGGNet Network. The VGGNet network suitable for this test is shown in Fig. 4. Compared with the classic CNN network, VGGNet network is composed of two convolution layers and one pooling layer repeatedly superimposed.

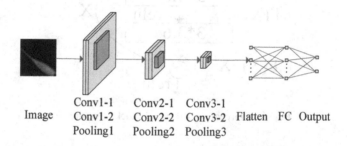

Image   Conv1-1   Conv2-1   Conv3-1
         Conv1-2   Conv2-2   Conv3-2   Flatten FC Output
         Pooling1   Pooling2   Pooling3

Fig. 4. VGGNet network.

In Fig. 4, the VGGNet network structure has a total of 12 layers, including 6 convolution layers, 3 maximum pooling layers, 1 Flatten layer, 1 full connection layer, and 1 output layer. The size of the convolutional kernel of the convolutional layer is all 5 * 5, and the step size is all 1. The size of the pooling area of the pooling layer is 2 * 2, and the step size is 2. The output dimension sizes of the network convolution layer, Flatten layer and full connection layer are 32, 32, 64, 64, 128, 128, 2048 and 2 respectively.

ResNet Network. The ResNet network of this test is shown in Fig. 5. Compared with the above model, the residual block structure is introduced to improve the system performance through residual learning.

Figure 5 shows that the ResNet network structure consists of 1 convolution layer, 3 residual layers, 2 average pooling layers, 1 Global Average Pooling layer, 1 full

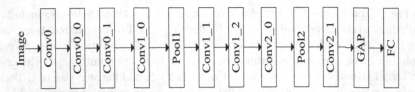

Fig. 5. ResNet network.

connection layer. The convolution kernel size of convolutional layer Conv0 is 5 ∗ 5. Due to the small image of the data set, the step size of the convolutional layer before input to the residual structure is set as 1, and the maximum pooled layer of is not passed. The three residual layers Conv0_x, Conv1_x and Conv2_x all adopt conventional residual block structure, and the number of residual blocks is 2, 3 and 2, respectively. The residual layer adopts the conventional residual block structure, as shown in Fig. 6. X is the input of the residual block, and F(X) is the residual learning. Learning makes F(X) go to 0, ignoring the depth.

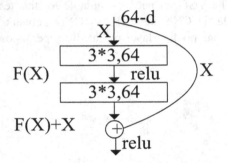

Fig. 6. Conventional residual block structure.

Among the 3 convolutional neural networks mentioned above, for the classic CNN network and VGGNet network, the Dropout layer is added after the full connection layer to reduce the parameters of network training and the complexity of the model.

The above three networks are classified by calculating the category probability of softmax function, which can be expressed as

$$y_{im} = \frac{e^{z_{im}}}{\sum_{k=1}^{K} e^{z_{ik}}} \tag{1}$$

Where, y_{im} is the prediction probability that the *ith* sample belongs to the *m* category; z_{im} is the product of the output vector of the *ith* sample and the parameter vector of class *m*; *K* is the number of categories; z_{ik} is the product of the output vector of the ith sample and the parameter vector of class *k*.

The classification cross entropy is taken as the loss function, and the calculation formula is

$$L = -\sum_{i=1}^{N} \hat{y}_{im} lg y_{im}$$ (2)

Where, L is the loss function; N is batch size; $\hat{y}_{im}$ is the expected value of the predicted probability of the ith sample belonging to class m.

3.2   Model Parameter Selection

The experiment used TensorFlow framework and Python 3.6 programming language to build wheat grain and impurity recognition model on PyCharm platform. The batch size for network training was set to 144 and the number of iterations (epoch) was set to 100. Set the Dropout value to 0.5 for the classic CNN network and VGGNet network. The model parameters were optimized by the adaptive gradient descent method, where the learning rate was set at 0.001 and the momentum factor was set at 0.9.

4   Test Results and Analysis

Using the wheat grains and impurities image database established in this paper, 7200 (80%) images of wheat grain and impurity images were selected as the training set, and 1800 (20%) images of wheat grain and impurity images were selected as the test set. Classic CNN, VGGNet and ResNet models were used to train the training set, and the change curves of training accuracy and loss were shown in Fig. 7(a), Fig. 7(b) and Fig. 7(c), respectively. It can be seen from the figure that the training accuracy of the classic CNN network tends to 1 and the loss tends to 0 when the number of iterations reaches about 20. Compared with the classic CNN network, VGGNet network has a complex structure. When the number of iterations reaches about 30, the training accuracy and loss tend to be stable. The number of iterations of the ResNet network tends to be stable is about 35.

The classical CNN, VGGNet and ResNet models after training were tested on the test set. The performance comparison of the three models is shown in Table 1.

In Table 1, compared with the classic CNN network model and VGGNet network model, the ResNet network model has the highest accuracy in wheat impurity images recognition. At the same time, it can be found that the classical CNN network model has the shortest recognition time for each wheat grain (or impurity) image. Although the ResNet network model is more time-consuming than the classic CNN network model in wheat impurity image recognition, it can still meet the practical application of wheat impurity detection.Therefore, the performance of the ResNet network model constructed in this experiment is better than that of the classic CNN and VGGNet network models.

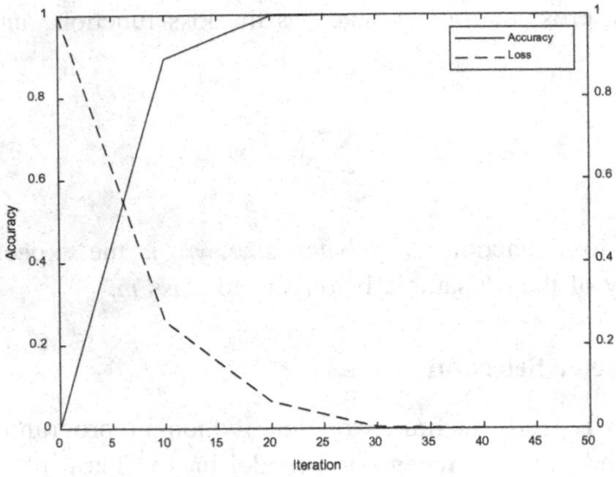

(a) Classic CNN network

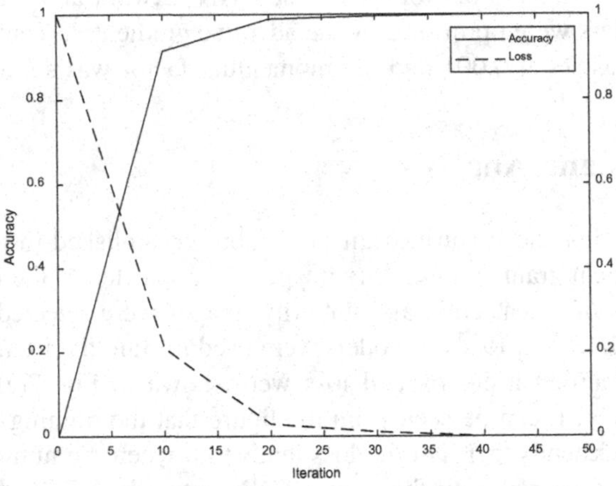

(b) VGGNet network

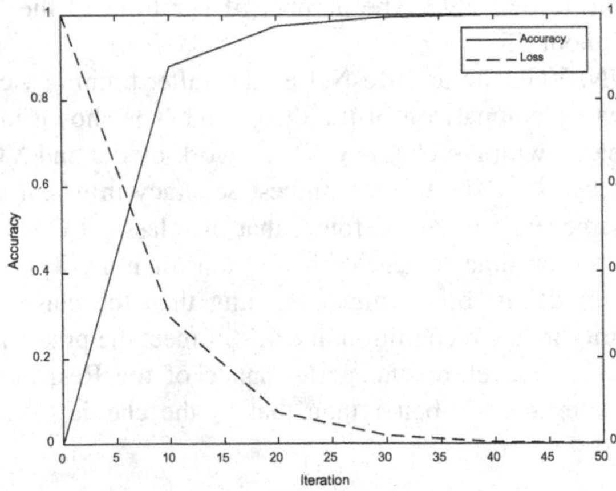

(c) ResNet network

Fig. 7. Variation of network training accuracy and loss.

Table 1. Performance comparison of different network models.

Network model	Recognition accuracy (%)	Recognition time (ms)
Classic CNN	93.33	1.04
VGGNet	95.72	5.30
ResNet	96.94	5.60

5 Conclusion

This paper mainly discusses the application of convolutional neural network in wheat impurity recognition. Through the self-built wheat grain and impurity image database, the classical CNN, VGGNet and ResNet network models established in this paper were compared and analyzed. The results show that the recognition accuracy of the three convolutional neural network models is above 90%. In conclusion, the ResNet network model is more suitable for wheat impurity recognition.

Author Contributions. Chunhua Zhu and Tiantian Miao proposed the original idea and Tiantian Miao carried out the experiment. Chunhua Zhu and Tiantian Miao wrote the paper. Tiantian Miao supervised and reviewed the manuscript. All authors read and approved the final manuscript.

Funding. This research was financially supported by National Science Foundation of China (61871176): Research of Abnormal Grain Conditions Detection using Radio Tomographic Imaging based on Channel State Information; National Science Foundation of China (61901159): Research on Beamspace Channel Estimation in Massive MIMO Systems by Fusing Multi-Dimensional Characteristic Information; Applied research plan of key scientific research projects in Henan colleges and Universities (19A510011): Research of Abnormal Grain Conditions Detection Based on Radio Tomographic Imaging based on RSSI; Scientific Research Foundation Natural Science Project In Henan University of Technology (2018RCJH18): Research of Abnormal Grain Conditions Detection using Radio Tomographic Imaging based on Received Signal Strength Information; the Innovative Funds Plan of Henan University of Technology Plan (2020ZKCJ02): Data-Driven Intelligent Monitoring and Traceability Technique for Grain Reserves.

Conflicts of Interest. The authors declare no conflict of interest.

References

1. Standardization Administration of China. GB 1351-2008 Wheat. Standards Press of China, Beijing (2001)
2. Yafei, X., Defu, R., Zhijun, Q., Xianping, Y., Haiquan, H.: Study on the detection method of impurity in imported grain crops. J. Agric. Process. (Acad.) **08**, 135–136 (2012)
3. Zhang, B.: Research on wheat appearance quality detection by machine vision based on deep learning. Northwest A&F University (2019)

4. Yurong, Z., Saisai, C., Xianqing, Z.: Advances in wheat image detection technology. J. Chin. Cereals Oils Assoc. **29**(04), 118–123 (2014)
5. Chemists A: Cereal Chem 1989 | Discrimination of Wheat and Nonwheat Components in Grain Samples by Image Analysis. Publications (1989)
6. Chen, S.S.: Research on machine vision technology for wheat quality index, Henan University of Technology (2014)
7. Jayas, D.S., Visen, N.S., Paliwal, J., et al.: Cereal grain and dockage identification using machine vision. Biosys. Eng. **85**(1), 51–57 (2003)
8. Su, Y.N.: Study on detection of water content and identification of impurity and imperfect grain based on machine vision and hyperspectral image technology, Zhejiang University (2011)
9. Ferentinos, K.P.: Deep learning models for plant disease detection and diagnosis. Comput. Electron. Agric. **145**, 311–318 (2018)
10. Zhang, S., Huang, W., Zhang, C.: Three-channel convolutional neural networks for vegetable leaf disease recognition. Cogn. Syst. Res. **53**(JAN), 31–41 (2019)
11. Arnal, B.: Impact of dataset size and variety on the effectiveness of deep learning and transfer learning for plant disease classification. Comput. Electron. Agric. **153**, 46–53 (2018)
12. Alvaro, F., Sook, Y., Sang, K., et al.: A robust deep-learning-based detector for real-time tomato plant diseases and pests recognition. Sensors **17**(9), 2022 (2017)
13. Artzai Picon, A., et al.: Deep convolutional neural networks for mobile capture device-based crop disease classification in the wild. Comput. Electron. Agric. **161**, 280–290 (2019)
14. Yang, L., et al.: Identification of rice diseases using deep convolutional neural networks. Neurocomputing **267**, 378–384 (2017)
15. Rangarajan, A.K., Purushothaman, R., Ramesh, A.: Tomato crop disease classification using pre-trained deep learning algorithm. Procedia Comput. Sci. **133**, 1040–1047 (2018)

Based on Energy Router Energy Management Control Strategy in Micro-grid

Xuemei Zheng[✉] ⓘ, Zhongshuai Zhang ⓘ, Haoyu Li,
and Yong Feng ⓘ

Engineering Department, Harbin Institute of Technology, No. 92 Xidazhi Street,
Harbin, China
xmzheng@hit.edu.cn

Abstract. As the key part of the Energy Internet (EI), the energy router (ER) needs to achieve the purpose of distribution and balance of power, making the entire power system more safe and stable. This paper proposes several energy management strategies for ER. Photovoltaic array is used as the basic power generation unit, wind power is used as the auxiliary unit, and energy storage unit realized the power balance through charging and recharging. At the same time, the maximum power tracking control and constant power of the photovoltaic power generation system and the wind power generation system are carried out, respectively. At last, simulation and control strategy are verified in the MATLAB simulation platform. The simulation results show the proposed management is effective and correct.

Keywords: Energy router · Power management · Microgrid · MPPT

1 Introduction

Consequently, with the development of large-scale integration of Distributed Renewable Energy Resources (DRERs), Distributed Energy Storage Devices (DESDs) and emerging DC loads, the power network structure has become more and more complex. It also caused a big challenge to the conventional grid. Therefore, inspired by the development of smart grid and information Internet, many experts from various countries put forward the idea of creating the "Energy Internet" (EI) conception. This may eventually shift the power and energy industry from the currently centralized mainframes to a client-based, distributed power infrastructure, and need the power and energy can be controlled and flow reasonably [1, 4, 5].

On the way to the Energy Internet, current research work towards to EI, falls into three major categories: one is focus on the design and development of silicon based Solid State Transformer (SST) [8–13]. Others study about the control strategies of Microgrid. Normally, the DRERs, DESDs and DC loads all connected to the DC-bus, which will connect to the grid through the inverter unit again, thus the stability of the DC-bus control is very important [1, 2]. In reference [3], the working modes of each converter are introduced under various working conditions, and then the setting of DC-bus voltage reference value under this condition is analyzed. Reference [4] proposed an algorithm for stabilizing the DC-bus voltage in an island case, and fuzzy control and

W. Xiang et al. (Eds.): BROADNETS 2021, LNICST 413, pp. 329–339, 2022.
https://doi.org/10.1007/978-3-030-93479-8_24

gain adjustment control are introduced in the control to achieve the control target. Reference [5] proposed a control algorithm for bidirectional converters, and according to different possible operating modes, the control methods of modules such as photovoltaic (PV) and batteries in the system are studied and designed. Besides on DC-side management control, some researchers also focus on AC ports by controlling the power electronic inverter. Traditionally, three control methods are used to control grid-connected inverters., that is the constant power control method [8], the V/F control method [9] and the droop control [10].The others are doing research about the standard based software and communication platform for traditional substations [6, 7].

In this paper, an EI and Energy Router (ER) topology, consisting a PV power generation, a wind turbine (WT) power generation system and Energy Storage System (ESS) is proposed. In the proposed EI system, the PV and WT power system can either switch in Maximum Power Point Tracking (MPPT) control mode or in constant power control mode according to the demands of ER. In order to realize the energy management and control of ER, the paper proposed four operating states control strategy and six energy management strategy according to the sunlight and wind speed to ensure the ER to work in the optimal states and utilize the PV and WT efficiently. At last, simulation verification is carried out in the MATLAB simulation platform to simulate the 6 modes and carry out the desired control strategy. The simulation results show the proposed management is effective and correct.

2   Model and Control for Multi-port ER System

The proposed multi-Port Control (MPC) ER topology is shown in Fig. 1. It consists four ports, one for PV generating unit, one for WT power system, these two units are connected to the common DC-bus through boost converter and realize MPPT and constant voltage control. The battery storage system, which is controlled by charging and recharging control and realize the power balanced. The last port for the grid, which connected the DC/AC converter and Solid State Transformer (SST). The whole MPC ER system can realize the energy exchange to the grid, but also can realize islanded running according to the demands.

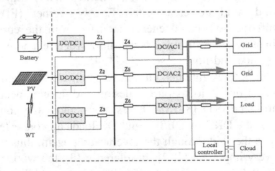

Fig. 1. Topology structure of multiport ER system

2.1   The Model of PV System and Control

In the proposed topology in Fig. 1, PV is the main supply unit, which usually works in the MPPT mode, but in some special cases, it is required to switch to the constant power mode according to the system power requirement. The control system block for PV power unit is shown in Fig. 2. The switching signal decides the operating mode of the system. Based on the state of the switching signal state, the system can switch either from constant power mode to the MPPT mode or vice versa. The PWM remain unchanged for both operating mode.

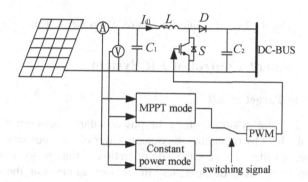

Fig. 2. PV power system control block diagram

2.2   Control of WT System

WT power generation system, works as an auxiliary power supply to support PV power generation system in case the PV and ESS cannot meet the load demand requirement. It usually works in the MPPT mode, but if the ESS cannot be charged, and the PV power generation system is insufficient to preserve power balancing, it is necessary for WT power system to switch from MPPT to the constant power control mode. The reference constant power is determined by the ER depending on the power required by the load and the power generated from PV. So the WT generation system need to work in both operating mode, either in MPPT mode or in constant power control mode according to the actual wind speed changes. The schematic diagram of the specific strategy for WT power system control is shown in Fig. 3.

If WT power system works in the MPPT mode, the pitch angle β is kept at zero. The dq inner current control strategy for PWM rectifier is adopted, where the reference for $i_d = 0$ and the i_q reference is obtained from the outer speed control, which tracks the optimal speed ω_{opt} for maximum power extraction. If WT power system is operating in a constant power mode, it is necessary to continuously adjust the utilization coefficient C_p, by controlling the pitch angle. The deviation between the given power P_{ref} and the actual output power P is fed to the pitch angle controller implemented as a, PI controller, which generates the variable pitch angle β to achieve the constant power.

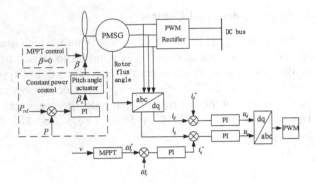

Fig. 3. The schematic diagram of WT power system

3   The Management Control of ER System

3.1   The Control Target of ER

The energy management system ensures the power balance between the power generation unit and the load by regulating the output power of each power generation unit. At the same time, in order to ensure the safe operation of the energy storage unit, it is necessary to monitor the SOC of the battery in real time to maintain the safe operating range of the battery storage. When the battery charges up to the high SOC upper limit, further charging of the battery is prohibited and when the battery discharges up to the lower SOC limit further discharging is prohibited. To guaranty the safe utilisation of the battery energy storage, the SOC monitoring control system must ensure the safe operating region of the battery storage, which relies between the upper SOC and the lower SOC limit. In the existing research, the upper and lower limits of charge and discharge of the ESS are different depending on the consideration. Considering the optimal range of system efficiency, in this paper, the maximum upper limit of SOC = 0.8, and the lower limit of SOC = 0.2 are adopted.

Figure 4 shows the basic block diagram of the energy management control strategy. The power balance relationship can be expressed as:

$$P_1 = P_{wind} + P_{PV} + P_{battery} \tag{1}$$

where P_1 is the load power, P_{wind} is the output power of WT power system, P_{PV} is the output power of PV system and $P_{battery}$ is the output power of the battery. For $P_{battery} < 0$ and $P_{battery} > 0$ represents the battery is being charged or discharged.

The logical decision control block uses P_1, SOC and P_{PV} as input, to generate the switching signal PV, required to control PV system. For the WT power system the switching signal wind is obtained from the logical decision that use P_1, SOC, P_{PV} and wind speed V_{wind} as the input. The WT power system generates the power P_{wind}.based on the wind. At the same time, the remained power of P_1-P_{wind}-P_{PV} is sent to the ESS and gets the amount of SOC.

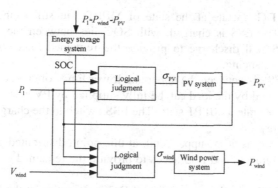

Fig. 4. The control block diagram of energy management system

The proposed system topology provide the following features. 1) It ensures the power balance and stable operation for the ER, and in addition the complete energy management and scheduling is achieved. 2) The stability of the ER is guaranteed in all operating modes and smoothly it can switch from one control mode to the other. 3) the efficiency of renewable energy utilization is maximized, and realize stabilize output power; 4) it ensures that the units of the ER work in the optimal working mode, with high quality of the output power.

3.2   ER'S Working State and Operating Mode

In this paper, the ER is able to operate into 4 states:

1. when all DG units operate MPPT mode, and cannot meet the load demand, the remained power is provided by the ESS, and the renewable energy utilization rate is maximized.
2. when the generated maximum power produced by the DG is higher than the DC load requirement, the excess energy is stored in the ESS.
3. when DG units are in the maximum output power, and cannot satisfy the DC side load demand, and ESS cannot provide energy. The load needs to be cut off from the system, the energy balanced control strategy will be determined according to the specific situation.
4. when DG units are in the maximum output power, and satisfy the DC side load demand, but cannot be charged to the ESS, the distributed generation unit can operate in constant power output state.

It can be seen that the ESS plays a key role in energy balancing. balanced node in the entire energy management strategy. The core of the control system of ER lies on controlling each DG unit to work in specified operating mode by the energy management system. Table 1 shows ER operation 6 operating modes.

Mode 1: with Both PV and WT generation system are all kept in MPPT mode, but still cannot meet the load demand, and the ESS is at its lower limit of discharge state, a part of the load must be disconnected from the ER.

Mode 2: The DG operate at the state of MPPT, but still cannot meet the load demand, and The ESS is charged, with SOC lies between the upper and lower limits, the ESS will discharge to provide the remained load power demand for system power balancing.

Mode 3: The ESS is between the upper and lower limits of charge and discharge. If the energy required by the load can be fully supplied by PV system and WT power system, which operate at MPPT state. The ESS switch to the charging mode to save the excess energy..

Modal 4: The ESS is at the upper limit, at this point, distributed generation cannot meet the load demand, and ESS needs to provide the remained energy. The ESS is in discharging state.

Mode 5: The ESS is at the upper limit, if DG is operating at the MPPT state, then select in the MPPT state, and the remained energy is provided by WT power system, at this point, ER is in the constant power state.

Modal 6: The ESS is at the upper limit, at this point, PV can meet the load demand. The PV system is selected to be the same as required by the load.

The above 6 operating modes can guarantee the energy router system in stable operation state. However, since DG is greatly affected by the external weather conditions, and the load demand value of the system will change with the scheduling command value, these external influences will interfere with ER, causing it to switch between different working modes. Therefore, to guaranty the accuracy power management, the real-time monitoring of the electrical quantity of each port is required for accuracy of control system and power allocation for each unit.

4 Simulations

To evaluate the effectiveness, feasibility and the performance of the proposed energy management control method, the simulation model is built in the MATLAB/Simulink platform. The simulation parameters are shown in Table 1.

Table 1. DC power supply simulation parameters

Parameter	Value
U_g/V	380
$U_{battery}$/V	400
U_{dc}/V	750
f/Hz	50
v/(m/s)	8,10
J	0.5
D	20
P_{ref}/kW	2
R_a/Ω	0.032
S/(W/m^2)	800,1000

4.1   Simulation Verification of PV Control

The control algorithm of PV system is Firstly simulated to evaluate the operating capability of the PV in either MPPT or constant power operating mode. To carry out simulation the disturbance observation method is adopted to implement the MPPT control. The solar irradiance and temperature variation are shown in Fig. 5a) and Fig. 5b) respectively. Figure 5c) shows the PV system given power, and Fig. 5d) shows the switching signal of the PV system switch. Figure 5e) shows the output power of the PV system after the switch is on and off. As seen in Fig. 5e), from t = 0.5 s–1.5 s and t = 4 s–5 s, the PV system works in the MPPT mode, while during t = 2 s– 4 s, the PV system works in constant power mode. It can be seen from Fig. 5d) and Fig. 5e), the PV system can follow the given power, this indicate effectiveness of the proposed PV system switching control.

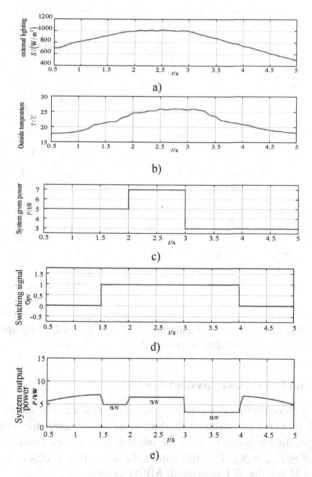

Fig. 5. PV character curve and output power a) Sunlight, b) temperature, c) PV given power, d) switching signal, e) PV output power

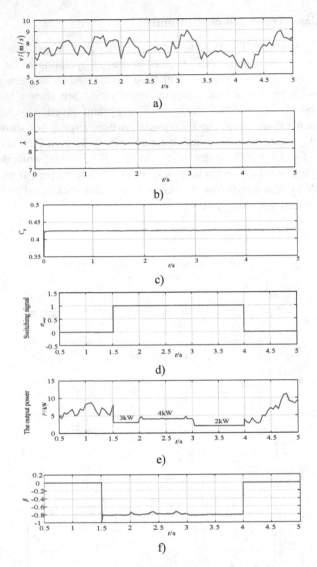

Fig. 6. WT power system input and output curve a) Random speed, b) tip speed ratio, c) Cp curver, d) switching signal, e) WT output power, f) pitch angle curve

4.2   Simulation of WT Power System Control

Next, the control algorithm of WT power system is evaluated. The results are shown in Fig. 6. Figure 6a) shows the input of random wind speed taken from the wind plant. Figure 6b) shows the tip speed ratio of the blade.it can be seen from Fig. 6b) that the optimal value of is $\lambda_{\text{opt}} = 8.1$, Fig. 6c) shows the utilization coefficient, which can be kept at $C_p = 0.425$ for the WT operate at MPPT control.

If the switch signal is added in the wind power system, as shown in Fig. 6d), the wind power output power as shown in Fig. 6e). It can be seen from Fig. 6e) that in the time interval of t = 0.5 s–1.5 s and t = 4 s–5 s, the wind power system works in the MPPT mode and in the time interval t = 1.5 s–4 s the wind power system operates at constant power mode. Figure 6f) shows the pitch angle β curve of the wind power system. The value of β is kept at zero in the time interval t = 0.5 s–1.5 s and t = 4 s–5 s, in which the WT operate at MPPT mode as can be observed in Fig. 6f). For time interval t = 1.5 s–4 s the wind power system is under pitch angle control mode, and the pitch angle β changed with respect to the wind speed to enhance constant power control.

4.3   The Simulation of Energy Management Strategy

In this part, the proposed 6 modes of ER control are evaluated. Firstly, supposed that the demand power of load is given in Fig. 7a). The output power of the PV system, wind power system, and battery are shown in Fig. 7b), Fig. 7c) and Fig. 7d), respectively. Figure 7e) shows the waveform of the SOC of battery.

As can be seen from Fig. 7, the system operates in mode 3 during t = 0.5 s and t = 1 s. The load demand power is 2 kW, at that time the battery SOC is less than 80%, so the battery will be charged. According to the energy management rules proposed in this paper, both PV and wind power systems carry out MPPT control, SOC of the ESS gradually increases Until t = 0.63 s, where the battery SOC reaches the upper limit of SOC (80%). The further charging of the is prohibited. To the system power, the PV switches to the constant power mode and generate 2 KW. During this period, the wind power system does not provide any power, it is deactivated.

Between t = 1 s and t = 2 s period, the system is in mode 6. The system power demand power is 5 kW, which is still less than the maximum tracked power of PV. At this time, the PV system switch to constant power control to maintain 5 kW power demand. The output power of WT power system is kept at 0 kW, and the battery is neither charged nor discharged. It can be seen that the battery provide a 0 kW to the load while its SOC is maintained at 80%. Between t = 2 s and t = 3 s period, the system operates in the mode 5. The system power demand changes from to 12 kW. At this time, the PV can no longer meet the load demand. The PV switches to MPPT mode to generate its maximum possible power And The remained power demand of the load is provided by WT generation system. The battery is neither charged nor discharged at this time. It can be seen that the output power of the battery is still 0 kW, SOC is maintained at 80%.Between t = 3 s and t = 4 s period, the system is in mode 4. The system demand power changes to 20 KW. At this time, PV and WT both switch to MPPT mode, but they are unable to provide enough power required by the load. Therefore. The remained power demanded by load is provided by the battery. It can be seen that the output power of the battery is positive, which means that the battery is discharging to support the PV and WT to meet the load requirement. meanwhile, the corresponding battery SOC continues to decrease, therefore, the system power is balanced, and the energy management rules are satisfied.

Between t = 4 s and t = 5 s time period, the system enter in mode 3. The system demand power is changed to 8 KW. At this time, the battery SOC is less than 80%, and

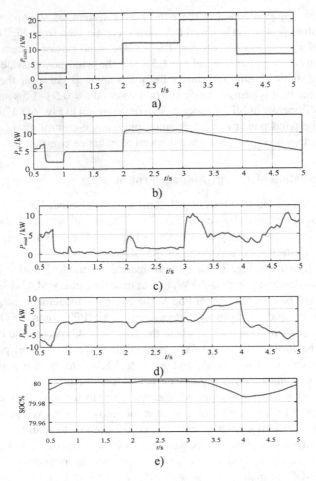

Fig. 7. Power of load, energy router, SOC curve a) Load demand power, b) output power of PV, c) output power of WT, d) output power of ESS, e) SOC curve

PV and WT continue to operate in MPPT state to charge the battery and provide required power to the load.

5 Conclusion

This paper firstly designed the ER control strategy of the PV system and the wind power system, so that each power generation unit can issue a certain amount of electric energy according to the demand command value. Then, the energy management strategy of the distributed power supply on the DC side of the energy router system is designed, determining the working state and output force of each power generating unit through logic judgment to achieve balanced flow of power. Finally, the simulation model is built in MATLAB/Simulink simulation software to verify the switching of each power generation mode and the proposed energy management strategy. The simulation verifies the correctness and effectiveness of the proposed method.

Acknowledgments. This work was supported by the National Natural Science Foundation of China (62073095).

References

1. Eren, S., Pahlevani, M., Bakhshai, A., et al.: An adaptive droop DC-bus voltage controller for grid-connected voltage source inverter with LCL filter. IEEE Trans. Power Electron. **30** (2), 547–560 (2015)
2. Lazroiu, G.C., Popescu, M.O., Dumbrava, V., et al.: Voltage control system and transient analysis of DG interfaced DC distribution system. In: IET Conference on Renewable Power Generation, Edinburgh, UK, pp. 1–6 (2011)
3. Kakigano, H., Nishino, A., Ise,T.: Distribution voltage control for DC microgrid with fuzzy controland gain-scheduling control. In: 8th International Conference on Power Electronics, Jeju, South Korea, pp. 256–263 (2011)
4. Zhang, L., Wu, T., Xing, Y., et al.: Power control of DC microgrid using DC bus signaling. In: 26th Annual IEEE Applied Power Electronics Conference and Exposition, Fort Worth, TX, USA, pp. 1926–193 (2011)
5. Liu, B., Zhuo, F., Bao, X.: Control method of the transient compensation process of a hybrid energy storage system based on battery and ultra-capacitor in micro-grid. In: IEEE International Symposium on Industrial Electronics, pp. 1325–1329, Hangzhou, China (2012)
6. Wu, D., Tang, F., Dragicevic, T., et al.: Coordinated control based on bus-signaling and virtual inertia for islanded DC microgrids. IEEE Trans. Smart Grid **64**(6), 2627–2638 (2015)
7. Liu, H., Zhang, Y., Mantooth, H.A.: Residential renewable energy distribution system with PQ control. In: 2015 IEEE International Conference on Building Efficiency and Sustainable Technologies, Singapore (2015)
8. Varsha,Y., Arunima, V.: Comparison of VF controlled wind energy system based on different sensing methods. In: 2016 International Conference on Emerging Trends in Communication Technologies (ETCT). Dehradun, India (2016)
9. Xue, X., Li, H., Lv, Z.: Research on new algorithm of droop control. In: 2018 Chinese Control And Decision Conference (CCDC).Shenyang, China (2018)
10. Kang, B.K., Kim, S.T., Sung, B.C., et al.: A Study on optimal sizing of superconducting magnetic energy storage in distribution power system. IEEE Trans. Appl. Supercond. **22**(3), 5701004 (2012)
11. Qian, H., Zhang, J., Lai, J., et al.: A high-efficiency grid-tie battery energy storagesystem. IEEE Trans. Power Electron. **26**(3), 886–896 (2011)
12. Etxeberria, A., Vechiu, I., Camblong, H., et al.: Hybrid energy storage systems for renewable energy sources integration in microgrids: a review. In: 2010 Conference Proceedings IPEC, Singapore (2010)
13. Phatipha, T., Luigi, P., Serge, P., et al.: Nonlinear intelligent DC grid stabilization for fuel cell vehicle applications with a supercapacitor storage device. Electr. Power Enegy Syst. **64**, 723–733 (2015)

Author Index

Printed in the United States
by Baker & Taylor Publisher Services